■ BETWEEN TRADITION AND MODERNITY ■

■ BETWEEN TRADITION AND MODERNITY ■

INDIA'S SEARCH FOR IDENTITY

A Twentieth Century Anthology

Editors

FRED DALLMAYR
G.N. DEVY

■ SAGE PUBLICATIONS ■
■ NEW DELHI ■ THOUSAND OAKS ■ LONDON ■

First published in 1998 by

Sage Publications India Pvt Ltd
M–32 Market, Greater Kailash–I
New Delhi–110 048

Sage Publications Inc
2455 Teller Road
Thousand Oaks, California 91320

Sage Publications Ltd
6 Bonhill Street
London EC2A 4PU

Published by Tejeshwar Singh for Sage Publications India Pvt Ltd, typeset by Line Arts, Pondicherry and printed at Chaman Enterprises, Delhi.

Library of Congress Cataloging-in-Publication Data
Between tradition and modernity / editors, Fred Dallmayr, G.N. Devy.
      p. cm. (c: alk. paper) (pbk: alk. paper)
    Includes bibliographical references.
     1. Nationalism — India. 2. India — Civilization. 3. India —
Politics and government — 1765–1947. I. Devy, G.N., 1950– .
DS463.B412   954 — dc21   1998   97–51895

ISBN: 0–7619–9243–X (US-hb) 81–7036–698–4 (India-hb)
      0–7619–9244–8 (US-pb) 81–7036–699–2 (India-pb)

Sage Production Team: Nilanjan Sarkar, Richard Brown and
Santosh Rawat

"While I appreciate modern thought, I find that an ancient thing, considered in the light of this thought, looks so sweet"

■ To the memory of Mahatma Gandhi ■

■ CONTENTS ■

■ PART TWO ■

■ MODERNIZATION AND ITS DISCONTENTS ■

■

■ PREFACE ■

This volume is the result of a collaborative endeavor stretching over several years. Given the background and native habitat of the two editors, the book also represents the outcome of cross-cultural collaboration between West and East—here between a German-American and a native Indian. For both, the collaboration has meant a genuine learning experience. For the former, the encounter with Indian culture and thought—initially quite unsettling—proved, in many ways, to be a turning point, away from a complacent, though half-conscious Eurocentrism toward a fuller appreciation of cultural diversity on our shrinking globe. For the Indian, the volume involved a confrontation and renewed engagement with his own cultural life-world, and the need to come to terms with its complex historical tapestry. Neither of the two editors could escape the intellectual and existential implications of their work, in the sense that the overall theme of 'India's search for identity' required of both a rethinking and renegotiation of their own self-understanding.

This is the place to thank a number of people for the continued support and encouragement provided for our endeavor. Without rank ordering their role these people include Bhikhu Parekh, Rajni Kothari, Ashis Nandy, Thomas Pantham, Nirmal Verma, Anantha Murthy, Rama Rao Pappu, and Arvind Sharma. Many others, too numerous to mention, had a more indirect, but by no means negligible influence on our undertaking. In our dealings with the publisher, we want to acknowledge with particular gratitude the indefatigable assistance of Omita Goyal, managing acquisitions editor for Sage Publications India; without her editorial labors this volume would not have seen the light of day. Finally—though not in the order of importance—we want to thank our respective families for granting us the nurturing environment conducive to scholarly work.

As it seems to us, the publication of the volume happens at a propitious time, for a number of reasons. The closing years of our century provide an appropriate setting for a retrospective scrutiny of salient events and ideas—which is one of the motives for our attempt to assemble a 'twentieth century anthology'. With particular respect to India, the closing years of the century also furnish the occasion for the celebration of fifty years of Indian national independence (1947–97), a celebration to which this volume seeks to make a modest contribution from an intellectual and existential angle. After fifty years, we believe, it is more than ever urgent and timely to reflect on the meaning of 'India' and on the sense and moral-political dimensions of Indian self-rule (swaraj). In our view, no one has seen and articulated these dimensions and challenges more clearly than Mahatma Gandhi, to whom this volume is fondly dedicated.

F.D.
G.N.D.

■

Note: Since this book is intended not for professional Indologists but for a general audience, the use of diacritical marks has been omitted throughout the text.

■ ACKNOWLEDGEMENTS ■

We gratefully acknowledge the following publishers for permission to include material originally published by them in this volume. The texts, with their complete citations, that have been included in this volume are:

■ Swami Vivekananda   ■ 'Modern India', reprinted from *The Complete Works of Swami Vivekananda*, Volume 4, © The Advaita Ashram, Calcutta.

■ Rabindranath Tagore   ■ 'Nationalism in India', © Visva-Bharati University, Santiniketan, West Bengal.

■ Sri Aurobindo   ■ 'The Renaissance in India', © Sri Aurobindo Ashram, Pondicherry.

■ Ananda K. Coomaraswamy   ■ 'The Vedanta and Western Tradition', © Princeton University Press, Princeton.

■ *Vinayak D. Savarkar   ■ 'Some of the Basic Principles and Tenets of the Hindu Movement', © Savarkar Prakashan, Bombay.

■ *J. Krishnamurti   ■ 'Freedom'; 'On Nationalism', © Gollancz, London.

■ Manavendranath Roy

■ 'Anti-Imperialist Struggle in India'; 'Preconditions of Indian Renaissance', © Indian Renaissance Institute, Calcutta.

■ *B.R. Ambedkar

■ 'Gandhism: The Doom of the Untouchables', © Thacker, Bombay.

■ Muhammad Iqbal

■ 'The Reconstruction of Religious Thought in Islam'; 'Presidential Address', reprinted from Stephen Hay (ed.), Sources of Indian Tradition, © Columbia University Press, 1988.

■ Abul Kalam Azad

■ 'Congress Presidential Speech', reprinted from Stephen Hay (ed.), Sources of Indian Tradition, © Columbia University Press, 1988.

■ Mohandas Gandhi

■ 'Hind Swaraj'; 'Medium of Instruction'; 'The Message of India', © Navjivan Trust, Ahmedabad.

■ Jawaharlal Nehru

■ 'A Tryst with Destiny'; 'Our Inheritance'; 'India—Old and New'; 'Synthesis is Our Tradition'; 'National Solidarity', © Jawaharlal Nehru Memorial Fund, New Delhi.

■ *A.K. Saran

■ 'Gandhi's Theory of Society and Our Times', reprinted from L.P. Vidyarthi et al. (eds), Gandhi and the Social Sciences, Bookhive Publishers, New Delhi, 1970.

■ Thomas Pantham

■ 'Understanding Nehru's Political Ideology', reprinted from A. Ray, N.B. Rao and V. Vyasulu (eds), *The Nehru Legacy: An Appraisal*, Oxford and IBH Publishing Company, New Delhi, 1991, © Institute for Social and Economic Change, Bangalore.

■ Rajni Kothari

■ 'Ethical Imperatives', reprinted from Rajni Kothari, *Growing Amnesia*, Penguin Books India Pvt. Ltd., New Delhi, 1993.

■ Ashis Nandy

■ 'Cultural Frames of Social Transformation: A Credo', © Alternatives,1987.

■ Romila Thapar

■ 'Tradition', reprinted from Romila Thapar, *Tradition*, The Qureishi Memorial Lectures, Oxford University Press, New Delhi.

■ Ranajit Guha

■ 'Some Aspects of the Historiography of Colonial India', reprinted from Ranajit Guha (ed.), *Selected Subaltern Studies*, Oxford University Press, New Delhi, 1988.

■ Sudhir Chandra

■ 'The Oppressive Present', reprinted from Sudhir Chandra, *The Oppressive Present*, Oxford University Press, New Delhi, 1992.

■ Ramchandra Gandhi

■ 'The Swaraj of India', © *The Indian Philosophical Quarterly*.

■ U.R. Anantha Murthy

■ 'Why Not Worship in the Nude? Reflections of a Novelist in His Time', reprinted from *Bahuvachan*, Bharat Bhavan, Bhopal, 1988.

■ Nirmal Verma

■ 'India and Europe—Some Reflections on Self and Other',

reprinted from *Kavita Asia*, Bharat Bhavan, Bhopal, 1990.

■ Maulana Wahiduddin Khan   ■ 'Religion and Politics'; 'A Silent Revolution', © The Islamic Centre, New Delhi.

■ Susie Tharu and K. Lalita   ■ 'Women Writing in India', reprinted from Susie Tharu and K. Lalita (eds), *Women Writing in India: 600 B.C. to the Early Twentieth Century*, The Feminist Press at the City University of New York, 1991.

■

* Every effort has been made to obtain the necessary permissions to reproduce these articles. The publishers apologize if inadvertently any sources remain unacknowledged.

■ INTRODUCTION ■

I

We live in a shrinking world. No doubt, our age displays a rich welter of diverse, often conflicting strands and tendencies; yet, beneath the turbulent panorama of world wars, cold war, and North–South conflicts a dominant trend or undercurrent can readily be detected: the process of globalization, of the emergence of a 'global city'.[1] Occasionally deflected and sometimes nearly eclipsed by the din of armed struggle, this strand has the earmarkings of a relentless and near-providential force: seemingly disconnected events or episodes appear to coalesce almost mysteriously or fortuitously into a larger design. Although powerfully pervasive, however, this trend is not entirely self-propelled or akin to a natural *force majeure*: overtly or covertly its movement is backed up by political and economic strategies as well as intellectual trajectories of long standing. Most prominent among these strategies and directions are industrialization, market capitalism, and the ascendancy of science and technology—features pre-eminently connected with modern Western culture. To this extent, globalization can be regarded as a synonym for modernization or Westernization, that is, the dissemination of the standards of Western modernity around the globe.[2] Until roughly the middle of the present century, this dissemination was buttressed by the administrative structures of Western imperialism and colonialism. The demise of colonial empires—while changing manifest structures—has by no means altered the overall thrust of dissemination.

In its global reach, modernization is a gripping, monumental drama saturated with promises and risks. Seen from the angle of non-Western societies in particular, the drama is bound to be marked by profound ambiguity irreducible to neat formulas (of either progress or regress). On the one hand, modernization in these societies is liable to generate a new dynamism or social vigor, a dynamism prone to break open congealed or ossified customs and thus to liberate untapped energies, especially those of previously silenced or oppressed strata of the population. Modernization in this sense can be the harbinger of social transformation and emancipation. On the other hand, the boons of modernity come to these societies mainly through the vehicle of colonialism, or else post-colonial modes of Western (military, economic, and scientific) hegemony; unsurprisingly, modernity is hence also experienced as the result of foreign intervention, accompanied by the traumatic agonies of alienation, heteronomy, and Western control. In a slight variation of the phrase coined by Horkheimer and Adorno (regarding the Enlightenment trajectory), the global drama of our age can be appropriately captured under the label of a 'dialectic of modernization'. Given its intrinsic ambivalence, the process is contestable and, in fact, fiercely contested on all sides. To devotees of modernity, indigenous customs or traditions in non-Western societies are liable to appear as mere obstacles or obsolete relics destined to be eradicated by the onrush of Western-style rationality and efficiency. By contrast, members of indigenous life-worlds are prone to defend these same traditions (in their original or a suitable modified form) as bulwarks of resistance against the homogenizing bent of global management. Like the role of tradition, forms of ethnic and religious distinctiveness are also intensely controverted, with charges of atavism and backwardness hurled against the catchwords of cultural autonomy and national independence.[3]

The clash of slogans and ideas is bound to be particularly acrimonious in societies steeped in age-old and venerable cultural traditions. Nowhere is this more true than in India, a country where cultural memories have been preserved with more loyalty and steadfastness than almost anywhere in the world. As is well known, the beginnings of Indian life are coeval with the birth of human civilization as such, and ensuing centuries and millennia have witnessed not so much radical reversals as a process of accretion and a steady proliferation of cultural strands. At the same time, the Indian subcontinent has been touched pervasively—perhaps more pervasively than other parts of Asia—by the inroads of

Western colonialism and political-economic hegemony. Starting in the early seventeenth century, Western interests established a foothold on the subcontinent in the form of Portuguese, Dutch, French, and English trading posts and settlements; rivalry among these European powers resulted in the eventual ascendancy of the British East India Company which—abetted by British troops and naval forces—managed to gain political and economic control over much of India while undermining Moghul rule. During the ensuing period, the Company's grip on Indian affairs was steadily tightened until, in the middle of the nineteenth century (1858), India was placed under direct governmental authority—an arrangement which transformed India into the 'jewel in the crown' of the British empire. Needless to say, these developments produced profound agonies and perplexities among peoples on the subcontinent, especially among Indian intellectuals imbued with classical canons of learning but simultaneously exposed to Western educational models. Reactions varied widely, ranging from the complete rejection of Western culture, seen as an alien intrusion, all the way to the fervent embrace of Britain's victorious, and hence demonstrably 'superior' life-form.

The present volume does not propose to recount the story of India's encounter with the West in all its historical and social–political details. There is no shortage of able studies on these details written by historians, social scientists, and economists.[4] Instead, the focus of this volume rests on the existential dimension of the encounter, that is, on its role as catalyst in a process of self-scrutiny and in the search for self-rule and cultural identity. To this extent, the story narrated here represents not so much an 'objective' travelogue as rather a 'sentimental journey' reflecting the experiences undergone by leading participants in the encounter, particularly Indian participants. The latter accent has several motivations. Evidently, the subcontinent's exposure to, and domination by, the West was far more traumatic and wrenching for Indians than for their Western colonizers and rulers—a fact which lends added weight and depth to the Indian perspective. The accent also reverses (and is meant to reverse) a long-standing Western bias. As many writers have noted, it has traditionally been a strictly Western privilege to investigate, understand or come to know the Other (specifically non-western cultures and societies)—a privilege which was predicated on the West's presumed superiority in cognitive or analytical terms and hence precluded reciprocity. As long as Western culture viewed itself as the promontory or (in Jacques Derrida's phrase) as the advanced 'heading' of human civilization as such, knowledge of others was necessarily seen as a one-way street militating against any kind of reciprocal learning between 'developed' and 'undeveloped', between modern and archaic or tradition-bound world-views.[5] Reversing this bias, the present volume explores Indian perceptions and interpretations of the West, perceptions which inevitably were linked with, or rebounded on, modes of Indian self-understanding and self-definition.

In recounting the story of cultural encounter, it is not our aim to subscribe to an 'orientalist' framework of discourse, that is, to assumptions regarding the essential 'nature' of orient and occident and their radical incompatibility; nor, in shifting the focus to the colonized, is there any intent to inaugurate a counter-discourse univocally stigmatizing the West as a synonym for imperialism. In recent times, these essentializing assumptions have been widely discarded—for good reasons—and replaced by a more nuanced awareness of the interpreted, constituted if not invented character of cultural traditions. Obviously, cultures are not naturally grown phenomena but the result both of shared learning experiences and of internal and external forms of contestation; in this sense, they are also 'imagined communities' (in Benedict Anderson's phrase).[6]

Still, carried to an extreme, the reaction against essentialism or compact identities can be self-defeating—mainly by subverting the aspect of difference or distinctiveness itself. Clearly, for Indians the impact of Western colonialism and imperialism was not simply a form of self-encounter; apart from military and economic power differentials, there were also significant differences in cultural traditions and concrete life-forms (no matter how porous or elusive the boundaries may have been). Moreover, these traditions and life-forms were not simply, individually, 'up for grabs'. Under the influence of a misconstrued Nietzscheanism, traditions and cultures are sometimes treated today as entirely willful constructions on the part of interpreters—which implies a slide into rampant subjectivism (and also into a Hobbesian notion of politics). No doubt, traditions and cultures are humanly lived and, as such, are always open to revised readings, rejections and renewals. Yet, to make sense, even the latter have to proceed within shared frameworks of significance, including semantic structures and historically evolved practices. To this extent, interpretations—no matter how creative—always have to respect, or respond to, the 'primacy of the *interpretandum*' (as Hans-Georg Gadamer has insisted). Properly conceived, hermeneutical readings thus involve a blending of continuity and discontinuity—a kind of studied symbiosis for which life-forms are not randomly transferable from time to time and place to place.[7]

None of this is meant to deny the internal variety and differentiation of all cultural traditions—a variety which also surfaces in the assessments of cross-cultural encounters. In India, where Western influence extends over several centuries, these assessments have been nuanced, insightful, and greatly diversified over time. The present volume cannot hope to capture the full breadth or scope of Indian responses to Western colonial and post-colonial intrusions. Mainly for the sake of manageability, our collection is limited to prominent statements articulated during the twentieth century. Beyond editorial considerations of feasibility, there is a further reason vindicating our selection: the status of our century as the watershed of overt colonialism. Although India's encounter with the West was always marked by tensions, and occasionally by armed conflict, it was only in our century that these tensions gathered sufficient momentum to erupt into a struggle for national independence. As a corollary, perceptions and assessments of the Other reached in our age an unprecedented level of intensity—an intensity reflecting deep existential traumas and something like a Hegelian 'struggle for recognition' on a large scale. Even after independence was achieved (in 1947), this tensional struggle did not abate—and could not possibly have abated given the steadily broadening scope of Western influence now proceeding under the banner of modernization and development.

To be sure, Indian reactions to the West cannot neatly be separated by the clock of centuries. In many ways, cross-cultural encounters resemble protracted conversations or debates where earlier points or arguments are freely picked up and modified during later rounds of the engagement. Thus, spokesmen of the struggle for independence were able to draw on a rich arsenal of themes first articulated by intellectuals and writers during the eighteenth and nineteenth centuries, especially the early pioneers of the so-called 'Hindu Reformism' or 'Hindu Renaissance'. By all accounts, one of the most widely respected and influential of these pioneers was Raja Ram Mohun Roy (1777–1833), an eminent scholar and journalist whose learning embraced in equal portions Eastern scriptures and modern Western forms of education (with a focus on science). Partly under the influence of Western deism and Enlightenment ideas, Ram Mohun sought to simplify and streamline Hindu beliefs in line with the spiritual teachings of the *Upanishads*; at the same time, he aimed to eradicate corrupt social practices, including caste abuses and widow burning (*sati*). To promote these goals, he founded the *Brahmo Samaj* in 1828, an organization or movement devoted to broad-scale social and religious reform.[8]

His work was ably continued by Debendranath Tagore (1817–1905), a scholar likewise imbued with both Eastern and Western learning, and later by Debendranath's son Rabindranath (1861–1941)—although the latter shifted the accent from scholarly intellectualism to more popular or populist modes of thought and belief. Somewhat less modernist than Ram Mohun's movement was the *Arya Samaj*, an organization founded in 1875 by Swami Dayanand Saraswati (1824–1883), a religious leader wedded to the motto 'back to the *Vedas*'. Despite his more traditionalist outlook, Saraswati's program was also dedicated to general literacy, modern education, and the improvement of the condition of oppressed castes and classes. Alongside these movements one should also mention the *guru* of 'Bengali Renaissance': Ramakrishna Paramahansa (1836–1886), a charismatic figure attached to the legacy of popular devotional Hinduism but interpreting the latter in a non-exclusive, cosmopolitan vein. His foremost disciple, Swami Vivekananda (1863–1902), gained considerable influence at home and abroad, both through his own writings and through the establishment of Ramakrishna Missions around the world.[9]

What the nineteenth century bequeathed to the later independence movement was thus a complex set of interpretive approaches and perspectives, together with a number of alternative blueprints or guideposts for the future course of India. By and large, what most of these approaches shared was a certain blending of Indian and Western life-forms and ideas, with dispute raging mainly over the precise dosage of ingredients; to this extent, most intellectuals of the period subscribed to a dialogical model of cross-cultural exchange—although the terms of the dialogue were sometimes cast in highly simplistic terms (for example, as involving an encounter of Western materialism and Indian spiritualism). Unsurprisingly, this model was rejected only at the extreme poles of the intellectual spectrum: by radical traditionalists (who viewed Western culture as unmitigated evil) and radical modernizers (who despised native practices as hopelessly obsolete).

In his study of 'colonialism, tradition and reform' during the pre-Gandhi era, Bhikhu Parekh perceptively distinguishes four main types of Indian attitudes—although he is himself quick to warn against a rigidly schematic use of his typology. The four perspectives are: traditionalism, modernism, critical modernism, and critical traditionalism. While the distinction between the first two is relatively straightforward, the difference between the last two is more complex and nuanced. In Parekh's account, traditionalists 'saw little wrong with their society, and consequently either took no interest in British rule or dismissed it as inconsequential'. By contrast, modernists were 'convinced that modernity was incompatible with India's traditional ways of life and thought, and felt that these must be rejected'. Accordingly, most of the leading modernists of the time saw the recipe for a regeneration of Indian public life in the creation of a 'strong, interventionist, democratic, secular, and centralized state' and in the establishment of uniform rules of citizenship as the groundwork of Indian national identity. As Parekh indicates, modernists came themselves in different shapes, covering the entire spectrum from classical (free enterprise) liberalism to socialism and Marxism; what chiefly united them was their Western-inspired belief 'that the state and society represented the opposite principles of light and darkness respectively. The state stood for modernity, society for tradition.'[10]

More difficult to sort out is the relation between critical modernism and critical traditionalism. In Parekh's portrayal, critical modernists—whose spokesmen included Ram Mohun Roy and Gopal Krishna Gokhale (1866–1915), among others—basically agreed with modernists that Indian society needed to be thoroughly revamped and transformed; yet, they also believed that India's time-honored traditions—especially when fused or synthesized with novel Western ideas—provided at least some resources for modernization and national resurgence. This reliance on cultural synthesis was not acceptable in this form to critical traditionalists who regarded cultural traditions as organic wholes and hence preferred to stress the potential of critical self-renewal of Indian culture from within—although this process might be triggered or abetted by external comparisons. Representatives of this outlook—among them Saraswati, Bankim Chandra Chatterjee

(1838–1894), Sri Aurobindo (1872–1950), and Vivekananda—suspected even synthetic merger as a form of heteronomy or external imposition and hence counseled greater efforts of cultural self-renovation (something pure traditionalists considered unnecessary). Despite their shared opposition to status-quo politics, the disagreements between the two critical camps were subtle and by no means marginal. Given the long-range implications of these perspectives, Parekh's analysis deserves to be quoted here at some length:

> The differences in the approaches of the critical modernists and critical traditionalists were deep and profound. Although they often advocated the same policies and institutions, their reasons for doing so were radically different. The critical modernists assumed that European and Indian civilizations could be comparatively assessed and synthesized; critical traditionalists considered the assumption preposterous. The former aspired to combine the 'best' features of both and to create a 'new' civilization; the latter considered such an enterprise absurd and concentrated on regenerating and reforming their own. Despite their sincere search for a creative synthesis, the critical modernists implicitly or explicitly accepted the superiority of European civilization and asked what aspects of Indian civilization could be fitted into it; the critical traditionalists adopted the opposite approach. The former aimed to preserve what was *valuable* in Indian civilization; the critical traditionalists were content to eliminate what was *evil*.[11]

II

One thing which stands out in the writings of most of the Indian Renaissance thinkers is their remarkably flexible, differentiated, and open-ended conception of Indian identity: the Indian 'nation' which they creatively 'imagined'—and whose future independence they anticipated—was by and large untainted by chauvinistic arrogance and self-indulgence. To this extent, the outlook of these thinkers did not exemplify the kind of atavistic backwardness which Hans Kohn—a leading Western writer on the topic—associated with 'non-Western nationalism' (as contrasted with the liberal-progressive variant in the West).[12] This flexible attitude was also and especially characteristic of critical traditionalism (to employ Parekh's term); precisely because they sought to invoke mainly internal resources, spokesmen of this outlook aimed their sharpest invectives not so much against colonial practices as against forms of domestic corruption and oppression which blocked the way to regeneration. This point is amply illustrated in the essay on 'Modern India' with which this volume opens. Written by Swami Vivekananda just before the turn of the century, the essay offers a sweeping and 'imaginative' overview of the entire course of Indian history—a narrative couched in terms of a kind of an indigenous class analysis.

As Vivekananda points out, public power in ancient times was concentrated in the hands of kings and priests, two castes which, though frequently in conflict, were united in keeping the people at bay. As laid down in ancient *shastras* (or public codes), people were granted 'no direct voice in the supreme government'; accordingly, it was impossible for them 'to acquire any sort of education by which they can learn to combine among themselves and be united for the accomplishment of any object for the common good'. The Brahmanical or priestly power was badly shaken by the rise of Buddhism and Jainism, and later even more severely undercut by the inroads of Islam and the succession of Sultanates and Moghul rulers. Yet, throughout these changes, the caste structure remained largely intact, with its exclusion of the common people from public life. Dramatic changes occurred, however, with the onset of colonialism and especially under the aegis of British domination: for now the class of merchants and traders (in Indian terms the *vaishyas*) who had subdued kings and priests in Europe, were extending their middle-class regime to the Indian subcontinent—thereby inaugurating a completely new model of social and political life. For Vivekananda, given the abuses of the old caste system, the advent of British rule was not a complete calamity, provided European ideas were not slavishly imitated to the exclusion of native resources. As a subjected nation, Indians in his view could gain a new sense of purpose and identity by associating with the low caste people still shunned by the middle-class merchants—the *shudras*:

What shall I say of India? Let alone her Shudra class; her Brahmans to whom belonged the acquisition of scriptural knowledge are now the foreign professor; her Kshatriyas [warriors] the ruling Englishmen; and Vaishyas, too, the English in whose bone and marrow is the instinct of trade, so that only the Shudra-ness—the beast-of-burdenness—is now left with the Indians themselves.

The condemnation of traditional abuses, coupled with openness to Western ideas and a primary reliance on native resources of renewal, is also the hallmark of the next two selections, penned again by leading Renaissance figures. Rabindranath Tagore finds the core of India's 'problem' or malaise not in governmental structures (mostly imported from abroad) but in inveterate social customs and practices; by the same token, the remedy for the malaise must also be sought not in passive imitation of external standards but in the rejuvenation of social life from within and from the bottom up. Both the illness and the promise of India lie in the complexity of her social structure, in the rich profusion of racial, ethnic, caste, and religious diversity; if cleansed of exploitation and mutual enmity, this diversity could become a model or prototype for the larger world community. For, Tagore notes, 'those who are gifted with the moral power of love and vision of spiritual unity, who have the least feeling of enmity against aliens, and the sympathetic insight to place themselves in the position of others, will be the fittest to take their permanent place in the age that is lying before us'. Regarding European colonialism, Tagore is not adamantly opposed to its lessons and practices; it may even be 'providential that the West has come to India'. What needs to be resisted, however, is the imposition of Western standards as imperial edicts; for 'India is no beggar of the West' and must find her own path toward modernity, thus making a distinctive contribution to human culture in general.

Yet, Tagore instantly cautions, self-reliance must not be confused with xenophobic self-enclosure; in fact, he is averse to the very idea of nationalism which he considers 'a great menace' and as 'the particular thing which for years has been at the bottom of India's troubles'. A similar tenor emerges in Sri Aurobindo's account of 'The Renaissance in India'. For Aurobindo, to be valid and meaningful this 'renaissance' must be a genuine spiritual rebirth of Indian life—which may be triggered from the outside but must properly be accomplished from within. Following the advent of Western colonialism, he distinguishes three main phases of India's response: first, a phase of fervent reception (in the mode of radical modernism); next, a stage of traditionalist rejection and denial; and finally a phase 'only now beginning' which involves 'a process of new creation in which the spiritual power of the Indian mind remains supreme, recovers its truths, accepts whatever it finds sound or true, useful or inevitable of the modern idea and form, but so transmutes and Indianizes it, so absorbs and so transforms it entirely into itself that its foreign character disappears'.[13]

As previously noted, the writings of leading Renaissance thinkers were marked by a remarkable blending or balance of accents or ingredients. Even and precisely when attached to the mode of 'critical traditionalism', their posture tended to combine appreciation of indigenous traditions with an openness to the 'winds' of modernity, especially the winds of intellectual and social–political change coming from the West. In the same measure, the kind of Indian 'identity' they imagined or sought to cultivate was far removed from xenophobic self-enclosure, but aimed to blend native customs and thought patterns—suitably revived or reformed—with selected 'modernist' trends and practices in the social and educational domains, a blending which testified to their cultural flexibility and their willingness to learn from, without succumbing to, the cultural Other. As one should also note, cultural flexibility in the case of leading Renaissance thinkers tended to resist the neat bifurcation between inner-spiritual renewal and concrete social-political renovation or transformation. Wedded to an integrated or holistic outlook on life, these thinkers on the whole refused to sacrifice the latter dimension to the former, thereby avoiding the traditional antinomies between essence and appearance, inwardness and outwardness, spirit and matter. As in the case of their nineteenth century precursors, however, this balanced weighting of accents was not shared by all the intellectuals or political leaders of pre-independence India. In some instances, the scales were tipped on the far sides of the tradition–modernity spectrum; in other instances—in a manner obliquely related to this same spectrum—intellectual holism gave way to a disaggregation of idea from practice, of spirit from material conditions of life.

Contrary to the claims or prejudices of radical modernizers, defenders of tradition are not always narrowly dogmatic or mindless devotees of the past. Among intellectuals in pre-independence

India, the most thoughtful and subtly nuanced defense of classical Indian thought was formulated by Ananda Coomaraswamy (1877–1947). A learned scholar, philosopher, and art historian, Coomaraswamy made important contributions both to the exegesis of classical texts and to a deeper understanding of non-Western, especially Asian, artworks. What he appreciated primarily in classical Indian thought (chiefly the *Vedas* and *Vedanta*) was its emphasis on 'metaphysics'—the term taken in its literal sense—meaning the attempt to transcend the realm of empirical contingency in the direction of a contemplative grasp of eternal essence or 'being' (*Brahman*). In this emphasis on metaphysics or *philosophia perennis*, Coomaraswamy discovered an affinity between Vedic teachings and classical and medieval European thought—an affinity which demarcates both traditions from Western modernity with its one-sided stress on pragmatic empiricism and psychological emotivism. In opposition to empiricist myopia, he noted, *Vedanta* celebrates 'an omniscience independent of any source of knowledge external to itself, and a beatitude independent of any external source of pleasure'. The same approach permeated his treatment or reinterpretation of classical Indian aesthetics which he saw dedicated to the production of permanent artworks patterned on supra-sensual or 'angelic' models and images. This outlook provided inspiration to his endeavor to assemble classical Indian artworks, an endeavor he was able to pursue as curator of Asian art in Boston during the last fifteen years of his life.[14]

In its emphasis on timeless, transcendental meanings, Coomaraswamy's 'traditionalism' was far removed from reactionary xenophobia and from any attempt to exploit Indian tradition for time-bound political purposes or strategies. In this respect, his posture stood in stark contrast to that of radical Indian (especially Hindu) nationalists bent on marshalling the classical past as a weapon in the struggle for political power. Among radical Hindu nationalists at the time, probably the most passionate—and occasionally vitriolic—spokesman was Vinayak D. Savarkar (1883–1966), a Brahman from Maharashtra and one of the chief leaders of the Hindu Mahasabha (a communal party competing with the Indian National Congress). In his nationalist fervor, Savarkar stood on the shoulders of earlier 'extremist' intellectuals, including Bal Gangadhar Tilak (1856–1920) who in many ways served as his model and mentor. In Savarkar's view, Hinduism as a religion comprised all forms of belief or faith which had their roots in the

Indian subcontinent (thereby including Buddhism, Jainism, and Sikhism). As a political leader, however, he was not so much concerned with religion as such, as with the possible use of faith as a political agenda. To highlight the confluence of religion, culture, and politics he coined the word *Hindutva*, a term which became a troubling legacy in post-independence India. As he noted, Hindus (in the broad sense) constituted a cultural-political collectivity, in fact a 'homogeneous and organic nation' excelling above other nations: 'Not only do we own a common fatherland, a territorial unity, but what is scarcely found anywhere else in the world, we have a common holyland which is identified with our common fatherland'. Hence, political self-rule or *swaraj* in India had to mean the self-assertion of Hindus over and above non-Hindu inhabitants. As the struggle for independence progressed, Savarkar's rhetoric became more strident, culminating in the slogan 'Hinduize all politics and militarize Hindudom'—which may have inspired one of his followers to assassinate Gandhi in early 1948.[15]

Savarkar's brand of nationalism and politicized Hindu traditionalism was not palatable to many intellectuals of the period who otherwise shared the desire for self-rule or *swaraj*. What primarily offended some of these intellectuals was the collectivism and quasi-military bent of Savarkar's program which was bound to damage cultural diversity and personal initiative. A leading exponent of this perspective was the philosopher and sage Jiddu Krishnamurti (1895–1986) who developed from an early adept of the Theosophical Society (and a protégé of Annie Besant) into a resolute opponent of all forms of organized belief and collective action. Self-rule or *swaraj*, in Krishnamurti's view, had to be premised not on political slogans or programs but on inner spiritual renewal and individual self-liberation. In his stress on individualism, Krishnamurti added a 'modernist' strand to the path of spiritualism—a strand which, in this form, was absent from Coomaraswamy's spiritual metaphysics. Some of his formulations, in fact, carry echoes more of Nietzsche's 'overman' (if not of Ayn Rand's libertarianism) than of Indian yoga.

Actually, in pursuing the spiritualist path, Krishnamurti aimed to exit from all binary oppositions, including those of tradition and modernity, or of East and West. Spirituality in his account equaled individual freedom and the latter meant an exodus from all forms of ethnic, caste-based, or religious contexts and limitations; the result of inner training and discipline, self-rule involved an ascent from contingent embroilments to the level of a quasi-transcendental universalism and cosmopolitanism. As he pointed out to a questioner: In order to be truly free, 'you must be very clear that you are free from fragmentation, that you are no longer an Englishman, an American, a Jew—you follow?—that you are free from your conditioning in a particular religion or culture, which tethers you, according to which you have your experiences, which only lead you to further conditioning'. A particularly obnoxious form of conditioning was nationalism or the search for a distinct national identity. As he said: 'Nationalism not only creates outward conflict but inward frustrations; when one understands nationalism the whole process of nationalism drops away'.

Although inspirational and personally uplifting, Krishnamurti's accent on self-help was bound to appeal only to a segment of the educated Indian elite; in particular, his individualistic brand of spiritualism was liable to be uncongenial and even charring to the vast majority of India's toiling masses. If self-rule was to reach and involve these toiling masses—many intellectuals felt—other 'modernist' resources had to be mobilized, above and beyond Krishnamurti's liberalism. In the wake of the Russian Revolution and the spreading of socialism and syndicalism throughout Europe, the resources which offered themselves most readily at the time were Marxist communism and democratic socialism—although these ideologies had to be suitably adapted to the Indian context (given the proponderant size of the Indian peasantry *vis-à-vis* the barely embryonic industrial working class). In their attack on caste structures and economic exploitation, advocates of Marxist-type programs typically embraced a radically modernist outlook disdainful of indigenous traditions; to this extent they concurred with liberal-bourgeois reformers, whose economic ideas they otherwise contested. A good example of this outlook was Manavendra Nath Roy (1887–1954), a one-time executive of the Comintern and founder of a Marxist wing of the Indian National Congress.[16] Strongly anti-traditionalist in temper, Roy concentrated all his energies on the propagation of a futurist vision: the vision of a classless society under Marxist auspices. In his programmatic statement on the 'preconditions of Indian Renaissance', he adopted, approvingly, for his own country the words of the Chinese writer Hu Shih: 'China has nothing worth preserving.... You foreigners, who tell China that she has something worth preserving, are doing her a disservice, for you are only adding to our pride. We must make a clean sweep and adopt Western culture and outlook.'

By making a 'clean sweep' and adopting a Western outlook Roy meant doing away with all forms of religion and metaphysical faith in favor of a strictly scientific and empiricist orientation as found in scientific Marxism and materialism. In this connection, Roy severely castigated some Indian intellectuals—without mentioning names—for ascribing to Indian tradition a distinctive spiritual or metaphysical quality. To a scientifically trained mind, such a claim was deeply suspect and, in fact, nothing but pretentious humbug and an obstacle to progress. Once 'man gains confidence in himself', he wrote, spiritualism falls away and only 'subsists as a prejudice': 'While stubbornly resisting new forms of thought, while combating the co-ordination of ever increasing varieties of empirically acquired knowledge into a rationalist and scientific philosophy, spiritualism becomes a powerful ally of reaction against the human urge for freedom and progress'. Intellectuals and scholars who extolled spirit over material social conditions were hence not uplifting India but were engaged in a 'disgraceful mission'. For Roy, the impending Renaissance of India was going to take place 'not under the leadership of the "great men" who, consciously or unconsciously, champion reaction, but in spite of their moralizing mysticism and stale spiritualist dogmas'; if at all, it was going to happen only 'under the banner of a revolutionary philosophy'. Among the 'great men' misleading India, Roy, on other occasions, also included Gandhi whose sympathies for religion, especially Hinduism, he bemoaned and whom he charged with petty bourgeois reformism.[17]

Equally opposed to Gandhi, but for somewhat different motives, was B.R. Ambedkar (1891–1956), an outcaste from Maharashtra who—educated at elite institutions in Bombay, New York, and London—bypassed a profitable legal career by devoting himself, instead, tirelessly to the life-long struggle to uplift the 'Untouchables' or (what came to be known as) the 'Scheduled Castes'. For Ambedkar, Gandhi's policies toward the Untouchables were half-hearted and self-defeating, given that Gandhi sought to remove the stigma of untouchability without abolishing castes or the *varna* system as such. Caste domination, in his view, was clearly connected with economic or class exploitation, an argument which approximated his position to that of M.N. Roy, with whom he differed, however, on two main points. First, wary of

Stalinist communism, he favored a brand of democratic socialism (patterned on the Labour Party in England); next, he did not share the Marxists' complete disdain for traditional religion (he converted to Buddhism shortly before his death, triggering a mass conversion of Untouchables).

As the time of independence drew near, Ambedkar (on pragmatic grounds) came out openly in favor of a partitioning of the subcontinent into Hindu India and Muslim Pakistan—a posture which deepened the rift between him and Gandhi into an unbridgeable gulf. The various issues dividing the two leaders surfaced with bitter eloquence in Ambedkar's postwar attack on 'Gandhism', entitled *What Congress and Gandhi have done to the Untouchables*. What earned Ambedkar's scorn in this text was both Gandhi's continued, though modified embrace of the caste system and his opposition to class struggle (even in mild form) between landlords and tenants, capitalists and workers. For Ambedkar, Gandhi's economic approach, with its resistance to industrialization, was 'hopelessly fallacious'. Although machinery and industry may have produced 'many evils', he wrote, these evils were 'no argument against them' for they were really due to 'wrong social organization which has made private property and pursuit of personal gain matters of absolute sanctity'. Rejection of industry amounted, in fact, to a call 'back to nature' which in turn meant a return back to nakedness, squalor, and poverty.

As one should note, not all progressive or Leftist intellectuals or political leaders of the time were equally hostile to Gandhi's ideas and policies. Several important intellectuals were able to build a bridge between Marx and Gandhi—which in effect amounted to building a bridge between a relatively state-centered socialism and Gandhi's more decentralized economic agenda. Particularly noteworthy in this category is Jayaprakash Narayan (1902–1979), whose work is not excerpted in the present volume and whose main influence emerged in the post-independence era. Studious and intelligent, young Narayan encountered Marx while studying in Wisconsin and immediately was drawn to the ideas of class struggle and revolutionary social change. In the Indian context, he sympathized (for a while) with M.N. Roy's program, although he was repelled by the Stalinist features of the communist movement. After his return from America he founded the Congress Socialist Party (in 1934) as a leftist branch or wing of the National Congress. During the height of the independence struggle,

Jayaprakash and his socialist group steered a precarious course between Gandhi's policy of non-violence and revolutionary guerrilla activities. Following independence, Jayaprakash—now popularly known as 'JP'—abandoned national politics and began to devote himself wholeheartedly to a Gandhian-style program at the grass roots or village level, especially to the program of *sarvodaya* (constructive work) dedicated to the promotion of social welfare and the common good in a decentralized setting. In this turn to *sarvodaya*, Narayan joined a group of other engaged intellectuals and politicians—including Vinoba Bhave (1895–1982)—who, against many odds, endeavored to carry forward Gandhi's legacy into a new era.[18]

In many ways, Narayan's intellectual and political career illustrates the tensions and ambiguities characterizing the Indian struggle for independence, as well as their possible management or resolution. Obviously, there were profound rifts and antagonisms between the leaders of this struggle; yet, on the whole, these rifts were not so much debilitating as rather fruitful and productive as guideposts in the search for self-rule and an 'identity' congruent with the complexity of the subcontinent. Many of the top leaders of the struggle were keenly aware of this tensional complexity and attempted, in their own way, to negotiate a settlement, or a least a *modus vivendi*, between competing gravitational pulls. To this extent, their endeavors emulated the example of the great 'Renaissance' figures who (as indicated before) had sought to maintain a tolerable balance between competing forces and demands, including the demands for self-assertion and openness to the Other, and for spiritual renewal and social–economic change. As the journey toward independence gathered momentum, one of the most vexing problems looming on the horizon was the issue of inter-religious rivalry, and especially the antagonism between Hindu and Muslim political aspirations. Unsurprisingly, this issue came to occupy near center-stage in public deliberations. In the end, the Hindu–Muslim conflict eluded peaceful settlement—but not without strenuous efforts at negotiation and reconciliation. Prior to partitioning, in fact, this conflict elicited among national leaders, on both sides of this divide, some eminently thoughtful and probing reflections on the relation between religion and politics, or between secular modernity and religious tradition—reflections which deserve to be remembered today. On the Muslim side, the present volume excerpts and commemorates the views of two outstanding intellectuals and politicians: the philosopher and poet Muhammad Iqbal (1877–1938) and the philosopher–politician Abul Kalam Azad (1888–1958).

The son of devout Muslims in the Punjab, Iqbal received his education in philosophy first in Lahore and later in Cambridge and Germany—a training which led him first to a teaching career and then to a life-time of independent writing and (occasional) political activity. In outlook and stature, Iqbal ranks with the pioneers of Hindu Renaissance like Vivekananda and Aurobindo; in his capacity as a poet, he can be (and has often been) compared with Rabindranath Tagore, with whom he was linked in distant friendship. Like these Renaissance figures, he tried to strike a balance between indigenous self-assertion and openness to the Other, chiefly the lessons of modern Europe. His stay in Germany had exposed him to the teachings of Nietzsche, Bergson and other 'life philosophers'—teachings he later sought to marshall for the goal of revitalizing and 'reconstructing' Islamic thought in a dynamic fashion. As he observed in his 'reconstructive' studies, Islamic religious thought—which had been nearly 'stationary for half a millennium'—needed to 'reawaken' and to examine carefully 'in an independent spirit, what Europe has taught'.

For Iqbal, the challenge which lay ahead was to 'rethink the whole system of Islam without completely breaking with the past', which meant a mediation between tradition and modernity. While tradition was governed mainly by revealed faith, modernity was wedded to critical inquiry and concrete life experience. In this respect, the lifework of the Prophet marked a watershed: 'In so far as the source of his revelation is concerned he belongs to the ancient world; in so far as the spirit of his revelation is concerned he belongs to the modern world'. In making this distinction Iqbal did not in any way endorse a segregation of faith and reason, or of religious tradition and secular politics. As he stated in 1930, what was unacceptable in modern Western society was the complete privatization of religion and its exile from public life: 'Islam does not bifurcate the unity of man into an irreconcilable duality of spirit and matter. In Islam, God and the universe, spirit and matter, church and state, are organic to each other'. Applied to the subcontinent this meant that Indian self-rule could be built not on the neglect but only on the public negotiation of religious diversity: 'The unity of an Indian nation, therefore, must be sought not in the negation but in the mutual harmony and cooperation of the many'.[19]

When making these statements, Iqbal still upheld the prospect of a multireligious India spanning Hindus and Muslims alike—a conception which increasingly came under attack from the Muslim League and supporters of the two nation theory advocated by Muhammed Ali Jinnah (1876–1948), the political architect of Pakistan. It deserves to be recalled, however, that not all Muslim leaders embraced Jinnah's separatist program. Prominent among these dissenting voices was Maulana Abul Kalam Azad who, like Iqbal, was equally versed in traditional Muslim thought and in modern Western literature and ideas. Under the impact of Western ideas Azad, as a young man, broke with dogmatic religious traditionalism (his adopted pen name 'Azad' means 'free') without, however, renouncing the inner spirit of his religious heritage. In defiance of communal pressures, he joined the Indian National Congress in his early adulthood and later served as president of the Congress during the difficult years of the Second World War and its aftermath (from 1940 to 1946). As he observed in 1940 in a speech to the Congress, Indian Muslims were not really a small, vulnerable minority and, hence, there was no need to contemplate an exodus. In Azad's view, Muslims were as much a part of a future 'democratic India' as were other faiths and traditions. Indian self-rule did not require the abandonment of any part of the Muslim heritage but only its integration into a larger diversified whole. As for himself, Azad declared himself 'proud of being an Indian', of being a 'part of the indivisible unity that is Indian nationality'. Just as a Hindu could say with pride 'that he is an Indian and follows Hinduism, so we also can say with pride that we are Indians and follow Islam'. Faithful to these pronouncements, Azad after independence remained in India and served as national minister of education until his death.

In his commitment to a multireligious India and his opposition to partition, Azad clearly placed himself alongside Gandhi's policies—whose leadership in the independence struggle he firmly supported. Born into a family of merchants and government officials in Gujarat, Mohandas Karamchand Gandhi (1869–1948)—later known as 'Mahatma'—followed in the footsteps of Renaissance leaders by balancing the struggle for native self-rule with an openness to the 'winds' of the world, while also combining the search for moral-spiritual renewal with a commitment to social–economic change and action. Like many of his precursors, Gandhi was an inhabitant of several universes: those of traditional India and modern Europe, augmented by a prolonged stay in South Africa where he first developed his political talents and strategies. As a youngster, he was first educated in his mother tongue (Gujarati) and then trained extensively in the English medium—a training later supplemented by his legal studies in London. As a nationalist leader (sometimes termed the 'father' of independent India) Gandhi was strongly opposed to chauvinistic militancy, evident in some 'extremist' policies, and preferred to continue the path of Congress 'moderates'—among whom Gokhale served as his 'political guru'.

In his overall lifework, Gandhi reflects, more than anyone else, the enormous complexity and tensional ambivalence of pre-independence India wedged 'between tradition and modernity'. By all accounts, he was a deeply religious person wedded to traditional modes of faith (he defined himself as a *karmayogin*, a practitioner of active religious service); but he was also a relentless critic of religious abuses, including those afflicting the caste system—differing with Ambedkar over strategy. Like M.N. Roy, he was strongly dedicated to social–economic equity and change, but was wary of the collectivism and regimentation endemic to some socialist programs. On numerous occasions, he angrily attacked the vices besetting modern Western culture, especially the vices of greed, exploitation, and domination (his *Hind Swaraj* is one of the severest indictments of Western modernity ever penned); but he was himself a Western-educated man who was fond of citing Ruskin, Tolstoy, and Thoreau. While emphatically insisting on the virtues of vernacular education and the cultivation of indigenous languages, he eloquently used English in addressing a global audience.

Regarding politics or practical policies, the following paradoxes should be noted: Although clearly the most well-known and influential figure in the nationalist movement, Gandhi never accepted any official position in that movement. While seeking Indian self-rule and national independence from the British, he was deeply suspicious of the hegemonic bent of the modern nation state, favoring instead a decentralized web of village governments. On many of these issues, Jawaharlal Nehru (1889–1964) differed from Gandhi and eventually adopted divergent policies, although their contrast should probably not be overstated. Born into a wealthy family in Allahabad, Nehru was the beneficiary of the best Western-style training, being first tutored by English governesses and later educated at Harrow, Cambridge, and in London. As a result of his background and training, Nehru was decidedly more 'modernist' in outlook than Gandhi—although his modernism was of the critical variety inaugurated by Ram Mohun Roy. By temper and intellectual disposition, he was leaning toward secular agnosticism; but he was not insensitive to the empowering qualities of religious faith. Partly under the influence of M.N. Roy, Nehru embraced socialism as an ideology, although he favored the democratic variety and was averse to any doctrinaire class war. In terms of strategy, he did not subscribe to Gandhian non-violence (*ahimsa*) as a normative principle, but he honored it as a practically expedient approach. The chief difference between Nehru and Gandhi—as reflected in the selections in this volume—resided probably in their attitudes toward the modern state: with Nehru favoring a strongly centralized apparatus seen as the engine of planned economic and social change and as the arbiter between contending faiths (as well as the 'nonaligned' mediator between the contending powers of the Cold War).

III

The second part of the volume is devoted to interpretive essays dating mainly from the post-independence period. Written by social theorists, historians, philosophers, religious leaders, and novelists, the essays assembled in that part offer reflective appraisals or assessments: appraisals of the ongoing process of modernization, of communal, ethnic, and interfaith relations, of the legacy of leading nationalist figures, and of the future course of social and political life in post-independence India. In the opening essay, social theorist A.K. Saran reflects on 'Gandhi's theory of society' and its continued relevance in our time. In Saran's assessment, Gandhi as a national leader basically had to navigate between competing trends or pulls: first of all, between the 'moderate' and 'extremist' factions of Congress, and secondly and more importantly, between the vision of secular nationalism (sponsored by

Gokhale) and the program of religious, especially Hindu, revivalism (promoted by Tilak, Savarkar, and others). The two pulls amounted to a schism in the very conception of Indian self-rule. In Saran's view, Gandhi was able to bridge and surmount this schism through a number of moves: by mobilizing the Indian masses, Hindu and Muslim alike, in the freedom struggle; by injecting moral and quasi-religious principles (like *satya* and *ahimsa*) into the heart of politics; and by universalizing or globalizing the significance of Indian *swaraj*.

As Saran notes, by emphasizing 'the truth in Hinduism and Islam, indeed in all religions', and by extending political thought and action to the 'common people', Gandhi accomplished a refocusing of *swaraj* in the direction of moral *and* social-political self-rule and renewal. Basically Gandhi aimed at two goals: 'the restoration of a spiritual or normal social order in India and by extension in the world, and secondly to free India from foreign rule'; the latter freedom was for him a 'precondition for his first goal'. Regarding the continuing importance of Gandhi's legacy, Saran strongly opposes a liberal-individualist reading which stresses the cultivation of private spirituality in the midst of public oppression and injustice. Countering this divorce, individual morality (for Gandhi) was a corollary of a good social order just as the latter depended on the ordinary practice of *satyagraha*. Taken seriously, this outlook aims at a profound individual and collective change: 'Gandhism calls for a radical revolution, for a complete transformation of man's thinking and way of life, social as well as individual. In a word, it aims of *metanoia*'.

In the next selection, political theorist Thomas Pantham seeks to clarify the character and thrust of 'Nehru's political ideology'. Basically, Pantham tries to correct a one-sided and simplistic portrayal of Nehru as a secular modernist in favor of a more nuanced appraisal attentive to different strands in his thought. In his reading, Nehru—not too far removed from Gandhi—aimed to bridge and overcome a number of competing pulls, especially those of 'indigenous reactionary groups' and of imperialist capitalism imposed or imported from the West; hence, struggle for self-rule, for Nehru, meant a 'revolutionary movement directed as much against reactionary traditionalism as against the decaying structures of Western post-Enlightenment capitalist-industrial modernity'. By embracing democratic socialism, Nehru—in Pantham's account—meant to extend 'the *bright side* of European post-Enlightenment modernity' while challenging its *dark* or imperialist side. As the essay makes clear, this nuanced assessment takes exception to the interpretations of both 'liberal rationalists' and 'Marxist subalternists'; while the former coopt Nehru's politics into the standard liberal model, the latter have tended to denounce him as a lackey of capitalism. Critiquing these views, the essay emphasizes the 'odd mixture of liberalism, Marxism and Gandhism' present in Nehru's thought, a mixture which, far from being subservient to liberal-capitalist or Marxist ideologies, harbored a 'radical transformative thrust against Western modernity'. The same thrust also colored his overall intellectual stance, including his critical secularism. Steering a course between liberalism and Indian traditions (recast along socialist lines), Nehru—Pantham writes—perceived the need for a 'fusion of horizons between the scientific spirit of post-Enlightenment modernity and the deeper lessons of life, which have absorbed the minds of thinkers in all ages and in all countries'.

Echoes of this Nehruvian critical modernism (minus its nation state ideology) can also be found in the next selection by Rajni Kothari, one of the most respected Indian social theorists and long-time director of the Centre for the Study of Developing Societies in Delhi. Following partly in the footsteps of the later M.N. Roy, Kothari has published a series of important books defending the perspective of a radical-democratic humanism and the pursuit of 'humane governance'—with an ethical commitment chiefly to the under-classes on both the domestic and global levels.[20] Over the years, Kothari has become increasingly disenchanted with grand ideological panaceas, especially the panacea of 'development' engineered by a managerial elite operating on the nation state level. As he argues in the selection (taken from *Growing Amnesia*), the essential task before India today is 'to render the actions of the State and other corporate entities humane' and 'to ensure that the processes generated by "development" do not destroy diverse cultures and their roots both in nature and in unique human beings' in the name of some abstract ideology.

Looking toward the future, Kothari sees two different paths for India. One path is to continue the model of development from the top down, a model which has led 'to more and more resources and opportunities being available for smaller and smaller sections of the people' and which has been used 'for perpetuating and enhancing the parasitic lifestyles of both Indians and non-Indians through an "integration" of the Indian economy into the "world market"'. The other path, favored by Kothari, is a more decentralized or grass roots approach in which the poor and underprivileged—instead of being merely treated as a 'problem'—actually become 'the main instrument of creating an alternative, both for themselves and hence necessarily for the world around them'. Such an approach, he emphasizes, is both social–economic and existential in character, because it involves 'a search for new identities, new relationships across existing identities, a new understanding of emerging shifts in relationships'.

In its stress on decentralization and peoples' aspirations, Kothari's approach moves into the close vicinity of the Gandhian legacy (to which he repeatedly pays tribute). In an emphatic manner the Gandhian affinity surfaces in the essay by Ashis Nandy, entitled 'Cultural Frames of Social Transformation: A Credo'. Like Kothari a senior member of the Centre for the Study of Developing Societies in Delhi, Nandy has taken a strongly critical stance toward modernism and the modernist 'development' model, a stance which he himself describes as one of 'critical traditionalism'. As in the case of Kothari, this critical stance involves a focus on decentralized local contexts, here amplified by close attention to indigenous cultural resources seen as harbingers of peoples' liberation (as opposed to management from the top). In the words of the essay, the stress on culture and cultural traditions 'reinstates the categories used by the victims' while calling into question 'the modern idea of expertise' which demands 'that even resistance be uncontaminated by the "inferior" cognition or "unripe" revolutionary consciousness of the oppressed'.

Rejecting managerial expertise means, for Nandy, according primacy to local contexts and to the political consciousness of those 'who have been forced to develop categories to understand their own suffering'. Such a shift of focus, he insists, involves 'in our part of the world, some resistance to modernity' and especially to the connotative meanings of concepts like 'development, growth, history, science and technology' which, in non-Western societies, have become 'not only new "reasons of state" but mystifications for new forms of violence and injustice'. As a model of such localized, anti-hegemonic resistance Nandy invokes the legacy of Gandhi who, in many of his writings and speeches, was 'by far the most consistent and savage critic of modernity', while refusing to retreat into a nostalgic traditionalism (in the manner of Coomaraswamy). According to the essay, Gandhi rejected 'modern innovations such as the nation state system, modern science and technology, urban industrialism and evolutionism', yet without abandoning traditional notions of 'the state, science and technology, civic living and social transformation'.

The next three selections are written by eminent Indian historians of ideas and social–cultural practices. In her contribution, Romila Thapar—emeritus professor of history at Jawaharlal Nehru University in Delhi—explores the meaning and status of 'tradition' as used by traditionalists, reformers and modernists alike. As she observes with keen hermeneutical insight, tradition is not an object or empirical thing but rather a mode of cultural self-understanding which, in turn, is the result of continuing transmission and creative reinterpretation from one generation to the next. Given the (at least partial) dependence of interpretation on prevailing social needs and conditions, traditions are selective and always open to challenge in the light of new evidence (or the same evidence placed in a new context). Thapar focuses attention particularly on the discrepancy between 'normative' traditions, usually sanctioned and perpetuated by ruling elites, and actually 'lived' traditions as experienced by ordinary people placed in concrete historical settings. As she shows, such a discrepancy surfaces in the role and status of the 'renouncer' (*sannyasin*) in traditional society, in the presumed attachment of Hindus to non-violence (*ahimsa*)—a presumption disconfirmed by repeated violent clashes—and in the conception of 'Hinduism' as an inclusive religion of Indians, a conception fashioned only in recent times in disregard of earlier forms of fragmentation. In her account, it is important to differentiate 'between common civilizational symbols which are recognized over an area, and the consciousness of a community acting towards common social and religious goals'. Once this is acknowledged, history emerges as imbued with a greater degree of ambivalence, polysemy, and internal contestation than is commonly assumed.

Thapar's essay refers to the linkage between cultural self-understanding and prevailing social–economic conditions—without insisting on a causal dependence of the former on the latter. The assumption of such a dependence is the hallmark of Marxist theory, including the school of 'subaltern' historiography inaugurated by Ranajit Guha. Educated in India and London but working and teaching mainly in Australia, Ranajit Guha—and the school of thought following his lead—has vigorously challenged the predominance of elitist historiography in India as practised by colonial administrators in the past and by 'bourgeois-nationalist' intellectuals after independence. While the former portrayed India's struggle as a 'stimulus–response' kind of reaction to colonial power, the latter present the same struggle as 'an idealist venture in which the indigenous elite led the people from subjugation to freedom'. What elitist historiography of both types ignores is the class structure of Indian society, and especially the contributions made by the common people or 'subaltern' classes 'on their own, that is, independently of the elite' to the achievement of national independence. (As one may note, Guha includes in the term 'elite' both 'dominant foreign' and 'dominant indigenous' groups, while applying the term 'subaltern classes' mainly to the peasantry and industrial working class.) What is left out of account in elitist historiography is the 'politics of the people', and especially the reality of 'popular mobilization', a mobilization involving large masses of the working class (and petty bourgeoisie) under the primary impetus of peasant insurgency. In Marxist terms, this disregard signals a basic theoretical defect: namely, the neglect of the economic 'structural dichotomy' of Indian society and of the 'failure of the Indian bourgeoisie to speak for the nation'—a failure which, for Guha, constitutes the 'central problematic' of the historiography of colonial India.

The assumption of a basic 'structural dichotomy' in Indian society is not uniformly shared by Indian historians, and has even come to be questioned in recent 'subaltern' writings—partly under the influence of post-structuralist trends. In his widely acclaimed The Oppressive Present, historian Sudhir Chandra launches a critical attack on historical accounts operating with simple dichotomies or 'binary pairs', especially accounts categorizing groups or movements as either 'progressive or revivalist, reformist or reactionary, secular or communal, nationalist or communalist, and so on.' As he notes, accounts operating with these schemes are far from neutral, since the first categories of the binary pairs are usually invested with positive meaning while the counter-categories are negatively devalued—thereby disclosing the 'normative bias' of the entire framework, namely, the 'valorization of modernity at the expense of tradition'. In Chandra's view, the historical situation is much more complex and nuanced, since the dimensions of tradition and modernity, continuity and change, are closely entwined and mutually contaminated. For example, the term 'change' is not simply or unequivocally synonymous with modernity or modernization; if seen as not external to tradition, change may also be grasped as inhabiting the latter.

To illustrate the complexity and mutual entwinement of presumed opposites, Chandra turns to some early Renaissance figures, such as the 'modernist' Ram Mohun Roy and the 'revivalist' Radhakanta Deb (1784–1867), showing that their relation was less one of polarity than of 'different mixes of acceptance and rejection'. The foremost example of tensional, even paradoxical, ambivalence and embroilment was Gandhi's lifework—who, while pursuing a nationalist (and hence modernist) strategy, was also deeply critical of aspects of Western modernity. In Chandra's portrayal, Gandhi's posture bore resemblance to that of the philosopher K.C. Bhattacharya (1875–1949) who, like Gandhi, supported the aim of Indian political self-rule or *swaraj*, but who—going beyond political agendas—also stressed the need for a '*swaraj* in ideas', that is, the attempt of colonized people to extricate themselves from cultural subjugation and the sway of the colonizers' hegemonic world-view. Without blindly rejecting the alien nor blindly accepting the indigenous, Bhattacharya sought to cultivate the 'vernacular mind' through open engagement and contestation.

The reference to Bhattacharya serves as a transition to contemporary philosophical discussions in India, and especially to the essay included in this volume by Ramchandra Gandhi on the '*swaraj* of India'. A grandson of the Mahatma, Ramchandra Gandhi takes up again the crucial issue dominating the life-work both of his forebear and of Bhattacharya: the proper meaning of decolonization and of mature Indian self-rule or autonomy. As matters stand, Indian philosophy today is deeply divided into antagonistic trends or camps: on the one side, trends emulating 'modernist' Western thought, especially Anglo-American analytical philosophy (with a stress on logic and scientific epistemology); on the other side, traditional Sanskrit-speaking pundits completely unfamiliar with, and disinterested in, the modern idiom. In fairness, one should mention the work of a number of thinkers innovatively contesting the prevailing antinomy, a group including, among others, Daya Krishna, the late J.L. Mehta, and Sundara

Rajan.[21] A prominent figure in this group is Ramchandra Gandhi, known for his proclivity for escaping school labels.

In the chosen essay, Ramchandra invokes the teachings of Bhattacharya, Ramana Maharshi (1879–1950) and others in an effort to clarify the genuine meaning of *swaraj* as disclosed in the classical tradition. As he indicates, *swaraj* denotes, indeed, self-reliance but not in a selfish or self-centered sense—since the 'self' is both singular and holistic. Drawing on the legacy of *Advaita* (non-dualism) and the Upanishadic mantra *'tat tvam asi'* ('thou art that'), he defines *swaraj* as autonomy free from any xenophobia. In all seeking of *swaraj*, he writes, '*sva* [self] seeks to be the ruler, center, source of all things'; but this seeking is '*sarvodaya* and not selfishness' due to the insight of *Advaita* 'that you and I are not other than one another'. This truth is opposed to the modern 'monadic' view of selfhood according to which 'everyone is what he is and not someone else'. For Ramchandra, '*advaitin* India' should boldly embrace this 'new testament of identity' which is 'new only in rediscovery' and which, in revealing *swaraj* as 'simultaneously autonomy *and* love, radical *and* universal', points the way beyond 'isolationism and hegemonism, tribalism and imperialism'.

The next two selections are by two leading Indian novelists, renowned for their 'vernacular' writings respectively in Kannada and Hindi. Perhaps better still than historians and social theorists, novelists and storytellers are able to capture the rich complexity and tensional rifts characterizing contemporary India. In his contribution, the Kannada novelist Anantha Murthy illustrates in dramatic fashion the tension marking the encounter between rationalist modern discourse, on the one hand, and indigenous beliefs and practices, on the other. Taking his cues from real-life happenings, he recounts in vivid detail the clash between enlightened onlookers (journalists, social scientists, reform activists) and participants in a religious practice—re-enacted annually in a certain Indian village—of worshipping a deity in the nude. 'The encounter', he writes, 'between illiterate believers and the educated middle-class rationalists was both fierce and unexpected. The worshippers broke through the physical barricade of the rationalists who stood on the bank of the river pleading with them to wear clothes'. Faced with the complexities of this drama, the novelist in Anantha Murthy's view is bound to be torn in multiple directions and cannot afford himself the comforts of 'either status-quoist acceptance or revolutionary ruthlessness'. Without pretending to offer a facile solution of the issue, his account instead captures the deep agonies and traumas involved in this clash of life-forms, thereby preserving the basic ambivalence of a situation which cannot be flattened into a linear story of progress. As he notes candidly: 'We are all in love with Modern Civilization in India, whether we are capitalists, communists or liberals'. But life in the villages and among the poor is different and cannot coercively be changed without loss and without resort to massive (totalitarian) violence and a brutalization of social life: 'Yes—all of us are modernizers in one way or the other, but with an uneasy conscience, if we are sensitive. The great writers among us see it as inevitable and search for ways to preserve what is best and unique in Indian civilization'.

In his essay on 'India and Europe', the novelist Nirmal Verma picks up the theme of the clash of life-forms, focusing directly on the relation between India and Western modernity. Like Anantha Murthy, he takes his bearings from the real-life happening of cultural encounter in a shrinking world; and again, like the former, he perceives the agony, trauma, and violence implicit in that encounter. For Verma, India's contact with the West was not a meeting among equals but a 'violent cultural rupture' in Indian ways of life; for, as he writes, European colonization was not merely an act of spatial–territorial expansion but an attempt 'to colonize India's sense of *time*' by pressing her into the Western model of evolutionary progress. This forced intrusion had the effect of disaggregating the customary fabric of meanings: 'As an Indian was "historicized" in the European context, he was de-Indianized in the context of his own "traditional" self'. As a corollary of the Western gospel of science and progress, the traditional texture of meanings and rituals—the 'network of myths and symbols' through which Hindus 'interpreted and deciphered the "text" of the world'—was steadily undermined. In its persistence through two centuries, European colonization cast 'a cleavage right in the middle of the Indian consciousness'. As a corrective to this schism, Verma—like Nandy and Sudhir Chandra—turns to the legacy of Gandhi who, as he writes, was both a severe critic of Western civilization and a passionate gadfly stirring the 'colonized consciousness of Indians' in the direction of *swaraj*. Through Gandhi's influence the encounter between cultures became a form of self-scrutiny or self-interrogation—a scrutiny which alone can create an open space allowing for mutual listening. As Verma concludes in a memorable passage: 'Such "listening" is both a discovery and a revelation, a discovery of the Other within ourselves and the revelation of ourselves through the Other. After all the utterances have been made by the anthropologists, historians and philosophers on either side, perhaps time has come for both India and Europe to pause a little, listening to one another in silence, which may be as "sound" a method of discourse as any other'.[22]

Despite its rich subtlety, Verma's essay—unintentionally—may give the impression of conceiving Indian *swaraj* narrowly in terms of 'Hindu' self-rule. To counteract this impression, the volume offers next some essays by Maulana Wahiduddin Khan, a leading Muslim writer and cleric in contemporary India. A senior member of the Islamic Centre in Delhi and editor-in-chief of the journal *Al-Risala*, Wahidduddin Khan for many years now has been a staunch defender of an open-minded 'liberal' posture while remaining firmly grounded in the genuine teachings of Islam. Following in the footsteps of Muhammed Iqbal and Kalam Azad, his writings have continuously pursued a dual path: by critiquing both a secular modernism hostile to religion and a religious fundamentalism hostile to constitutional politics. In this manner, the Maulana's work—like that of the novelists—reflects and respects the tensional ambivalence of contemporary India which requires prudent negotiation.

One of Khan's chief critical targets has been the subordination of religion to politics, that is, the exploitation of religious faith for power-political purposes. His essay on 'Religion and Politics' strongly attacks politicization attempts in both India and Pakistan. As he writes: 'The Islamization of Pakistan and the Hinduization of India simply failed to take shape; despite a fifty-year bloody struggle neither could Pakistan be Islamized nor India Hinduized.' While opposing the fusion of state and religion, Khan gives ample room to religious faith in civil society—but to a genuine, non-aggressive faith which would encourage people (of different beliefs) to 'begin to pray for each other'. In his essay 'A Silent Revolution' the Maulana applies this approach to the experiences of Muslims in Kashmir and the experiences of Hindus after the demolition of the Babri Masjid in late 1992. In both cases, people were mobilized by fanatical demagogues, with extremely painful results. But as Khan surmises, perhaps these experiences had a salutary and sobering effect—by prompting people to extricate themselves from 'the clutches of self-serving and incompetent leaders' and to reorient themselves toward civic reconciliation. Such a change would indeed hold out the 'greatest hope' for the future of India.

The concluding essay in the present volume expands the complex tapestry of Indian intellectual life by turning attention to the emerging feminist movement and especially to the voice of women in contemporary Indian literature. In this field again, a tensional ambivalence surfaces—one which, though often side-stepped, is carefully articulated by Susie Tharu and K. Lalita in their excerpted essay (which serves as Introduction to the second volume of their *Women Writing in India*). As Tharu and Lalita point out, the feminist movement around the world is in significant ways shaped and spearheaded by Western, particularly American, feminism—which, in the literary domain, takes the form of avant-garde 'gynocriticism'. While acknowledging the critical edge animating Western feminism, both authors are disturbed by certain hegemonic or elitist features in avant-gardism, features which are troubling for Indian (and other non-Western) women seeking literary *swaraj*. What is particularly dubious, for Tharu and Lalita, is the tendency of Western feminist writers to 'naturalize' and universalize their particular experiences, thereby erasing historical and cultural differences—and also concealing the (possible) complicity of their outlook in global structures of hegemonic domination. As they write, gender relations in prominent Western texts tend to be portrayed in 'domestic, middle class terms' and to revolve around one 'fundamental antagonism', that of a 'monolithic, unchanging patriarchy', which seemingly has 'no connections with other hegemonies, say, of class or race'. Faced with Western gynocriticism, Indian women writers, therefore, have to practise a double gesture: that of both appreciating and challenging the Western model. For Tharu and Lalita, the task ahead is to develop an awareness that 'there are many "mainstream" literatures', that women writing in English 'cannot be so casually gathered into the same fold', and, above all, that 'it is not the same essential female nature that is struggling, the world over, to free itself from male bondage'.

In assembling the present volume, the editors have been guided by the hope of presenting a fair and reasonably broad—though of course not all-inclusive—portrait of Indian social and intellectual life in our century and of the ongoing search for identity or genuine *swaraj*. As it seems to us, the portrait sketched in this volume is instructive and revealing on many levels. In its collection of criss-crossing and often antagonistic perspectives, the volume introduces the reader to a monumental drama of our age—a drama which is often blandly styled as 'development' or 'modernization' but which really involves a clash of competing life-forms and competing conceptions of the 'good life'. To this extent, the volume exposes and hopefully sensitizes the reader to (what we called earlier) a vast 'sentimental journey', a journey which for millions of people has been, and continues to be, the source of immense agony and profound perplexity. This agony is felt world-wide, but has been particularly intense in the Indian context, the context of a society where the most ancient memories and traditions collide head-on with the most acute pressures of Western modernity, introduced first by European colonialism and later continued by modernization experts. Seen from this angle, the process of development is really a struggle over the heart and soul of India, and, by extension, over the sense and direction of humanity or humankind. What is remarkable in the Indian case, and what makes this story so revealing, is the fact that, over the past century and more, India's struggle has given relatively free expression to the most varied perspectives and the most divergent pulls and counter-pulls—thus offering a gripping panoramic view of (what existentialists termed) the 'human predicament' in our time. Although undergoing parallel experiences, other non-Western societies—less democratic in disposition—have often been too rigidly regimented (by political or clerical elites) to allow for the open display of this human and social drama.

For Western readers the present volume offers an insight into a complex cultural life-world which—by modernist standards—may seem exceedingly remote or alien. Yet, if we take seriously Nirmal Verma's point regarding the embroilment of cultural encounter and self-knowledge, the volume may also help Western readers to gain a better understanding of their own culture and of the (intended or unintended) repercussions of Western modernity around the world. Seriously pursued, such self-knowledge can also be wrenching. In many ways, Western modernity has become so habitual and self-assured that readers may be unprepared or ill-equipped to question some of its premises or to explore (what Horkheimer and Adorno called) the 'dialectic of enlightenment'. Yet, precisely by virtue of its claim to be 'critical' (of habitual prejudice), Western modernity cannot refuse the challenge of internal self-critique. Without necessarily leading to disorientation or self-abnegation, such internal scrutiny might stimulate in Western culture a comparable search for self-rule or *swaraj*, far removed from colonial or neo-colonial forms of dominance. Pursued as a generalized quest, improved self-rule and self-understanding may well turn out to be the most promising antidote to the danger of global conflagration and to the destructive virus of communal hatred and ethnic or religious violence. By fully endorsing this alternative, our volume pays tribute to the legacy of Gandhi who, in A.K. Saran's terms, emphasized the 'world-historical character' of the Indian struggle, without denying the salience of local-historical contexts. In embracing this Gandhian legacy we, the editors, are also encouraged by these lines from the *Shvetashvatara Upanishad*:

> *He who is one and who dispenses*
> *The inherent needs of all peoples and all times,*
> *Who is in the beginning and the end of all things,*
> *May He unite us with the bond of goodwill.*[23]

■

■ Notes ■

[1] Regarding globalization see Mike Featherstone (ed.), *Global Culture: Nationalism, Globalization and Modernity; A Theory, Culture and Society Special Issue*, London, Sage Publications Ltd, 1990; Roland Robertson, *Globalization: Social Theory and Global Culture*, London, Sage Publications Ltd, 1992; Martin J. Gannon, *Understanding Global Cultures: Metaphorical Journeys Through 17 Countries*, Newbury Park, Sage Publications, Inc. 1994; also Stephen Toulmin, *Cosmopolis: The Hidden Agenda of Modernity*, New York, Free Press, 1990.

[2] As Lucian W. Pye wrote, in a display of rare candor: The process of modernization 'might also be called Westernization, or simply advancement and progress; it might, however, be more accurately termed the diffusion of a world

culture—a world culture based on advanced technology and the spirit of science, on a rational view of life, a secular approach to social relations.... At an ever-accelerating rate, the direction and the volume of cross-cultural influence has become nearly a uniform pattern of the Western industrial world imposing its practices, standards, techniques, and values upon the non-Western world'. See his *Aspects of Political Development* Boston, Little Brown, 1966, pp. 8–9, 44–45.

[3] Compare Mark Juergensmeyer, *The New Cold War? Religious Nationalism Confronts the Secular State*, Berkeley, University of California Press, 1993; and Franke Wilmer, *The Indigenous Voice in World Politics: Since Time Immemorial*, Newbury Park, Sage Publications, Inc., 1993.

[4] See, e.g., R.C. Majumdar, ed., *History and Culture of the Indian People*, 7 vols (Bombay: Bharatiya Vidya Bhavan, 1951–1969); R.C. Majumdar et al., *An Advanced History of India*, 2nd edn, New York, St. Martin's Press, 1959; Romila Thapar, *A History of India*, Harmondsworth, Viking, 1966; Stanley A. Wolpert, *A New History of India*, 3rd edn, New York, Oxford University Press, 1989; idem, *An Introduction to India*, Berkeley, University of California Press, 1991; idem, *Jinnah of Pakistan*, New York, Oxford University Press, 1984; Richard Sisson and Stanley A. Wolpert (eds), *Congress and Indian Nationalism: The Pre-Independence Phase*, Berkeley, University of California Press, 1988; David Kopf, *British Orientalism and the Bengal Renaissance: The Dynamics of Indian Modernization, 1733–1834*, Berkeley, University of California Press, 1969; S.M. Ikram, *Muslim Civilization in India* (ed.) A.T. Embree, New York, Columbia University Press, 1964; Lloyd I. Rudolph and Susanne H. Rudolph, *The Modernity of Tradition*, Chicago, University of Chicago Press, 1967; Milton Singer, *When a Great Tradition Modernizes: An Anthropological Approach to Indian Civilization*, New York, Praeger Publishers, 1972; M.N. Srinivas, *Caste in Modern India and Other Essays*, Bombay, Asia Publishing House, 1962; idem., *Social Change in Modern India*, Berkeley, University of California Press, 1966; G.S. Ghurye, *Caste and Class in India*, Bombay, Popular Book Depot, 1957; *Caste and Race in India*, 5th edn, Bombay, Popular Prakashan, 1969; David G. Mandelbaum, *Society in India, 2 Vols* Berkeley, University of California Press, 1970; B.L.C. Johnson, *Development in South Asia*, Harmondsworth, Viking, 1983.

[5] Compare Jacques Derrida, *The Other Heading: Reflections on Today's Europe*, trans. Pascale-Anne Brault and Michael N. Naas, Bloomington, Indiana University Press, 1992; also Edward W. Said, *Covering Islam: How the Media and the Experts Determine How We See the Rest of the World*, New York, Pantheon Books, 1981, esp. the chapter on 'Knowledge and Power', pp. 126–164.

[6] See Benedict Anderson, *Imagined Communities*, New York, Pergamon Press, 1991; also Richard Cronin, *Imagining India*, New York, St. Martin's Press, 1989.

[7] See in this context Hans-Georg Gadamer, *Truth and Method*, 2nd rev. edn, trans. & rev. Joel Weinsheimer and Donald G. Marshall, New York, Crossroad, 1989; and regarding 'horizons of significance', Charles Taylor, *The Ethics of Authenticity*, Cambridge, MA, Harvard University Press, 1992, pp. 31–41. In one sense, the notion of the arbitrary construction of traditions and cultures presupposes a kind of transcendental spectator, that is, an interpreter located outside all cultures and traditions; absolved from contexts, this interpreter dwells in undifferentiated sameness. If this presupposition is abandoned, a strictly constructivist interpretation coincides with power politics or strategic manipulation.

[8] Regarding Ram Mohun Roy see especially Kalidas Nag and D. Burman (eds), *English Works of Raja Rammohan Roy, Part I–VI*, Calcutta, Sadharan Brahmo Samaj, 1945–1951; Sophia D. Collet, *The Life and Letters of Raja Rammohan Roy*, 3rd edn, Calcutta, Sadharan Brahmo Samaj, 1962; also Thomas Pantham, 'The Socio-Religious and Political Thought of Rammohan Roy', in Thomas Pantham and Kenneth L. Deutsch, eds, *Political Thought in Modern India*, New Delhi, Sage Publications India Pvt Ltd, 1986, pp. 32–52.

[9] For a short overview of these nineteenth century developments see K.M. Sen, *Hinduism*, London, Penguin, 1986, pp. 108–111; and for a more detailed account Donald Bishop (ed), *Thinkers of the Indian Renaissance*, Delhi, Wiley Eastern Ltd., 1982. As one should note, the above list of Renaissance figures is by no means complete—just as the selections in this volume should only be viewed as illustrative of prominent perspectives or approaches. Other important Renaissance figures were Keshub Chundra Sen (1838–1884) who aimed to combine Hinduism and Christianity, and Mahadev Govind Ranade (1842–1901), one of the founders of the Prarthana Samaj (Prayer Society) in 1867. It is important to realize that the Hindu revival was paralleled by an equally energetic Islamic reformism or renaissance whose leaders included Syed Ahmed Khan (1817–1898), the Muslim counterpart of Ram Mohun Roy; and Mohammed Ali (1878–1931), a spokesman of the Khilafat movement. For selections from these figures see Stephen Hay (ed.), *Sources of Indian Tradition*, 2nd edn, New York, Columbia University Press, 1988, Vol. 2, pp. 44–52, 102–113, 180–222.

[10] Bhikhu Parekh, *Colonialism, Tradition and Reform: An Analysis of Gandhi's Political Discourse*, New Delhi, Sage Publications India Pvt Ltd, pp. 35, 57–58.

[11] Parekh, *Colonialism, Tradition and Reform*, pp. 59, 63–64. As Parekh keenly observes, one important difference between the two perspectives was their treatment of the state–society relation: while critical modernists saw the state as the chief engine of modernization (with traditional society functioning only as a partial ally), critical traditionalists placed their trust mainly in the resources of society (which alone could provide legitimacy to the state). Regarding Bankim Chandra see especially Sudipta Kaviraj, *The Unhappy Consciousness: Bankimchandra Chattopadhyay and the Formation of Nationalist Discourse in India*, New York, Oxford University Press, 1995; also Partha Chatterjee, 'Culture and Power in the Thought of Bankimchandra', in Pantham and Deutsch, eds, *Political Thought in Modern India*, pp. 67–91.

[12] See Hans Kohn, *The Idea of Nationalism: A Study in Its Origins and Background*, New York, Macmillan, 1944; and John Plamenatz, 'Two Types of Nationalism', in Eugene Kamenka (ed.), *Nationalism: The Nature and Evolution of an Idea*, London, Edward Arnold, 1976, pp. 23–26. In recent decades, the study of nationalism has been greatly refined, beyond Kohn's liberal-regressive dichotomy, partly through reliance on the constructed nature of national identities. Compare Ernest Gellner, *Nations and Nationalism*, Ithaca, Cornell University Press, 1983; Anthony D. Smith, *Theories of Nationalism*, New York, Homes & Meier Publishers, 1983; Eric Hobsbawm, *Nations and Nationalism Since 1780*, Cambridge, Cambridge University Press, 1990; James Mayall, *Nationalism and International Society*, Cambridge, Cambridge University Press, 1990; William Bloom, *Personal Identity, National Identity, and International Relations*, Cambridge, Cambridge University Press, 1990; Homi K. Bhabha (ed.), *Nation*

and Narration, New York, Routledge, 1990; John Breuilly, *Nationalism and the State*, New York, St. Martin's Press, 1992; also Johann P. Arnason, 'Nationalism, Globalization and Modernity', in M. Featherstone (ed.), *Global Culture*, pp. 207–236.

[13] As should be noted, Sri Aurobindo, at an earlier point of his life, espoused a radical kind of Hindu nationalism both in his writings and his political activities, but this stance lasted only a few years. For selections from this period (1907–1908) see Hay (ed.), *Sources of Indian Tradition*, Vol. 2, pp. 150–154.

[14] Coomaraswamy was curator in the Department of Asiatic Art of the Boston Museum of Fine Arts from 1932 to his death. In its emphasis on a timeless, transcendental realm, his thought carried an (implicit) critical or liberating impulse—which distanced him from any vulgar kind of Indian nationalism. At the same time, he was curiously attracted to the metaphysical 'socialism' of William Morris. For an instructive comparison of Coomaraswamy with spokesmen of 'neo-Hinduism' (or critical traditionalism) like Sri Aurobindo and Sarvepalli Radhakrishnan (1888–1975) see Wilhelm Halbfass, *India and Europe: An Essay in Understanding*, Albany, NY, SUNY Press, 1988, pp. 254–55, 371.

[15] Compare Vinayak D. Savarkar, *Hindutva*, 1923; 4th edn, Poona, S.P. Gokhale, 1949. Building on earlier 'extremist' views, Savarkar's ideas in turn served as inspiration to subsequent political and even para-military Hindu organizations like the *Rashtriya Swayamsevak Sangh* (National Assembly of Volunteers, RSS) and the *Bharatiya Jan Sangh* (All-India People's League). See, in this context, Prabha Dixit, 'The Ideology of Hindu Nationalism', in Pantham and Deutsch (eds), *Political Thought in Modern India*, pp. 122–41.

[16] The Indian National Congress had been founded as a national party in Bombay in 1885. In 1906 the Muslim League was founded, dividing the nationalist movement along religious lines. In 1907, the Congress itself was split by the quarrel between 'Moderates' and 'Extremists' who differed on strategies to overcome British colonialism. Among 'moderate' Congress leaders are usually counted Dadabhai Naoroji (1825–1917), Surendranath Banerjee (1848–1925), Mahadev Govind Ranade (1842–1901), Gopal Krishna Gokhale (1866–1915), and Romesh Chunder Dutt (1848–1909). Among 'extremist' figures these stand out: Bankim Chandra Chatterji (1838–1894), Bal Gangadhar Tilak (1856–1920), Lala Lajpat Rai (1865–1928), in addition to the early Sri Aurobindo. For selections from these figures see Hay (ed.), *Sources of Indian Tradition*, Vol. 2, pp. 84–172. As one should note, the distinction made by Parekh between critical modernists and critical traditionalists is not identical with, but cuts across the difference between moderates and extremists in terms of political strategy.

[17] Following World War II, realizing the extent of Stalinist oppression, M.N. Roy became disenchanted with communism and began to advocate a radical secular humanism. See, in this context, his *New Humanism: A Manifesto*, Calcutta, Renaissance, 1947. Through his radical humanist stance, Roy became influential for a number of later thinkers, including Ram Manohar Lohia (1910–1967) and, to some extent, Rajni Kothari.

[18] Compare in this context Jayaprakash Narayan (1902–1979), *Socialism, Sarvodaya and Democracy* (ed.) Bimla Prasad, New York, Asia Publishing House, 1964; also Dennis Dalton, 'The Ideology of Sarvodaya', in Pantham and Deutsch (eds), *Political Thought in Modern India*, pp. 275–96.

[19] These statements are taken from Iqbal's 'Presidential Address' before the All-India Muslim League in 1930. At that time, Iqbal still envisaged the formation of semi-autonomous religious communities within a comprehensive Indian state. However, despairing of this possibility he seems to have moved later on to an endorsement of partitioning of the subcontinent along Muslim/Hindu lines. Compare Moin Shakir, *Khilafat to Partition*, New Delhi, Kalamkar Prakashan, 1970; also his 'Dynamics of Muslim Political Thought', in Pantham and Deutsch (eds), *Political Thought in Modern India*, pp. 142–60.

[20] See especially Rajni Kothari, *State against Democracy: In Search of Humane Governance*, Delhi, Ajanta, 1988; *Transformation and Survival: In Search of a Humane World Order*, Delhi, Ajanta, 1988; *Rethinking Development: In Search of Humane Alternatives*, New York, New Horizons, 1989; *Growing Amnesia: An Essay on Poverty and the Human Consciousness*, Delhi, Viking, 1993, published in England under the title *Poverty: Human Consciousness and the Amnesia of Development*, London, Zed Books, 1993. For a fuller discussion of the work of both Kothari and Ashis Nandy see Fred Dallmayr, 'Global Development? Alternative Voices from Delhi', *Alternatives*, Vol. 21 (1996), pp. 259–82.

[21] Compare Daya Krishna, *Indian Philosophy: A Counter-Perspective*, Delhi, Oxford University Press, 1991, *Political Development: A Critical Perspective*, Delhi, Oxford University Press, 1979, *Considerations Toward a Theory of Social Change*, Bombay, Manaktalas, 1965; R. Sundara Rajan, *The Primacy of the Political*, Delhi, Oxford University Press, 1991; *Towards a Critique of Cultural Reason*, Delhi, Oxford University Press, 1987; *Innovative Competence and Social Change*, Ganeshkind, Poona University Press, 1986; J.L. Mehta, *Philosophy and Religion: Essays in Interpretation*, New Delhi, Munshiram Manoharlal Publishers, 1990, *India and the West: The Problem of Understanding*, Chico, CA: Scholars Press, 1985, *Martin Heidegger: The Way and the Vision*, Honolulu, University Press of Hawaii, 1976. On Mehta see also William J. Jackson (ed.), *J.L. Mehta on Heidegger, Hermeneutics and Indian Tradition*, Leiden, Brill, 1992 and Fred Dallmayr, 'Heidegger, Bhakti, and Vedanta: A Tribute to J.L. Mehta', in his *Beyond Orientalism: Essays on Cross-Cultural Encounter*, Albany, NY, SUNY Press, 1996, pp. 89–114.

[22] As one may note, Verma repeatedly criticizes the philosopher J.L. Mehta for sponsoring a complicated self-search through 'otherness', involving a possible peregrination through foreign lands. Yet, Verma's own view of self-scrutiny is sufficiently complex, involving an intimate self–other embroilment, so as to render the distinction more a matter of accent or nuance. His stress on listening, in any event, is strongly supported by Kenneth L. Schmitz when he writes that cross-cultural understanding 'will be helped, no doubt, by dialogue such as that which occurs at scientific and cultural meetings.... But the exchange calls for listening as well as speaking, for we are being called to venture out into relatively unexplored seas, into unknown space between cultures, in which we must recognize the freedom of others to contribute to what can only be the *joint* building up of the unity-in-diversity of humankind.' See 'The Unity of Human Nature and The Diversity of Cultures', in George F. McLean and John Kromkowski, eds, *Relations Between Cultures*, Washington, DC: Council for Research in Values and Philosophy, 1991, p. 320.

[23] *Shvetashvatara Upanishad*, IV, 1; cited in Sen, *Hinduism*, p. 111. Regarding communal conflict and related trends in present-day India compare Gyanendra

Pandey (ed.), *Hindus and Others: The Question of Identity in India Today*, New Delhi, Viking–Penguin Books, 1993; Ashutosh Varshney, *Contested Meanings: India's National Identity, Hindu Nationalism and the Politics of Anxiety*, Cambridge, Center for International Affairs, 1992; Felix Wilfred, (ed.), *Leave the Temple: Indian Paths to Human Liberation*, New York, Orbis, 1992; Norbu Dawa, *Culture and the Politics of Third World Nationalism*, New York, Routledge, 1992; Koenraad Elst, *Ayodhya and After: Issues before Hindu Society*, New Delhi, Voice of India Publications, 1991; Bruce Desmond Graham, *Hindu Nationalism*, New York, Cambridge University Press, 1990; Ainslee T. Embree, *Utopias in Conflict: Religion and Nationalism in Modern India*, Berkeley, University of California Press, 1990; Arvind P. Nirmal (ed.), *Towards a Dalit Ideology*, Delhi, Indian Society for the Promotion of Christian Knowledge, 1988; E.A. Kappen, *Communism and Culture in India*, Madras, Christian Literature Society, 1984.

■

■ PART ONE ■

■ COLONIALISM AND THE STRUGGLE FOR NATIONAL INDEPENDENCE ■

1

■ SWAMI VIVEKANANDA ■

Narendranath Datta (1863–1902), later known as Vivekananda, was born in Calcutta in a high-caste family of lawyers. As a boy he received a good Western-style education, and he was planning to study law in England when he met Sri Ramakrishna in 1881. Although previously inclining toward Western rationalism and science, the encounter profoundly changed his outlook; giving up the idea of a worldly career, he adopted the life of a 'renouncer' (sannyasi), dedicating himself to spreading Ramakrishna's message of God-realization, especially among the poor and underprivileged masses. After having traveled throughout India in pursuit of this mission, he was invited to represent Vedantic Hinduism at the First World Parliament of Religions held in Chicago in 1893, a visit which earned him world-wide acclaim. Following extensive lecture tours in America and England, he returned to India a national hero, and devoted himself again with great zeal to social work and religious education among Indians of all castes. He died at the age of 39.

For primary and secondary sources see *The Complete Works of Swami Vivekananda*, 8 volumes, Calcutta, Advaita Ashrama, 1972–1978; Swami Vidyatmananda (ed.), *What Religion is in the Words of Swami Vivekananda*, Calcutta, Advaita Ashrama, 1972; Swami Nikhilananda (ed.), *Vivekananda: The Yogas and Other Works*, New York, Ramakrishna–Vivekananda Center, 1953; Ann Myren and Dorothy Madison (eds), *Yoga Teachings of Vivekananda*, Boston, Shambhala, 1993. The following selection is taken from the journal *Udbodhana* (March 1899).

MODERN INDIA

The Vedic priests base their superior strength on the knowledge of the sacrificial Mantras.[1] By the power of these Mantras, the Devas are made to come down from their heavenly abodes, accept the drink and food offerings, and grant the prayers of the Yajamanas.[2] The kings as well as their subjects are, therefore, looking up to these priests for their welfare during their earthly life. Raja Soma[3] is worshipped by the priest and is made to thrive by the power of his Mantras.... The king might have paramount power; attaining a great glory in his reign, he might prove himself as the father and mother in one to his subjects; but if the priest is not appeased, his sun of glory goes down with his last breath for ever; all his worth and usefulness deserving of universal approbation are lost in the great womb of time, like unto the fall of gentle dew on the ocean....

To protect the State, to meet the expenses of the personal comforts and luxuries of himself and his long retinue, and, above all, to fill to overflowing the coffers of the all-powerful priesthood for its propitiation, the king is continually draining the resources of his subjects, even as the sun sucks up moisture from the earth. His especial prey—his milk cows—are the Vaishyas.

Neither under the Hindu kings, nor under the Buddhist rule, do we find the common subject-people taking any part in expressing their voice in the affairs of the State. True, Yudhishthira visits the houses of Vaishyas and even Shudras when he is in Varanavata; true, the subjects are praying for the installation of Ramachandra to the regency of Ayodhya; nay, they are even criticizing the conduct of Sita and secretly making plans for the bringing about of her exile, but as a recognized rule of the State they have no direct voice in the supreme government. The power of the populace is struggling to express itself in indirect and disorderly ways without any method. The people have not, as yet, the conscious knowledge of the existence of this power. There is neither the attempt on their part to organize it into a united action, nor have they got the will to do so; there is also a complete absence of that capacity, that skill, by means of which small and incoherent centers of force are united together, creating insuperable strength as their resultant.

Is this due to want of proper laws?—no, that is not it. There are laws, there are methods, separately and distinctly assigned for the guidance of different departments of government, there are laws laid down in the minutest detail for everything, such as the collection of revenue, the management of the army, the administration of justice, punishments and rewards. But at the root of all is the injunction of the Rishi—the word of divine authority, the revelation of God coming through the inspired Rishi. The laws have, it can almost be said, no elasticity in them. Under the circumstances, it is never possible for the people to acquire any sort of education by which they can learn to combine among themselves and be united for the accomplishment of any object for the common good of the people, or by which they can have the concerted intellect to conceive the idea of popular right in the treasures collected by the king from his subjects, or even such education by which they can be fired with the aspiration to gain the right of representation in the control of State revenues and expenditure. Why should they do such things? Is not the inspiration of the Rishi responsible for their prosperity and progress?

Again, all those laws are in books. Between laws as codified in books and their operation in practical life, there is a world of difference. One Ramachandra is born after thousands of Agnivarnas[4] pass away! Many kings show us the life of Chandashoka;[5] Dharmashokas are rare! The number of kings like Akbar, in whom the subjects find their life, is far less than that of kings like Aurangzeb who live on the blood of their people!

Even if the kings be of as godlike nature as that of Yudhishthira, Ramachandra, Dharmashoka, or Akbar, under whose benign rule the people enjoyed safety and prosperity, and were looked after with paternal care by their rulers, the hand of him who is always fed by another gradually loses the power of taking the food to his mouth. His power of self-preservation can never become fully manifest who is always protected in every respect by another. Even the strongest youth remains but a child if he is always looked after as a child by his parents. Being always governed by kings of godlike nature, to whom is left the whole duty of protecting and providing for the people, they can never get any occasion for understanding the principles of self-government. Such a nation, being entirely dependent on the king for everything and never caring to exert itself for the common good or for self-defense, becomes gradually destitute of inherent energy and strength. If this state of dependence and protection continues long, it becomes the cause of the destruction of the nation, and its ruin is not far to seek.

Of course, it can be reasonably concluded that, when the government of a country is guided by codes of laws enjoined by Shastras which are the outcome of knowledge inspired by the divine genius of great sages, such a government must lead to the unbroken welfare of the rich and the poor, the wise and the ignorant, the king and the subjects alike. But we have seen already how far the operation of those laws was, or may be, possible in practical life. The voice of the ruled in the government of their land—which is the watchword of the modern Western world, and of which the last expression has been echoed with a thundering voice in the declaration of the American Government, in the words: 'That the government of the people of this country must be by the people and for the good of the people'—cannot however be said to have been totally unrecognized in ancient India. The Greek travelers and others saw many independent small states scattered all over this country, and references are also found to this effect in many places of the Buddhistic literature. And there cannot be the least doubt about it that the germ of self-government was at least present in the shape of the village panchayat,[6] which is still to be found in existence in many places of India. But the germ remained for ever the germ; the seed, though put in the ground, never grew into a tree. This idea of self-government never passed beyond the embryo state of the village panchayat system and never spread into society at large....

With the deluge which swept the land at the advent of Buddhism, the priestly power fell into decay and the royal power was in the ascendant. Buddhist priests are renouncers of the world, living in monasteries as homeless ascetics, unconcerned with secular affairs. They have neither the will nor the endeavor to bring and keep the royal power under their control through the threat of curses or magic arrows. Even if there were any remnant of such a will, its fulfillment has now become an impossibility. For Buddhism has shaken the thrones of all the oblation-eating gods and brought them down from their heavenly positions. The state of being a Buddha is superior to the heavenly positions of many a Brahma or an Indra, who vie with each other in offering their worship at the feet of the Buddha, the God-man! And to this Buddhahood, every man has the privilege to attain; it is open to all even in this life. From the descent of the gods, as a natural consequence, the superiority of the priests who were supported by them is gone.

Accordingly, the reins of that mighty sacrificial horse—the royal power—are no longer held in the firm grasp of the Vedic priest; and being now free, it can roam anywhere by its unbridled will. The center of power in this period is neither with the priests chanting the sama hymns and performing the yajnas [sacrifices] according to the Yajurveda; nor is the power vested in the hands of Kshatriya kings separated from each other and ruling over small independent states. But the center of power in this age is in emperors whose unobstructed sway extends over vast areas bounded by the ocean, covering the whole of India from one end to the other. The leaders of this age are no longer Vishvamitra or Vasishtha, but emperors like Chandragupta, Dharmashoka, and others. There never were emperors who ascended the throne of India and led her to the pinnacle of her glory such as those lords of the earth who ruled over her in paramount sway during the Buddhistic period. The end of this period is characterized by the appearance of Rajput power on the scene, and the rise of modern Hinduism. With the rise of Rajput power, and the decline of Buddhism, the scepter of the Indian empire, dislodged from its paramount power, was again broken into a thousand pieces and wielded by small powerless hands. At this time, the Brahmanical [priestly] power again succeeded in raising its head, not as an adversary as before, but this time as an auxiliary to the royal supremacy.

During this revolution, that perpetual struggle for supremacy between the priestly and the royal classes, which began from the Vedic times and continued through ages till it reached its climax at the time of the Jain and Buddhist revolutions, has ceased for ever. Now these two mighty powers are friendly to each other; but neither is there any more that glorious kshatra (warlike) valor of the kings, nor that spiritual brilliance which characterized the Brahmans; each has lost his former intrinsic strength. As might be expected, this new union of the two forces was soon engaged in the satisfaction of mutual self-interests, and became dissipated by spending its vitality on extirpating their common opponents, especially the Buddhists of the time, and on similar other deeds. Being steeped in all the vices consequent on such a union, e.g., the sucking of the blood of the masses, taking revenge on the enemy, spoliation of others' property, etc., they in vain tried to imitate the Rajasuya and other Vedic sacrifices of the ancient kings, and only made a ridiculous farce of them. The result was that they were bound hand and foot by a formidable train of sycophantic attendance and its obsequious flatteries, and being entangled in an interminable net of rites and ceremonies with flourishes of mantras and the like, they soon became a cheap and ready prey to the Mohammedan invaders from the West.

That priestly power which began its strife for superiority with the royal power from the Vedic times and continued it down the ages, that hostility against the kshatra power, Bhagwan Shri Krishna succeeded by his superhuman genius in putting a stop to, at least for the time being, during his earthly existence. That Brahmanya power was almost effaced from its field of work in India during the Jain and Buddhist revolutions, or, perhaps, was holding its feeble stand by being subservient to the strong antagonistic religions. That Brahmanya power made its last effort to recover its lost greatness; and in its effort to establish that supremacy, it sold itself at the feet of the fierce hordes of barbarians newly come from Central Asia, and to win their pleasure introduced in the land their hateful manners and customs. Moreover, it, the Brahmanya power, solely devoting itself to the easy means to dupe ignorant barbarians, brought into vogue mysterious rites and ceremonies backed by its new mantras and the like; and in doing so, itself lost its former wisdom, its former vigor and vitality, and its own chaste habits of long acquirement. Thus, it turned the whole Aryavarta into a deep and vast whirlpool of the most vicious, the most horrible, the most abominable, barbarous customs; and as the inevitable consequence of countenancing these detestable customs and superstitions, it soon lost all its own internal strength and stamina and became the weakest of the weak. What wonder that it should be broken into a thousand pieces and fall at the mere touch of the storm of Mussulman invasions from the West! That great Brahmanya power fell—who knows, if ever to rise again?

The resuscitation of the priestly power under the Mussulman rule was, on the other hand, an utter impossibility. The Prophet Mohammed himself was dead set against the priestly class in any shape and tried his best for the total destruction of this power by formulating rules and injunctions to that effect. Under the Mussulman rule, the king himself was the supreme priest; he was the chief guide in religious matters; and when he became the emperor, he cherished the hope of being the paramount leader in all matters over the whole Mussulman world. To the Mussulman, the Jews or the Christians are not objects of extreme detestation; they are, at the worst, men of little faith. But not so the Hindu. According to him, the Hindu is idolatrous, the hateful Kafir; hence in this life he deserves to be butchered; and in the next, eternal hell is in store for him. The utmost the Mussulman kings could do as a favor to the priestly class—the spiritual guides of these Kafirs—was to allow them somehow to pass their life silently and wait for the last moment. This was again sometimes considered too much kindness! If the religious ardor of any king was a little more uncommon, there would immediately follow arrangements for a great yajna by way of Kafir slaughter!

On one side, the royal power is now centered in kings professing a different religion and given to different customs. On the other, the priestly power has been entirely displaced from its influential position as the controller and lawgiver of the society. The Koran and its code of laws have taken the place of the Dharma Shastras of Manu and others. The Sanskrit language has made room for the Persian and the Arabic. The Sanskrit language has to remain confined only to the purely religious writings and religious matters of the conquered and detested Hindu, and, as such, has since been living a precarious life at the hands of the neglected priest. The priest himself, the relic of the Brahmanya power, fell back upon the last resource of conducting only the comparatively unimportant family ceremonies, such as the matrimonial etc., and that also only so long and as much as the mercy of the Mohammedan rulers permitted....

Thus, the priestly power—which sages like Kumarila, Shankara, and Ramanuja tried to re-establish, which for some time was supported by the sword of the Rajput power, and which tried to rebuild its structure on the fall of its Jain and Buddhist adversaries—was under Mohammedan rule laid to sleep for ever, knowing no awakening. In this period, the antagonism or warfare is not between kings and priests, but between kings and kings. At the end of this period, when Hindu power again raised its head, and, to some extent, was successful in regenerating Hinduism through the Mahrattas and the Sikhs, we do not find much play of the priestly power with these regenerations. On the contrary, when the Sikhs admitted any Brahman into their sect, they, at first, compelled him publicly to give up his previous Brahmanical signs and adopt the recognized signs of their own religion.

In this manner, after an age-long play of action and reaction between these two forces, the final victory of the royal power was echoed on the soil of India for several centuries, in the name of foreign monarchs professing an entirely different religion from the faith of the land. But at the end of this Mohammedan period, another entirely new power made its appearance on the arena and slowly began to assert its prowess in the affairs of the Indian world.

This power is so new, its nature and workings are so foreign to the Indian mind, its rise so inconceivable, and its vigor so insuperable that though it wields the suzerain power up till now, only a handful of Indians understand what this power is.

We are talking of the occupation of India by England.

From very ancient times, the fame of India's vast wealth and her rich granaries has enkindled in many powerful foreign nations the desire for conquering her. She has been, in fact, again and again conquered by foreign nations. Then why should we say that the occupation of India by England was something new and foreign to the Indian mind?

From time immemorial Indians have seen the mightiest royal power tremble before the frown of the ascetic priest, devoid of worldly desire, armed with spiritual strength—the power of mantras [sacred formulas] and religious lore—and the weapon of curses. They have also seen the subject people silently obey the commands of their heroic all-powerful suzerains, backed by their arms and armies, like a flock of sheep before a lion. But that a handful of Vaishyas [traders] who, despite their great wealth, have ever crouched awestricken not only before the king but also before any member of the royal family, would unite, cross for purposes of business rivers and seas, would, solely by virtue of their intelligence and wealth, by degrees make puppets of the long-established Hindu and Mohammedan dynasties; not only so, but that they would buy as well the services of the ruling powers of their own country and use their valor and learning as powerful instruments for the influx of their own riches—this is a spectacle entirely novel to the Indians, as also the spectacle that the descendants of the mighty nobility of a country, of which a proud lord, sketched by the extraordinary pen of its great poet, says to a common man, 'Out, dunghill! Darest thou brave a nobleman?' would, in no distant future, consider it the zenith of human ambition to be sent to India as obedient servants of a body of merchants, called

The East India Company—such a sight was, indeed, a novelty unseen by India before!....

Among the Chinese, the Sumerians, the Babylonians, the Egyptians, the Chaldeans, the Aryas, the Iranians, the Jews, the Arabs—among all these ancient nations, the supreme power of guiding society is, in the first period of their history, in the hands of the Brahman or the priest. In the second period, the ruling power is the Kshatriya, that is, either absolute monarchy or oligarchical government by a chosen body of men. Among the modern Western nations, with England at their head, this power of controlling society has been, for the first time, in the hands of the Vaishyas or mercantile communities, made rich through the carrying on of commerce....

As in the ancient days the priestly power, in spite of its long-continued struggle, was subdued by the more powerful royal power, so, in modern times, before the violent blow of the newly-risen Vaishya power, many a kingly crown has to kiss the ground, many a scepter is forever broken to pieces. Only those few thrones which are allowed still to exercise some power in some of the civilized countries and make a display of their royal pomp and grandeur are all maintained solely by the vast hordes of wealth of these Vaishya communities—the dealers in salt, oil, sugar, and wine—and kept up as a magnificent and an imposing front, and as a means of glorification to the really governing body behind, the Vaishyas.

That mighty newly-risen Vaishya power—at whose command, electricity carries messages in an instant from one pole to another, whose highway is the vast ocean, with its mountain-high waves, at whose instance, commodities are being carried with the greatest ease from one part of the globe to another, and at whose mandate, even the greatest monarchs tremble—on the white foamy crest of that huge wave, the all-conquering Vaishya power, is installed the majestic throne of England in all its grandeur.

Therefore the conquest of India by England is not a conquest by Jesus or the Bible as we are often asked to believe. Neither is it like the conquest of India by the Moguls and the Pathans. But behind the name of the Lord Jesus, the Bible, the magnificent palaces, the heavy tramp of the feet of armies consisting of elephants, chariots, cavalry, and infantry, shaking the earth, the sounds of war trumpets, bugles, and drums, and the splendid display of the royal throne, behind all these, there is always the virtual presence of England—that England whose war flag is the factory chimney, whose troops are the merchantmen, whose bat-tlefields are the marketplaces of the world, and whose Empress is the shining Goddess of Fortune herself! It is on this account I have said before that it is indeed an unseen novelty, this conquest of India by England. What new revolution will be effected in India by her clash with the new giant power, and as the result of that revo-lution what new transformation is in store for future India, cannot be inferred from her past history....

The foundation of the priestly power rests on intellectual strength, and not on the physical strength of arms. Therefore, with the supremacy of the priestly power, there is a great prevalence of intellectual and literary culture.... With the ascendancy of the priestly supremacy are seen the first advent of civilization, the first victory of the divine nature over the animal, the first mastery of spirit over matter, and the first manifestation of the divine power which is potentially present in this very slave of nature, this lump of flesh, to wit, the human body. The priest is the first discrimina-tor of spirit from matter, the first to help to bring this world in com-munion with the next, the first messenger from the gods to man, and the intervening bridge that connects the king with his sub-jects. The first offshoot of universal welfare and good is nursed by his spiritual power, by his devotion to learning and wisdom, by his renunciation, the watchword of his life and, watered even by the flow of his own life-blood. It is therefore that in every land it was he to whom the first and foremost worship was offered. It is there-fore that even his memory is sacred to us!

There are evils as well. With the growth of life is sown simulta-neously the seed of death. Darkness and light always go together. Indeed, there are great evils which, if not checked in proper time, lead to the ruin of society.... Where the repository of power and the center of its play are wholly mental, where the power is con-fined to certain special words, to certain special modes of uttering them, to the mental repetition of certain mysterious syllables, or to other similar processes and applications of the mind, there light is mixed with shade, there the ebb and flow naturally disturb the otherwise unshaken faith, and there even when things are actually seen or directly perceived, still sometimes doubts arise as to their real occurrence....

There is implanted in every man, naturally, a strong desire for progress; and those who, finding that the fulfillment of this desire is an impossibility so long as one is trammelled in the shackles of priesthood, rend this net and take to the profession of other castes in order to earn money thereby—them, the society immediately dispossesses of their priestly rights. Society has no faith in the Brahmanhood of the so-called Brahmans who, instead of keeping the Shikha,[7] part their hair, who, giving up their ancient habits and ancestral customs, clothe themselves in semi-European dress and adopt the newly introduced usages from the West in a hybrid fashion. Again, in those parts of India, wherever this newcomer, the English Government, is introducing new modes of education and opening up new channels for the coming in of wealth, there, hosts of Brahman youths are giving up their hereditary priestly profession and trying to earn their livelihood and become rich by adopting the callings of other castes, with the result that the habits and customs of the priestly class, handed down from their distant forefathers, are scattered to the winds and are fast disappearing from the land.... Those who lay the fault of attempting to bring down the supremacy of the priestly class at the door of any particular person or body of persons other than themselves ought to know that, in obedience to the inevitable law of nature, the Brahman caste is erecting with its own hands its own sepulcher; and this is what ought to be. It is good and appropriate that every caste of high birth and privileged nobility should make it its principal duty to raise its own funeral pyre with its own hands....

On the other side, the king is like the lion; in him are present both the good and evil propensities of the lord of beasts. Never for a moment his fierce nails are held back from tearing to pieces the heart of innocent animals, living on herbs and grass, to allay his thirst for blood when occasion arises; again, the poet says, though himself stricken with old age and dying with hunger, the lion never kills the weakest fox that throws itself in his arms for protection. If the subject classes, for a moment, stand as impediments in the way of the gratification of the senses of the royal lion, their death knell is inevitably tolled; if they humbly bow down to his commands, they are perfectly safe....

As during the Brahmanical supremacy, at the first stage is the awakening of the first impulse for search after knowledge, and later the continual and careful fostering of the growth of that impulse still in its infancy—so, during the Kshatriya supremacy, a strong desire for pleasure pursuits has made its appearance at the first stage, and later have sprung up inventions and developments of arts and sciences as the means for its gratification. Can the king, in the height of his glory, hide his proud head within the lowly cottages of the poor? Or can the common good of his subjects ever minister to his royal appetite with satisfaction?

He whose dignity bears no comparison with anyone else on earth, he who is divinity residing in the temple of the human body—for the common man, to cast even a mere glance at his, the king's objects of pleasure is a great sin; to think of ever possessing them is quite out of the question. The body of the king is not like the bodies of other people, it is too sacred to be polluted by any contamination; in certain countries it is even believed never to come under the sway of death. A halo of equal sacredness shines around the queen, so she is scrupulously guarded from the gaze of the common folk, not even the sun may cast a glance on her beauty! Hence the rising of magnificent palaces to take the place of thatched cottages. The sweet harmonious strain of artistic music, flowing as it were from heaven, silenced the disorderly jargon of the rabble. Delightful gardens, pleasant groves, beautiful galleries, charming paintings, exquisite sculptures, fine and costly apparel began to displace by gradual steps the natural beauties of rugged woods and the rough and coarse dress of the simple rustic. Thousands of intelligent men left the toilsome task of the ploughman and turned their attention to the new field of fine arts, where they could display the finer play of their intellect in less laborious and easier ways. Villages lost their importance; cities rose in their stead....

The king, the center of the forces of the aggregate of his subjects, soon forgets that those forces are only stored with him so that he may increase and give them back a thousandfold in their potency, so that they may spread over the whole community for its good. Attributing all Godship to himself, in his pride, like the king Vena,[8] he looks upon other people as wretched specimens of humanity who should grovel before him; any opposition to his will, whether good or bad, is a great sin on the part of his subjects. Hence oppression steps into the place of protection—sucking their blood in place of preservation. If the society is weak and debilitated, it silently suffers all ill-treatment at the hands of the king, and as the natural consequence, both the king and his people go down and down and fall into the most degraded state, and thus become an easy prey to any nation stronger than themselves. Where the society is healthy and strong, there soon follows a fierce contest between the king and his subjects, and, by its reaction and convulsion, are flung away the scepter and the crown; and the throne and the royal paraphernalia become like past curiosities preserved in the museum galleries.

As the result of this contest—as its reaction—is the appearance of the mighty power of the Vaishya, before whose angry glance the crowned heads, the lords of heroes, tremble like an aspen leaf on their thrones—whom the poor as well as the prince humbly follow in vain expectation of the golden jar in his hands, that like Tantalus' fruit always recedes from the grasp.

The Brahman said, 'Learning is the power of all powers; that learning is dependent upon me. I possess that learning, so the society must follow my bidding.' For some days such was the case. The Kshatriya said, 'But for the power of my sword, where would you be, O Brahman, with all your power of lore? You would in no time be wiped off the face of the earth. It is I alone that am the superior.' Out flew the flaming sword from the jingling scabbard—society humbly recognized it with bended head. Even the worshipper of learning was the first to turn into the worshipper of the king. The Vaishya is saying, 'You, madmen! What you call the effulgent all-pervading deity is here, in my hand, the ever-shining gold, the almighty sovereign. Behold, through its grace, I am also equally all-powerful. O Brahman! Even now, I shall buy through its grace all your wisdom, learning, prayers, and meditation. And, O great king! Your sword, arms, valor, and prowess will soon be employed, through the grace of this, my gold, in carrying out my desired objects. Do you see those lofty and extensive mills? Those are my hives. See, how, swarms of millions of bees, the Shudras, are incessantly gathering honey for those hives. Do you know for whom? For me, this me, who in due course of time will squeeze out every drop of it for my own use and profit.'

As during the supremacy of the Brahman and the Kshatriya there is a centralization of learning and advancement of civilization, so the result of the supremacy of the Vaishya is accumulation of wealth. The power of the Vaishya lies in the possession of that coin, the charm of whose clinking sound works with an irresistible fascination on the minds of the four castes. The Vaishya is always in fear lest the Brahman swindles him out of this, his only possession, and lest the Kshatriya usurps it by virtue of his superior strength of arms. For self-preservation, the Vaishyas as a body are, therefore, of one mind. The Vaishya commands the money; the exorbitant interest that he can exact for its use by others, as with a lash in his hand, is his powerful weapon which strikes terror in the heart of all. By the power of his money, he is always busy curbing the royal power. That the royal power may not anyhow stand in the way of the inflow of his riches, the merchant is ever watchful. But, for all that, he has never the least wish that the power should pass on from the kingly to the Shudra class.

To what country does not the merchant go? Though himself ignorant, he carries on his trade and transplants the learning, wisdom, art, and science of one country to another. The wisdom, civilization, and arts that accumulated in the heart of the social body during the Brahman and the Kshatriya supremacies are being diffused in all directions by the arteries of commerce to the different marketplaces of the Vaishya. But for the rising of this Vaishya power, who would have carried today the culture, learning, acquirements, and articles of food and luxury of one end of the world to the other?

And where are they through whose physical labor only are possible the influence of the Brahman, the prowess of the Kshatriya, and the fortune of the Vaishya? What is their history, who, being the real body of society, are designated at all times in all countries as 'baseborn'?—for whom kind India prescribed the mild punishments, 'Cut out his tongue, chop off his flesh', and others of like nature, for such a grave offense as any attempt on their part to gain a share of the knowledge and wisdom monopolized by her higher classes—those 'moving corpses' of India and the 'beasts of burden' of other countries—the Shudras, what is their lot in life? What shall I say of India? Let alone her Shudra class, her Brahmans to whom belonged the acquisition of scriptural knowledge are now the foreign professors, her Kshatriyas the ruling Englishmen, and Vaishyas, too, the English in whose bone and marrow is the instinct of trade, so that, only the Shudra-ness—the beast-of-burdenness—is now left with the Indians themselves.

A cloud of impenetrable darkness has at present equally enveloped us all. Now there is neither firmness of purpose nor boldness of enterprise, neither courage of heart nor strength of mind, neither aversion to maltreatments by others nor dislike for slavery, neither love in the heart nor hope nor manliness: but what we have in India are only deep-rooted envy and strong antipathy against one another, morbid desire to ruin by hook or by crook the weak, and to lick dog-like the feet of the strong. Now the highest satisfaction consists in the display of wealth and power, devotion in self-gratification, wisdom in the accumulation of transitory objects, yoga in hideous diabolical practices, work in the slavery of others, civilization in base imitation of foreign nations, eloquence in the use of abusive language, the merit of literature in extravagant flatteries of the rich or in the diffusion of ghastly obscenities! What to speak separately of the distinct Shudra class of such a land, where the whole population has virtually come down to the level of the Shudra? The Shudras of countries other than India have become, it seems, a little awake; but they are wanting in proper education and have only the mutual hatred of men of their own class—a trait common to Shudras. What avails it if they greatly outnumber the other classes? That unity, by which ten men collect the strength of a million, is yet far away from the Shudra; hence, according to the law of nature, the Shudras invariably form the subject race.

But there is hope. In the mighty course of time, the Brahman and the other higher castes, too, are being brought down to the lower status of the Shudras, and the Shudras are being raised to higher ranks. Europe, once the land of Shudras enslaved by Rome, is now filled with Kshatriya valor. Even before our eyes, powerful China, with fast strides, is going down to Shudra-hood, while insignificant Japan, rising with the sudden start of a rocket, is throwing off her Shudra nature and is invading by degrees the rights of the higher castes. The attaining of modern Greece and Italy to Kshatriya-hood and the decline of Turkey, Spain, and other countries, also, deserve consideration here.

Yet, a time will come when there will be the rising of the Shudra class, *with their Shudra-hood*; that is to say, not like that as at present when the Shudras are becoming great by acquiring the characteristic qualities of the Vaishya or the Kshatriya, but a time will come when the Shudras of every country, with their inborn Shudra nature and habits—not becoming in essence Vaishya or Kshatriya, but remaining as Shudras—will gain absolute supremacy in every society. The first glow of the dawn of this new power has already begun to break slowly upon the Western world, and the thoughtful are at their wits' end to reflect upon the final issue of this fresh phenomenon. Socialism, Anarchism, Nihilism, and other like sects are the vanguard of the social revolution that is to follow.

In spite of the spread of education in the West, there is a great hindrance in the way of the rising of the Shudra class, and that is the recognition of caste as determined by the inherence of more or less good or bad qualities. By this very qualitative caste system which obtained in India in ancient days, the Shudra class was kept down, bound hand and foot. In the first place, scarcely any opportunity was given to the Shudra for the accumulation of wealth or the earning of proper knowledge and education; to add to this disadvantage, if ever a man of extraordinary parts and genius were born of the Shudra class, the influential higher sections of the society forthwith showered titular honors on him and lifted him up to their own circle. His wealth and the power of his wisdom were employed for the benefit of an alien caste—and his own caste-people reaped no benefits of his attainments....

Whether the leadership of society be in the hands of those who monopolize learning or wield the power of riches or arms, the source of its power is always the subject masses. By so much as the class in power severs itself from this source, by so much is it sure to become weak. But such is the strange irony of fate, such is the queer working of Maya, that they from whom this power is directly or indirectly drawn, by fair means or foul—by deceit, stratagem, force, or by voluntary gift—they soon cease to be taken into account by the leading class. When, in course of time, the priestly power totally estranged itself from the subject masses, the real dynamo of its power, it was overthrown by the then kingly power taking its stand on the strength of the subject people; again, the kingly power, judging itself to be perfectly independent, created a gaping chasm between itself and the subject people, only to be itself destroyed or become a mere puppet in the hands of the Vaishyas, who now succeeded in securing a relatively greater cooperation of the mass of the people. The Vaishyas have now gained their end; so they no longer deign to count on help from the subject people and are trying their best to dissociate themselves from them; consequently, here is being sown the seed of the destruction of this power as well.

Though themselves the reservoir of all powers, the subject masses, creating an eternal distance between one another, have been deprived of all their legitimate rights; and they will remain so as long as this sort of relation continues....

The present government of India has certain evils attendant on it, and there are some very great and good parts in it as well. Of highest good is this, that after the fall of the Pataliputra Empire till now, India was never under the guidance of such a powerful machinery of government as the British, wielding the scepter throughout the length and breadth of the land. And under this Vaishya supremacy, thanks to the strenuous enterprise natural to the Vaishya, as the objects of commerce are being brought from one end of the world to another, so at the same time, as its natural sequence, the ideas and thoughts of different countries are forcing their way into the very bone and marrow of India. Of these ideas and thoughts, some are really most beneficial to her, some are harmful, while others disclose the ignorance and inability of the foreigners to determine what is truly good for the inhabitants of this country.

But piercing through the mass of whatever good or evil there may be is seen rising the sure emblem of India's future prosperity—that as the result of the action and reaction between her own old national ideals on the one hand, and the newly-introduced strange ideals of foreign nations on the other, she is slowly and gently awakening from her long deep sleep. Mistakes she will make, let her—there is no harm in that; in all our actions, errors and mistakes are our only teachers. Who commits mistakes, the path of truth is attainable by him only. Trees never make mistakes, nor do stones fall into error; animals are hardly seen to transgress the fixed laws of nature; but man is prone to err, and it is man who becomes God-on-earth....

It has been said before that India is slowly awakening through her friction with the outside nations; and as the result of this little awakening, is the appearance, to a certain extent, of free and independent thought in modern India. On one side is modern Western science, dazzling the eyes with the brilliancy of myriad suns and driving in the chariot of hard and fast facts collected by the application of tangible powers direct in their incision; on the other are the hopeful and strengthening traditions of her ancient forefathers, in the days when she was at the zenith of her glory—traditions that have been brought out of the pages of her history by the great sages of her own land and outside, that run for numberless years and centuries through her every vein with the quickening of life drawn from universal love—traditions that reveal unsurpassed valor, superhuman genius, and supreme spirituality, which are the envy of the gods—these inspire her with future hopes. On one side, rank materialism, plenitude of fortune, accumulation of gigantic power, and intense sense-pursuits have, through foreign literature, caused a tremendous stir; on the other, through the confounding din of all these discordant sounds, she hears, in low yet unmistakable accents, the heartrending cries of her ancient gods, cutting her to the quick.

There lie before her various strange luxuries introduced from the West—celestial drinks, costly well-served food, splendid apparel, magnificent palaces, new modes of conveyance, new manners, new fashions dressed in which moves about the well-educated girl in shameless freedom—all these are arousing unfelt desires. Again, the scene changes, and in its place appear, with stern presence, Sita, Savitri, austere religious vows, fastings, the forest retreat, the matted locks and orange garb of the semi-naked Sannyasin, Samadhi and the search after the Self. On one side is the independence of Western societies based on self-interest; on the other is the extreme self-sacrifice of the Aryan society. In this violent conflict, is it strange that Indian society should be tossed up and down? Of the West, the goal is individual independence, the language money-making education, the means politics; of India, the goal is Mukti, the language the Veda, the means renunciation. For a time, Modern India thinks, as it were, I am ruining this worldly life of mine in vain expectation of uncertain spiritual welfare hereafter which has spread its fascination over me; and again, lo! spellbound she listens—'Here, in this world of death and change, O Man, where is thy happiness?'

On one side, new India is saying, 'We should have full freedom in the selection of husband and wife; because the marriage, in which are involved the happiness and misery of all our future life, we must have the right to determine according to our own free will.' On the other, old India is dictating, 'Marriage is not for sense-enjoyment, but to perpetuate the race. This is the Indian conception of marriage. By the producing of children, you are contributing to, and are responsible for, the future good or evil of the society. Hence society has the right to dictate whom you shall marry and whom you shall not. That form of marriage obtains in society which is conducive most to its well-being; do you give up your desire of individual pleasure for the good of the many.'

On one side, new India is saying, 'If we only adopt Western ideas, Western language, Western food, Western dress, and Western manners, we shall be as strong and powerful as the Western nations'; on the other, old India is saying, 'Fools! By imitation, other's ideas never become one's own; nothing, unless earned, is your own. Does the ass in the lion's skin become the lion?'

On one side, new India is saying, 'What the Western nations do is surely good, otherwise how did they become so great?' On the other side, old India is saying, 'The flash of lightning is intensely bright, but only for a moment; look out, boys, it is dazzling your eyes. Beware!'

Have we not then to learn anything from the West? Must we not needs try and exert ourselves for better things? Are we perfect? Is our society entirely spotless, without any flaw? There are many things to learn, we must struggle for new and higher things till we die—struggle is the end of human life. Shri Ramakrishna used to say, 'As long as I live, so long do I learn.' That man or that society which has nothing to learn is already in the jaws of death. Yes, learn we must many things from the West; but there are fears as well.

A certain young man of little understanding used always to blame the Hindu Shastras before Shri Ramakrishna. One day he praised the Bhagavad Gita, on which Shri Ramakrishna said, 'Methinks, some European Pandit has praised the Gita, and so he has also followed suit.'

O India, this is your terrible danger. The spell of imitating the West is getting such a strong hold upon you that what is good or what is bad is no longer decided by reason, judgment, discrimination, or reference to the Shastras. Whatever ideas, whatever manners the white men praise or like are good; whatever things they dislike or censure are bad. Alas! What can be a more tangible proof of foolishness than this?

The Western ladies move freely everywhere, therefore that is good; they choose for themselves their husbands, therefore that is the highest step of advancement; the Westerners disapprove of our dress, decorations, food, and ways of living, therefore they must be very bad; the Westerners condemn image-worship as sinful, surely then, image-worship is the greatest sin, there is no doubt of it!

The Westerners say that worshipping a single deity is fruitful of the highest spiritual good, therefore let us throw our gods and goddesses into the river Ganga? The Westerners hold caste distinctions to be obnoxious, therefore let all the different castes be jumbled into one! The Westerners say that child-marriage is the root of all evils, therefore that is also very bad, of a certainty it is!

We are not discussing here whether these customs deserve continuance or rejection; but if the mere disapproval of the Westerners be the measure of the abominableness of our manners and customs, then it is our duty to raise our emphatic protest against it....

I have observed in the West also that the children of weaker nations, if born in England, give themselves out as Englishmen, instead of Greek, Portuguese, Spaniard, etc., as the case may be. All drift towards the strong. That the light of glory which shines in the glorious may anyhow fall and reflect on one's own body, i.e., to shine in the borrowed light of the great, is the one desire of the weak. When I see Indians dressed in European apparel and costumes, the thought comes to my mind, perhaps they feel ashamed to own their nationality and kinship with the ignorant, poor, illiterate, downtrodden people of India! Again, the Westerners have now taught us that those stupid, ignorant, low caste millions of India, clad only in loin-cloths, are non-Aryans. They are therefore no more our kith and kin!

O India! With this mere echoing of others, with this base imitation of others, with this dependence on others, this slavish weakness, this vile detestable cruelty—wouldst thou, with these provisions only, scale the highest pinnacle of civilization and greatness? Wouldst thou attain, by means of thy disgraceful cowardice, that freedom deserved only by the brave and the heroic? O India! Forget not that the ideal of thy womanhood is Sita, Savitri, Damayanti; forget not that the God thou worshippest is the great Ascetic of ascetics, the all-renouncing Shankara, the Lord of Uma; forget not that thy marriage, thy wealth, thy life are not for sense-pleasure, are not for thy individual personal happiness; forget not that thou are born as a sacrifice to the Mother's altar; forget not that thy social order is but the reflex of the Infinite Universal Motherhood; forget not that the lower classes, the ignorant, the poor, the illiterate, the cobbler, the sweeper, are thy flesh and blood, thy brothers. Thou brave one, be bold, take courage, be proud that thou art an Indian, and proudly proclaim, 'I am an Indian, every Indian is my brother'. Say, 'The ignorant Indian, the poor and destitute Indian, the Brahman Indian, the Pariah Indian, is my brother'. Thou, too, clad with but a rag round thy loins proudly proclaim at the top of thy voice: 'The Indian is my brother, the Indian is my life, India's gods and goddesses are my God. India's society is the cradle of my infancy, the pleasure garden of my youth, the sacred heaven, the Varanasi of my old age.' Say, brother: 'The soil of India is my highest heaven, the good of India is my good', and repeat and pray day and night, 'O Thou Lord of Gauri, O Thou Mother of the Universe, vouchsafe manliness unto me! O Thou Mother of Strength, take away my weakness, take away my unmanliness, and make me a Man!'

■

■ Notes ■

[1] Vedic hymns uttered by the priests to invoke the Devas at the time of sacrifice.

[2] The men who perform sacrifices.

[3] The name of the Soma plant as commonly found in the Vedas. The priests offered to the Devas the juice of this plant at the time of sacrifice.

[4] Agnivarna was a prince of the Solar race, who never used to come out of the seraglio, and died of consumption due to excessive indulgence.

[5] The great king Ashoka was at first called Chandashoka, i.e., Fierce Ashoka, because of his ascending the throne by killing his brother and his other cruel deeds. After nine years of reign he became a convert to Buddhism, and his character underwent a complete transformation; he was thenceforth known for his good deeds by the name of Dharmashoka, Virtuous Ashoka.

[6] Literally, 'government by five', in which the village-men sit together and decide, among themselves, all disputes.

[7] The sacred tuft or lock of hair left on the crown of the head at tonsure.

[8] His story occurs in the *Bhagavata*. The King Vena thought himself higher than Brahma, Vishnu, and Maheshvara, and declared accordingly that all worship should be offered to him. The Rishis once sought him and tried by good advice to make him give up such egoism, but he in return insulted them and ordered them to worship him, whereupon, it is said, he was destroyed by the fire of the anger of the Rishis.

■

2

■ RABINDRANATH TAGORE ■

One of fifteen children, Rabindranath Tagore (1861–1941) was the son of Debendranath Tagore, a wealthy Bengali landowner and a leader of the Brahmo Samaj. Growing up in a highly cultured and artistic family setting, Rabindranath as an adolescent turned to writing poetry and at age 20 won renown by publishing a volume of Bengali poems. Following the death of his wife and some of his children, he published in 1912 a collection entitled *Gitanjali (Song Offerings)*—and was awarded the Nobel Prize for Literature a year later. Next to his love for poetry, music and painting, Rabindranath was strongly committed to educational pursuits, a commitment reflected in his effort to develop a learning center in Shantiniketan (converted into a university in 1921) dedicated to the ideals of universal brotherhood and cultural exchange. His cosmopolitan outlook—strengthened by lecture tours abroad—produced tension between him and extremist nationalist leaders, and even from some time friction with Gandhi. In 1940, a year before his death, he was awarded an honorary doctoral degree by Oxford University.

For primary and secondary sources see *Collected Poems and Plays of Rabindranath Tagore*, London, Papermac, 1989; Rabindranath Tagore, *The Religion of Man*, Hibbert Lectures of 1930, New York, Macmillan, 1931; *Towards Universal Man*, Bombay, Asia Publishing House, 1961; *Gitanjali (Song Offerings)*, London, Macmillan, 1926; *Nationalism*, Westport, CT, Greenwood Press, 1973; R.K. Prabhu and Ravindra Kelekar, eds, *Truth Called Them Differently (Tagore–Gandhi controversy)*, Ahmedabad, Navajivan, 1961; Edward J. Thompson, *Rabindranath Tagore: His Life*

and Work, London, Oxford University Press, 1921. The following
selection is taken from *Nationalism*.

NATIONALISM IN INDIA

Our real problem in India is not political. It is social. This is a condition not only prevailing in India, but among all nations. I do not
believe in an exclusive political interest. Politics in the West have
dominated Western ideals, and we in India are. trying to imitate
you. We have to remember that in Europe, where peoples had
their racial unity from the beginning, and where natural resources
were insufficient for the inhabitants, the civilization has naturally
taken on the character of political and commercial aggressiveness.
For on the one hand they had no internal complications, and on
the other they had to deal with neighbors who were strong and
rapacious. To have perfect combination among themselves and a
watchful attitude of animosity against others was taken as the solution of their problems. In former days they organized and plun-
dered; in the present age the same spirit continues—and they
organize and exploit the whole world.

But from the earliest beginnings of history India has had her
own problem constantly before her—it is the race problem. Each
nation must be conscious of its mission, and we in India must realize that we cut a poor figure when we try to be political, simply
because we have not yet been finally able to accomplish what was
set before us by our providence.

This problem of race unity which we have been trying to solve
for so many years has likewise to be faced by you here in America. Many people in this country ask me what is happening to the
caste distinctions in India. But when this question is asked me, it is
usually done with a superior air. And I feel tempted to put the
same question to our American critics with a slight modification:
'What have you done with the Red Indian and the Negro?' For
you have not got over your attitude of caste towards them. You
have used violent methods to keep aloof from other races, but
until you have solved the question, here in America, you have no
right to question India.

In spite of our great difficulty, however, India has done something.
She has tried to make an adjustment of races, to acknowledge the

real differences between them where these exist, and yet seek for some basis of unity. This basis has come through our saints, like Nanak, Kabir, Chaitanya,[1] and others, preaching one God to all races of India.

In finding the solution of our problem we shall have helped to solve the world problem as well. What India has been, the whole world is now. The whole world is becoming one country through scientific facility. And the moment is arriving when you must also find a basis of unity which is not political. If India can offer to the world her solution, it will be a contribution to humanity. There is only one history—the history of man. All national histories are merely chapters in the larger one. And we are content in India to suffer for such a great cause.

Each individual has his self-love. Therefore his brute instinct leads him to fight with others in the sole pursuit of his self-interest. But man has also his higher instincts of sympathy and mutual help. The people who are lacking in this higher moral power and who therefore cannot combine in fellowship with one another must perish or live in a state of degradation. Only those peoples have survived and achieved civilization who have this spirit of co-operation strong in them. So we find that from the beginning of history men had to choose between fighting with one another and combining, between serving their own interest or the common interest of all....

The most important fact of the present age is that all the different races of men have come close together. And again we are confronted with two alternatives. The problem is whether the different groups of peoples shall go on fighting with one another or find out some true basis of reconciliation and mutual help; whether it will be interminable competition or cooperation.

I have no hesitation in saying that those who are gifted with the moral power of love and vision of spiritual unity, who have the least feeling of enmity against aliens, and the sympathetic insight to place themselves in the position of others, will be the fittest to take their permanent place in the age that is lying before us, and those who are constantly developing their instincts for fight and intolerance of aliens will be eliminated. For this is the problem before us, and we have to prove our humanity by solving it through the help of our higher nature. The gigantic organizations for hurting others and warding off their blows, for making money by dragging others back, will not help us. On the contrary, by their crushing weight, their enormous cost and their deadening effect upon living humanity, they will seriously impede our freedom in the larger life of a higher civilization.

During the evolution of the nation the moral culture of brotherhood was limited by geographical boundaries, because at that time those boundaries were true. Now they have become imaginary lines of tradition divested of the qualities of real obstacles. So the time has come when man's moral nature must deal with this great fact with all seriousness or perish. The first impulse of this change of circumstance has been the churning up of man's baser passions of greed and cruel hatred. If this persists indefinitely, and armaments go on exaggerating themselves to unimaginable absurdities, and machines and storehouses envelop this fair earth with their dirt and smoke and ugliness, then it will end in a conflagration of suicide. Therefore, man will have to exert all his power of love and clarity of vision to make another great moral adjustment which will comprehend the whole world of men and not merely the fractional groups of nationality. The call has come to every individual in the present age to prepare himself and his surroundings for this dawn of a new era, when man shall discover his soul in the spiritual unity of all human beings.

If it is given at all to the West to struggle out of these tangles of the lower slopes to the spiritual summit of humanity then I cannot but think that it is the special mission of America to fulfill this hope of God and man. You are the country of expectation, desiring something else than what is. Europe has her subtle habits of mind and her conventions. But America, as yet, has come to no conclusions. I realize how much America is untrammeled by the traditions of the past, and I can appreciate that experimentalism is a sign of America's youth. The foundation of her glory is in the future, rather than in the past, and if one is gifted with the power of clairvoyance, one will be able to love the America that is to be.

America is destined to justify Western civilization to the East. Europe has lost faith in humanity, and has become distrustful and sickly. America, on the other hand, is not pessimistic or blasé. You know, as a people, that there is such a thing as a better and a best, and that knowledge drives you on. There are habits that are not merely passive but aggressively arrogant. They are not like mere walls, but are like hedges of stinging nettles. Europe has been cultivating these hedges of habits for long years, till they have grown round her, dense and strong and high. The pride of her traditions has sent its roots deep into her heart. I do not wish to contend that it is unreasonable. But pride in every form breeds blindness at the end. Like all artificial stimulants its first effect is a heightening of consciousness, and then with the increasing dosage it muddles it and brings an exultation that is misleading. Europe has gradually grown hardened in her pride in all her outer and inner habits. She not only cannot forget that she is Western, but she takes every opportunity to hurl this fact against others to humiliate them. This is why she is growing incapable of imparting to the East what is best in herself, and of accepting in a right spirit the wisdom that the East has stored for centuries.

In America national habits and traditions have not had time to spread their clutching roots round your hearts. You have constantly felt and complained of your disadvantages when you compared your nomadic restlessness with the settled traditions of Europe—the Europe which can show her picture of greatness to the best advantage because she can fix it against the background of the past. But in this present age of transition, when a new era of civilization is sending its trumpet-call to all peoples of the world across an unlimited future, this very freedom of detachment will enable you to accept its invitation and to achieve the goal for which Europe began her journey but lost herself mid-way. For she was tempted out of her path by her pride of power and greed of possession....

A parallelism exists between America and India—the parallelism of welding together into one body various races. In my country we have been seeking to find out something common to all races, which will prove their real unity. No nation looking for a mere political or commercial basis of unity will find such a solution sufficient. Men of thought and power will discover the spiritual unity, will realize it, and preach it.

India has never had a real sense of nationalism. Even though from childhood I have been taught that idolatry of the nation is almost better than reverence for God and humanity, I believe I have outgrown that teaching, and it is my conviction that my countrymen will truly gain their India by fighting against the education which teaches them that a country is greater than the ideals of humanity.

The educated Indian at present is trying to absorb some lessons from history contrary to the lessons of our ancestors. The East, in fact, is attempting to take unto itself a history, which is not the outcome of its own living. Japan, for example, thinks she is getting powerful through adopting Western methods but, after she has exhausted her inheritance, only the borrowed weapons of civilization will remain to her. She will not have developed herself from within.

Europe has her past. Europe's strength therefore lies in her history. We in India must make up our minds that we cannot borrow other people's history, and that if we stifle our own we are committing suicide. When you borrow things that do not belong to your life, they only serve to crush your life. And therefore I believe that it does India no good to compete with Western civilization in its own field. But we shall be more than compensated if, in spite of the insults heaped upon us, we follow our own destiny.

There are lessons which impart information or train our minds for intellectual pursuits. These are simple and can be acquired and used with advantage. But there are others which affect our deeper nature and change our direction of life. Before we accept them and pay their value by selling our own inheritance, we must pause and think deeply. In man's history there come ages of fireworks which dazzle us by their force and movement. They laugh not only at our modest household lamps but also at the eternal stars. But let us not for that provocation be precipitate in our desire to dismiss our lamps. Let us patiently bear our present insult and realize that these fireworks have splendor but not permanence, because of the extreme explosiveness which is the cause of their power, and also of their exhaustion. They are spending a fatal quantity of energy and substance compared to their gain and production.

Anyhow, our ideals have been evolved through our own history, and even if we wished we could only make poor fireworks of them because their materials are different from yours, as is also their moral purpose. If we cherish the desire of paying our all to buy a political nationality it will be as absurd as if Switzerland had staked her existence on her ambition to build up a navy powerful enough to compete with that of England. The mistake that we make is in thinking that man's channel of greatness is only one—the one which has made itself painfully evident for the time being by its depth of insolence.

We must know for certain that there is a future before us and that future is waiting for those who are rich in moral ideals and not in mere things. And it is the privilege of man to work for fruits that are beyond his immediate reach, and to adjust his life not in slavish conformity to the examples of some present success or even to his own prudent past, limited in its aspiration, but to an infinite future bearing in its heart the ideals of our highest expectations.

We must recognize that it is providential that the West has come to India. And yet someone must show the East to the West, and convince the West that the East has her contribution to make to the history of civilization. India is no beggar of the West. And yet even though the West may think she is, I am not for thrusting off Western civilization and becoming segregated in our independence. Let us have a deep association. If providence wants England to be the channel of that communication, of that deeper association, I am willing to accept it with all humility. I have great faith in human nature, and I think the West will find its true mission. I speak bitterly of Western civilization when I am conscious that it is betraying its trust and thwarting its own purpose. The West must not make herself a curse to the world by using her power for her own selfish needs but, by teaching the ignorant and helping the weak, she should save herself from the worst danger that the strong is liable to incur by making the feeble acquire power enough to resist her intrusion. And also she must not make her materialism to be the final thing, but must realize that she is doing a service in freeing the spiritual being from the tyranny of matter.

I am not against one nation in particular, but against the general idea of all nations. What is the nation?

It is the aspect of a whole people as an organized power. This organization incessantly keeps up the insistence of the population on becoming strong and efficient. But this strenuous effort after strength and efficiency drains man's energy from his higher nature where he is self-sacrificing and creative. For thereby man's power of sacrifice is diverted from his ultimate object, which is moral, to the maintenance of this organization, which is mechanical. Yet, in this he feels all the satisfaction of moral exaltation and therefore becomes supremely dangerous to humanity. He feels relieved of the urging of his conscience when he can transfer his responsibility to this machine which is the creation of his intellect and not of his complete moral personality. By this device the people which loves freedom perpetuates slavery in a large portion of the world with the comfortable feeling of pride in having done its duty; men who are naturally just can be cruelly unjust both in their act and their thought, accompanied by a feeling that they are helping the world to receive its deserts; men who are honest can blindly go on robbing others of their human rights for self-aggrandizement, all the while abusing the deprived for not deserving better treatment. We have seen in our everyday life even small organizations of business and profession produce callousness of feeling in men who are not naturally bad, and we can well imagine what a moral havoc it is causing in a world where whole peoples are furiously organizing themselves for gaining wealth and power.

Nationalism is a great menace. It is the particular thing which for years has been at the bottom of India's troubles. And inasmuch as we have been ruled and dominated by a nation that is strictly political in its attitude, we have tried to develop within ourselves, despite our inheritance from the past, a belief in our eventual political destiny.

There are different parties in India, with different ideals. Some are struggling for political independence. Others think that the time has not arrived for that, and yet believe that India should have the rights that the English colonies have. They wish to gain autonomy as far as possible.

In the beginning of the history of political agitation in India there was not the conflict between parties which there is today. At that time there was a party known as the Indian Congress;[2] they had no real program. They had a few grievances for redress by the authorities. They wanted larger representation in the Council House, and more freedom in Municipal Government. They wanted scraps of things, but they had no constructive ideal. Therefore, I was lacking in enthusiasm for their methods. It was my conviction that what India most needed was constructive work coming from within herself. In this work we must take all risks and go on doing the duties which by right are ours, though in the teeth of persecution, winning moral victory at every step, by our failure and suffering. We must show those who are over us that we have in ourselves the strength of moral power, the power to suffer for truth. Where we have nothing to show, we have only to beg. It would be mischievous if the gifts we wish for were granted to us at once, and I have told my countrymen, time and again, to combine for the work of creating opportunities to give vent to our spirit of self-sacrifice, and not for the purpose of begging.

The party, however, lost power because the people soon came to realize how futile was the half policy adopted by them. The party split,[3] and there arrived the Extremists, who advocated independence of action, and discarded the begging method—the easiest method of relieving one's mind from his responsibility towards his country. Their ideals were based on Western history. They had no sympathy with the special problems of India. They did not recognize the patent fact that there were causes in our social organization which made the Indian incapable of coping with the alien. What should we do if, for any reason, England was driven away? We should simply be victims for other nations. The same social weaknesses would prevail. The thing we in India have to think of is this: to remove those social customs and ideals which have generated a want of self-respect and a complete dependence on those above us—a state of affairs which has been brought about entirely by the domination in India of the caste system, and the blind and lazy habit of relying upon the authority of traditions that are incongruous anachronisms in the present age.

Once again I draw your attention to the difficulties India has had to encounter and her struggle to overcome them. Her problem was the problem of the world in miniature. India is too vast in its area and too diverse in its races. It is many countries packed in one geographical receptacle. It is just the opposite of what Europe truly is: namely, one country made into many. Thus, Europe in its culture and growth has had the advantage of the strength of the many as well as the strength of the one. India, on the contrary, being naturally many, yet adventitiously one, has all along suffered from the looseness of its diversity and the feebleness of its unity. A true unity is like a round globe; it rolls on, carrying its burden easily. But diversity is a many-cornered thing which has to be dragged and pushed with all force. Be it said to the credit of India that this diversity was not her own creation; she has had to accept it as a fact from the beginning of her history. In America and Australia, Europe has simplified her problem by almost exterminating the original population. Even in the present age this spirit of extermination is making itself manifest, in the inhospitable shutting out of aliens, by those who themselves were aliens in the lands they now occupy. But India tolerated difference of races from the first, and that spirit of toleration has acted all through her history.

Her caste system is the outcome of this spirit of toleration. For India has all along been trying experiments in evolving a social unity within which all the different peoples could be held together, while fully enjoying the freedom of maintaining their own differences. The tie has been as loose as possible, yet as close as the circumstances permitted. This has produced something like a United States of a social federation, whose common name is Hinduism.

India had felt that diversity of races there must be and should be, whatever may be its drawbacks, and you can never coerce nature into your narrow limits of convenience without paying, one day, very dearly for it. In this India was right; but what she failed to realize was that in human beings differences are not like the physical barriers of mountains, fixed for ever—they are fluid with life's flow, they are changing their courses and their shapes and volumes.

Therefore, in her caste regulations India recognized differences, but not the mutability which is the law of life. In trying to avoid collisions she set up boundaries of immovable walls, thus giving to her numerous races the negative benefit of peace and order but not the positive opportunity of expansion and movement. She accepted nature where it produces diversity, but ignored it where it uses that diversity for its world-game of infinite permutations and combinations. She treated life in all truth where it is manifold, but insulted it where it is ever-moving. Therefore, life departed from her social system and in its place she is worshipping with all ceremony the magnificent cage of countless compartments that she has manufactured.

The same thing happened where she tried to ward off the collisions of trade interests. She associated different trades and professions with different castes. This had the effect of allaying for good the interminable jealousy and hatred of competition—the competition which breeds cruelty and makes the atmosphere thick with lies and deception. In this also India laid all her emphasis upon the law of heredity, ignoring the law of mutation, and thus, gradually, reduced arts into crafts and genius into skill.

However, what Western observers fail to discern is that in her caste system India, in all seriousness, accepted her responsibility to solve the race problem in such a manner as to avoid all friction, and yet to afford each race freedom within its boundaries. Let us admit India has not in this achieved a full measure of success. But this you must also concede: that the West, being more favorably situated as to homogeneity of races, has never given her attention to this problem, and whenever confronted with it she has tried to make it easy by ignoring it altogether. And this is the source of her anti-Asiatic agitations for depriving aliens of their right to earn their honest living on these shores. In most of your colonies you only admit them on condition of their accepting the menial positions of hewers of wood and drawers of water. Either you shut your doors against the aliens or reduce them into slavery. And this is your solution to the problem of race conflict. Whatever may be its merits you will have to admit that it does not spring from the higher impulses of civilization, but from the lower passions of greed and hatred. You say this is human nature—and India also thought she knew human nature when she strongly barricaded her race distinctions by the fixed barriers of social gradations. But we have found out to our cost that human nature is not what it seems, but what it is in truth, which is in its infinite possibilities. And when we in our blindness insult humanity for its ragged appearance, it sheds its disguise to disclose to us that we have insulted our God. The degradation which we cast upon others in our pride or self-interest degrades our own humanity—and this is the punishment which is most terrible, because we do not detect it till it is too late.

Not only in your relation with aliens but with the different sections of your own society you have not achieved harmony of reconciliation. The spirit of conflict and competition is allowed the full freedom of its reckless career. And because its genesis is the greed of wealth and power it can never come to any other end but to a violent death. In India, the production of commodities was brought under the law of social adjustments. Its basis was cooperation, having for its object the perfect satisfaction of social needs. But in the West it is guided by the impulse of competition, whose end is the gain of wealth for individuals. But the individual is like the geometrical line; it is length without breadth. It has not got the depth to be able to hold anything permanently. Therefore, its greed or gain can never come to finality. In its lengthening process of growth it can cross other lines and cause entanglements, but will ever go on missing the ideal of completeness in its thinness of isolation....

The ideals that strive to take form in social institutions have two objects. One is to regulate your passions and appetites for the harmonious development of man, and the other is to help him to cultivate disinterested love for his fellow-creatures. Therefore, society is the expression of those moral and spiritual aspirations of man which belong to his higher nature.

Our food is creative, it builds our body; but not so wine, which stimulates. Our social ideals create the human world, but when our mind is diverted from them to greed of power, then, in that state of intoxication, we live in a world of abnormality where our strength is not health and our liberty is not freedom. Therefore, political freedom does not give us freedom when our mind is not free. An automobile does not create freedom of movement, because it is a mere machine. When I myself am free I can use the automobile for the purpose of my freedom.

We must never forget in the present day that those people who have got their political freedom are not necessarily free; they are merely powerful. The passions which are unbridled in them are creating huge organizations of slavery in the disguise of freedom. Those who have made the gain of money their highest end are unconsciously selling their life and soul to rich persons or to the combinations that represent money. Those who are enamored of their political power and gloat over their extension of dominion over foreign races gradually surrender their own freedom and humanity to the organizations necessary for holding other peoples in slavery. In the so-called free countries the majority of the people are not free; they are driven by the minority to a goal which is not even known to them. This becomes possible only because people do not acknowledge moral and spiritual freedom as their object. They create huge eddies with their passions, and they feel dizzily inebriated with the mere velocity of their whirling movement, taking that to be freedom. But the doom which is waiting to overtake them is as certain as death—for man's truth is moral truth and his emancipation is in the spiritual life.

The general opinion of the majority of the present-day nationalists in India is that we have come to a final completeness in our social and spiritual ideals, the task of the constructive work of society having been done several thousand years before we were born, and that now we are free to employ all our activities in the political direction. We never dream of blaming our social inadequacy as the origin of our present helplessness, for we have accepted as the creed of our nationalism that this social system has been perfected for all time to come by our ancestors, who had the superhuman vision of all eternity and supernatural power for making infinite provision for future ages. Therefore, for all our miseries and shortcomings, we hold responsible the historical surprises that burst upon us from outside. This is the reason why we think that our one task is to build a political miracle of freedom upon the quicksand of social slavery. In fact, we want to dam up the true course of our own historical stream, and only borrow power from the sources of other peoples' history.

Those of us in India who have come under the delusion that mere political freedom will make us free have accepted their lessons from the West as the gospel truth and lost their faith in humanity. We must remember that whatever weakness we cherish in our society will become the source of danger in politics. The same inertia which leads us to our idolatry of dead forms in social institutions will create in our politics prison-houses with immovable walls. The narrowness of sympathy which makes it possible for us to impose upon a considerable portion of humanity the galling yoke of inferiority will assert itself in our politics in creating the tyranny of injustice.

When our nationalists talk about ideals they forget that the basis of nationalism is wanting. The very people who are upholding these ideals are themselves the most conservative in their social practice. Nationalists say, for example: look at Switzerland where, in spite of race differences, the people have solidified into a nation. Yet, remember that in Switzerland the races can mingle, they can intermarry, because they are of the same blood. In India, there is no common birthright. And when we talk of Western nationality we forget that the nations there do not have that physical repulsion, one for the other, that we have between different castes. Have we an instance in the whole world where a people who are not allowed to mingle their blood shed their blood for one another except by coercion or for mercenary purposes? And can we ever hope that these moral barriers against our race amalgamation will not stand in the way of our political unity?

Then, again, we must give full recognition to this fact that our social restrictions are still tyrannical, so much so as to make men cowards. If a man tells me that he has heterodox ideas, but that he cannot follow them because he would be socially ostracized, I excuse him for having to live a life of untruth, in order to live at all. The social habit of mind which impels us to make the life of our fellow-beings a burden to them where they differ from us even in such a thing as their choice of food, is sure to persist in our political organization and result in creating engines of coercion to crush every rational difference which is the sign of life. And tyranny will only add to the inevitable lies and hypocrisy in our political life. Is the mere name of freedom so valuable that we should be willing to sacrifice for its sake our moral freedom?

The intemperance of our habits does not immediately show its effects when we are in the vigor of our youth. But it gradually consumes that vigor, and when the period of decline sets in then we have to settle accounts and pay off our debts, which leads us to insolvency. In the West you are still able to carry your head high, though your humanity is suffering every moment from its dipsomania of organizing power. India, also in the heyday of her youth, could carry in her vital organs the dead weight of her social organizations stiffened to rigid perfection, but it has been fatal to her, and has produced a gradual paralysis of her living nature. And this is the reason why the educated community of India has become insensible of her social needs. They are taking the very immobility of our social structures as the sign of their perfection—and because the healthy feeling of pain is dead in the limbs of our social organism they delude themselves into thinking that it needs no ministration. Therefore, they think that all their energies need their only scope in the political field. It is like a man whose legs have become shriveled and useless, trying to delude himself that these limbs have grown still because they have attained their ultimate salvation, and all that is wrong about him is the shortness of his sticks....

In our mythology we have the legend that the man who performs penances for attaining immortality has to meet with temptations sent by Indra, the Lord of the Immortals. If he is lured by them, he is lost. The West has been striving for centuries after its goal of immortality. Indra has sent her the temptation to try her. It is the gorgeous temptation of wealth. She has accepted it, and her civilization of humanity has lost its path in the wilderness of machinery....

The temptation which is fatal for the strong is still more so for the weak. And I do not welcome it in our Indian life, even though it be sent by the Lord of the Immortals. Let our life be simple in its outer aspect and rich in its inner gain. Let our civilization take its firm stand upon its basis of social cooperation and not upon that of economic exploitation and conflict. How to do it in the teeth of the drainage of our life-blood by the economic dragons is the task set before the thinkers of all oriental nations who have faith in the human soul. It is a sign of laziness and impotency to accept conditions imposed upon us by others who have other ideals than ours. We should actively try to adapt the world powers to guide our history to its own perfect end.

From the above you will know that I am not an economist. I am willing to acknowledge that there is a law of demand and supply and an infatuation of man for more things than are good for him. And yet, I will persist in believing that there is such a thing as the harmony of completeness in humanity, where poverty does not take away his riches, where defeat may lead him to victory, death to immortality, and where in the compensation of Eternal Justice those who are the last may yet have their insult transmuted into a golden triumph.

■

■ Notes ■

[1] Nanak (1469–1533), Kabir (1440–1518), Chaitanya (1485–1533).
[2] The Indian National Congress was founded in 1885.
[3] In 1907, at the annual session of the Indian National Congress, held at Surat.

■

3

■ SRI AUROBINDO ■

Aurobindo Ghose (1872–1950), better known as Sri Aurobindo, was born in West Bengal into an influential family closely linked with the Brahmo Samaj. Reared in an anglophile household, Aurobindo was educated entirely in European style, first in a convent school in Darjeeling and later in public schools in England. After studies at King's College in Cambridge he returned to India in 1893 to enter civil service in the progressive princely state of Baroda. Feeling himself uprooted or 'denationalized', he proceeded to immerse himself in the cultural legacy of India—and in due course also in Indian politics. His newly found patriotism drove him into the arms of 'extremist' national leaders, especially Tilak—an association which prompted him to leave Baroda and to take up fervently the cause of Bengali and Indian political autonomy. In 1908 he was jailed on charges of advocating terrorism and violence—an experience which occasioned a profound transformation. Not long after his release he left Bengal and took up residence in the French settlement of Pondicherry where he remained for the rest of his life engaged in writing and spiritual exercises.

For primary and secondary sources see Aurobindo Ghose, *Life Divine*, New York, Greystone Press, 1949; *The Human Cycle, The Ideal of Human Unity, War and Self-Determination*, Pondicherry, Sri Aurobindo Ashram, 1971; *The Synthesis of Yoga*, Pondicherry, Sri Aurobindo Ashram, 1973; *The Secret of Veda*, Pondicherry, Sri Aurobindo Ashram, 1971; *Essays on the Gita*, Pondicherry, Sri Aurobindo Ashram, 1976; Kewal Motwani, ed., *Sri Aurobindo on Social Sciences and Humanities for the New*

Age, Bombay, Orient Longman, 1962; D.P. Chattopadhyay, History, Society and Polity: Integral Sociology of Sri Aurobindo, New Delhi, Macmillan, 1976; Stephen H. Philipps, Aurobindo's Philosophy of Brahman, Leiden, Brill, 1986. The following selection is taken from The Foundations of Indian Culture, in Sri Aurobindo, Works, Vol. 14, Pondicherry, Sri Aurobindo Birth Centenary Library, 1972.

THE RENAISSANCE IN INDIA

I

There has been recently some talk of a renaissance in India. A number of illuminating essays with that general title and subject have been given to us by a poet and subtle critic and thinker, Mr James H. Cousins, and others have touched suggestively various sides of the growing movement towards a new life and a new thought that may well seem to justify the description. This Renaissance, this new birth in India, if it is a fact, must become a thing of immense importance both to herself and the world: to herself because of all that is meant for her in the recovery or the change of her time-old spirit and national ideals, to the world because of the possibilities involved in the re-arising of a force that is in many respects unlike any other and its genius very different from the mentality and spirit that have hitherto governed the modern idea in mankind, although not so far away perhaps from that which is preparing to govern the future. It is rather the first point of view that I shall put forward at present: for the question what India means to make of her own life must precede the wider question of what her new life may mean to the human race. And it is, besides, likely to become before long an issue of pressing importance.

There is a first question, whether at all there is really a renaissance in India. That depends a good deal on what we mean by the word; it depends also on the future, for the thing itself is only in its infancy and it is too early to say to what it may lead. The word carries the mind back to the turning-point of European culture to which it was first applied; that was not so much a reawakening as an overturn and reversal, a seizure of Christianized, Teutonized, feudalized Europe by the old Graeco-Latin spirit and form with all the complex and momentous results which came from it. That is certainly not a type of renaissance that is at all possible in India. There is a closer resemblance to the recent Celtic movement in Ireland, the attempt of a reawakened national spirit to find a new impulse of self-expression which shall give the spiritual force for a great reshaping and rebuilding: in Ireland this was discovered by a return to the Celtic spirit and culture after a long period of eclipsing English influences, and in India something of the same kind of movement is appearing and has especially taken a pronounced turn since the political outburst of 1905. But even here the analogy does not give the whole truth.

We have to see, moreover, that the whole is at present a great formless chaos of conflicting influences with a few luminous points of formation here and there where a new self-consciousness has come to the surface. But it cannot be said that these forms have yet a sufficient hold on the general mind of the people. They represent an advance movement; they are the voices of the vanguard, the torch-lights of the pioneers. On the whole, what we see is a giant Shakti who, awakening into a new world, a new and alien environment, finds herself shackled in all her limbs by a multitude of gross or minute bonds, bonds self-woven by her past, bonds recently imposed from outside, and is struggling to be free from them, to arise and proclaim herself, to cast abroad her spirit and set her seal on the world. We hear on every side a sound of the slow fraying of bonds, here and there a sharp tearing and snapping; but freedom of movement has not yet been attained. The eyes are not yet clear, the bud of the soul has only partly opened. The Titaness has not yet arisen.

Mr Cousins puts the question in his book whether the word 'renaissance' at all applies, since India has always been awake and stood in no need of reawakening. There is a certain truth behind that and to one coming in with a fresh mind from outside and struck by the living continuity of past and present India, it may be especially apparent; but that is not quite how we can see it who are her children and are still suffering from the bitter effects of the great decline which came to a head in the eighteenth and nineteenth centuries. Undoubtedly, there was a period, a brief but very disastrous period, of the dwindling of that great fire of life, even a moment of incipient disintegration, marked politically by the anarchy which gave European adventure its chance, inwardly by an increasing torpor of the creative spirit in religion and

art—science and philosophy and intellectual knowledge had long
been dead or petrified into a mere scholastic Punditism—all
pointing to a nadir of setting energy, the evening-time from which,
according to the Indian idea of the cycles, a new age has to start.
It was that moment and the pressure of a superimposed European
culture which followed it that made the reawakening necessary.

We have practically to take three facts into consideration: the
great past of Indian culture and life with the moment of inadaptive
torpor into which it had lapsed; the first period of the Western
contact in which it seemed for a moment likely to perish by slow
decomposition; and the ascending movement which first broke
into some clarity of expression only a decade or two ago. Mr Cousins
has his eye fixed on Indian spirituality which has always maintained itself even in the decline of the national vitality; it was certainly that which saved India always at every critical moment of
her destiny, and it has been the starting-point too of her renascence. Any other nation under the same pressure would have
long ago perished soul and body. But certainly the outward members were becoming gangrened; the powers of renovation seemed
for a moment to be beaten by the powers of stagnation, and stagnation is death. Now that the salvation, the reawakening has
come, India will certainly keep her essential spirit, will keep her
characteristic soul, but there is likely to be a great change of the
body. The shaping for itself of a new body, of new philosophical,
artistic, literary, cultural, political, social forms by the same soul
rejuvenescent will, I should think, be the type of the Indian renascence—forms not contradictory of the truths of life which the old
expressed, but rather expressive of those truths restated, cured of
defect, completed.

What was this ancient spirit and characteristic soul of India?
European writers, struck by the general metaphysical bent of the
Indian mind, by its strong religious instincts and religious idealism,
by its other-worldliness, are inclined to write as if this were all the
Indian spirit. An abstract, metaphysical, religious mind overpow-
ered by the sense of the infinite, not apt for life, dreamy, unpractical, turning away from life and action as Maya, this, they said, is
India; and for a time Indians in this, as in other matters, submis-
sively echoed their new Western teachers and masters. They
learned to speak with pride of their metaphysics, of their literature, of their religion, but in all else they were content to be learn-
ers and imitators. Since then Europe has discovered that there

was too an Indian art of remarkable power and beauty; but the rest of what India meant, it has hardly at all seen. But meanwhile the Indian mind began to emancipate itself and to look upon its past with a clear and self-discerning eye, and it very soon discovered that it had been misled into an entirely false self-view. All such one-sided appreciations indeed almost invariably turn out to be false. Was it not the general misconception about Germany at one time, because she was great in philosophy and music, but had blundered in life and been unable to make the most of its materials, that this was a nation of unpractical dreamers, idealists, erudites and sentimentalists, patient, docile and industrious certainly, but politically inept—'admirable, ridiculous Germany'? Europe has had a terrible awakening from that error. When the renascence of India is complete, she will have an awakening, not of the same brutal kind, certainly, but startling enough, as to the real nature and capacity of the Indian spirit.

Spirituality is indeed the master-key of the Indian mind; the sense of the infinite is native to it. India saw from the beginning—and even in her ages of reason and her age of increasing ignorance, she never lost hold of the insight—that life cannot be rightly seen in the sole light, cannot be perfectly lived in the sole power of its externalities. She was alive to the greatness of material laws and forces; she had a keen eye for the importance of the physical sciences; she knew how to organize the arts of ordinary life. But she saw that the physical does not get its full sense until it stands in right relation to the supra-physical; she saw that the complexity of the universe could not be explained in the present terms of man or seen by his superficial sight, that there were other powers behind, other powers within man himself of which he is normally unaware, that he is conscious only of a small part of himself, that the invisible always surrounds the visible, the suprasensible the sensible, even as infinity always surrounds the finite. She saw too that man has the power of exceeding himself, of becoming himself more entirely and profoundly than he is—truths which have only recently begun to be seen in Europe and seem even now too great for its common intelligence. She saw the myriad gods beyond man, God beyond the gods, and beyond God his own ineffable eternity; she saw that there were ranges of life beyond our life, ranges of mind beyond our present mind and above these she saw the splendors of the spirit. Then, with that calm audacity of her intuition which knew no fear or littleness and shrank from no act whether of spiritual or intellectual, ethical or vital courage, she declared that there was none of these things which man could not attain if he trained his will and knowledge; he could conquer these ranges of mind, become the spirit, become a god, become one with God, become the ineffable Brahman. And with the logical practicality and sense of science and organized method which distinguished her mentality, she set forth immediately to find out the way. Hence, from long ages of this insight and practice there was ingrained in her spirituality, her powerful psychic tendency, her great yearning to grapple with the infinite and possess it, her ineradicable religious sense, her idealism, her yoga, the constant turn of her art and her philosophy.

But this was not and could not be her whole mentality, her entire spirit; spirituality itself does not flourish on earth in the void, even as our mountain-tops do not rise like those of an enchantment of dream out of the clouds without a base. When we look at the past of India, what strikes us next is her stupendous vitality, her inexhaustible power of life and joy of life, her almost unimaginably prolific creativeness. For three thousand years at least—it is indeed much longer—she has been creating abundantly and incessantly, lavishly, with an inexhaustible many-sidedness, republics and kingdoms and empires, philosophies and cosmogonies and sciences and creeds and arts and poems and all kinds of monuments, palaces and temples and public works, communities and societies and religious orders, laws and codes and rituals, physical sciences, psychic sciences, systems of Yoga, systems of politics and administration, arts spiritual, arts worldly, trades, industries, fine crafts—the list is endless and in each item there is almost a plethora of activity. She creates and creates and is not satisfied and is not tired; she will not have an end of it, seems hardly to need a space for rest, a time for inertia and lying fallow. She expands too, outside her borders; her ships cross the ocean and the fine superfluity of her wealth brims over to Judea and Egypt and Rome; her colonies spread her arts and epics and creeds in the archipelago; her traces are found in the sands of Mesopotamia; her religions conquer China and Japan and spread westward as far as Palestine and Alexandria, and the figures of the Upanishads and the sayings of the Buddhists are re-echoed on the lips of Christ. Everywhere, as on her soil, so in her works there is the teeming of a super-abundant energy of life. European critics complain that in her ancient architecture, sculpture and art there is no reticence, no holding back of riches, no blank spaces, that she labors to fill every rift with ore, occupy every inch with plenty. Well, but defect or no, that is the necessity of her super-abundance of life, of the teeming of the infinite within her. She lavishes her riches because she must, as the infinite fills every inch of space with the stirring of life and energy because it is the infinite.

But this supreme spirituality and this prolific abundance of the energy and joy of life and creation do not make all that the spirit of India has been in its past. It is not a confused splendor of tropical vegetation under heavens of a pure sapphire infinity. It is only to eyes unaccustomed to such wealth that there seems to be a confusion in this crowding of space with rich forms of life, a luxurious disorder of excess, or a wanton lack of measure, clear balance and design. For the third power of the ancient Indian spirit was a strong intellectuality, at once austere and rich, robust and minute, powerful and delicate, massive in principle and curious in detail. Its chief impulse was that of order and arrangement, but an order founded upon a seeking for the inner law and truth of things and having in view always the possibility of conscientious practice. India has been pre-eminently the land of the Dharma and the Shastra. She searched for the inner truth and law of each human or cosmic activity, its Dharma; that found, she labored to cast into elaborate form and detailed law of arrangement its application in fact and rule of life. Her first period was luminous with the discovery of the Spirit; her second completed the discovery of the Dharma; her third elaborated into detail the first simpler formulation of the Shastra; but none was exclusive, the three elements are always present.... Thus, an ingrained and dominant spirituality, an inexhaustible vital creativeness and gust of life and, mediating between them, a powerful, penetrating and scrupulous intelligence combined of the rational, ethical and aesthetic mind, each at a high intensity of action, created the harmony of the ancient Indian culture....

I have dwelt on these facts because they are apt to be ignored by those who look only at certain sides of the Indian mind and spirit which are most prominent in the last epochs. By insisting only upon these we get an inaccurate or incomplete idea of the past of India and of the integral meaning of its civilization and the spirit that animated it. The present is only a last deposit of the past at a time of ebb; it has no doubt also to be the starting-point of the future, but in this present all that was in India's past is still dormant, it is not destroyed; it is waiting there to assume new forms. The decline was the ebb-movement of a creative spirit which can only be understood by seeing it in the full tide of its greatness; the renascence is the return of the tide and it is the same spirit that is likely to animate it, although the forms it takes may be quite new. To judge, therefore, the possibilities of the renascence, the powers that it may reveal and the scope that it may take, we must dismiss the idea that the tendency of metaphysical abstraction is the one note of the Indian spirit which dominates or inspires all its cadences. Its real keynote is the tendency of spiritual realization, not cast at all into any white monotone, but many-faceted, many-colored, as supple in its adaptability as it is intense in its highest pitches....

The evening of decline was prepared by three movements of retrogression. First there is, comparatively, a sinking of that superabundant vital energy and a fading of the joy of life and the joy of creation. Even in the decline this energy is still something splendid and extraordinary and only for a very brief period sinks nearest to a complete torpor; but still a comparison with its past greatness will show that the decadence was marked and progressive. Second, there is a rapid cessation of the old free intellectual activity, a slumber of the scientific and the critical mind as well as the creative intuition; what remains becomes more and more a repetition of ill-understood fragments of past knowledge. There is a petrifaction of the mind and life in the relics of the forms which a great intellectual past had created. Old authority and rule become rigidly despotic and, as always then happens, lose their real sense and spirit. Finally, spirituality remains but burns no longer with the large and clear flame of knowledge of former times, but in intense jets and in a dispersed action which replaces the old magnificent synthesis and in which certain spiritual truths are emphasized to the neglect of others. This diminution amounts to a certain failure of the great endeavor which is the whole meaning of Indian culture, a falling short in the progress towards the perfect spiritualization of the mind and the life....

It was at this moment that the European wave swept over India. The first effect of this entry of a new and quite opposite civilization was the destruction of much that had no longer the power to live, the deliquescence of much else, a tendency to the devitalization of the rest. A new activity came in, but this was at first crudely and confusedly imitative of the foreign culture. It was a crucial moment and an ordeal of perilous severity; a less vigorous energy of life might well have foundered and perished under the double weight of the deadening of its old innate motives and a servile imitation of alien ideas and habits. History shows us how disastrous this situation can be to nations and civilizations. But fortunately the energy of life was there, sleeping only for a moment, not dead, and, given that energy, the evil carried within itself its own cure. For whatever temporary rotting and destruction this crude impact of European life and culture has caused, it gave three needed impulses. It revived the dormant intellectual and critical impulse; it rehabilitated life and awakened the desire of new creation; it put the reviving Indian spirit face to face with novel conditions and ideals and the urgent necessity of understanding, assimilating and conquering them. The national mind turned a new eye on its past culture, reawoke to its sense and import, but also, at the same time, saw it in relation to modern knowledge and ideas. Out of this awakening vision and impulse the Indian Renaissance is arising, and that must determine its future tendency. The recovery of the old spiritual knowledge and experience in all its splendor, depth and fullness is its first, most essential work; the flowing of this spirituality into new forms of philosophy, literature, art, science and critical knowledge is the second; an original dealing with modern problems in the light of Indian spirit and the endeavor to formulate a greater synthesis of a spiritualized society is the third and most difficult. Its success on these three lines will be the measure of its help to the future of humanity....

II

The process which has led up to the Renaissance, now inevitable, may be analyzed, both historically and logically, into three steps by which a transition is being managed, a complex breaking, reshaping and new building, with the final result yet distant in prospect—though here and there the first bases may have been already laid—a new age of an old culture transformed, not an affiliation of a newborn civilization to one that is old and dead, but a true rebirth, a renascence. The first step was the reception of the European contact, a radical reconsideration of many of the prominent elements and some revolutionary denial of the very principles of the old culture. The second was a reaction of the

Indian spirit upon the European influence, sometimes with a total denial of what it offered and a stressing both of the essential and the strict letter of the national past, which yet masked a movement of assimilation. The third, only now beginning or recently begun, is rather a process of new creation in which the spiritual power of the Indian mind remains supreme, recovers its truths, accepts whatever it finds sound or true, useful or inevitable of the modern idea and form, but so transmutes and Indianizes it, so absorbs and so transforms it entirely into itself that its foreign character disappears and it becomes another harmonious element in the characteristic working of the ancient goddess, the Shakti of India mastering and taking possession of the modern influence, no longer possessed or overcome by it....

This was not the idea of the earliest generation of intellectuals, few in number but powerful by their talent and originative vigor, that arose as the first result of Western education in India. Theirs was the impatient hope of a transformation such as took place afterwards with so striking a velocity in Japan; they saw in welcome prospect a new India modernized wholesale and radically in mind, spirit and life. Intensely patriotic in motive, they were yet denationalized in their mental attitude. They admitted practically, if not in set opinion, the occidental view of our past culture as only a half-civilization, and their governing ideals were borrowed from the West or at least centrally inspired by the purely Western spirit and type of their education. From medieval India they drew away in revolt and inclined to discredit and destroy whatever it had created; if they took anything from it, it was as poetic symbols to which they gave a superficial and modern significance. To ancient India they looked back, on the contrary, with a sentiment of pride, at least in certain directions, and were willing to take from it whatever material they could subdue to their new standpoint, but they could not quite grasp anything of it in its original sense and spirit and strove to rid it of all that would not square with their Westernized intellectuality. They sought for a bare, simplified and rationalized religion, created a literature which imported very eagerly the forms, ideas and whole spirit of their English models—the value of the other arts was almost entirely ignored—put their political faith and hope in a wholesale assimilation or rather an exact imitation of the middle class pseudo-democracy of nineteenth century England, that would have revolutionized Indian society by introducing into it all the social ideas and main features of the

European form. Whatever value for the future there may be in the things they grasped at with this eager conviction, their method was, as we now recognize, a false method—an anglicized India is a thing we can no longer view as either possible or desirable—and it could only, if pursued to the end, have made us painful copyists, clumsy followers always stumbling in the wake of European evolution and always fifty years behind it. This movement of thought did not and could not endure; something of it still continues, but its engrossing power has passed away beyond any chance of vigorous revival.

Nevertheless, this earliest period of crude reception left behind it results that were of value and indeed indispensable to a powerful renaissance. We may single out three of them as of the first order of importance. It reawakened a free activity of the intellect which, though at first confined within very narrow bounds and derivative in its ideas, is now spreading to all subjects of human and national interest and is applying itself with an increasing curiosity and a growing originality to every field it seizes. This is bringing back to the Indian mind its old unresting thirst for all kinds of knowledge and must restore to it before long the width of its range and the depth and flexible power of its action; and it has opened to it the full scope of the critical faculty of the human mind, its passion for exhaustive observation and emancipated judgment which, in older times exercised only by a few and within limits, has now become an essential equipment of the intellect. These things the imitative period did not itself carry very far, but it cast the germ which we now see beginning to fructify more richly. Second, it threw definitely the ferment of modern ideas into the old culture and fixed them before our view in such a way that we are obliged to reckon and deal with them in far other sort than would have been possible if we had simply proceeded from our old fixed traditions without some such momentary violent break in our customary view of things. Finally, it made us turn our look upon all that our past contains with new eyes which have not only enabled us to recover something of their ancient sense and spirit, long embedded and lost in the unintelligent practice of received forms, but to bring out of them a new light which gives to the old truths fresh aspects and therefore novel potentialities of creation and evolution. That in this first period we misunderstood our ancient culture, does not matter; the enforcement of a reconsideration, which even orthodox thought has been obliged to accept, is the fact of capital importance.

The second period of reaction of the Indian mind upon the new elements, its movement towards a recovery of the national poise, has helped us to direct these powers and tendencies into sounder and more fruitful lines of action. For the anglicizing impulse was very soon met by the old national spirit and began to be heavily suffused by its influence. It is now a very small and always dwindling number of our present-day intellectuals who still remain obstinately Westernized in their outlook; and even these have given up the attitude of blatant and uncompromising depreciation of the past which was at one time a common poise. A larger number have proceeded by a constantly increasing suffusion of their modernism with much of ancient motive and sentiment, a better insight into the meaning of Indian things and their characteristics, a free acceptance more of their spirit than of their forms, and an attempt at new interpretation. At first the central idea still remained very plainly of the modern type and betrayed everywhere the Western inspiration, but it drew to itself willingly the ancient ideas and it colored itself more and more with their essential spirit; and latterly, this suffusing element has overflooded, has tended more and more to take up and subdue the original motives until the thought and spirit, turn and tinge are now characteristically Indian. The works of Bankim Chandra Chatterji and Tagore, the two minds of the most distinctive and original genius in our recent literature, illustrate the stages of this transition.[1]

Side by side with this movement, and more characteristic and powerful, there has been flowing an opposite current. This first started on its way by an integral reaction, a vindication and re-acceptance of everything Indian as it stood and because it was Indian. We have, still, waves of this impulse and many of its influences continuing among us; for its work is not yet completed. But in reality the reaction marks the beginning of a more subtle assimilation and fusing; for in vindicating ancient things it has been obliged to do so in a way that will at once meet and satisfy the old mentality and the new, the traditional and the critical mind. This in itself involves no mere return, but consciously or unconsciously hastens a restatement. And the riper form of the return has taken as its principle a synthetical restatement; it has sought to arrive at the spirit of the ancient culture and, while respecting its forms and often preserving them to revivify, has yet not hesitated also to remould, to reject the outworn and to admit whatever new motive seemed assimilable to the old spirituality or apt to widen the channel of its larger evolution. Of this freer dealing with past and present, this preservation by reconstruction, Vivekananda was in his lifetime the leading exemplar and the most powerful exponent.

But this too could not be the end; of itself it leads towards a principle of new creation. Otherwise, the upshot of the double current of thought and tendency might be an incongruous assimilation, something in the mental sphere like the strangely assorted half-European, half-Indian dress which we now put upon our bodies. India has to get back entirely to the native power of her spirit at its very deepest and to turn all the needed strengths and aims of her present and future life into materials for that spirit to work upon and integrate and harmonize. Of such vital and original creation we may cite the new Indian art as a striking example. The beginning of this process of original creation in every sphere of her national activity will be the sign of the integral self-finding of her Renaissance.

III

To attempt to penetrate through the indeterminate confusion of present tendencies and first efforts in order to foresee the exact forms the new creation will take, would be an effort of very doubtful utility. One might as well try to forecast a harmony from the sounds made by the tuning of the instrument. In one direction or another we may just detect certain decisive indications, but even these are only first indications and we may be quite sure that much lies behind them that will go far beyond anything that they yet suggest. This is true whether in religion and spirituality or thought and science, poetry and art or society and politics. Everywhere there is, at most, only a beginning of beginnings.

One thing seems at any rate certain, that the spiritual motive will be in the future of India, as in her past, the real, originative and dominating strain. By spirituality we do not mean a remote metaphysical mind or the tendency to dream rather than to act. That was not the great India of old in her splendid days of vigor—whatever certain European critics or interpreters of her culture may say—and it will not be the India of the future. Metaphysical thinking will always, no doubt, be a strong element in her mentality, and it is to be hoped that she will never lose her great, her sovereign powers in that direction; but Indian metaphysics is as far removed from the brilliant or the profound idea-spinning of the French or the German mind as from the broad intellectual generalizing on the basis of the facts of physical science which for some time did duty for philosophy in modern Europe. It has always been in its essential parts an intellectual approach to spiritual realization....

In the things of the mind we have, then, within however limited an area, certain beginnings, preparatory or even initially definitive. But in the outward life of the nation we are still in a stage of much uncertainty and confusion. Very largely this is due to the political conditions which have ceased in spirit to be those of the past, but are not yet in fact those of the future. Indian society is in a still more chaotic stage; for the old forms are crumbling away under the pressure of the environment, their spirit and reality are more and more passing out of them, but the façade persists by the force of inertia of thought and will and the remaining attachment of a long association, while the new is still powerless to be born. There is much of slow and often hardly perceptible destruction, a dull preservation effective only by immobility, no possibility yet of sound reconstruction. We have had a loud proclaiming—only where supported by religion, as in the reforming Samajas,[2] any strong effectuation—of a movement of social change, appealing sometimes crudely to Western exemplars and ideals, sometimes to the genius or the pattern of ancient times; but it has quite failed to carry the people, because it could not get at their spirit and itself lacked, with the exceptions noted, in robust sincerity. We have had, too, a revival of orthodox conservatism, more academic and sentimental than profound in its impulse or in touch with the great facts and forces of life. We have now in emergence an increasing sense of the necessity of a renovation of social ideas and expressive forms by the spirit of the nation awaking to the deeper yet unexpressed implications of its own culture, but as yet no sufficient will or means of execution. It is probable that only with the beginning of a freer national life will the powers of the Renaissance take effective hold of the social mind and action of the awakened people....

■ Notes ■

1 The reference is to Bankim Chandra Chatterji (1838–1894) and Rabindranath Tagore (1861–1941).
2 The reference is to reform movements like the Brahmo Samaj and Arya Samaj.

■

4

■ ANANDA K. COOMARASWAMY ■

Ananda Kentish Coomaraswamy (1877–1947) was born in Colombo, Sri Lanka (then Ceylon), into a wealthy and influential family (his father being a successful barrister and his mother of English descent). After the early death of his father in 1879, he was raised by his mother in England, first by private tutors and then at a preparatory school in Kent. In 1897 he entered University College in London where he studied geology and botany and subsequently, in 1906, he obtained a doctor of science degree from London University. In preparation for his degree he spent several years in Ceylon as a geologist and as editor of a journal of the Ceylon Social Reform Society. After returning to England, he visited India repeatedly between 1909 and 1916, where he became involved in the circle around Tagore. Facing legal problems because of his stand as a conscientious objector, he left England in 1917 for the United States, where he began work at the Boston Museum of Fine Arts, assisting in the department of Oriental Collections. From 1932 to 1947 he served as curator in the Department of Asiatic Art of the Museum of Fine Arts in Boston.

For primary and secondary sources see A.K. Coomaraswamy, *Medieval Sinhalese Art*, Broad Campden, Essex House, 1908; *Myths of the Hindus and Buddhists*, New York, Holt, 1914; *Buddha and the Gospel of Buddhism*, London, Harrap, 1916; *The Dance of Shiva*, New York, Holt, 1918; *A New Approach to the Vedas*, London, Harrap, 1933; *Figures of Speech or Figures of Thought*, London, Luzac, 1946; Roger Lipsey, ed., *Coomaraswamy*, Vol. 1, *Traditional Art & Symbolism*, Princeton, Princeton University Press, 1977; *Coomaraswamy*, Vol. 2, *Metaphysics*,

Princeton, Princeton University Press, 1977; Roger Lipsey, *Coomaraswamy*, Vol. 3, *His Life and Work*, Princeton, Princeton University Press, 1977. The following selection is taken from *Coomaraswamy: Metaphysics*, pp. 3–22.

THE VEDANTA AND WESTERN TRADITION

The sacred literature of India is available to most of us only in translations made by scholars trained in linguistics rather than in metaphysics; and it has been expounded and explained—or as I should rather say, explained away—mainly by scholars provided with the assumptions of the naturalist and anthropologist, scholars whose intellectual capacities have been so much inhibited by their own powers of observation that they can no longer distinguish the reality from the appearance, the Supernal Sun of metaphysics from the physical sun of their own experience. Apart from these, Indian literature has either been studied and explained by Christian propagandists whose main concern has been to demonstrate the falsity and absurdity of the doctrines involved, or by theosophists by whom the doctrines have been caricatured with the best intentions and perhaps even worse results.

The educated man of today is, moreover, completely out of touch with those European modes of thought and those intellectual aspects of the Christian doctrine which are nearest those of the Vedic traditions. A knowledge of modern Christianity will be of little use because the fundamental sentimentality of our times has diminished what was once an intellectual doctrine to a mere morality that can hardly be distinguished from a pragmatic humanism. A European can hardly be said to be adequately prepared for the study of the Vedanta unless he has acquired some knowledge and understanding of at least Plato, Philo, Hermes, Plotinus, the Gospels (especially John), Dionysius, and finally Eckhart who, with the possible exception of Dante, can be regarded from an Indian point of view as the greatest of all Europeans.

The Vedanta is not a 'philosophy' in the current sense of the word, but only as the word is used in the phrase *philosophia perennis*, and only if we have in mind the hermetic 'philosophy' or that 'wisdom' by whom Boethius was consoled. Modern philosophies are closed systems, employing the method of dialectics, and taking for granted that opposites are mutually exclusive. In modern philosophy things are either so or not so; in eternal philosophy this depends upon our point of view. Metaphysics is not a system, but a consistent doctrine; it is not merely concerned with conditioned and quantitative experience, but with universal possibility. It therefore considers possibilities that may be neither possibilities of manifestation, nor, in any sense, formal, as well as ensembles of possibility that can be realized in a given world. The ultimate reality of metaphysics is a Supreme Identity in which the opposition of all contraries, even of being and not-being, is resolved; its 'worlds' and 'gods' are levels of reference and symbolic entities which are neither places nor individuals but states of being realizable within you.

Philosophers have personal theories about the nature of the world; our 'philosophical discipline' is primarily a study of the history of these opinions and of their historical connections. We encourage the budding philosopher to have opinions of his own on the chance that they may represent an improvement on previous theories. We do not envisage, as does the *philosophia perennis*, the possibility of knowing the Truth once and for all; still less do we set before us as our goal to become this Truth.

The metaphysical 'philosophy' is called 'perennial' because of its eternity, universality, and immutability; it is Augustine's 'wisdom uncreate, the same now as it ever was and ever will be'; the religion which, as he also says, only came to be called 'Christianity' after the coming of Christ. What was revealed in the beginning contains implicitly the whole truth; and so long as the tradition is transmitted without deviation, so long, in other words, as the chain of teachers and disciples remains unbroken, neither inconsistency nor error is possible. On the other hand, an understanding of the doctrine must be perpetually renewed; it is not a matter of words. That the doctrine has no history by no means excludes the possibility, or even the necessity, for a perpetual explicitation of its formulae, an adaptation of the rites originally practised, and an application of its principles to the arts and sciences. The more humanity declines from its first self-sufficiency, the more the necessity for such an application arises. Of these explicitations and adaptations a history is possible. Thus, a distinction is drawn between what was 'heard' at the outset and what has been 'remembered'.

A deviation or heresy is only possible when the essential teaching has been in some respect misunderstood or perverted. To say, for example, that 'I am a pantheist' is merely to confess that 'I am not a metaphysician', just as to say that 'two and two make five' would be to confess 'I am not a mathematician'. Within the tradition itself there cannot be any contradictory or mutually exclusive theories or dogmas. For example, what are called the 'six systems of Indian philosophy' (a phrase in which only the words 'six' and 'Indian' are justified) are not mutually contradictory and exclusive theories. The so-called 'systems' are no more or less orthodox than mathematics, chemistry, and botany which, though separate disciplines more or less scientific amongst themselves, are not anything but branches of one 'science'. India, indeed, makes use of the term 'branches' to denote what the Indologist misunderstands to be 'sects'. It is precisely because there are no 'sects' within the fold of Brahmanical orthodoxy that an intolerance in the European sense has been virtually unknown in Indian history—and for the same reason, it is just as easy for me to think in terms of the hermetic philosophy as in terms of Vedanta. There must be 'branches' because nothing can be known except in the mode of the knower; however strongly we may realize that all roads lead to one Sun, it is equally evident that each man must choose that road which starts from the point at which he finds himself at the moment of setting out. For the same reasons, Hinduism has never been a missionary faith. It may be true that the metaphysical tradition has been better and more fully preserved in India than in Europe. If so, it only means that the Christian can learn from the Vedanta how to understand his own 'way' better....

Taken in their materiality, as 'literature', the texts and symbols are inevitably misunderstood by those who are not themselves in quest. Without exception, the metaphysical terms and symbols are the technical terms of the chase. They are never literary ornaments, and as Malinowski has so well said in another connection, '[t]echnical language, in matters of practical pursuit, acquires its meaning only through personal participation in this type of pursuit'. That is why, the Indian feels, the Vedantic texts have been only *verbally* and *grammatically* and never *really* understood by European scholars, whose methods of study are avowedly objective and noncommittal. The Vedanta can be known only to the extent that it has been lived. The Indian, therefore, cannot trust a teacher whose doctrine is not directly reflected in his very being. Here is something very far removed from the modern European concept of scholarship.

We must add, for the sake of those who entertain romantic notions of the 'mysterious East', that the Vedanta has nothing to do with magic or with the exercise of occult powers. It is true that the efficacy of magical procedure and the actuality of occult powers are taken for granted in India. But the magic is regarded as an applied science of the basest kind; and while occult powers, such as that of operation 'at a distance', are incidentally acquired in the course of contemplative practice, the use of them—unless under the most exceptional circumstances—is regarded as a dangerous deviation from the path.

Nor is the Vedanta a kind of psychology or Yoga a sort of therapeutics except quite accidentally. Physical and moral health are prerequisites to spiritual progress. A psychological analysis is employed only to break down our fond belief in the unity and immateriality of the 'soul', and with a view to a better distinguishing of the spirit from what is not the spirit but only a temporary psycho-physical manifestation of one of the most limited of its modalities. Whoever, like Jung, insists upon translating the essentials of Indian or Chinese metaphysics into a psychology is merely distorting the meaning of the texts. Modern psychology has, from an Indian point of view, about the same values that attach to spiritualism and magic and other 'superstitions'. Finally, I must point out that the metaphysics, the Vedanta, is not a form of mysticism, except in the sense that with Dionysius we can speak of a *theologia mystica*. What is ordinarily meant by 'mysticism' involves a passive receptivity—'we must be able to let things happen in the psyche' is Jung's way of putting it (and in this statement he proclaims himself a 'mystic'). But metaphysics repudiates the psyche altogether. The words of Christ, that 'No man can be my disciple who hateth not his own soul', have been voiced again and again by every Indian guru; and so far from involving passivity, contemplative practice involves an activity that is commonly compared to the blazing of a fire at a temperature so high as to show neither flickering nor smoke. The pilgrim is called a 'toiler', and the characteristic refrain of the pilgrim song is 'keep on going, keep on going'. The 'Way' of the Vedantist is above all an activity....

The Vedanta takes for granted an omniscience independent of any source of knowledge external to itself, and a beatitude independent of any external source of pleasure. In saying 'That art thou', the Vedanta affirms that man is possessed of, and is himself, 'that one thing which when it is known, all things are known' and 'for the sake of which alone all things are dear'. It affirms that man is unaware of this hidden treasure within himself because he has inherited an ignorance that inheres in the very nature of the psycho-physical vehicle which he mistakenly identifies with himself. The purpose of all teaching is to dissipate this ignorance; when the darkness has been pierced nothing remains but the Gnosis of the Light. The technique of education is, therefore, always formally destructive and iconoclastic; it is not the conveyance of information but the education of a latent knowledge.

The 'great dictum' of the Upanishads is, 'That art thou'. 'That' is here, of course, *atman* or Spirit, *Sanctus Spiritus*, Greek *pneuma*, Arabic *ruh*, Hebrew *ruah*, Egyptian *amon*, Chinese *ch'i*; *atman* is spiritual essence, impartite whether transcendent or immanent; and however many and various the directions to which it may extend or from which it may withdraw, it is unmoved mover in both intransitive and transitive senses. It lends itself to all modalities of being but never itself becomes anyone or anything. That than which all else is a vexation—'That art thou'. 'That', in other words, is the Brahman, or God in the general sense of Logos or Being, considered as the universal source of all being—expanding, manifesting and productive, font of all things, all of which are 'in' him as the finite in the infinite, though not a 'part' of him, since the infinite has no parts.

For the most part, I shall use the word *atman* hereafter. While this *atman*, as that which blows and enlightens, is primarily 'Spirit', because it is this divine Eros that is the quickening essence in all things and thus their real being, the word *atman* is also used reflexively to mean 'self'—either 'oneself' in whatever sense, however gross, the notion may be entertained, or with reference to the spiritual self or person (which is the only knowing subject and essence of all things, and must be distinguished from the affected and contingent 'I' that is a compound of the body and of all that we mean by 'soul' when we speak of a 'psychology'). Two very different 'selves' are thus involved, and it has been the custom of translators, accordingly, to render *atman* as 'self', printed either with a small or with a capital 'S' according to the context. The same distinction is drawn, for example, by St. Bernard between what is my 'property' (*proprium*) and what is my very being (*esse*). An alternative Indian formulation distinguishes the 'knower of the field'—viz. the Spirit as the only knowing subject in `all things and the same in all—from the 'field' or body-and-soul as defined above (taken together with the pastures of the senses and embracing, therefore, all things that can be considered objectively). The *atman* or Brahman itself cannot be thus considered: 'How couldst thou know the knower of knowing?'—or, in other words, how can the first cause of all things be one of them?

The *atman* is impartite, but it is apparently divided and identified into variety by the differing forms of its vehicles, mouse or man, just as space within a jar is apparently signate and distinguishable from space without it. In this sense it can be said that 'he is one as he is in himself but many as he is in his children', and that 'participating himself, he fills these worlds'. But this is only in the sense that light fills space while it remains itself without discontinuity; the distinction of things from one another thus depending not on differences in the light but on differences in reflecting power. When the jar is shattered, when the vessel of life is unmade, we realize that what was apparently delimited had no boundaries and that 'life' was a meaning not to be confused with 'living'. To say that the *atman* is thus at once participated and impartible, 'undivided amongst divided things', without local position and at the same time everywhere, is another way of stating what we are more familiar with as the doctrine of Total Presence....

■

5

VINAYAK D. SAVARKAR

Vinayak Damodar Savarkar (1883–1966) was born in Maharashtra as the second son of a landowning Brahman. From his early youth he was attracted to Hindu nationalism in its extremist form and, as a student at Ferguson College in Pune, he quickly organized a nationalist cadre among his fellow students—which eventually led to his dismissal from college. With Tilak's help he obtained a scholarship to study law in London, and used this opportunity to engage in subversive activities and assassination plots (aimed at Lord Curzon). Arrested and deported by the British, he was shipped in 1911 to the Andaman Islands for confinement. Although released in 1924, he was effectively barred from taking part in politics until 1937 when he joined the Hindu Mahasabha (Great Assembly of Hindus) which elected him as their president for seven consecutive years. During the second World War, Savarkar issued the slogan 'Hinduize all politics and militarize Hindudom', in direct opposition to Gandhi's principle of non-violence and efforts at Hindu-Muslim reconciliation. During the remainder of his life Savarkar remained staunchly attached to his program of 'Hindutva'.

For primary and secondary sources see V.D. Savarkar, *Hindutva*, 4th edn, Poona, Gokhale, 1946; Dhananja Keer, *Savarkar and His Times*, Bombay, A.V. Keer, 1950. The following selection is taken from Savarkar, *Hindu Rashtra Darshan*, 2nd edn, Bombay, Savarkar Prakashan, 1984, pp. 76–83.

SOME OF THE BASIC PRINCIPLES AND TENETS OF THE HINDU MOVEMENT

It is encouraging to note that thousands of those who were brought up from their early days under the influence of the pseudo-nationalistic ideology current in the Congress camp and were consequently so thoroughly prejudiced against anything that was connected with Hindutva that they militated against the very word 'Hindu' as something superstitious, out-of-date, unworthy of a progressive patriot to own, should now be evincing a genuine desire to know all about the Hindu Mahasabha, its policy and immediate program. The case of no less a personality than Mr Tairsee, whose sad death all Bombay lamented only a couple of months ago, can serve as a case in point. He was reputed to be one amongst the first ten citizens of Bombay, a rationalist of rationalists, one of the foremost Congress-ites. Yet, after I had casually explained to him the Hindu Sanghatan-ist ideology as expounded in my Nagpur speech, he publicly confessed that the rationalism which made him shun the word 'Hindu' or Hindu Sanghatan as a crass superstition was itself the crassest of superstitions. He not only joined our party but proudly accepted the presidentship of the Bombay Provincial Hindu Sabha.

Throughout my extensive tours I have come across thousands of the intellectual class who simply militated against the Hindu idea at its first mention, [but] when cogently explained, rubbed their eyes in a doubting mood at its second mention and half of them pressed for a closer acquaintance with it while the other half simply capitulated at its third mention. There has grown, of late, enormous curiosity throughout India to know something of the Hindu Mahasabha, its aims and as to what is its program and this demand at times comes from foreign countries as well. That is the reason why I wish to devote this address mainly to enumerate categorically the leading principles and tenets on which the Hindu movement is based, and to outline its general policy and some outstanding details of its immediate program. It will serve as a cogent statement of our case, and may be utilized as a basis for a manifesto in future to an organized Hindu party in the legislatures as well as a handy guide to our workers and propagandists in the press and platform.

The following are some of the basic tenets and aspects of the Hindu movement:

(i) Every person is a Hindu who regards and owns this Bharat Bhumi, this land from the Indus to the seas, as his fatherland as well as his holyland—i.e., the land of the origin of his religion, the cradle of his faith.

The followers therefore of Vedicism, Sanatanism, Jainism, Buddhism, Lingaitism, Sikhism, the Arya Samaj, the Brahmo Samaj, the Devasamaj, the Prarthana Samaj and such other religions of Indian origin are Hindus and constitute Hindudom, i.e., the Hindu people as a whole.

Consequently the so-called aboriginal or hill tribes also are Hindus: because India is their fatherland as well as their holyland of whatever form of religion or worship they follow.

This definition, therefore, should be recognized by the government and made the test of Hindutva in enumerating the population of Hindus in the government census to come....

(ii) *The word 'Hindu' is not of a foreign origin nor it is connected with the advent of the Moslems in India*, as was erroneously suspected for a time under the mischievous influence of some alien scribes. Our land and our people were at times called Sapta Sindhus or Sindhus even by our Vedic rishis.

Thousands of years before Muhammad, the Moslem prophet was born, the ancient Babylonians knew us as 'Sindhus' and the ancient Zend Avesta refers to us as 'Hindus'. One of our provinces on this side of the Indus has retained this ancient appellation of our land and people down to this day as 'Sindhu Desh' and its people as 'Sindhus' (Sindh).

(iii) *Hinduism, Hindutva and Hindudom*: In expounding the ideology of the Hindu movement, it is absolutely necessary to have a correct grasp of the meaning attached to these three terms. From the word 'Hindu' has been coined the word 'Hinduism' in English. It means the school or system of religions the Hindus follow. The second word, 'Hindutva', is far more comprehensive and refers not only to the religious aspect of the Hindu people as the word 'Hinduism' does but comprehends even their cultural, linguistic, social and political aspects as well. It is more or less akin to 'Hindu polity', and its nearly exact translation would be 'Hinduness'. The third word, 'Hindudom', means the Hindu people spoken of collectively. It is a collective name for the Hindu world, just as Islam denotes the Moslem world or Christiandom denotes the Christian world.

(iv) *We Hindus are a nation by ourselves*: In my presidential speech at Nagpur I had, for the first time in the history of our recent politics, pointed out in bold relief that the whole Congress ideology was vitiated *ab initio* by its unwitting assumption that the territorial unity, a common habitat, was the only factor that constituted and ought to constitute a nation. This conception of a territorial nationality has since then received a rude shock in Europe itself from which it was imported wholesale to India and the present war has justified my assertion by exploding the myth altogether. All nations carved out to order on the territorial design without any other common bond to mold each of them into a national being have gone to rack and ruin, tumbled down like a house of cards. Poland and Czechoslovakia will ever serve as a stern warning against any such efforts to frame heterogeneous peoples into such hotch-potch nations, based on the shifting sands of the conception of territorial nationality, not cemented by any cultural, racial or historical affinities and consequently having no common will to incorporate themselves into a nation. These treaty-nations broke up at the first opportunity they got: the German part of them went over to Germany, the Russian to Russia, Czechs to Czechoslovakia and Poles to Poland. The cultural, linguistic, historical and such other organic affinities proved stronger than the territorial one. Only those nations have persisted in maintaining their national unity and identity during the last three to four centuries in Europe which had developed racial, linguistic, cultural and such other organic affinities in addition to their territorial unity or even at times in spite of it, and consequently willed to be homogeneous national units—such as England, France, Germany, Italy, Portugal, etc.

Judged by any and all of these tests which go severally and collectively to form such a homogeneous and organic nation, in India we Hindus are marked out as an abiding nation by ourselves. Not only do we own a common fatherland, a territorial unity, but what is scarcely found anywhere else in the world, we have a common holyland which is identified with our common fatherland.... Our patriotism, therefore, is doubly sure. Then, we have common affinities, cultural, religious, historical, linguistic and racial which, through the process of countless centuries of association and assimilation, molded us into a homogeneous and organic nation and, above all, induced a will to lead a corporate and common national life. The Hindus are no treaty nation—but an organic national being.

One more pertinent point must be met as it often misleads our Congress-ite Hindu brethren in particular. The homogeneity that wields a people into a national being does not imply the total absence of all internal differences, religious, racial or linguistic, of sects and sections amongst themselves. It only means that they differ more from other people as a national unit than they differ amongst themselves. Even the most unitarian nations of today— say the British or the French—cannot be free from any religious, linguistic, cultural, racial or other different sects or sections or even some antipathies existing amongst themselves. National homogeneity connotes oneness of a people in relation to the contrast they present to any other people as a whole.

We Hindus, in spite of thousand and one differences within our fold, are bound by such religious, cultural, historical, racial, linguistic and other affinities in common as to stand out as a definitely homogeneous people as soon as we are placed in contrast with any other non-Hindu people—say the English or Japanese or even the Indian Muslims. That is the reason why today we Hindus from Kashmir to Madras and Sindh to Assam will to be a nation by ourselves—while the Indian Muslims are on the whole more inclined to identify themselves and their interests with Muslims outside India than Hindus who lived next door, like the Jews in Germany.

Some well-meaning but simple-minded Hindus amuse themselves with the thought and hope against hope that inasmuch as the majority of Indian Muslims also are in fact allied to us by race and language and in some cases had gone over to the Muslim fold in living memory of this very generation, they could easily be persuaded to acknowledge this homogeneity and even blood relation with the Hindus, and merge themselves into a common national being if but we only remind them of these affinities and appeal to them in their name. These innocent souls are really to be pitied. As if the Muslims do not know of it all! The fact is that the Muslims know of these affinities all too well: the only difference to be taken into account being that while the Hindus love these affinities which bind the Hindu to a Hindu and dwell on them with pride—the Muslims hate the very mention of them and are trying to eradicate the very memory of it all.... I am telling the simple fact which no Muslim can honestly contest that Islam as a whole wants on a deliberate design to assert itself in India as a nation altogether heterogeneous with the Hindus and having nothing in common with them. Consequently, it ought to be clear even to these well-meaning Hindu simpletons that this refusal of the Indian Muslims to merge in a common national unit leaves the Hindus, negatively too, as a nation by themselves.

(v) *Swarajya to the Hindus must mean only that 'Rajya' in which their 'Swatva', their 'Hindutva' can assert itself without being overlorded by any non-Hindu people, whether they be Indian territorials or extra-territorials:* Some Englishmen are and may continue to be territorially-born Indians. Can, therefore, the over-lordship of these Anglo-Indians be a 'swarajya' to the Hindus? Aurangzeb or Tippu were hereditary Indians, nay, were the sons of converted Hindu mothers. Did that mean that the rule of Aurangzeb or Tippu was a 'swarajya' to the Hindus? No! Although they were territorially Indians they proved to be the worst enemies of Hindudom and therefore, a Shivaji, a Gobind Singh, a Pratap or the Peshwas had to fight against the Muslim domination and establish a real Hindu *swarajya*.

Consequently, under the present circumstances too, all that an Indian national state can mean is that the Muslim minority in India will have the right to be treated as equal citizens, enjoying equal protection and civic rights in proportion to their population. The Hindu majority will not encroach on the legitimate rights of any non-Hindu minority. But in no case can the Hindu majority resign its right which, as a majority, it is entitled to exercise under any democratic and legitimate constitution. The Muslim minority in particular has not obliged the Hindus by remaining in minority and therefore, they must remain satisfied with the status they occupy and with the legitimate share of civic and political rights that is their proportionate due. It would be simply preposterous to endow the Muslim minority with the right of exercising a practical veto on the legitimate rights and privileges of the majority and call it a 'swarajya'. The Hindus do not want a change of masters, are not going to struggle and fight and die only to replace an Edward by an Aurangzeb simply because the latter happens to be born within Indian borders; but they want henceforth to be masters themselves in their own house, in their own land.

(vi) *Consequently, the name 'Hindusthan' must continue to be the appellation of our country:* Such other names as India, Hind, etc., being derived from the same original word 'Sindhu' may be used, but only to signify the same sense—the land of the Hindus— a country which is the abode of the Hindu nation. Aryavarta, Bharat Bhumi and such other names are of course the ancient and the most cherished epithets of our motherland, and will continue to appeal to the cultured elite. In this insistence that the motherland of the Hindus must be called but 'Hindusthan', no encroachment or humiliation is implied in connection with any of our non-Hindu countrymen. Our Parsee and Christian countrymen are already too akin to us culturally and are too patriotic, and the Anglo-Indians too sensible to refuse to fall in line with us Hindus on so legitimate a ground.

So far as our Muslim countrymen are concerned it is useless to conceal the fact that some of them are already inclined to look upon this molehill also as an insuperable mountain in their way to Hindu–Muslim unity. But they should remember that the Muslims do not dwell only in India; nor are the Indian Muslims the only heroic remnants of the faithful in Islam. China has crores of Muslims; Greece, Palestine and even Hungary and Poland have thousands of Muslims amongst their nationals. But being there a minority, only a community, their existence in these countries has never been advanced as a ground to change the ancient names of these countries which indicate the abodes of those races whose overwhelming majority own the land. The country of the Poles continues to be Poland, and of the Greeks Greece. The Muslims there did not or dare not distort them but are quite content to distinguish themselves as Polish Muslims or Greek Muslims or Chinese Muslims when occasion arises. So also our Muslim countrymen may distinguish themselves nationally or territorially whenever they want, as 'Hindusthani Muslims' without compromising in the least their separateness as a religious or cultural entity. Nay, the Muslims have been calling themselves 'Hindusthanis' ever since their advent in India, of their own accord.

But if, in spite of it all, some irrational Muslim sections amongst our countrymen object even to this name of our country, that is no reason why we should play cowards to our own conscience. We Hindus must not betray or break up the continuity of our nation from the Sindhus in Rigvedic days to the Hindus of our own generation which is implied in 'Hindusthan', the accepted appellation of our motherland. Just as the land of the Germans is Germany, of the English England, of the Turks Turkisthan, of the

Afghans Afghanisthan—even so we must have indelibly impressed on the map of the earth for all times to come a 'Hindusthan'—the land of the Hindus....

(*vii*) *The Hindu Mahasabha is a National Organization of Hindudom*: It has come to my notice that a very large section of the English-educated Hindus hold back from joining the Hindu Mahasabha and political circles in India and outside in general feel themselves totally unconcerned about it under the erroneous idea that it is an exclusively religious organization—something like a Christian Mission. Nothing could be farther from the truth. The Hindu Mahasabha is not a Hindu Mission. It leaves religious questions regarding theism, monotheism, pantheism or even atheism to be discussed and determined by the different Hindu schools of religious persuasions. It is not a Hindu Dharma Mahasabha, but a Hindu National Mahasabha. Consequently, by its very constitution it is debarred to associate itself exclusively as a partisan with any particular religious school or sect even within the Hindu fold.... The Hindu Mahasabha identifies itself with the national life of Hindudom in all its entirety, in all its social, economic, cultural, and, above all, political aspects, and is pledged to protect and promote all that contributes to the freedom, strength and glory of the Hindu nation; and as an indispensable means to that end to attain *purna swarajya* [complete self-rule], absolute political independence of Hindusthan by all legitimate and proper means.

■

6

JIDDU KRISHNAMURTI

Jiddu Krishnamurti (1895–1986) was born into a family of South Indian Brahmans. As a boy he became acquainted with Mrs Annie Besant, the English social reformer and president of the Theosophical Society (founded earlier by Madame Blavatsky). In 1911, at the age of 15, he was brought to England by Mrs Besant where he received a very intensive education by private tutors; in fact, he was being groomed for the role of a spiritual 'World Teacher' (*jagadguru*) and thrust into a leadership position in the theosophical movement. However, in 1929 he disbanded the organization which he was supposed to lead, and declared that he did not want disciples. After this, and for the rest of his life, he traveled ceaselessly all over the world giving public talks and private interviews, spreading the message of individual self-realization and moral self-improvement, while keeping a main residence in Ojai, California. He died in 1986 at the age of ninety-one.

For primary and secondary sources see J. Krishnamurti, *On Freedom*, San Francisco, Harper, 1991; *The Awakening of Intelligence*, London, Gollancz, 1973; *Beyond Violence*, New York, Harper & Row, 1973; *Education and the Significance of Life*, New York, Harper, 1953; *The First and Last Freedom*, with Foreword by Aldous Huxley, London, Gollancz, 1954; Mary Lutyers, ed., *The Only Revolution*, New York, Harper & Row, 1970; Mary Cadogan, Alan Kishbaugh, Mark Lee and Ray McCoy, eds, *Total Freedom: The Essential Krishnamurti*, San Francisco, Harper, 1996. The following selections are taken from *The Impossible Question*, London, Gollancz, 1972, pp. 20–29, and *The First and Last Freedom*, London, Gollancz, 1954, pp. 148–49.

FREEDOM

'The dependence on any form of subjective imagination, fantasy or knowledge, breeds fear and destroys freedom.'

There are many things we have to talk over, but first, it seems to me, we have to consider very deeply what freedom is. Without understanding freedom, not only outwardly, but especially inwardly, deeply and seriously—not merely intellectually, but actually feeling it—whatever we talk about will have very little meaning.

The other day we were considering the nature of the mind. It is the serious mind that really lives and enjoys life—not the mind that is merely seeking entertainment, some particular gratification or fulfilment. Freedom implies the total abnegation and denial of all inward psychological authority. The younger generation thinks freedom is to spit in the face of the policeman, to do whatever it wants. But the denial of outward authority does not mean complete freedom from all inward, psychological authority. When we understand inward authority, the mind and heart are wholly and completely free; then, we will be able to understand the action of freedom outwardly.

Freedom of action outwardly depends entirely on a mind that is free from inward authority. This requires a great deal of patient enquiry and deliberation. It is a matter of primary importance; if it is understood, then we will approach other things which are involved in life and daily living with quite a different quality of mind.

According to the dictionary the meaning of the word 'Authority' is: 'one who starts an original idea', 'the author of something entirely new'. He sets up a pattern, a system based on his ideation; others follow it, finding some gratification in it. Or, he starts a religious mode of life which others follow blindly, or intellectually. So patterns, or ways of life, of conduct are set up, politically or psychologically, outwardly and inwardly. The mind, which is generally very lazy and indolent, finds it easy to follow what somebody else has said. The follower accepts 'authority' as a means to achieve what is promised by the particular system of philosophy or ideation; he clings to it, depends on it and thereby confirms the 'authority'. A follower, then, is a second-hand human being; and most people are completely second-hand. They may think they have some original ideas with regard to painting, writing and so on, but essentially, because they are conditioned to follow, to imitate, to conform, they have become second-hand, absurd human beings. That is one aspect of the destructive nature of authority.

As a human being, do you follow somebody psychologically? We are not talking of outward obedience, the following of the law—but inwardly, psychologically, do you follow? If you do, then you are essentially second-hand; you may do good works, you may lead a very good life, but it all has very little meaning.

There is also the authority of tradition. Tradition means: 'to carry over from the past to the present'—the religious tradition, the family tradition, or the racial tradition. And there is the tradition of memory. One can see that to follow tradition at certain levels has value; at other levels, it has no value at all. Good manners, politeness, consideration born out of the alertness of the mind that is watching, can gradually become tradition; the pattern having been set, the mind repeats it. One opens the door for someone, is punctual for meals, and so on. But it has become tradition and is no longer born out of alertness, sharpness and clearness.

The mind which has cultivated memory, functions from tradition like a computer—repeating things over and over again. It can never receive anything new, it can never listen to anything in a totally different way. Our brains are like tape recorders: certain memories have been cultivated through centuries and we keep on repeating them. Through the noise of that repetition one is unable to listen to something new. So one asks: 'What am I to do?', 'How am I to get rid of the old machinery, the old tape?'. The new can be heard only when the old tape becomes completely silent without any effort, when one is serious to listen, to find out, and can give one's attention.

So there is the authority of another on whom we are dependent, the authority of tradition, and the authority of past experience as memory, as knowledge. There is also the authority of the immediate experience, which is recognized from one's past accumulated knowledge; and being recognized, it is no longer something new. How can a mind, a brain, which is so conditioned by authority, imitation, conformity and adjustment, listen to anything completely new? How can one see the beauty of the day, when the mind and the heart and brain are so clouded by the past as authority? If one can actually perceive the fact that the mind is burdened by the past and conditioned by various forms of authority, that it is not free and therefore incapable of seeing completely, then the past is set aside without effort.

Freedom implies the complete cessation of all inward authority. From that quality of mind comes an outward freedom—something which is entirely different from the reaction of opposing or resisting. What we are saying is really quite simple, and it is because of its very simplicity that you will miss it. The mind, the brain, is conditioned through authority, through imitation and conformity—that is a fact. The mind that is actually free, has no inward authority whatsoever; it knows what it means to love and to meditate.

In understanding freedom one understands also what discipline is. This may seem rather contradictory because we generally think freedom means freedom from all discipline. What is the quality of mind that is highly disciplined? Freedom cannot exist without discipline; which does not mean that you must first be disciplined and then you will have freedom. Freedom and discipline go together, they are not two separate things. So what does 'discipline' mean? According to the dictionary, the meaning of the word 'discipline' is 'to learn'—not a mind that forces itself into a certain pattern of action according to an ideology or a belief. A mind that is capable of learning is entirely different from a mind which is capable only of conforming. A mind that is learning, that is observing, seeing actually 'what is', is not interpreting 'what is' according to its own desires, its own conditioning, its own particular pleasures.

Discipline has not meant suppression and control, nor is it adjustment to a pattern or an ideology; it means a mind that sees 'what is' and learns from 'what is'. Such a mind has to be extraordinarily alert, aware. In the ordinary sense, 'to discipline oneself' implies that there is an entity that is disciplining itself according to something. There is a dualistic process: I say to myself, 'I must get up early in the morning and not be lazy', or 'I must not be angry'. That involves a dualistic process. There is the one who with his will tries to control what he should do, as opposed to what he actually does. In that state, there is conflict.

The discipline laid down by parents, by society, by religious organizations means conformity. And there is revolt against conformity—the parent wanting one to do certain things, and the revolt against that, and so on. It is a life based on obedience and conformity; and there is the opposite of it, denying conformity and to do what one likes. So, we are going to find out what the quality of the mind is that does not conform, does not imitate, follow and obey, yet has a quality in itself which is highly disciplined—'disciplined' in the sense of constantly learning.

Discipline is learning, not conforming. Conformity implies comparing myself with another, measuring myself as to what I am, or think I should be, against the hero, the saint, and so on. Where there is conformity there must be comparison—please see this. Find out whether you can live without comparison which means, not to conform. We are conditioned from childhood to compare—'You must be like your brother, or your great-aunt'; 'You must be like the saint', or 'Follow Mao'. We compare in our education; in schools there is the giving of marks and the passing of examinations. We do not know what it means to live without comparison and without competition, therefore non-aggressively, non-competitively, non-violently. Comparing yourself with another is a form of aggression and a form of violence. Violence is not only killing or hitting somebody, it is in this comparative spirit, 'I must be like somebody else', or 'I must perfect myself'. Self-improvement is the very antithesis of freedom and learning. Find out for yourself how to live a life without comparing, and you will see what an extraordinary thing happens. If you really become aware, choicelessly, you will see what it means to live without comparison, never using the words 'I will be'. We are slaves to the verb 'to be', which implies: 'I will be somebody sometime in the future'. Comparison and conformity go together; they breed nothing but suppression, conflict and endless pain. So it is important to find a way of daily living in which there is no comparison. Do it, and you will see what an extraordinary thing it is: it frees you from so many burdens. The awareness of that brings about a quality of mind that is highly sensitive and therefore disciplined, constantly learning—not what it wants to learn, or what is pleasurable, gratifying to learn, but *learning*. So you become aware of inward conditioning resulting from authority, conformity to a pattern, to tradition, to propaganda, to what other people have said, and of your own accumulated experience and that of the race and the family. All of that has become the authority. Where there is authority, the mind can never be free to discover whatever there is to be discovered—something timeless, entirely new.

A mind that is sensitive is not limited by any set pattern; it is constantly moving, flowing like a river, and in that constant movement there is no suppression, no conformity, no desire to fulfil. It is very important to understand clearly, seriously and deeply, the nature of a mind that is free and therefore truly religious. A mind that is free sees that dependency on something—on people, on friends, on husband or wife, on ideation, authority and so on— breeds fear; there is the source of fear. If I depend on you for my comfort, as an escape from my own loneliness and ugliness, from shallowness and pettiness, then that dependence breeds fear. Dependence on any form of subjective imagination, fantasy, or knowledge, breeds fear and destroys freedom.

When you see what it all implies—how there is no freedom when there is dependence inwardly and therefore fear, and how it is only a confused and unclear mind that depends—you say: 'How am I to be free from dependency?' Which is again another cause of conflict. Whereas, if you observe that a mind that depends must be confused, if you know the truth that a mind that depends inwardly on any authority only creates confusion—if you see that, without asking how to be free of confusion—then you will cease to depend. Then your mind becomes extraordinarily sensitive and therefore capable of learning and it disciplines itself without any form of compulsion or conformity....

Questioner: From what you have said, it seems that an action which at one point can be thought to be a reaction to some outward authority, can be a total action at another point, by another individual.

KRISHNAMURTI: Intellectually, verbally, we can compete with each other, explain each other away, but that does not mean a thing; what to you may be a complete action may appear to me as incomplete action—that is not the point. The point is whether your mind, as that of a human being, acts completely. A human being of the world—you understand?—is not an individual. 'Individual' means indivisible. An individual is one who is undivided in himself, who is non-fragmentary, who is whole, sane, healthy; also 'whole' means holy. When you say 'I am an individual', you are nothing of the kind. Live a life of no authority, of no comparison, and you will find out what an extraordinary thing it is; you have tremendous energy when you are not competing, not comparing and not suppressing; you are really alive, sane, whole and therefore sacred....

Questioner: How is it possible for a total, whole, sane individual who is not fragmented but indivisible, to love another? How can a whole human being love a fragmented human being? Further, how can a whole individual love another whole individual?

KRISHNAMURTI: You cannot be whole if you do not know what love is. If you are whole—in the sense we are talking about—then there is no question of loving another. Have you ever watched a flower by the roadside. It exists, it lives in the sun, in the wind, in the beauty of light and colour, it does not say to you: 'Come and smell me, enjoy me, look at me'—it lives and its very action of living is love.

■

ON NATIONALISM

Question: What is it that comes when nationalism goes?
KRISHNAMURTI: Obviously, intelligence. But I am afraid that is not the implication in this question. The implication is, what can be substituted for nationalism? Any substitution is an act which does not bring intelligence. If I leave one religion and join another, or leave one political party and later on join something else, this constant substitution indicates a state in which there is no intelligence.

How does nationalism go? Only by our understanding its full implications, by examining it, by being aware of its significance in outward and inward action. Outwardly, it brings about divisions between people, classifications, wars and destruction, which is obvious to anyone who is observant. Inwardly, psychologically, this identification with the greater, with the country, with an idea, is obviously a form of self-expansion. Living in a little village or a big town or whatever it may be, I am nobody; but if I identify myself with the larger, with the country, if I call myself a Hindu, it flatters my vanity, it gives me gratification, prestige, a sense of well-being; and that identification with the larger, which is a psychological necessity for those who feel that self-expansion is essential, also creates conflict, strife, between people. Thus, nationalism not only creates outward conflict but inward frustrations; when one understands nationalism, the whole process of nationalism, it falls away.

The understanding of nationalism comes through intelligence, by carefully observing, by probing into the whole process of nationalism, patriotism. Out of that examination comes intelligence and then there is no substitution of something else for nationalism. The moment you substitute religion for nationalism, religion becomes another means of self-expansion, another source of psychological anxiety, a means of feeding oneself through a belief. Therefore, any form of substitution, however noble, is a form of ignorance. It is like a man substituting chewing gum or betel nut or whatever it is for smoking, whereas if one really understands the whole problem of smoking, of habits, sensations, psychological demands and all the rest of it, then smoking drops away. You can understand only when there is a development of intelligence, when intelligence is functioning, and intelligence is not functioning when there is substitution. Substitution is merely a form of self-bribery, to tempt you not to do this but to do that. Nationalism, with its poison, with its misery and world strife, can disappear only when there is intelligence, and intelligence does not come merely by passing examinations and studying books. Intelligence comes into being when we understand problems as they arise. When there is understanding of the problem at its different levels, not only of the outward part but of its inward, psychological implications, then, in that process, intelligence comes into being. So, when there is intelligence there is no substitution; and when there is intelligence, then nationalism, patriotism, which is a form of stupidity, disappears.

∎

India's Message.

7

■ MANAVENDRANATH ROY ■

Narendranath Bhattacharya (1887–1954), better known as
M.N. Roy, was born in Bengal into an educated middle class
family. As a young man he engaged in 'extremist' nationalist activities, not shunning terrorist tactics—activities for which he was
arrested by the British. After managing to slip out of India in 1915,
he traveled to the United States and finally to Mexico where he
assumed his new name. Following the Bolshevik Revolution in
1917, he helped found the Mexican Communist Party, and then
proceeded to Moscow where he met Lenin, who placed him on
the Executive Committee of the Communist International (Comintern). As an international Communist leader he was involved in
training Indians in Central Asia, but after Stalin's rise to power he
eventually fell from favor and was expelled from the Comintern in
1929. On his return to India he was promptly arrested and impris-
oned for six years. Not yet disillusioned, despite Stalin's maneu-
vers, he proceeded, on his release, to found a Marxist party inside
the Indian National Congress, with limited success. Finally, disenchanted with communism, he turned, after the Second World
War, to the rational and secular humanism of the European Enlightenment for inspiration. Until the end of his life he was actively
involved in a Radical Humanist network extending from India to
many parts of the Western world.

For primary and secondary sources see M.N. Roy, *New Humanism: A Manifesto*, Calcutta, Renaissance, 1947; *India's Message*, 2nd rev. edn, Calcutta, Renaissance, 1950; *I Accuse*, New
York, Roy Defense Committee of India, 1932; *Science and Philosophy*, Calcutta, Renaissance, 1947; *Reason, Romanticism and*

Revolution, 2 Vols, Calcutta, Renaissance, 1952; *Heresies of the Twentieth Century*, Moradabad, Pradeep Karyalaya, 1940; *India in Transition*, Bombay, Nachiketa, 1971; *The Philosophy and Practice of Radical Humanism*, New Delhi, Radical Humanist Association, 1970; John P. Haithcox, *Communism and Nationalism in India: M.N. Roy and Comintern Policy, 1920–39*, Princeton, Princeton University Press, 1971. The following selections are taken from *The Communist International*, Number 6, 1924, and *India's Message.*

ANTI-IMPERIALIST STRUGGLE IN INDIA

Slowly, but surely British domination in India is being undermined. It is true that this historic process is not so speedy as many expected or even prophesied. Nevertheless, the process is going on unceasingly. The depression that followed the sudden collapse of the great Non-Cooperation Movement lasted rather long, only to be enlivened, not by an intensified revolutionary activity, but by a concerted effort on the part of the bourgeoisie to challenge the absolute position of imperialism, on constitutional lines. The development of this new stage has been the outstanding feature of the Indian nationalist struggle during the last twelve months. It has culminated in a political deadlock which has not only nonplussed the nationalist bourgeoisie, but has also placed the British government in a somewhat uncomfortable position. Some decisive action must be taken from one side or the other to break this deadlock. For the nationalists, it is necessary either to compromise with imperialism or to go a few steps further towards revolution. Imperialism, on the other hand, is faced with the alternatives: to placate the nationalist bourgeoisie with concessions or to adopt openly the policy of blood and iron. It is likely that the initiative will come from the imperialist side, which today does not dare take the latter course lest the seething volcano of popular discontent erupt, and even the timid bourgeoisie be driven to revolution....

Should this temporary solution be looked upon with pessimism? Certainly not; because it is but a stage in the process of undermining imperialism. Historic reasons prevent the Indian bourgeoisie from launching upon a revolutionary path; but at the same time, their very existence is an objective menace to imperialism. In every compromise made the former win, however beggarly the compromise may be, and the latter gives up a little of its ground. Therefore, a compromise made does not end the antagonism, but simply prepares the ground for another one eventually. One concession is inevitably followed by the demand for another concession. This is certainly a very long and tedious process, and the historic necessity of a National Revolution cannot be circumvented within the narrow limits of this contemptible barter. But the Indian bourgeoisie, as they are situated, do not want to strike a short-cut. They are not bold enough to throw down the final challenge and unfurl the flag of revolution.

The Indian bourgeoisie are conspicuous for confusion of political thought and timidity of action. The former is expressed through the intellectual poverty of the nationalist movement and the failure to formulate a comprehensive program of nationalism; while the latter causes such a surprising phenomenon as the absence of any faction within the nationalist camp which openly stands for a complete break with the imperial connection. The reason for this confusion of thought and timidity of action is to be sought in the history of the last two hundred years.

Timidity of action is caused by ideological confusion. Objectively, the Indian bourgeoisie are a revolutionary factor; but they are totally unconscious of this revolutionary role of theirs, and what is worse still, they are remarkably inclined towards counter-revolution, or rather, reaction. They desire a politico-economic reconstruction of the country, without disturbing the social status quo. This strongly reactionary social character of the Indian bourgeoisie makes them timid in political action, because it does not allow them to countenance any revolutionary upheaval of the masses. They not only fail to undertake the historic role of the bourgeoisie—to lead the serf in the revolutionary fight against feudalism—but, on the contrary, are defenders of the modern forms of the latter that prevail in India. The landed aristocracy—both the scions of the old feudal class as well as that created by British imperialism in its earlier days—is one of the pillars that supports British rule. By failing to deal a mortal blow to this pillar, the nationalist bourgeoisie separate themselves from the social foundation of a revolutionary movement. This being the case, they find themselves hopelessly weak when at close grips with the forces of imperialism. Hence their timidity of action, typified by the absurd program of ousting British domination by constitutional warfare, and the conspicuous failure of the vanguard of a subject nation to put forth the demand for complete independence.

The struggle of a subject people to free itself from the yoke of foreign domination, however, is not based solely upon the antagonism between the interests of the native bourgeoisie and imperialism. The objective necessity for the progress of the entire people is the fundamental factor that gives occasion to this struggle. Any social class that happens at the given period to stand at the vanguard of the entire people, and which gives expression to this objective necessity, automatically becomes the leader of the struggle. Under normal circumstances, therefore, the bourgeoisie should be the leaders of the anti-imperialist struggle in India. Until now, they have been the leaders; but experience has proved their failure to give an account of themselves. They have failed to rise to the situation. Consequently, a movement fraught with immense objective revolutionary possibilities has not developed speedily enough, and imperialism still appears to prosper, while sitting on the summit of a seething volcano.

To determine the strength or weakness of the Indian nationalist struggle by the action of the bourgeoisie, therefore, would be misleading. The present position of the nationalist bourgeoisie does not indicate the correct revolutionary perspectives in India. On the other hand, it would be equally mistaken to persist in the notion that the bourgeoisie is the standard-bearer of revolution. This notion has its origin in the fact that, at a certain period of history, the bourgeoisie plays a revolutionary role; since it has been so in those countries which today stand at the van of human progress, it is bound to be so in the rest of the world. A particular inter-relation of social forces rendered the bourgeoisie revolutionary in certain countries at a certain epoch of history. It would be a mechanical reading of history to assert that an identical juxtaposition of social forces will occur in every other country. In fact, here in India the social forces are somewhat differently related, and this difference has made itself felt upon the political thoughts and movement of the country.

Nor is India a solitary instance. Russia, in broad outlines, belonged to the same category. The revolutionary significance of her bourgeoisie was not very considerable. It was left for the proletariat to carry through the bourgeois revolution—to lead the peasantry in the final struggle against the landed aristocracy. If it was so in Russia, it is likely to be more so in India, where the bourgeoisie is even more backward than their Russian confreres. The Indian bourgeoisie is even innocent of the radicalism which prevailed among the intellectual wing of the Russian bourgeoisie in the latter decades of the nineteenth century. All the reactionary cults, which find expression in Gandhism, are more hostile to revolutionary ideas than was the pan-Slavism of the Russian intellectuals. The Indian bourgeoisie are closely bound up with landlordism, and the majority of the intellectuals are generally conservative in their social outlook.

This being the case, if we accept the action of the bourgeoisie as the only indicator of revolutionary perspectives in India, there rises before us a rather discouraging vision. It is notorious how the Gandhi-ite leadership got frightened at the revolutionary sweep of the movement it pretended to lead. This fright, coupled with an innate anti-revolutionary conviction, induced the petty bourgeoisie to set their face against the great mass movement which threatened the security of the Empire. They systematically sabotaged the movement, and finally succeeded in throwing it into hopeless confusion....

This slow process of reformism, which at first sight looks very futile, possesses a deeper significance, owing to the fact that it is carried out upon a revolutionary background. Although the nationalist bourgeoisie fail to mobilize the revolutionary energy of the masses to back up their demands for reform, imperialism is fully conscious of the existence of the powder magazine, capable, at the slightest ignition, of blowing it up. It also knows that the dynamic force of nationalism does not lie either in the reactionary doctrines of the lower middle class intellectuals, nor in the 'national demand' of the bourgeoisie, but in the partially manifested will of the masses of revolt against their miserable condition. Imperialism is reluctantly inclined to make petty concessions to the reformist bourgeoisie (whose impotency it is fully aware of) to prevent the possible determination of the bourgeoisie to fall back upon these forces of revolution.

In view of this essentially revolutionary character of the situation in India, every phase of the anti-imperialist struggle has its value in the general scheme of events. In the last year, the nationalist bourgeoisie have been busy in organizing the fighting qualities of their class inside a powerful political party. As stated above, owing to deep-seated reasons, the program and tactics of this party still remain essentially reformist. The party leaders do not fail to indulge in bombastic language and veiled threats which, however, are empty. The party is young, lacking the assets of a radical social outlook, constructive political ideology and a firm determination to act. It has not even succeeded in drawing all the bourgeois elements together. Nevertheless, for the first time in the history of the Indian national movement, it has acted as the conscious spokesman of an entire class, and has, therefore, sounded the close of that epoch when imperialism could play the one section of the bourgeoisie against the other. This is certainly a long step forward....

■

PRECONDITIONS OF INDIAN RENAISSANCE

The spiritualist revivalism, mystic extravagances and religious atavism in the recent and contemporary intellectual life of the West are interpreted as indications of repentance on the part of the sinner, and have a galvanizing effect on our prejudices in India. A necessary condition for the Renaissance of India, that is to say, for India's coming into the inheritance of the blessings of modern civilization, is the liberation of the objectively progressive forces from this prejudice. The idle vanity of the would-be savior of a repenting materialist world turns our vision to the imaginary Golden Age of India's past, which is supposed to hold the cure for all the evils of modern civilization. Looking backwards in the foolish zeal of a self-arrogated mission, we ironically forget our journey forward and, as a blindfolded herd, go round and round in the vicious circle of our ideological confusion.

Even a cursory glance at the cultural background of modern Europe will convince all but the hopeless fanatics that it would not be necessary for Western civilization to wait for the medicine man from India, were its malady really curable by the magic elixir of spiritualism. Europe could find plenty of that drug in the dusty cellars of its own past. As a matter of historical fact, the roots of all the exuberant spiritualist growth on the decaying body of the bourgeois society can all be traced to the subsoil of Christianity and of the pagan speculative thought and religious views that went into the making of the Western civilization.

Once it is seen that India has little to offer even in the field which is supposed to be her speciality, the crusading spirit of the forces objectively making for her renaissance will be dampened, and they will begin to act according to the good old dictum: Doctor, heal thyself. What young India needs is the conviction of Hu Shih, the greatest Chinese philosopher living, who is called the father of the Chinese Renaissance, and the courage with which he expressed his conviction: 'China has nothing worth preserving. If she has anything, it will preserve itself. You foreigners, who tell China that she has something worth preserving, are doing her a disservice, for you are only adding to our pride. We must make a clean sweep and adopt Western culture and outlook.' Young India may also be referred to the address of Sir C.V. Raman at the Convocation of the Bombay University in 1932, which contained a message immensely more valuable than the reactionary confusion and lyrical futility of all those who are woefully misleading India by the nose, away from the road of progress. The deplorable intellectual stagnation of young India is evidenced by the singular fact that an epoch-making message of one of the greatest living Indians goes practically unnoticed, while potty platitudes and reactionary rigmaroles pronounced by demagogues, charlatans and muddleheads are applauded as the acme of wisdom.

But there are a few Indians who raise their voice of reason and wisdom from time to time. Speaking at the Ravenshaw College at Cuttack in January 1934, Dr R.P. Paranjpye, Vice-Chancellor of Lucknow, for example, said: 'Our old literature, philosophy and civilization in general serve for serious study and appreciation, but we find many directions in which we have lost a real hold over the kernel of that civilization and are often clinging to its mere shell. There is an aggressive kind of nationalism which considers everything worthy of retention simply because it is old. But the present state of our country is mainly due to our not having moved with the time, not having learned from the progress made by other nations. Some of the greatest evils from which the world is suffering at the present moment are due to this intense feeling of aggressive nationalism and racialism as exemplified in the case of Germany and Italy.'

To visualize others in their greatness, measured by the standards of spiritualism, should cure the vanity of Indians, and enable them to look at the world with a reasonable desire to learn from others, and approach their own problems with a sense of realism.

The doctrine of the spiritual superiority of Indian culture disregards the history of Europe from the downfall of the Graeco-Roman antiquity to the sixteenth century of the Christian era, when rationalism and scientific knowledge began to dispel the depressing darkness of the Middle Ages and claimed predominance over human thought. The life and culture of the European peoples throughout that long period were intensely spiritualistic, completely dominated by priests, lay or professional—those purveyors of spiritual power as against the temporal. It was strikingly possessed of all the features which are fondly believed by the Hindus to be their proud heritage—the special genius of their race. For more than a thousand years, since the conclusion of the period of Alexandrian learning, faith completely dominated the European mind; revealed knowledge completely eclipsed reason. The materialist philosophy of ancient Greece had been eclipsed by the metaphysics and moral philosophy of the Athenian era; this, in its turn, having laid down the philosophical foundation of Christian theology, was itself eclipsed by the new religion.

An acquaintance with the European history of that long period shows that the religious form of thought is not the special genius of any chosen people, but is associated with certain forms of social relations irrespective of the geographical location of peoples living under such relations. As a matter of fact, at a certain stage of his intellectual development, man can think only in terms of religion, and can express his striving for progress only in terms of a moralizing mysticism. In those conditions, religion, mysticism, metaphysical speculation, become a social necessity. Every people in such a stage of social evolution must necessarily think in religious, mystic, metaphysical terms. The contents of their thought are identical; its basic forms are analogous; difference of geographical environment may create only superficial peculiarities. As long as ignorance prevents man from being conscious of the endless potentialities inherent in his own being, man must seek the support of a supernatural power in the hope of rising above his limitations and overcoming the obstacles to his aspirations. In proportion, as the knowledge of nature and of his own self as a part of nature dissipates his ignorance, man gains confidence in himself. Spiritualism ceases to be an intellectual necessity. But it subsists as a prejudice. While stubbornly resisting new forms of thought, while combatting the coordination of the ever increasing varieties of empirically acquired knowledge into a rationalist and scientific philosophy, spiritualism becomes a powerful ally of reaction against the human urge for freedom and progress. It provides the moral sanction to the vulgarest forms of materialism in practice.

In Europe, spiritualism attained such a socially reactionary and ideologically enslaving significance already in the early Middle Ages after Christianity had played out its revolutionary role in the history of civilization and established itself as the powerful Catholic Church, which transformed itself into an ally of feudal barbarism.

In the history of India, the Buddhist revolution draws the dividing line between the period when the religious form of thought was a necessary intellectual phenomenon, served a positive social purpose, and the period in which spiritualism became an instrument of reaction, a bulwark against higher civilization. The growth of rational and quasi-materialist systems of thought (Vaisheshika, Sankhya, Nyaya, etc.) which went into the revolutionary philosophy of Buddhism, indicated that the older form of religious thought as contained in the Upanishads had outlived their social utility. Their continuation as the predominating ideology meant a dark period of intellectual reaction. A critical historian would find post-Buddhist India (including the period of Buddhist decline and degeneration) just as full of incongruous contradictions as the Middle Ages in Europe. A study of the history of India, not with the preconceived notion of vindicating her past greatness, as an apology for the present shame, not with the purpose of rewriting it to prove a thesis, but in quest of historical truth, will discover ample material showing that the spiritualist extravagances of Mahayana Buddhism as well as of triumphant Hinduism, as finally re-established by Shankaracharya, were closely associated with the vulgarest material practices of life. When the patriarchal, feudal, and priestly ruling classes revelled in corruption, sensualism, luxury and barbarian chivalry, sanctimonious religiosity, moralizing mysticism and spiritualist philosophical doctrines were the characteristic features of the prevailing ideology. The history of the European Middle Ages might serve as a mirror to many who lack the courage of directly facing the ugly realities of India's past, and inspire them to cast a critical look at their own idealized background. Then, the fascinating rainbow of imagination will disappear, many bubbles of beautiful dreams will burst, freeing young India from cherished illusions, clearing its vision of the mist of preconceived notions, enabling it finally to look boldly ahead and march with determination on the road of progress, casting off the shackles of the past and the unnecessary ballasts of hoary tradition.

With a superficial knowledge of the subject (often without that), the average Hindu intellectual regards Christianity with a lofty contempt. He finds the Biblical doctrines to be crude and childish in comparison with the subtlety and what he considers to be deepness of his ancestral faith. He is amused, for example, by the doctrine of creation as contained in the *Genesis*, forgetful or ignorant of the fact that the Vedic cosmology, not to mention the ludicrous *puranic* tales, appear no less fantastic in the light of knowledge subsequently acquired by mankind....

This doctrine of creation has of late been interpreted and rationalized so as to make it appear as anticipating the most modern scientific theories. The old popular saying that what is not mentioned in the Vedas does not exist, has come to be a serious article of Hindu faith. It is claimed that the Hindu scriptures contain the maximum of human knowledge. Modern science and philosophy have nothing to say about what was not known to the inspired Rishis. But this practice of pouring new wine in old bottles is simply ridiculous, because the scientific view of things knows no sudden beginning of the world. It dispenses with the primitive notion of creation. There is no difference whatever between those who believe that God said, 'Let there be light, etc., and there was light, etc.,' and those who believe that in the beginning there was one who became many simply because he wished to do so. In any case, the point of departure in either case is a supernatural will, which conjures up the universe out of nothing. This magical power, again, can only be assumed. It can never be known, its existence cannot be proved, since in that case it would cease to be what it is imagined to be....

No religion is really born in a particular moment of time, revealed to a particular prophet. The doctrines and dogmas of any religion crystallize themselves in a process, over a whole period of time, determined by the social conditions of the given period. In certain stages of human evolution, religion in some form or other is a social necessity, and as all other social phenomena, it is changeable and transitory. No religion is based upon any eternal, immutable and absolute truths. The basis of all religions being the material conditions of life, not only are their forms bound to change from time to time, but religion itself, that is, faith in some supernatural agency, becomes useless when the spiritual development of man

attains a sufficiently high level. The advance of positive knowledge, as distinct from speculative thought and the so-called revealed wisdom, enables man to depend on himself. It is no longer
necessary for him to seek some superhuman support....

A change in the material conditions of life brings about a corresponding readjustment of ideal standards. The disruption of an
established set of social relations shakes the foundation of the traditional form of faith. Man's relation to the God or gods, as the
case may be, is determined by the relation amongst men themselves. Natural religion, as for example of the Vedas, or of the
Greek mythology—deification of the diverse phenomena of nature as objects of worship—originally was the religion of decentralized tribal society. Monotheism—the belief in one God—rose
as the ideological reflex of the striving for the political organization
of society under a centralized state. The worship of a glittering gal-
laxy of gods, all equally powerful idealized superhuman beings,
was the spiritual expression of man living in the conditions of
primitive democracy. The conception of a super-God became a
spiritual necessity when monarchist states began to rise out of the
ruins of tribal republics. An overlord in Heaven is postulated as
the moral sanction for the overlordship on earth.

This process of involved religious development from the poly-
theistic faith to a mystic cult took place in ancient India, in Egypt
and Assyria. The Vedantic monotheism—the evolution of which is
to be traced in the tales of the *Upanishads*—was a creation of the
Brahmans, and became a force for the stabilization of society under sacerdotal supremacy. It did not replace the Vedic natural religion, which had partially lost its hold on the people under the
conditions of the decay of the tribal social order. It did not appear
as a revolt against the established rites and rituals. The priesthood
could not advocate the abolition of a form of faith and worship
which had placed it at the head of the society.... An airy structure
of a mystical monotheistic cult was thus reared upon the foundation of a decayed natural religion, which was preserved, on the
authority of the new cult, as the faith suitable for the vulgar multitude. It became a new weapon in the hands of the sacerdotal
rulers of society. It fortified the shaken position of the anthropo-
morphic deities by placing them in a Pantheon, the inner mysteries of which were accessible only to the privileged Brahmans....

The Western civilization, being even today largely dominated by
the moral principles and spiritual standards of Christianity, cannot

be charged of materialism, in the philosophical sense. Europe has been all along, and even today is, true to its Christian faith, just as much as India has abided by the spiritual principles of Hinduism. The spiritual principles in either case being essentially identical, there is absolutely no reason to assume that they degenerated in one place, whereas in the other they retained their pristine purity. In both the cases, they degenerated necessarily, having outlived their historical usefulness. In the case of Europe, a new mode of thought developed to dispute the authority of spiritualist dogmas and to replace them as the determining factor of human life and progress. The new revolutionary philosophy steadily gained ground as the embodiment of all the positive outcome of the preceding forms of culture. In that prolonged struggle antiquated spiritualism was forced to cast off, one after another, the deceptive trappings of philosophical forms, rationalist terminology and pseudo-scientific professions.

In India, religious ideology retained its domination of culture even after its historical usefulness had been exhausted. Not subjected to the criticism born of scientific knowledge, in India, spiritualism was not exposed in all its absurdities, nor was it forced to rationalize its forms (as modern idealist philosophy), in order to adapt itself to changing social conditions, destroying itself in the process. Consequently, it appeared to retain its pristine purity—as the special genius of Indian culture. The domination of religious ideology was the result of a prolonged period of social stagnation.

If it is true that the decaying materialist civilization of the West is appealing to India to come to its aid with the panacea of spiritualism, which she has preserved in pristine purity at the cost of several centuries of social progress, let those who thrive on the prostrate and putrid body of Indian society be proud of this disgraceful mission. The impending Renaissance of India, however, will take place, not under the leadership of the 'great men' who, consciously or unconsciously, champion reaction, but in spite of their moralizing mysticism and stale spiritualist dogmas. The Renaissance of India will take place under the banner of a revolutionary philosophy. Those who are not able to rise above the spiritualist prejudice will be thrown into oblivion by the inexorable logic of historical development, however great they may appear to be today....

■

8

■ B.R. AMBEDKAR ■

Bhimrao Ramji Ambedkar (1891–1956), later known as Baba-saheb ('respected master') Ambedkar, was born into the untouch-able Mahar caste in Maharashtra. In a sharp departure from the general illiteracy of his caste, Ambedkar was able to obtain an outstanding, Western-style education: first at a college in Bombay, next at Columbia University in New York (where he received a doctoral degree), and finally in London (where he secured a doc-tor of science in addition to passing the bar). On his return to India he plunged himself into political and organizational activities aimed at uplifting the Untouchables and (what then were called) the 'Depressed Classes'. Following a confrontation over the issue of separate electorates, he reached a compromise with Gandhi in 1932 which gave special representation to Untouchables (now known as 'Scheduled Castes'). Progressively turning away both from Hinduism and the dominant Congress Party, Ambedkar tried to organize an independent Labour Party, but with limited suc-cess. Following independence, he served as chairman of the com-mittee drafting the constitution and, in a gesture of reconciliation, Nehru appointed him minister of law. However, in 1951, he re-signed from the cabinet protesting the government's continuing neglect of the Scheduled Castes. He devoted himself more inten-sively than ever to educational activities and visited a number of Buddhist countries. On October 1956, a few weeks before his death, he converted to Buddhism in a massive ceremony in Nagpur.

For primary and secondary sources see B.R. Ambedkar, *Thoughts on Pakistan*, Bombay, Thacker, 1941; *What Gandhi and Congress Have Done to the Untouchables*, Bombay, Thacker,

1945; R.C. Prasad, *Ambedkarism*, Delhi, Motilal Banarsidass, 1996; D.R. Jatava, *The Political Philosophy of B.R. Ambedkar*, Agra, Phoenix Publishers, 1965; A.J. Rajasekhariah, *B.R. Ambedkar: The Politics of Emancipation*, Bombay, Sindhu Publications, 1971; C. Bharill, *Social and Political Ideas of B.R. Ambedkar*, Jaipur, Aalekk Publications, 1977; Dhananjay Keer, *Dr Ambedkar: Life and Mission*, 3rd edn, Bombay, Popular Prakashan, 1971. The following selection is taken from *What Gandhi and Congress Have Done to the Untouchables*.

GANDHISM: THE DOOM OF THE UNTOUCHABLES

Hitherto when Indians have been talking about the reconstruction of Indian social and economic life, they have been talking in terms of individualism *versus* collectivism, capitalism *versus* socialism, conservatism *versus* radicalism, and so on. But quite recently, a new 'ism' has come on the Indian horizon. It is called Gandhism. It is true that very recently Mr Gandhi had denied that there is such a thing as Gandhism. This denial is nothing more than the usual modesty, which Mr Gandhi wears so well. It does not disprove the existence of Gandhism. There have been quite a number of books with the title of Gandhism without any protest from Mr Gandhi. It has already caught the imagination of some people, both inside and outside India. Some have so much faith in it that they do not hesitate to offer it as an alternative to Marxism....

What is Gandhism? What does it stand for? What are its teachings about economic problems? What are its teachings about social problems?

At the outset, it is necessary to state that some Gandhists have conjured up a conception of Gandhism which is purely imaginary. According to this conception, Gandhism means return to the village and making the village self-sufficient. It makes Gandhism a mere matter of regionalism. Gandhism, I am sure, is neither so simple nor so innocent as regionalism is. Gandhism has a much bigger content than regionalism. Regionalism is a small insignificant part of it. It has a social philosophy, and it has an economic philosophy. To omit to take into account the economic and social philosophy of Gandhism is to present deliberately a false picture of Gandhism. The first and foremost requisite is to present a true picture of Gandhism. In 1922, Mr Gandhi was a defender of the caste system. Pursuing the inquiry, one comes across a somewhat critical view of the caste system by Mr Gandhi in the year 1925. This is what Mr Gandhi said on 3 February 1925:

> I gave support to caste because it stands for restraint. But at present caste does not mean restraint, it means limitations. Restraint is glorious and helps to achieve freedom. But limitation is like [a] chain. It binds. There is nothing commendable in castes as they exist today. They are contrary to the tenets of the shastras. The number of castes is infinite and there is a bar against intermarriage. This is not a condition of elevation. It is a state of fall.

In reply to the question: What is the way out? Mr Gandhi said:

> The best remedy is that small castes should fuse themselves into one big caste. There should be four such big castes so that we may reproduce the old system of four varnas.

In short, in 1925, Mr Gandhi became an upholder of the varna system.

The old varna system prevalent in ancient India had the society divided into four orders: (i) Brahmans, whose occupation was learning; (ii) Kshatriyas, whose occupation was warfare; (iii) Vaishyas, whose occupation was trade; and (iv) Shudras, whose occupation was service of the other classes....

Turning to the field of economic life, Mr Gandhi stands for two ideals.

One of these is the opposition to machinery. As early as 1921, Mr Gandhi gave vent to his dislike for machinery. Writing in the *Young India* of 19 January 1921, Mr Gandhi said:

> Do I want to put back the hand of the clock of progress? Do I want to replace the mills by hand-spinning and hand-weaving? Do I want to replace the railway by the country-cart? Do I want to destroy machinery altogether? These questions have been asked by some journalists and public men. My answer

is: I would not weep over the disappearance of machinery or consider it a calamity.

His opposition to machinery is well evidenced by his idolization of [the] *charkha* (the spinning wheel), and by insistence upon hand-spinning and hand-weaving. His opposition to machinery and his love for *charkha* are not a matter of accident. They are a matter of his philosophy of life. This philosophy Mr Gandhi took special occasion to propound in his presidential address at the Kathiawad political conference held on 8 January 1925. This is what Mr Gandhi said:

> Nations are tired of the worship of lifeless machines multi-plied *ad infinitum*. We are destroying the matchless living ma-chines, viz., our own bodies by leaving them to rust and trying to substitute lifeless machinery for them. It is a law of God that the body must be fully worked and utilized. We dare not ignore it. The spinning wheel is the auspicious symbol of *sharir yajna*—body labor. He who eats his food without offer-ing this sacrifice steals it. By giving up this sacrifice we be-came traitors to the country and banged the door in the face of the Goddess of Fortune.

Anyone who has read Mr Gandhi's booklet on *Hind Swaraj* (Indian Home Rule) will know that Mr Gandhi is against modern civilization. The book was first published in 1908. But there has been no change in his ideology. Writing in 1921 Mr Gandhi said:

> The booklet is a severe condemnation of 'modern civiliza-tion'. It was written in 1908. My conviction is deeper today than ever. I feel that, if India would discard 'modern civiliza-tion', she can only gain by doing so.

The second ideal of Mr Gandhi is the elimination of class war, and even class struggle, in the relationship between employers and employees, and between landlords and tenants. Mr Gandhi's views on the relationship between employers and employees were set forth by him in an article on the subject, which appeared in the *Nava Jivan* of 8 June 1921, and from which the following is an extract:

> Two paths are open before India, either to introduce the Western principle of 'might is right', or to uphold the Eastern

principle that truth alone conquers, that truth knows no mis-hap, that the strong and the weak have alike a right to secure justice. The choice is to begin with the laboring class. Should the laborers obtain an increment in their wages by violence? Even if that be possible, they cannot resort to anything like violence, howsoever legitimate may be their claims. To use violence for securing rights may seem an easy path, but it proves to be thorny in the long run. Those who live by sword die also by sword. The swimmer often dies by drowning. Look at Europe. No one seems to be happy there, for not one is contented. The laborer does not trust the capitalist, and the capitalist has no faith in the laborer. Both have a sort of vigor and strength but even the bulls have it. They fight to the very bitter end. All motion is not progress. We have got no reason to believe that the people of Europe are progress-ing. Their possession of wealth does not argue the possession of any moral or spiritual qualities.

What shall we do then? The laborers in Bombay made a fine stand. I was not in a position to know all the facts. But this much I could see that they could fight in a better way. The millowner may be wholly in the wrong. In the struggle between capital and labor, it may be generally said that more often than not the capitalists are in the wrong box. But when labor comes fully to realize its strength, I know it can become more tyrannical than capital. The millowners will have to work on the terms dictated by labor, if the latter could com-mand intelligence of the former. It is clear, however, that la-bor will never attain to that intelligence. If it does, labor will cease to be labor and become itself the master. The capitalists do not fight on the strength of money alone. They do possess intelligence and tact.

The question before us is this: When the laborers, remain-ing what they are, develop a certain consciousness, what should be their course? It would be suicidal if the laborers rely upon their numbers or brute force, i.e., violence. By so doing, they will do harm to industries in the country. If, on the other hand, they take their stand on pure justice and suffer in their person to secure it, not only will they always succeed but they will reform their masters, develop industries and both master and men will be as members of one and the same family....

Mr Gandhi does not wish to hurt the propertied class. He is even opposed to a campaign against them. He has no passion for economic equality. Referring to the propertied class Mr Gandhi said quite recently that he does not wish to destroy the hen that lays the golden egg. His solution for the economic conflict between the owners and the workers, between the rich and the poor, between the landlords and the tenants, and between the employers and the employees is very simple. The owners need not deprive themselves of their property. All that they need do is to declare themselves trustees for the poor. Of course, the trust is to be a voluntary one carrying only a spiritual obligation.

Is there anything new in the Gandhian analysis of economic ills? Are the economics of Gandhism sound? What hope does Gandhism hold out to the common man, to the down and out? Does it promise him a better life, a life of joy and culture, a life of freedom, not merely freedom from want but freedom to rise, to grow to the full stature which his capacities can reach?

There is nothing new in the Gandhian analysis of economic ills, in so far as it attributes them to machinery and the civilization that is built upon it. That machinery and modern civilization help to concentrate management and control into relatively few hands, and with the aid of banking and credit facilitate the transfer into still fewer hands of all materials and factories and mills in which millions are bled white in order to support huge industries thousands of miles away from their cottages, or that machinery and modern civilization cause deaths, maimings and cripplings far in excess of the corresponding injuries by war, and are responsible for disease and physical deterioration due directly and indirectly to the development of large cities with their smoke, dirt, noise, foul air, lack of sunshine and outdoor life, slums, prostitution and unnatural living which they bring about, are all old and worn out arguments. There is nothing new in them. Gandhism is merely repeating the views of Rousseau, Ruskin, Tolstoy, and their school.

The ideas which go to make up Gandhism are just primitive. It is a return to nature, to animal life. Their only merit is their simplicity. As there is always a large corps of simple people who are attracted by them, such simple ideas do not die, and there is always some simpleton to preach them. There is, however, no doubt that the practical instincts of men—which seldom go wrong—have found them unfruitful and which society in search of progress has thought it best to reject.

The economics of Gandhism are hopelessly fallacious. The fact that machinery and modern civilization have produced many evils may be admitted. But these evils are no argument against them. For the evils are not due to machinery and modern civilization. They are due to wrong social organization, which has made private property and pursuit of personal gain matters of absolute sanctity. If machinery and civilization have not benefited everybody, the remedy is not to condemn machinery and civilization but to alter the organization of society so that the benefits will not be usurped by the few but will accrue to all.

In Gandhism, the common man has no hope. It treats man as an animal and no more. It is true that man shares the constitution and functions of animals, nutritive, reproductive, etc. But these are not distinctively human functions. The distinctively human function is reason, the purpose of which is to enable man to observe, meditate, cogitate, study and discover the beauties of the universe and enrich his life and control the animal elements in his life. Man thus occupies the highest place in the scheme of animate existence. If this is true what is the conclusion that follows? The conclusion that follows is that while the ultimate goal of a brute's life is reached once his physical appetites are satisfied, the ultimate goal of man's existence is not reached unless and until he has fully cultivated his mind. In short, what divides the brute from man is culture. Culture is not possible for the brute, but it is essential for man. That being so, the aim of human society must be to enable every person to lead a life of culture, which means the cultivation of mind as distinguished from the satisfaction of mere physical wants. How can this happen?

Both for society as well as for the individual there is always a gulf between merely living and living worthily. In order that one may live worthily one must first live. The time and energy spent upon mere life, upon gaining of subsistence detracts from that available for activities of a distinctively human nature, and which go to make up a life of culture. How, then, can a life of culture be made possible? It is not possible unless there is sufficient leisure. For, it is only when there is leisure that a person is free to devote himself to a life of culture. The problem of all problems, which human society has to face, is how to provide leisure to every individual. What does leisure mean? Leisure means the lessening of the toil and effort necessary for satisfying the physical wants of life. How can leisure be made possible? Leisure is quite impossible unless some means are found whereby the toil required for producing goods necessary to satisfy human needs is lessened.

What can lessen such toil? Only when machine takes the place of man. There is no other means of producing leisure. Machinery and modern civilization are thus indispensable for emancipating man from leading the life of a brute, and for providing him with leisure and for making a life of culture possible. The man who condemns machinery and modern civilization simply does not understand their purpose and the ultimate aim which human society must strive to achieve.

Gandhism may be well suited to a society which does not accept democracy as its ideal. A society which does not believe in democracy may be indifferent to machinery and the civilization based upon it. But a democratic society cannot. The former may well content itself with a life of leisure and culture for the few and a life of toil and drudgery for the many. But a democratic society must assure a life of leisure and culture to each one of its citizens. If the above analysis is correct then the slogan of a democratic society must be machinery, and more machinery, civilization and more civilization. Under Gandhism the common man must keep on toiling ceaselessly for a pittance and remain a brute. In short, Gandhism with its call of back to nature, means back to nakedness, back to squalor, back to poverty and back to ignorance for the vast mass of the people.

■

9

■ MUHAMMAD IQBAL ■

Muhammad Iqbal (1877–1938) was born in the Punjab into a family of devout Muslims. After receiving education at the Government College at Lahore, he went on to study philosophy at Cambridge and in Germany and also to prepare for the bar. On his return to India in 1908 he taught philosophy for a few years at Lahore, but then gave up this position and started a private law practice—an occupation meant to allow him more time for studying and writing poetry. In the ensuing years his literary reputation steadily increased and he was soon recognized as the leading Urdu poet of his generation (as well as an outstanding poet in the Persian language). Iqbal involved himself only intermittently in politics. In 1926 he was elected to the Punjab provincial legislature, but refrained from pursuing a more ambitious political career. Although initially supporting the idea of a separate Muslim community within a larger India, he progressively despaired of the possibility of Muslim–Hindu co-existence. In the end he came to endorse the creation of an independent Pakistan under the leadership of Jinnah.

For primary and secondary sources see Muhammad Iqbal, *The Secrets of the Self*, trans. R.A. Nicholson, Lahore, Ashraf, 1944; *The Reconstruction of Religious Thought in Islam*, Lahore, Ashraf, 1944; *The Mysteries of Selflessness*, trans. Arthur J. Arberry, London, Murray, 1953; *Poems from Iqbal*, trans. V.G. Kiernan, London, Murray, 1955; *Speeches and Statements of Iqbal*, Lahore, Al-Manar Academy, 1948; Luce-Claude Maitre, *Mohammed Iqbal*, Paris, Segers, 1964. The following selections are taken from *The Reconstruction of Religious Thought in Islam*, pp. 7–8, 97, 125–27; *Speeches and Statements*, pp. 3–15, 34–36.

THE RECONSTRUCTION OF RELIGIOUS THOUGHT IN ISLAM

During the last five hundred years religious thought in Islam has been practically stationary. There was a time when European thought received inspiration from the world of Islam. The most remarkable phenomenon of modern history, however, is the enormous rapidity with which the world of Islam is spiritually moving towards the West. There is nothing wrong in this movement, for European culture, on its intellectual side, is only a further development of some of the most important phases of the culture of Islam. Our only fear is that the dazzling exterior of European culture may arrest our movement and we may fail to reach the true inwardness of that culture. During all the centuries of our intellectual stupor, Europe has been seriously thinking on the great problems in which the philosophers and scientists of Islam were so keenly interested. Since the Middle Ages, when the schools of Muslim theology were completed, infinite advance has taken place in the domain of human thought and experience. The extension of man's power over nature has given him a new faith and a fresh sense of superiority over the forces that constitute his environment. New points of view have been suggested, old problems have been restated in the light of fresh experience, and new problems have arisen. It seems as if the intellect of man is outgrowing its own most fundamental categories—time, space, and causality. With the advance of scientific thought even our concept of intelligibility is undergoing a change. The theory of Einstein has brought a new vision of the universe and suggests new ways of looking at the problems common to both religion and philosophy. No wonder, then, that the younger generation of Islam in Asia and Africa demand a fresh orientation of their faith. With the reawakening of Islam, therefore, it is necessary to examine, in an independent spirit, what Europe has thought and how far the conclusions reached by her can help us in the revision and, if necessary, reconstruction, of theological thought in Islam. Besides this it is not possible to ignore the generally anti-religious and especially anti-Islamic propaganda in Central Asia which has already crossed the Indian frontier.

The task before the modern Muslim is, therefore, immense. He has to rethink the whole system of Islam without completely breaking with the past.... The only course open to us is to approach modern knowledge with a respectful but independent attitude and to appreciate the teachings of Islam in the light of that knowledge, even though we may be led to differ from those who have gone before us....

Now, during the minority of mankind, psychic energy develops what I call prophetic consciousness—a mode of economizing individual thought and choice by providing ready-made judgments, choices, and ways of action. With the birth of reason and critical faculty, however, life, in its own interest, inhibits the formation and growth of non-rational modes of consciousness through which psychic energy flowed at an earlier stage of human evolution. Man is primarily governed by passion and instinct. Inductive reason, which alone makes man master of his environment, is an achievement; and, when once born, it must be reinforced by inhibiting the growth of other modes of knowledge. There is no doubt that the ancient world produced some great systems of philosophy at a time when man was comparatively primitive and governed more or less by suggestion. But we must not forget that this system-building in the ancient world was the work of abstract thought which cannot go beyond the systematization of vague religious beliefs and traditions, and gives us no hold on the concrete situations of life.

Looking at the matter from this point of view, then, the Prophet of Islam seems to stand between the ancient and the modern world. In so far as the source of his revelation is concerned, he belongs to the ancient world; in so far as the spirit of his revelation is concerned, he belongs to the modern world. In him life discovers other sources of knowledge suitable to its new direction. The birth of Islam, as I hope to be able presently to prove to your satisfaction, is the birth of inductive intellect. In Islam prophecy reaches its perfection in discovering the need of its own abolition. This involves the keen perception that life cannot forever be kept in leading strings; that in order to achieve full self-consciousness man must finally be thrown back on his own resources. The abolition of priesthood and hereditary kingship in Islam, the constant appeal to reason and experience in the Qur'an, and the emphasis that it lays on Nature and History as sources of human knowledge, are all different aspects of the same idea of finality. The idea, however, does not mean that mystic experience, which qualitatively does not differ from the experience of the Prophet, has now ceased to exist.... God reveals His signs in inner as well as outer experience, and it is the duty of man to judge the knowledge-yielding capacity of all aspects of experience. The idea of finality, therefore, [the belief that Muhammad was the final Prophet] should not be taken to suggest that the ultimate fate of life is complete displacement of emotion by reason. Such a thing is neither possible nor desirable. The intellectual value of the idea is that it tends to create an independent critical attitude towards mystic experience by generating the belief that all personal authority, claiming a supernatural origin, has come to an end in the history of man.... The function of the idea is to open up fresh vistas of knowledge in the domain of man's inner experience, just as the first half of the formula of Islam ['There is no god but God'] has created and fostered the spirit of a critical observation of man's outer experience by divesting the forces of nature of that divine character with which earlier culture had clothed them. Mystical experience, then, however unusual and abnormal, must now be regarded by a Muslim as a perfectly natural experience, open to critical scrutiny like other aspects of human experience. This is clear from the Prophet's own attitude towards Ibn-i-Sayyad's psychic experiences....

The third source of Mohammedan [i.e., Islamic] Law is *ijma* [consensus] which is in my opinion perhaps the most important legal notion in Islam. It is, however, strange that this important notion, while invoking great academic discussions in early Islam, remained practically a mere idea, and rarely assumed the form of a permanent institution of any Mohammedan country. Possibly, its transformation into a permanent legislative institution was contrary to the political interests of absolute monarchy that grew up in Islam.... It is, however, extremely satisfactory to note that the pressure of new world forces and the political experience of European nations are impressing on the mind of modern Islam the value and possibilities of the idea of *ijma*. The growth of republican spirit, and the gradual formation of legislative assemblies in Muslim lands constitutes a great step in advance. The transfer of the power of *ijtihad* [interpretation] from individual representatives of schools to a Muslim legislative assembly which, in view of the growth of opposing sects, is the only possible form *ijma* can take in modern times, will secure contributions to legal discussion from laymen who happen to possess a keen insight into affairs. In this way alone we can stir into activity the dormant spirit of life in our legal system, and give it an evolutionary outlook. In India, however, difficulties are likely to arise; for it is doubtful whether a non-Muslim legislative assembly can exercise the power of *ijtihad.*

■

PRESIDENTIAL ADDRESS

It cannot be denied that Islam, regarded as an ethical ideal plus a certain kind of polity—by which expression I mean a social structure regulated by a legal system and animated by a specific ethical ideal—has been the chief formative factor in the life-history of the Muslims of India. It has furnished those basic emotions and loyalties which gradually unify scattered individuals and groups and finally transform them into a well-defined people. Indeed, it is no exaggeration to say that India is perhaps the only country in the world where Islam, as a people-building force, has worked at its best. In India, as elsewhere, the structure of Islam as a society is almost entirely due to the working of Islam as a culture inspired by a specific ethical ideal. What I mean to say is that Muslim society, with its remarkable homogeneity and inner unity, has grown to be what it is under the pressure of the laws and institutions associated with the culture of Islam. The ideas set free by European thinking, however, are now rapidly changing the outlook of the present generation of Muslims both in India and outside India. Our younger men, inspired by these ideas, are anxious to see them as living forces in their own countries without any critical appreciation of the facts which have determined their evolution in Europe....

The conclusion to which Europe is [...] driven is that religion is a private affair of the individual and has nothing to do with what is called man's temporal life. Islam does not bifurcate the unity of man into an irreconcilable duality of spirit and matter. In Islam, God and the universe, spirit and matter, church and state, are organic to each other. Man is not the citizen of a profane world to be renounced in the interest of a world of spirit situated elsewhere. To Islam matter is spirit realizing itself in space and time.... In the world of Islam we have a universal polity whose fundamentals are believed to have been revealed, but whose structure, owing to our legists' want of contact with [the] modern world, stands today in need of renewed power by fresh adjustments. I do not know what will be the final fate of the national idea in the world of Islam. Whether Islam will assimilate and transform it, as it has assimilated and transformed before many ideas expressive of different spirits, or allow a radical transformation of its own structure by the force of this idea, is hard to predict....

What, then, is the problem and its implications? Is religion a private affair? Would you like to see Islam, as a moral and political ideal, meeting the same fate in the world of Islam as Christianity has already met in Europe? Is it possible to retain Islam as an ethical ideal and to reject it as a polity in favor of national politics, in which a religious attitude is not permitted to play any part? This question becomes of special importance in India where the Muslims happen to be in a minority. The proposition that religion is a private individual experience is not surprising on the lips of a European. In Europe the conception of Christianity as a monastic order, renouncing the world of matter and fixing its gaze entirely on the world of spirit led, by a logical process of thought, to the view embodied in this proposition. The nature of the Prophet's religious experience, as disclosed in the Qur'an, however, is wholly different. It is not mere experience in the sense of a purely biological event, happening inside the experiment and necessitating no reactions on his social environment. It is individual experience creative of a social order. Its immediate outcome is the fundamentals of a polity with implicit legal concepts whose civic significance cannot be belittled merely because their origin is revelational. The religious ideal of Islam, therefore, is organically related to the social order which it has created. The rejection of the one will eventually involve the rejection of the other. Therefore the construction of a polity on national lines, if it means a displacement of the Islamic principle of solidarity, is simply unthinkable to a Muslim. This is a matter which at the present moment directly concerns the Muslims of India.... The unity of an Indian nation, therefore, must be sought, not in the negation but in the mutual harmony and cooperation of the many. True statemanship cannot ignore facts, however unpleasant they may be. The only practical course is not to assume the existence of a state of things which does not exist, but to recognize facts as they are, and to exploit them to our greatest advantage....

Events seem to be tending in the direction of some sort of internal harmony. And as far as I have been able to read the Muslim mind, I have no hesitation in declaring that if the principle that the Indian Muslim is entitled to full and free development on the lines of his own culture and tradition in his own Indian homelands is recognized as the basis of a permanent communal settlement, he will be ready to stake his all for the freedom of India. The principle that each group is entitled to free development on its own lines is not inspired by any feeling of narrow communalism. There are communalisms and communalisms. A community which is inspired by feelings of ill-will toward other communities is low and ignoble. I entertain the highest respect for the customs, laws, religions, and social institutions of other communities. Nay, it is my duty, according to the teaching of the Qur'an, even to defend their places of worship, if need be. Yet, I love the communal group which is the source of my life and behavior and which has formed me what I am by giving me its religion, its literature, its thought, its culture and thereby recreating its whole past as a living factor in my present consciousness....

Communalism in its higher aspect, then, is indispensable to the formation of a harmonious whole in a country like India. The units of Indian society are not territorial as in European countries. India is a continent of human groups belonging to different races, speaking different languages and professing different religions. Their behavior is not at all determined by a common race-consciousness. Even the Hindus do not form a homogeneous group. The principle of European democracy cannot be applied to India without recognizing the fact of communal groups. The Muslim demand for the creation of a Muslim India within India is, therefore, perfectly justified. The [1929] resolution of the All-Parties Muslim Conference at Delhi is, to my mind, wholly inspired by this noble ideal of a harmonious whole which, instead of stifling the respective individualities of its component wholes, affords them chances of fully working out the possibilities that may be latent in them. And I have no doubt that this House will emphatically endorse the Muslim demands embodied in this resolution. Personally, I would go further than the demands embodied in it. I would like to see the Punjab, North-West Frontier Province, Sind and Baluchistan amalgamated into a single state. Self-government within the British empire or without the British empire, the formation of a consolidated North-West Indian Muslim state appears to me to be the final destiny of the Muslims, at least of North-West India....

The idea need not alarm the Hindus or the British. India is the greatest Muslim country in the world. The life of Islam, as a cultural force, in this country very largely depends on its centralization in a specified territory. This centralization of the most living portion of the Muslims of India, whose military and police service has, notwithstanding unfair treatment from the British, made the British rule possible in this country, will eventually solve the problem of India as well as of Asia. It will intensify their sense of responsibility and deepen their patriotic feeling. Thus, possessing full opportunity of development within the body politic of India, the North-West India Muslims will prove the best defenders of India against a foreign invasion, be the invasion one of ideas or of bayonets....

I therefore demand the formation of a consolidated Muslim state in the best interests of India and Islam. For India, it means security and peace resulting from an internal balance of power; for Islam an opportunity to rid itself of the stamp that Arabian imperialism was forced to give it, to mobilize its law, its education, its culture, and to bring them into closer contact with its own original spirit and with the spirit of modern times.

Thus, it is clear that in view of India's infinite variety in climates, races, languages, creeds and social systems, the creation of autonomous states based on the unity of language, race, history, religion and identity of economic interests, is the only possible way to secure a stable constitutional structure in India.....

In conclusion, I cannot but impress upon you that the present crisis in the history of India demands complete organization and unity of will and purpose in the Muslim community, both in your own interest as a community, and in the interest of India as a whole....

Our disorganized condition has already confused political issues vital to the life of the community. I am not hopeless of an intercommunal understanding, but I cannot conceal from you the feeling that in the near future our community may be called upon to adopt an independent line of action to cope with the present crisis. And an independent line of political action, in such a crisis, is possible only to a determined people, possessing a will focalized by a single purpose. Is it possible for you to achieve the organic wholeness of a unified will? Yes, it is. Rise above sectional interests and private ambitions, and learn to determine the value of your individual and collective action, however directed on material ends, in the light of the ideal which you are supposed to represent. Pass from matter to spirit. Matter is diversity; spirit is light, life and unity. One lesson I have learnt from the history of Muslims: at critical moments in their history it is Islam that has saved Muslims, and not vice versa. If today you focus your vision on Islam and see inspiration from the ever-vitalizing idea embodied in it, you will be only reassembling your scattered forces, regaining your lost integrity, and thereby saving yourself from total destruction. One of the profoundest verses in the Holy Qur'an teaches us that the birth and rebirth of the whole of humanity is like the birth of a single individual. Why cannot you who, as a people, can well claim to be the first practical exponents of this superb conception of humanity, live and move and have your being as a single individual?...In the words of the Qur'an: 'Hold fast to yourself; no one who erreth can hurt you, provided you are well guided.' [5:104]

■

10

■ ABUL KALAM AZAD ■

Abul Kalam Azad (1888–1958) was born in Mecca, of an Indian father and an Arabian mother. He first received a traditional Islamic education in Calcutta but then devoted himself to intensive English-language studies focused on European culture. Partly under the influence of Sri Aurobindo, the young Azad joined a Hindu revolutionary group devoted to 'extremist' nationalism—and was promptly arrested and detained by the British. After World War I he embraced the pro-caliphate Non-Cooperation Movement under Gandhi's leadership, and subsequently remained a faithful member of the National Congress, serving as its president from 1940 to 1946. Believing in the possibility of Hindu–Muslim co-existence he did not support partitioning and, following independence, served as India's minister of education from 1947 until his death.

For primary and secondary sources see Maulana Abul Kalam Azad, *India Wins Freedom: An Autobiographical Narrative*, Bombay, Orient Longman, 1959; *Basic Concepts of the Quran*, Hyderabad, Academy of Islamic Studies, 1958; *Speeches of Maulana Azad*, New Delhi, Government of India, Publications Division, 1956; Sankar Ghose, ed., *Congress Presidential Speeches*, Calcutta, West Bengal Pradesh Committee, 1972; Ian Henderson Douglas, *Abul Kalam Azad: An Intellectual and Religious Biography*, Delhi, Oxford University Press, 1993. The following selection is taken from Ghose, *Congress Presidential Speeches*, pp. 356–63.

CONGRESS PRESIDENTIAL SPEECH

We have considered the problem of the minorities of India. But are the Muslims such a minority as to have the least doubt or fear about their future? A small minority may legitimately have fears and apprehensions, but can the Muslims allow themselves to be disturbed by them? I do not know how many of you are familiar with my writings, twenty-eight years ago, in the *Al-Hilal*. If there are any such here, I would request them to refresh their memories. Even then I gave expression to my conviction, and I repeat this today, that in the texture of Indian politics, nothing is further removed from the truth than to say that Indian Muslims occupy the position of a political minority. It is equally absurd for them to be apprehensive about their rights and interests in a democratic India. This fundamental mistake has opened the door to countless misunderstandings. False arguments were built up on wrong premises. This error, on the one hand, brought confusion into the minds of Musalmans about their own true position and, on the other hand, it involved the world in misunderstandings, so that the picture of India could not be seen in right perspective.

If time had permitted, I would have told you in detail how, during the last sixty years, this artificial and untrue picture of India was made, and whose hands traced it. In effect, this was the result of the same policy of divide and rule which took particular shape in the minds of British officialdom in India after the Congress launched the national movement. The object of this was to prepare the Musalmans for use against the new political awakening. In this plan, prominence was given to two points. First, that India was inhabited by two different communities, the Hindus and the Musalmans, and for this reason no demand could be made in the name of a united nation. Second, that numerically the Musalmans were far less than the Hindus, and because of this, the necessary consequence of the establishment of democratic institutions in India would be to establish the rule of the Hindu majority and to jeopardise the existence of the Muslims.

Thus were sown the seeds of disunity by British imperialism on Indian soil. The plant grew and was nurtured and spread its nettles, and even though fifty years have passed since then, the roots are still there.

Politically speaking, the word 'minority' does not mean just a group that is so small in number and so lacking in other qualities that give strength, that it has no confidence in its own capacity to protect itself from the much larger group that surrounds it. It is not enough that the group should be relatively the smaller, but that it should be absolutely so small as to be incapable of protecting its interests. Thus, this is not merely a question of numbers; other factors count also. If a country has two major groups numbering [one] million and two millions respectively, it does not necessarily follow that because one is half the other, therefore it must call itself politically a minority, and consider itself weak.

If this is the right test, let us apply it to the position of the Muslims in India. You will see at a glance a vast concourse, spreading out all over the country; they stand erect, and to imagine that they exist helplessly as a 'minority' is to delude oneself. The Muslims in India number between eighty and ninety millions. The same type of social or racial divisions, which affect other communities, do not divide them. The powerful bonds of Islamic brotherhood and equality have protected them to a large extent from the weakness that flows from social divisions. It is true that they number only one-fourth of the total population; but the question is not one of population ratio, but of the large numbers and the strength behind them. Can such a vast mass of humanity have any legitimate reason for apprehension that in a free and democratic India, it might be unable to protect its rights and interest?

These numbers are not confined to any particular area but spread out unevenly over different parts of the country. In four provinces out of eleven in India there is a Muslim majority, the other religious groups being minorities. If British Baluchistan is added, there are five provinces with Muslim majority. Even if we are compelled at present to consider this question on a basis of religious groupings, the position of the Muslims is not that of a minority only. If they are in a minority in seven provinces, they are in a majority in five. This being so, there is absolutely no reason why they should be oppressed by the feeling of being a minority.

Whatever may be the details of the future constitution of India, we know that it will be an all-India federation which is, in the fullest sense, democratic, and every unit of which will have autonomy in regard to internal affairs. The federal center will be concerned only with all-India matters of common concern, such as, foreign relations, defence, customs, etc. Under these circumstances, can any one who has any conception of the actual working of a democratic constitution, allow himself to be led astray by this false issue of majority and minority? I cannot believe for an instant that there can be any room whatever for these misgivings in the picture of India's future. These apprehensions are arising because, in the words of a British statesman regarding Ireland, we are yet standing on the banks of the river and, though wishing to swim, are unwilling to enter the water. There is only one remedy: we should take the plunge fearlessly. No sooner is this done, we shall realize that all our apprehensions were without foundation....

Do we, Indian Musalmans, view the free India of the future with suspicion and distrust or with courage and confidence? If we view it with fear and suspicion, then, undoubtedly, we have to follow a different path. No present declaration, no promise for the future, no constitutional safeguards, can be a remedy for our doubts and fears. We are then forced to tolerate the existence of a third power. This third power is already entrenched here and has no intention of withdrawing and, if we follow this path of fear, we must need look forward to its continuance. But if we are convinced that for us fear and doubt have no place, and that we must view the future with courage and confidence in ourselves, then our course of action becomes absolutely clear. We find ourselves in a new world which is free from the dark shadows of doubt, vacillation, inaction and apathy, and where the light of faith and determination, action and enthusiasm never fails. The confusions of the times, the ups and downs that come our way, the difficulties that beset our thorny path, cannot change the direction of our steps. It becomes our bounden duty, then, to march with assured steps to India's national goal....

I am a Musalman and am proud of that fact. Islam's splendid traditions of thirteen hundred years are my inheritance. I am unwilling to lose even the smallest part of this inheritance. The teaching and history of Islam, its arts and letters and civilization are my wealth and my fortune. It is my duty to protect them.

As a Musalman I have a special interest in Islamic religion and culture, and I cannot tolerate any interference with them. But in addition to these sentiments, I have others also which the realities and conditions of my life have forced upon me. The spirit of Islam does not come in the way of these sentiments; it guides and helps me forward. I am proud of being an Indian. I am a part of the indivisible unity that is Indian nationality. I am indispensable to this noble edifice and without me this splendid structure of India is incomplete. I am an essential element which has gone to build India. I can never surrender this claim.

It was India's historic destiny that many human races and cultures and religions should flow to her, finding a home in her hospitable soil, and that many a caravan should find rest here. Even before the dawn of history, these caravans trekked into India and wave after wave of newcomers followed. This vast and fertile land gave welcome to all and took them to her bosom. One of the last of these caravans, following the footsteps of its predecessors, was that of the followers of Islam. This came here and settled here for good. This led to a meeting of the culture-currents of two different races. Like the Ganga and Jumna, they flowed for a while through separate courses, but nature's immutable law brought them together and joined them in a *sangam* [confluence]. This fusion was a notable event in history. Since then, destiny, in her own hidden way, began to fashion a new India in place of the old. We brought our treasures with us, and India too was full of the riches of her own precious heritage. We gave our wealth to her and she unlocked the doors of her own treasures to us. We gave her, what she needed most, the most precious of gifts from Islam's treasury, the message of democracy and human equality.

Full eleven centuries have passed by since then. Islam has now as great a claim on the soil of India as Hinduism. If Hinduism has been the religion of the people here for several thousands of years, Islam also has been their religion for a thousand years. Just as a Hindu can say with pride that he is an Indian and follows Hinduism, so also we can say with equal pride that we are Indians and follow Islam. I shall enlarge this orbit still further. The Indian Christian is equally entitled to say with pride that he is an Indian and is following a religion of India, namely Christianity.

Eleven hundred years of common history have enriched India with our common achievement. Our languages, our poetry, our literature, our culture, our art, our dress, our manners and customs, the innumerable happenings of our daily life, everything bears the stamp of our joint endeavor. There is indeed no aspect of our life which has escaped this stamp. Our languages were different, but we grew to use a common language; our manners and customs were dissimilar, but they acted and reacted on each other and thus produced a new synthesis. Our old dress may be seen only in ancient pictures of bygone days; no one wears it today.

This joint wealth is the heritage of our common nationality and we do not want to leave it and go back to the times when this joint life had not begun. If there are any Hindus amongst us who desire to bring back the Hindu life of a thousand years ago and more, they dream, and such dreams are vain fantasies. So also if there are any Muslims who wish to revive their past civilization and culture, which they brought a thousand years ago from Iran and Central Asia, they dream also and the sooner they wake up the better. These are unnatural fancies which cannot take root in the soil of reality. I am one of those who believe that revival may be a necessity in a religion but in social matters it is a denial of progress.

This thousand years of our joint life has molded us into a common nationality. This cannot be done artificially. Nature does her fashioning through her hidden processes in the course of centuries. The cast has now been molded and destiny has set her seal upon it. Whether we like it or not, we have now become an Indian nation, united and indivisible. No fantasy or artificial scheming to separate and divide can break this unity. We must accept the logic of fact and history and engage ourselves in the fashioning of our future destiny.

I shall not take any more of your time. My address must end now. But before I do so, permit me to remind you that our success depends upon three factors: unity, discipline and full confidence in Mahatma Gandhi's leadership. The glorious past record of our movement was due to his great leadership, and it is only under his leadership that we can look forward to a future of successful achievement.

The time of our trial is upon us. We have already focused the world's attention. Let us endeavor to prove ourselves worthy.

■

11

■ MOHANDAS GANDHI ■

Mohandas Karamchand Gandhi (1869–1948), later known as the Mahatma, was born in Porbandar, Gujarat, the son of a Vaishnava family of merchants and small government officials. He went to school in Rajkot, receiving education mostly in the English medium. At age 18 he traveled to London to earn a law degree (after having taken triple vows not to touch meat, wine, or women). Having been admitted to the bar in 1891, he returned to India to start a legal practice, but had little success. On the invitation of a Muslim trading firm he traveled to South Africa—where he suffered severe racial abuse and humiliation. In opposition to such abuse he founded the Natal Indian Congress to improve the condition of Natal Indians and other disenfranchised people. In the course of his struggle he developed a number of norms and strategies which became decisive for his later life, like *satyagraha* (truth force), and *ahimsa* (non-violent resistance). After twenty years in South Africa, Gandhi (now 45) returned to India and plunged himself into the anti-British struggle: by organizing a 'Non-Cooperation Movement' in the 1920s, by leading the 'Salt March' in 1930, and later struggling against plans to partition the subcontinent. In August of 1947, on the day of independence, he refused to come to New Delhi, preferring to stay in Calcutta in order to pacify communal violence between Muslims and Hindus. On January 30, 1948 he was shot and killed by a Hindu fanatic.

For primary and secondary literature see *The Collected Works of Mahatma Gandhi*, 72 Vols, New Delhi, Government of India, Publications Division, 1958–1978; *An Autobiography, or the Story of My Experiments with Truth*, trans. Mahadev Desai, Ahmedabad,

Navajivan, 1927; *Hind Swaraj or Home Rule*, Ahmedabad, Navajivan, 1946; *Young India*, New York, Huebsch, 1922; Louis Fischer, *Gandhi: His Life and Message for the World*, New York, Harper, 1950; Raghavan Iyer, *The Moral and Political Thought of Mahatma Gandhi*, New York, Oxford University Press, 1973; Dennis Dalton, *Mahatma Gandhi: Nonviolent Power in Action*, New York, Columbia University Press, 1993. The following selections are taken from *Hind Swaraj, Speeches and Writings of the Mahatma Gandhi, Young India, Harijan* (9 July 1938), and *Collected Works*.

HIND SWARAJ

What is *Swaraj*?

Reader: I have now learnt what the Congress has done to make India one nation, how the partition has caused an awakening, and how discontent and unrest have spread through the land. I would now like to know your views on *swaraj*. I fear that our interpretation is not the same as yours.

Editor [Gandhi]: It is quite possible that we do not attach the same meaning to the term. You and I and all Indians are impatient to obtain *swaraj*, but we are certainly not decided as to what it is. To drive the English out of India is a thought heard from many mouths, but it does not seem that many have properly considered why it should be so. I must ask you a question. Do you think that it is necessary to drive away the English, if we get all we want?

Reader: I should ask of them only one thing, that is: 'Please leave our country'. If, after they have complied with this request, their withdrawal from India means that they are still in India, I should have no objection. Then we would understand that, in their language, the word 'gone' is equivalent to 'remained'.

Editor: Well then, let us suppose that the English have retired. What will you do then?

Reader: That question cannot be answered at this stage. The state after withdrawal will depend largely upon the manner of it. If, as you assume, they retire, it seems to me we shall still keep their constitution and shall carry on the government. If they simply retire for the asking, we should have an army, etc., ready at hand. We should, therefore, have no difficulty in carrying on the government.

Editor: You may think so; I do not. But I will not discuss the matter just now. I have to answer your question and that I can do well by asking you several questions: why do you want to drive away the English?

Reader: Because India has become impoverished by their government. They take away our money from year to year. The most important posts are reserved for themselves. We are kept in a state of slavery. They behave insolently towards us and disregard our feelings.

Editor: If they do not take our money away, become gentle, and give us responsible posts, would you still consider their presence to be harmful?

Reader: That question is useless. It is similar to the question whether there is any harm in associating with a tiger if he changes his nature. Such a question is sheer waste of time. When a tiger changes his nature, Englishmen will change theirs. This is not possible, and to believe it to be possible is contrary to human experience.

Editor: Supposing we get self-government similar to what the Canadians and the South Africans have, will it be good enough?

Reader: That question also is useless. We may get it when we have the same powers; we shall then hoist our own flag. As is Japan, so must India be. We must own our navy, our army, and we must have our own splendor, and then will India's voice ring through the world.

Editor: You have drawn the picture well. In effect it means this: that we want English rule without the Englishman. You want the tiger's nature, but not the tiger; that is to say, you would make India English. And when it becomes English, it will be called not Hindustan but *Englistan*. This is not the *swaraj* that I want.

Reader: I have placed before you my idea of *swaraj* as I think it should be. If the education we have received be of any use, if the works of Spencer, Mill and others be of any importance, and if the English Parliament be the Mother of Parliaments, I certainly think that we should copy the English people, and this to such an extent that, just as they do not allow others to obtain a footing in their country, so we should not allow them or others to obtain it in ours. What they have done in their own country has not been done in any other country. It is, therefore, proper for us to import their institutions. But now I want to know your views.

Editor: There is need for patience. My views will develop of themselves in the course of this discourse. It is as difficult for me to understand the true nature of *swaraj* as it seems to you to be easy. I shall therefore, for the time being, content myself with endeavoring to show that what you call *swaraj* is not truly *swaraj*.

The Condition of England

Reader: Then, from your statement I deduce that the Government of England is not desirable and not worth copying by us.

Editor: Your deduction is justified. The condition of England at present is pitiable. I pray to God that India may never be in that plight. That which you consider to be the Mother of Parliaments is like a sterile woman and a prostitute. Both these are harsh terms, but exactly fit the case. That Parliament has not yet, of its own accord, done a single good thing. Hence I have compared it to a sterile woman. The natural condition of that Parliament is such that, without outside pressure, it can do nothing. It is like a prostitute because it is under the control of ministers who change from time to time. Today it is under Mr Asquith, tomorrow it may be under Mr Balfour.

Reader: You have said this sarcastically. The term 'sterile woman' is not applicable. The Parliament, being elected by the people, must work under public pressure. This is its quality.

Editor: You are mistaken. Let us examine it a little more closely. The best men are supposed to be elected by the people. The members serve without pay and, therefore, it must be assumed, only for the public weal. The electors are considered to be educated and therefore we should assume that they would not generally make mistakes in their choice. Such a Parliament should not need the spur of petitions or any other pressure. Its work should be so smooth that its effects would be more apparent day by day. But, as a matter of fact, it is generally acknowledged that the members are hypocritical and selfish. Each thinks of his own little interest. It is fear that is the guiding motive. What is done today may be undone tomorrow. It is not possible to recall a single instance in which finality can be predicted for its work. When the greatest questions are debated, its members have been seen to stretch themselves and to doze. Sometimes the members talk away until the listeners are disgusted. Carlyle has called it the 'talking shop of the world'. Members vote for their party without a thought. Their so-called discipline binds them to it. If any member, by way of exception, gives an independent vote, he is considered a renegade. If the money and the time wasted by Parliament were entrusted to a few good men, the English nation would be occupying today a much higher platform. Parliament is simply a costly toy of the nation. These views are by no means peculiar to me. Some great English thinkers have expressed them. One of the members of that Parliament recently said that a true Christian could not become a member of it. Another said that it was a baby. And if it has remained a baby after an existence of seven hundred years, when will it outgrow its babyhood?

Reader: You have set me thinking; you do not expect me to accept at once all you say. You give me entirely novel views. I shall have to digest them. Will you now explain the epithet 'prostitute'?

Editor: That you cannot accept my views at once is only right. If you will read the literature on this subject, you will have some idea of it. Parliament is without a real master. Under the prime minister, its movement is not steady but it is buffeted about like a prostitute. The prime minister is more concerned about his power than about the welfare of Parliament. His energy is concentrated upon securing the success of his party. His care is not always that Parliament shall do right. Prime ministers are known to have made Parliament do things merely for party advantage. All this is worth thinking over.

Reader: Then you are really attacking the very men whom we have hitherto considered to be patriotic and honest?

Editor: Yes, that is true; I can have nothing against prime ministers, but what I have seen leads me to think that they cannot be considered really patriotic. If they are to be considered honest because they do not take what are generally known as bribes, let them be so considered, but they are open to subtler influences. In order to gain their ends, they certainly bribe people with honors. I do not hesitate to say that they have neither real honesty nor a living conscience.

Reader: As you express these views about parliament, I would like to hear you on the English people, so that I may have your view of their government.

Editor: To the English voters their newspaper is their Bible. They take their cue from their newspapers which are often dishonest. The same fact is differently interpreted by different newspapers, according to the party in whose interests they are edited. One newspaper would consider a great Englishman to be a paragon of honesty, another would consider him dishonest. What must be the condition of the people whose newspapers are of this type?

Reader: You shall describe it.

Editor: These people change their views frequently. It is said that they change them every seven years. These views swing like the pendulum of a clock and are never steadfast. The people would follow a powerful orator or a man who gives them parties, receptions, etc. As are the people, so is their Parliament. They have certainly one quality very strongly developed. They will never allow their country to be lost. If any person were to cast an evil eye on it, they would pluck out his eyes. But that does not mean that the nation possesses every other virtue or that it should be imitated. If India copies England, it is my firm conviction that she will be ruined.

Reader: To what do you ascribe this state of England?

Editor: It is not due to any peculiar fault of the English people, but the condition is due to modern civilization. It is a civilization only in name. Under it the nations of Europe are becoming degraded and ruined day-by-day.

Civilization

Reader: Now you will have to explain what you mean by civilization.

Editor: It is not a question of what I mean. Several English writers refuse to call that civilization which passes under that name. Many books have been written upon that subject. Societies have been formed to cure the nation of the evils of civilization. A great English writer has written a work called *Civilization: Its Cause and Cure*. Therein he has called it a disease.

Reader: Why do we not know this generally?

Editor: The answer is very simple. We rarely find people arguing against themselves. Those who are intoxicated by modern civilization are not likely to write against it. Their care will be to find out facts and arguments in support of it, and this they do un-consciously, believing it to be true. A man whilst he is dreaming, believes in his dream; he is undeceived only when he is awakened from his sleep. A man laboring under the bane of civilization is like a dreaming man. What we usually read are the works of de-fenders of modern civilization, which undoubtedly claims among its votaries very brilliant and even some very good men. Their writings hypnotize us. And so, one by one, we are drawn into the vortex.

Reader: This seems to be very plausible. Now will you tell me something of what you have read and thought of this civilization?

Editor: Let us first consider what state of things is described by the word 'civilization'. Its true test lies in the fact that people living in it make bodily welfare the object of life. We will take some examples. The people of Europe today live in better built houses than they did [one] hundred years ago. This is considered an em-blem of civilization, and this is also a matter to promote bodily happiness. Formerly, they wore skins, and used spears as their weapons. Now, they wear long trousers, and, for embellishing their bodies, they wear a variety of clothing, and, instead of spears, they carry with them revolvers containing five or more chambers. If people of a certain country, who have hitherto not been in the habit of wearing much clothing, boots, etc., adopt European clothing, they are supposed to have become civilized out of savagery. Formerly, in Europe, people ploughed their lands mainly by manual labor. Now, one man can plough a vast tract by means of steam engines and can thus amass great wealth. This is called a sign of civilization. Formerly, only a few men wrote valu-able books. Now, anybody writes and prints anything he likes and poisons people's minds. Formerly, men traveled in wagons. Now, they fly through the air in trains at the rate of four hundred and more miles per day. This is considered the height of civilization. It has been stated that, as men progress, they shall be able to travel in airship and reach any part of the world in a few hours. Men will not need the use of their hands and feet. They will press a button, and they will have their clothing by their side. They will press an-other button, and they will have their newspaper. A third, and a motor car will be in waiting for them. They will have a variety of delicately dished up food. Everything will be done by machinery. Formerly, when people wanted to fight with one another, they measured between them their bodily strength; now it is possible to take away thousands of lives by one man working behind a gun from a hill. This is civilization.

Formerly, men worked in the open air only as much as they liked. Now thousands of workmen meet together and for the sake of maintenance work in factories or mines. Their condition is worse than that of beasts. They are obliged to work, at the risk of their lives, at most dangerous occupations, for the sake of million-aires. Formerly, men were made slaves under physical compulsion. Now they are enslaved by temptation of money and of the luxuries that money can buy. There are now diseases of which people never dreamt before, and an army of doctors is engaged in finding out their cures, and so hospitals have increased. This is a test of civilization. Formerly, special messengers were required and much expense was incurred in order to send letters; today, anyone can abuse his fellow by means of a letter for one penny. True, at the same cost, one can send one's thanks also. Formerly, people had two or three meals consisting of home-made bread and vegetables; now, they require something to eat every two hours so that they have hardly leisure for anything else. What more need I say? All this you can ascertain from several authoritative books. These are all true tests of civilization. And if anyone speaks to the contrary, know that he is ignorant. This civilization takes note neither of morality nor of religion. Its votaries calmly state that their business is not to teach religion. Some even consider it to be a superstitious growth. Others put on the cloak of religion, and prate about morality. But, after twenty years' experience, I have come to the conclusion that immorality is often taught in the name of morality. Even a child can understand that in all I have described above there can be no inducement to morality. Civilization seeks to increase bodily comforts, and it fails miserably even in doing so.

This civilization is irreligion, and it has taken such a hold on the people in Europe that those who are in it appear to be half mad. They lack real physical strength or courage. They keep up their energy by intoxication. They can hardly be happy in solitude. Women, who should be the queens of households, wander in the streets or they slave away in factories. For the sake of a pittance, half a million women in England alone are laboring under trying circumstances in factories or similar institutions. This awful fact is one of the causes of the daily growing suffragette movement.

This civilization is such that one has only to be patient, and it will be self-destroyed. According to the teaching of Mahomed this would be considered a satanic civilization. Hinduism calls it the Black Age. I cannot give you an adequate conception of it. It is eating into the vitals of the English nation. It must be shunned; Parliaments are really emblems of slavery. If you will sufficiently think over this, you will entertain the same opinion and cease to blame the English. They rather deserve our sympathy. They are a shrewd nation and I therefore believe that they will cast off the evil. They are enterprising and industrious, and their mode of thought is not inherently immoral. Neither are they bad at heart. I therefore respect them. Civilization is not an incurable disease, but it should never be forgotten that the English people are at present afflicted by it.

Why was India Lost?

Reader: You have said much about civilization—enough to make me ponder over it. I do not now know what I should adopt and what I should avoid from the nations of Europe, but one question comes to my lips immediately. If civilization is a disease and if it has attacked England, why has she been able to take India, and why is she able to retain it?

Editor: Your question is not very difficult to answer, and we shall presently be able to examine the true nature of *swaraj*; for I am aware that I have still to answer that question. The English have not taken India; we have given it to them. They are not in India because of their strength, but because we keep them. Let us now see whether these propositions can be sustained. They came to our country originally for purposes of trade. Recall the Company Bahadur. Who made it Bahadur? They had not the slightest intention at the time of establishing a kingdom. Who assisted the company's officers? Who was tempted at the sight of their silver? Who bought their goods? History testifies that we did all this. In order to become rich all at once we welcomed the Company's officers with open arms. We assisted them. If I am in the habit of drinking *bhang* and a seller thereof sells it to me, am I to blame him or myself? By blaming the seller, shall I be able to avoid the habit? And, if a particular retailer is driven away will not another take his place? A true servant of India will have to go to the root of the matter. If an excess of food has caused me indigestion, I shall certainly not avoid it by blaming water. He is a true physician who probes the cause of disease, and if you pose as a physician for the disease of India, you will have to find out its true cause.

Reader: You are right. Now I think you will not have to argue much with me to drive your conclusions home. I am impatient to know your further views. We are now on a most interesting topic. I shall, therefore, endeavor to follow your thought, and stop you when I am in doubt.

Editor: I am afraid that, in spite of your enthusiasm, as we proceed further, we shall have differences of opinion. Nevertheless, I shall argue only when you stop me. We have already seen that the English merchants were able to get a footing in India because we encouraged them. When our princes fought among themselves, they sought the assistance of Company Bahadur. That corporation was versed alike in commerce and war. It was unhampered by questions of morality. Its object was to increase its commerce and to make money. It accepted our assistance, and increased the number of its warehouses. To protect the latter it employed an army which was utilized by us also. Is it not then useless to blame the English for what we did at that time? The Hindus and the Muslims were at daggers drawn. This, too, gave the Company its opportunity and thus we created the circumstances that gave the Company its control over India. Hence it is truer to say that we gave India to the English than that India was lost.

Reader: Will you now tell me how they are able to retain India?

Editor: The causes that gave them India enable them to retain it. Some Englishmen state that they took and they hold India by the sword. Both these statements are wrong. The sword is entirely useless for holding India. We alone keep them. Napoleon is said to have described the English as a nation of shopkeepers. It is a fitting description. They hold whatever dominions they have for the sake of their commerce. Their army and their navy are intended to protect it. When the Transvaal offered no such attractions, the late Mr Gladstone discovered that it was not right for the English to hold it. When it became a paying proposition, resistance led to war. Mr Chamberlain soon discovered that England enjoyed a suzerainty over the Transvaal. It is related that someone asked the late President Kruger whether there was gold in the moon. He replied that it was highly unlikely because, if there were, the English would have annexed it. Many problems can be solved by remembering that money is their God. Then it follows that we keep the English in India for our base self-interest. We like their commerce; they please us by their subtle methods and get what they want from us. To blame them for this is to perpetuate their power. We further strengthen their hold by quarrelling amongst ourselves. If you accept the above statements, it is proved that the English entered India for the purposes of trade. They remain in it for the same purpose and we help them to do so. Their arms and ammunition are perfectly useless. In this connection I remind you that it is the British flag which is waving in Japan and not the Japanese. The English have a treaty with Japan for the sake of their commerce, and you will see that if they can manage it their commerce will greatly expand in that country. They wish to convert the whole world into a vast market for their goods. That they cannot do so is true, but the blame will not be theirs. They will leave no stone unturned to reach the goal.

The Condition of India

Reader: I now understand why the English hold India. I should like to know your views about the condition of our country.

Editor: It is a sad condition. In thinking of it my eyes water and my throat gets parched. I have grave doubts whether I shall be able sufficiently to explain what is in my heart. It is my deliberate opinion that India is being ground down, not under the English heel, but under that of modern civilization. It is groaning under the monster's terrible weight. There is yet time to escape it, but every day makes it more and more difficult. Religion is dear to me and my first complaint is that India is becoming irreligious. Here I am not thinking of the Hindu or the Muslim or the Zoroastrian religion but of that religion which underlies all religions. We are turning away from God.

Reader: How so?

Editor: There is a charge laid against us that we are a lazy people and that Europeans are industrious and enterprising. We have accepted the charge and we therefore wish to change our condition. Hinduism, Islam, Zoroastrianism, Christianity and all other religions teach that we should remain passive about worldly pursuits and active about godly pursuits, that we should set a limit to our worldly ambition and that our religious ambition should be illimitable. Our activity should be directed into the latter channel.

Reader: You seem to be encouraging religious charlatanism. Many a cheat has, by talking in a similar strain, led the people astray.

Editor: You are bringing an unlawful charge against religion. Humbug there undoubtedly is about all religions. Where there is light, there is also shadow. I am prepared to maintain that humbugs in worldly matters are far worse than the humbugs in religion. The humbug of civilization that I am endeavoring to show to you is not to be found in religion.

Reader: How can you say that? In the name of religion Hindus and Muslims fought against one another. For the same cause Christians fought Christians. Thousands of innocent men have been murdered, thousands have been burned and tortured in its name. Surely, this is much worse than any civilization.

Editor: I certainly submit that the above hardships are far more bearable than those of civilization. Everybody understands that the cruelties you have named are not part of religion although they have been practiced in its name; therefore there is no aftermath to these cruelties. They will always happen so long as there are to be found ignorant and credulous people. But there is no end to the victims destroyed in the fire of civilization. Its deadly effect is that people come under its scorching flames believing it to be all good, they become utterly irreligious and, in reality, derive little advantage from the world. Civilization is like a mouse gnawing while it is soothing us. When its full effect is realized, we shall see that religious superstition is harmless compared to that of modern civilization. I am not pleading for a continuance of religious superstitions. We shall certainly fight them tooth and nail, but we can never do so by disregarding religion. We can only do so by appreciating and conserving the latter.

Reader: Then you will contend that the *Pax Britannica* is a useless encumbrance?

Editor: You may see peace if you like; I see none.

Reader: You make light of the terror that the Thugs, the Pindaris and the Bhils were to the country.

Editor: If you give the matter some thought, you will see that the terror was by no means such a mighty thing. If it had been a very substantial thing, the other people would have died away before the English advent. Moreover, the present peace is only nominal, for by it we have become emasculated and cowardly. We are not to assume that the English have changed the nature of the Pindaris and the Bhils. It is, therefore, better to suffer the Pindari peril than that someone else should protect us from it and thus render us effeminate. I should prefer to be killed by the arrow of a Bhil than to seek unmanly protection. India without such protection was an India full of valor. Macaulay betrayed gross ignorance when he libelled Indians as being practically cowards. They never merited the charge. Cowards living in a country inhabited by hardy mountaineers and infested by wolves and tigers must surely find an early grave. Have you ever visited our fields? I assure you that our agriculturists sleep fearlessly on their farms even today; but the English and you and I would hesitate to sleep where they sleep. Strength lies in absence of fear, not in the quantity of flesh and muscle we may have on our bodies. Moreover, I must remind you who desire Home Rule that, after all, the Bhils, the Pindaris, and the Thugs are our own countrymen. To conquer them is your and my work. So long as we fear our own brethren, we are unfit to reach the goal.

■

MEDIUM OF INSTRUCTION

The Mother Tongue

I am hoping that this University (Banaras Hindu University) will see to it that the youths who come to it will receive their instruction through the medium of their vernaculars. Our language is the reflection of ourselves, and if you tell me that our languages are too poor to express the best thought, then I say that the sooner we are wiped out of existence the better for us. Is there a man who dreams that English can ever become the national language of India? (Cries of 'never'). Why this handicap on the nation? Just consider for one moment what an unequal race our lads have to run with every English lad. I had the privilege of a close conversation with some Poona professors. They assured me that every Indian youth, because he reached his knowledge through the English language, lost at least six precious years of life. Multiply that by the number of students and colleges and find out for yourselves how many thousand years have been lost to the nation.

The charge against us is, that we have no initiative. How can we have any if we are to devote the precious years of our life to the mastery of a foreign tongue? We fail in this attempt also.... I have heard it said that after all it is English-educated India which is leading and which is doing everything for the nation. It would be monstrous if it were otherwise. The only education we receive is English education. Surely we must show something for it. But suppose that we had been receiving during the past fifty years education through our vernaculars, what should we have today? We should have today a free India, we should have our educated men, not as if they were foreigners in their own land, but speaking to the heart of the nation; they would be working amongst the poorest of the poor, and whatever they would have gained during the past fifty years would be a heritage for the nation (Applause). Today even our wives are not sharers in our best thought.

The Foreign Medium

The foreign medium has caused brain fag, put an undue strain upon the nerves of our children, made them crammers and imitators, unfitted them for original work and thought, and disabled them for filtrating their learning to the family or the masses. The foreign medium has made our children practically foreigners in their own land. It is the greatest tragedy of the existing system. The foreign medium has prevented the growth of our vernaculars. If I had the powers of a despot, I would today stop the tuition of our boys and girls through a foreign medium, and require all the teachers and professors on pain of dismissal to introduce the change forthwith. I would not wait for the preparation of textbooks. They will follow the change. It is an evil that needs a summary remedy.

But for the fact that the only higher education, the only education worth the name has been received by us through the English medium, there would be no need to prove such a self-evident proposition that the youth of a nation to remain a nation must receive all instruction including the highest in its own vernacular or vernaculars. Surely, it is a self-demonstrated proposition that the youth of a nation cannot keep or establish a living contact with the masses unless their knowledge is received and assimilated through a medium understood by the people. Who can calculate the immeasurable loss sustained by the nation owing to thousands of its young men having been obligated to waste years in mastering a foreign language and its idiom of which in their daily life they have the least use and in learning by which they had to neglect their own mother tongue and their own literature? There never was a greater superstition than that a particular language can be incapable of expansion or expressing abstruse or scientific ideas. A language is an exact reflection of the character and growth of its speakers.

Among the many evils of foreign rule this blighting imposition of a foreign medium upon the youth of the country will be counted by history as one of the greatest. It has sapped the energy of the nation, it has shortened the lives of the pupils, it has estranged them from the masses, it has made education unnecessarily expensive. If this process is still persisted in, it bids fair to rob the nation of its soul. The sooner, therefore, educated India shakes itself free from the hypnotic spell of the foreign medium, the better it would be for them and the people.

My Own Experience

Let me give a chapter from my own experience. Up to the age of 12 all the knowledge I gained was through Gujarati, my mother tongue. I knew then something of arithmetic, history and geography. Then I entered high school. For the first three years the mother tongue was still the medium, but the schoolmaster's business was to drive English into the pupil's head. Therefore, more than half of our time was given to learning English and mastering its arbitrary spelling and pronunciation. It was a painful discovery to have to learn a language that was not pronounced as it was written. It was a strange experience to have to learn the spelling by heart. But that is by the way, and irrelevant to my argument. However, for the first three years, it was comparatively plain sailing.

The pillory began with the fourth year. Everything had to be learnt through English—geometry, algebra, chemistry, astronomy, history, geography. The tyranny of English was so great that even Sanskrit or Persian had to be learnt through English, not through the mother tongue. If any boy spoke in the class in Gujarati which he understood, he was punished. It did not matter to the teacher if a boy spoke bad English which he could neither pronounce correctly nor understand fully. Why should the teacher worry? His own English was by no means without blemish. It could not be otherwise. English was as much a foreign language to him as to his pupils. The result was chaos. We, the boys, had to learn many things by heart, though we could not understand them fully and often not at all.... I know now that what I took four years to learn of arithmetic, geometry, algebra, chemistry and astronomy, I should have learnt easily in one year, if I had not to learn them through English but Gujarati. My grasp of the subjects would have been easier and clearer. My Gujarati vocabulary would have been richer. I would have made use of such knowledge in my own home. This English medium created an impassable barrier between me and the members of my family, who had not gone through English schools. My father knew nothing of what I was doing. I could not, even if I had wished it, interest my father in what I was learning. For though he had ample intelligence, he knew not a word of English. I was fast becoming a stranger in my own home. I certainly became a superior person. Even my dress began to undergo imperceptible changes. What happened to me was not an uncommon experience. It was common to the majority....

A word about literature. We had to learn several books of English prose and English poetry. No doubt all this was nice. But that knowledge has been of no use to me in serving or bringing me in touch with the masses. I am unable to say that if I had not learnt what I did of English prose and poetry, I should have missed a rare treasure. If I had, instead, passed those precious seven years in mastering Gujarati and had learnt mathematics, science, and Sanskrit, and other subjects through Gujarati, I could easily have shared the knowledge so gained with my neighbors. I would have enriched Gujarati, and who can say that I would not have, with my habit of application and my inordinate love for the country and the mother tongue, made a richer and greater contribution to the service of the masses?

I must not be understood to decry English or its noble literature. The columns of the *Harijan* are sufficient evidence of my love of English. But the nobility of its literature cannot avail the Indian nation any more than the temperate climate or the scenery of England can avail her. India has to flourish in her own climate and scenery and her own literature, even though all the three may be inferior to the English climate, scenery and literature. We and our children must build on our own heritage. If we borrow another we impoverish our own. We can never grow on foreign victuals. I want the nation to have the treasures contained in that language, and for that matter the other languages of the world, through its own vernaculars. I do not need to learn Bengali in order to know the beauties of Rabindranath's matchless productions. I get them through good translations. Gujarati boys and girls do not need to learn Russian to appreciate Tolstoy's short stories. They learn them through good translations. It is the boast of Englishmen that the best of the world's literary output is in the hands of that nation in simple English inside of a week of its publication. Why need I learn English to get at the best of what Shakespeare and Milton thought and wrote?....

The medium of instruction should be altered at once and at any cost, the provincial languages being given their rightful place. I would prefer temporary chaos in higher education to the criminal waste that is daily accumulating. In order to enhance the status and the market value of the provincial languages, I would have the language of the law courts to be the language of the province where the court is situated. The proceedings of the provincial legislatures must be in the language, or even the languages of the province where a province has more than one language within its borders.

■

THE MESSAGE OF INDIA

I was wondering as to what I was to say to you. I wanted to collect my thoughts but, let me confess to you, I had no time. Yet I had promised yesterday that I would try to say a few words.... You, friends, have not seen the real India and you are not meeting in conference in the midst of real India. Delhi, Bombay, Madras, Calcutta, Lahore—all these are big cities and are, therefore, influenced by the West.

I then thought of a story. It was in French and was translated for me by an Anglo-French philosopher. He was an unselfish man. He befriended me without having known me because he always sided with the minorities. I was not then in my own country. I was not only in a hopeless minority but in a despised minority, if the

Europeans in South Africa will forgive me for saying so. I was a coolie lawyer. At that time we had no coolie doctors, no coolie lawyers. I was the first in the field. You know perhaps what is meant by the word coolie.

This friend—his mother was a French woman and his father an Englishman—said: 'I want to translate for you a French story. There were three scientists who went out from France in search of truth. They went to different parts of Asia. One of them found his way to India. He began to search. He went to the so-called cities of those times—naturally this was before British occupation, before even the Moghul period. He saw the so-called high caste people, men and women, and he felt at a loss. Finally, he went to a humble cottage in a humble village. That was the cottage of a *bhangi* and there he found the truth that he was in search of.'

If you really want to see India at its best, you have to find it in the humble *bhangi* homes of such villages. There are 7,000,000 of such villages and 38 crores of people inhabit them.

If some of you see the villages, you will not be fascinated by the sight. You will have to scratch below the dung heaps. I do not say that they ever were heavenly places. Today, they are really dung heaps. They were not like that before. What I say is not from history but from what I have seen myself. I have traveled from one end of India to the other and have seen the miserable specimen of humanity with lusterless eyes. They are India. In these humble cottages, in the midst of these dung heaps, are to be found the humble *bhangis* in whom you find the concentrated essence of wisdom....

[Stating that wisdom had come to the West from the East, Gandhi added:]

The first of these wise men was Zoroaster. He belonged to the East. He was followed by the Buddha who belonged to the East—to India. Who followed the Buddha? Jesus, who came from the East. Before Jesus was Moses who belonged to Palestine though he was born in Egypt. After Jesus came Mohammed. I omit any reference to Krishna and Rama and other lights. I do not call them lesser lights but they are less known to the literary world. All the same I do not know of a single person in the world to match these men of Asia. And then what happened? Christianity became disfigured when it went to the West. I am sorry to have to say that. I would not talk any further....

What I want you to understand is the message of Asia. It is not to be learnt through the Western spectacles or by imitating the atom bomb. If you want to give a message to the West, it must be the message of love and the message of truth. I want you to go away with the thought that Asia has to conquer the West through love and truth. I do not want merely to appeal to your heads. I want to capture your hearts.

Of course, I believe in 'one world'. How can I possibly do otherwise, when I became an inheritor of the message of love that these great unconquerable teachers left for us? In this age of democracy, in this age of awakening of the poorest of the poor, you can redeliver this message with the greatest emphasis. You will complete the conquest of the West not through vengeance because you have been exploited, but with real understanding. I am confident that if all of you put your hearts together—not merely heads—to understand the secret of the message these wise men of the East have left to us, and if we really become worthy of that great message, the conquest of the West will be complete. This conquest will be loved by the West itself.

The West is today pining for wisdom. It is despairing of the multiplication of the atom bomb, because atom bombs mean utter destruction not merely of the West but of the whole world, as if the prophesy of the Bible was going to be fulfilled and there was to be a perfect deluge. It is up to you to tell the world of its wickedness and sin—that is the teaching your teachers and my teachers have taught Asia.

■

12

■ JAWAHARLAL NEHRU ■

Jawaharlal Nehru (1889–1964) was born in Allahabad into a family of Kashmiri Brahmans, his father Motilal being a wealthy lawyer at the high court. After being tutored by English governesses, he was sent at age 15 to Harrow, and two years later to Cambridge. Having obtained a law degree in London, he returned to India in 1912 to practice law with his father, who, by that time, had emerged as a leading 'moderate' in the Indian National Congress. Following in his father's footsteps Nehru joined the Congress and, in 1920, Gandhi's 'Non-Cooperation Movement'. During the 1930s he came under the influence of socialist ideas, but remained loyal to the Congress as whose president he served for several successive terms. Following independence in 1947, he served as India's prime minister and minister for external affairs for seventeen years, pursuing such policies as democratization, economic development with 'socialist' safeguards, and international non-alignment.

For primary and secondary sources see Jawaharlal Nehru, *The Discovery of India*, New York, John Day, 1946; *An Autobiography*, London, John Lane, 1937; *Jawaharlal Nehru's Speeches, 1949–1964*, 5 Vols, New Delhi, Government of India, Publications Division, 1954–1968; *Selected Works*, New Delhi, Orient Longman, 1975; Anup Singh, *Nehru: The Rising Star of India*, New York, John Day, 1939; Michael Brecher, *Nehru: A Political Biography*, London, Oxford University Press, 1959; D.E. Smith, *Nehru and Democracy: The Political Thought of an Asian Democrat*, Calcutta, Orient Longman, 1958; Willard Range, *Jawaharlal Nehru's World View: A Theory of International Relations*, Athens,

University of Georgia Press, 1961; B.N. Pande, *Nehru*, London, Macmillan, 1977. The following selections are taken from Nehru, 'Speech in the Constituent Assembly' (14 August 1947), 'Address at the Aligarh Muslim University' (24 January 1948), 'Foreword' to Jean Filliozat, *India: The Country and Its Traditions*, London, Harrap, 1962; Azad Memorial Lectures, *India Today and Tomorrow*, Calcutta, Orient Longman, 1960, and 'Broadcast to the Nation' (19 October 1963).

A TRYST WITH DESTINY

Long years ago we made a tryst with destiny, and now the time comes when we shall redeem our pledge, not wholly or in full measure, but very substantially. At the stroke of the midnight hour, when the world sleeps, India will awake to life and freedom. A moment comes, which comes but rarely in history, when we step out from the old to the new, when an age ends, and when the soul of a nation, long suppressed, finds utterance. It is fitting that at this solemn moment we take the pledge of dedication to the service of India and her people and to the still larger cause of humanity.

At the dawn of history India started on her unending quest, and trackless centuries are filled with her striving and the grandeur of her success and her failures. Through good and ill fortune alike she has never lost sight of that quest or forgotten the ideals which gave her strength. We end today a period of ill fortune, and India discovers herself again. The achievement we celebrate today is but a step, an opening of opportunity, to the greater triumphs and achievements that await us. Are we brave enough and wise enough to grasp this opportunity and accept the challenge of the future?

Freedom and power bring responsibility. The responsibility rests upon this assembly, a sovereign body representing the sovereign people of India. Before the birth of freedom we have endured all the pains of labor and our hearts are heavy with the memory of this sorrow. Some of those pains continue even now. Nevertheless, the past is over and it is the future that beckons to us now.

That future is not one of ease or resting but of incessant striving so that we may fulfill the pledges we have so often taken and the one we shall take today. The service of India means the service of the millions who suffer. It means the ending of poverty and ignorance and disease and inequality of opportunity. The ambition of the greatest man of our generation has been to wipe every tear from every eye. That may be beyond us, but as long as there are tears and suffering, so long our work will not be over.

And so we have to labor and to work, and work hard, to give reality to our dreams. Those dreams are for India, but they are also for the world, for all the nations and peoples are too closely knit together today for any one of them to imagine that it can live apart. Peace has been said to be indivisible; so is freedom, so is prosperity now, and so also is disaster in this one world that can no longer be split into isolated fragments.

To the people of India, whose representatives we are, we make an appeal to join us with faith and confidence in this great adventure. This is no time for petty and destructive criticism, no time for ill will or blaming others. We have to build the noble mansion of free India where all her children may dwell.

■

OUR INHERITANCE

For every sensitive human being in India the last six months have brought pain and sorrow, and what is worst of all, a humiliation of the spirit. It has been bad enough for those who are old in years and experienced, but I often wonder how the young feel who, at the threshold of their lives, have seen and experienced catastrophe and disaster. They will, no doubt, survive it, for youth is resilient; but it may well be that they will carry the mark of it for the rest of their days. Perhaps if we are wise and strong enough to think and act rightly even now, we may succeed in erasing that mark.

For my part I wish to say that, in spite of everything, I have a firm faith in India's future. Indeed, if I did not have it, it would not have been possible for me to work effectively. Although many of my old dreams have been shattered by recent events, yet the basic objective still holds and I see no reason to change it. That objective is to build a free India of high ideals and noble endeavor where there is equality of opportunity for all and where many variegated streams of thought and culture meet together to form a mighty river of progress and advancement for her people.

I am proud of India, not only because of her ancient, magnificent heritage, but also because of her remarkable capacity to add to it by keeping the doors and windows of her mind and spirit open to fresh and invigorating winds from distant lands. India's strength has been twofold: her own innate culture which flowered through the ages, and her capacity to draw from other sources, and thus add to her own. She was far too strong to be submerged by outside streams, and she was too wise to isolate herself from them, and so there is a continuing synthesis in India's real history and the many political changes which have taken place have had little effect on the growth of this variegated and yet essentially unified culture.

I have said that I am proud of our inheritance and our ancestors who gave an intellectual and cultural pre-eminence to India. How do you feel about this past? Do you feel that you are also sharers in it and inheritors of it and, therefore, proud of something that belongs to you as much as to me? Or do you feel alien to it and pass it by without understanding it or feeling that strange thrill which comes from the realization that we are the trustees and inheritors of this vast treasure? I ask you these questions, because in recent years many forces have been at play diverting people's minds into wrong channels and trying to pervert the course of history. You are Muslims and I am a Hindu. We may adhere to different religious faiths or even to none; but that does not take away from that cultural inheritance that is yours as well as mine. The past holds us together; why should the present or the future divide us in spirit?

Political changes produce certain results, but the essential changes are in the spirit and outlook of a nation. What has troubled me very greatly during these past months and years is not the political changes, but rather the creeping sense of a change of spirit which has created enormous barriers between us. The attempt to change the spirit of India was a reversal of the historical process through which we had been passing for long ages past, and it is because we tried to reverse the current of history that disaster overwhelmed us. We cannot easily play about with geography or with the powerful trends which make history. And it is infinitely worse if we make hatred and violence the springs of action.

Pakistan has come into being, rather unnaturally I think. Nevertheless, it represents the urges of a large number of persons. I believe that this development has been a throw-back, but we accepted it in good faith. I want you to understand clearly what our present view is. We have been charged with desiring to strangle and crush Pakistan and to force it into a reunion with India. That charge, as many others, is based on fear and a complete misunderstanding of our attitude. I believe that, for a variety of reasons, it is inevitable that India and Pakistan should draw closer to each other, or else they will come into conflict. There is no middle way, for we have known each other too long to be indifferent neighbors. I believe indeed that in the present context of the world India must develop a closer union with many other neighboring countries. But all this does not mean any desire to strangle or compel Pakistan. Compulsion there can never be, and an attempt to disrupt Pakistan would recoil to India's disadvantage. If we had wanted to break Pakistan, why did we agree to the partition? It was easier to prevent it than to try to do so now, after all that has happened. There is no going back in history. As a matter of fact, it is to India's advantage that Pakistan should be a secure and prosperous state with which we can develop close and friendly relations. If today by any chance I were offered the reunion of India and Pakistan, I would decline it for obvious reasons. I do not want to carry the burden of Pakistan's great problems. I have enough of my own. Any closer association must come out of a normal process, and in a friendly way which does not end Pakistan as a state, but makes it an equal part of a larger union in which several countries might be associated.

I have spoken of Pakistan because that subject must be in your minds and you would like to know what our attitude towards it is. Your minds are probably in a fluid state at present, not knowing which way to look and what to do. All of us have to be clear about our basic allegiance to certain ideas. Do we believe in a national state which includes people of all religions and shades of opinion and is essentially secular as a state, or do we believe in the religious, theocratic conception of a state which regards people of other faiths as somebody beyond the pale? That is an odd question to ask, for the idea of a religious or theocratic state was given up by the world some centuries ago and has no place in the mind of the modern man. And yet the question has to be put in India today, for many of us have tried to jump back to a past age. I have no doubt that whatever our individual answers may be, it is not possible for us to go back to a conception that the world has outlived and that is completely out of tune with modern conceptions. As far as India is concerned, I can speak with some certainty. We shall proceed on secular and national lines in keeping with the powerful trends towards internationalism. Whatever confusion the present may contain, in the future, India will be a land, as in the past, of many faiths equally honored and respected, but of one national outlook, not, I hope, a narrow nationalism living in its own shell, but rather the tolerant creative nationalism which, believing in itself and the genius of its people, takes full part in the establishment of an international order. The only ultimate aim we can have is that of one world. That seems a far cry today with warring groups and preparations for and shouting of World War III. Yet, despite all this shouting, that is the only aim that we can keep in view, for the alternative to world cooperation is world disaster.

We must cultivate this broad outlook and not be led away by the narrowness of others into becoming narrow in spirit and outlook ourselves. We have had enough of what has been called communalism in this country, and we have tasted of its bitter and poisonous fruit. It is time that we put an end to it. For my part I do not like the intrusion of this communal spirit anywhere, and least of all in educational institutions. Education is meant to free the spirit of man and not to imprison it in set frames. I do not like this university being called the Muslim University just as I do not like the Benares University to be called the Hindu University. This does not mean that a university should not specialize in particular cultural subjects and studies. I think it is right that this university should lay special stress on certain aspects of Islamic thought and culture.

I want you to think about those problems and come to your conclusions. These conclusions cannot be forced upon you except to some extent, of course, by the compulsion of events which none of us can ignore. Do not think that you are outsiders here, for you are as much flesh and blood of India as anyone else, and you have every right to share in what India has to offer. But those who seek rights must share in the obligations also. Indeed, if the duties and obligations are accepted, then rights follow by themselves. I invite you as free citizens of free India to play your role in the building of this great country and to be sharers, in common with others, in the triumphs and setbacks alike that may come our way. The present with all its unhappiness and misery will pass. It is the future that counts, more especially to the young, and it is that future that beckons to you. How will you answer that call?

■

INDIA—OLD AND NEW

India is a curious mixture of an amazing diversity and an abiding unity. It has been fashioned by the initial urge of the Indian people at the dawn of history which has persisted through the ages and which has given them a certain individuality; it has also been molded by repeated impacts from outside. Throughout this long period of history, people have come to India from abroad and influenced their thinking and the ways of living of the Indian people, thus producing a composite culture which has yet been based on the initial urge that carried our people forward. Today, there is the powerful impact of the industrialized West, and India herself is becoming rapidly an industrial nation absorbing science and technology. There can be no doubt that this new urge for industrialization or the adoption of modern techniques will succeed and change the face of India. How far this will affect what might be called the basic individuality and uniqueness of India is a question which the future alone can answer....

But the fascinating question for all of us, not only for Indians but also for others, is what the final outcome will be in this conflict between the past and the changing present. There can be no doubt that India will be industrialized and will take on progressively more and more the appearance of a modern industrialized society. In doing so she will shed many of her superstitions and past practices and develop a new dynamism, as indeed she is doing today. But I doubt very much if this change will result in her losing her individuality, which has been her traditional feature throughout her history. Indeed, it would be a pity if she lost her uniqueness and individuality and became merely a copy of the industrialized West....

India has always seemed to me to have broadly more the feminine qualities than the masculine. Of course, masculine qualities

are there and have played an important part in her history. Nevertheless, the feminine qualities seem to me to predominate. Essentially she is gentle and peaceful even though on occasions she
may indulge in brutal and callous behavior. That is why I think
that Indian women, from whatever part of the country one may
select them, represent the essence of India more, perhaps, than
the men. India's women have excelled in her history in many of the
masculine qualities, even in war. But essentially they have remained
feminine. We have today brilliant women scholars in mathematics
and physics. And yet they do not lose their feminineness.

By the coming of modern techniques and industrialization both
rural and, even more so, urban, India is changing fast. I have described the India of today as being in the bicycle age. I have done
so because the bicycle is now everywhere to be seen in the villages. If I address a public meeting in a rural area, thousands of
people come to it on bicycles. It is perhaps a greater change to
take to the bicycle from the bullock cart than the automobile from
the bicycle. Yet the bullock cart persists just as primitive ploughs
persist at the same time as modern ploughs and tractors. The curious thing about India is the persistence of the old and the new at
the same time; all the centuries seem to be represented in the India of today. There does not seem to be any obvious conflict between them. They co-exist, though undoubtedly the past and its
methods are giving place to the new.

This concept of co-existence, in the political sphere, is thus basic to Indian thinking. It is not an outcome of some balancing feat
of today. It fits in with the basic philosophy that has come down to
us. We have not been, broadly speaking, a proselytizing people.
We accept other religions and faiths tolerantly. We do not think
that our view must necessarily prevail over others. There are
many aspects of truth, and how can we presume to limit it to one
particular aspect which appeals to us?

The political revolution which led to the independence of India
was a major event in our life. And yet it was not quite complete till
the French and Portuguese enclaves in India became parts of independent India. It is only now when these enclaves have become absorbed in India that the political revolution is complete.

Indian nationalism, however, had always a broader basis than
the achievement of freedom for India. Even as India had been the
classic land for modern imperialism, the freedom of India was looked
upon by us as a forerunner of the freedom of all other colonial

territories. Also, our nationalism had an economic aspect. We have been too powerfully influenced by the poverty and economic backwardness of India to think of political changes only. Inevitably, being an agricultural country, to begin with our agrarian policy absorbed our attention. This resulted in the abolition of landlords and the creation of peasant proprietors linked together by the cooperative movement. In industry we were inevitably led to state-owned or cooperative industries. Even though we gave freedom to the private sector in industry, our broad outlook was governed by the dominance of the public sector, and the progressive growth of a socialist pattern of society.

To this end we have fashioned our Five Year Plans. Industrialization has become essential in order to get rid of our poverty and unemployment, and the base of this is the development of heavy industries and the training of our people. Mass education, in addition to specialized and technical education, has grown greatly in recent years, and is likely to cover the entire school-going population soon.

The measure of our general progress can be seen by the marked progress made in the average age of the expectation of life. Previous to Independence this was thirty-two; now it is forty-eight, in spite of the vast growth in our population. This is not only due to better health services and the eradication of some widespread diseases such as malaria, but also to the consumption of more and better food.

Perhaps the most revolutionary feature in India today is the spread of what is called Panchayati Raj in the rural areas. This has led to the decentralization of authority and giving of greater power and resources to the village organizations. Also, there is a great spread of the cooperative movement. Primarily this is meant to better our agriculture and to encourage various development schemes in the rural areas. But, in the final analysis, it is aimed at the improvement of the individual and making him more self-reliant. Democracy is thus spreading down to the hundreds of millions of our people in the villages, and the old curse of officialdom is lessening.

To us in India this is a fascinating and absorbing spectacle. I believe it is important to the rest of the world too at a time when authoritarian and military rule is playing an important part in many parts of the world, especially in Asia and Africa. It is significant that in India we are proceeding on democratic lines and doing so with a large measure of success. We are not only industrializing the country through democratic processes, but also, at the same time, trying to maintain the unique features in Indian philosophy and way of life and the individuality of India. Thus, we believe we shall serve the Indian people best and perhaps the rest of the world also.

■

SYNTHESIS IS OUR TRADITION

To endeavor to understand and describe the India of today would be the task of a brave man. To describe tomorrow's India would verge on rashness.

What is India? That is a question which has come back again and again to my mind. The early beginnings of our history filled me with wonder. It was the past of a virile and vigorous race with a questing spirit and an urge for free inquiry and, even in its earliest known period, giving evidence of a mature and tolerant civilization. Accepting life and its joys and burdens, it was ever searching for the ultimate and the universal. It built up a magnificent language, Sanskrit, and through this language, its arts and architecture, it sent its vibrant message to far countries. It produced the Upanishads, the Gita and the Buddha.

Hardly any language in the world has probably played that vital part in the history of a race which Sanskrit has. It was not only the vehicle of the highest thought and some of the finest literature, but it became the uniting bond for India, in spite of its political divisions. The *Ramayana* and the *Mahabharata* were woven into the texture of millions of lives in every generation for thousands of years. I have often wondered, if our race forgot the Buddha, the Upanishads and the great epics, what then will it be like! It would be uprooted and would lose the basic characteristics which have clung to it and given it distinction throughout these long ages. India would cease to be India.

Gradually, deterioration set in. Thought lost its freshness and became stale, and the vitality and exuberance of youth gave place to crabbed age. Instead of the spirit of adventure there came lifeless routine, and the broad and exciting vision of the world was cabined and confined and lost in caste divisions, narrow social customs and ceremonials. Even so, India was vital enough to absorb the streams of people that flowed into her mighty ocean of humanity and she never quite forgot the thoughts that had stirred her in the days of her youthful vigor.

Subsequently, India was powerfully influenced by the coming of Islam and Muslim invasions. Western colonial powers followed, bringing a new type of domination and a new colonialism and, at the same time, the impact of fresh ideas and of the industrial civilization that was growing up in Europe. This period culminated, after a long struggle, in Independence and now we face the future with all this burden of the past upon us and the confused dreams and stirrings of the future that we seek to build.

We have all these ages represented in us and in our country today. We have the growth of nuclear science and atomic energy in India, and we also have the cowdung age. In the tumult and confusion of our time, we stand facing both ways, forward to the future and backwards to the past, being pulled in both directions. How can we resolve this conflict and evolve a structure for living which fulfills our material needs and, at the same time, sustains our mind and spirit? What new ideals or old ideals varied and adapted to the new world can we place before our people, and how can we galvanize the people into wakefulness and action?

For the present, in India we are rightly absorbed in the Five Year Plans and in a tremendous effort to raise our people's living standards. Economic progress is essential and a prerequisite for any other type of advance. But a doubt creeps into our minds. Is this by itself enough or is something else to be added on to it? The welfare state is a worthwhile ideal, but it may well be rather drab. The examples of states which have achieved that objective bring out new problems and difficulties, which are not solved by material advance alone or by a mechanical civilization. Whether religion is necessary or not, a certain faith in a worthwhile ideal is essential to give substance to our lives and to hold us together.

Change is essential, but continuity is also necessary. The future has to be built on the foundations laid in the past and in the present. To deny the past and break with it completely is to uproot ourselves and, sapless, dry up. It was the virtue of Gandhiji to keep his feet firmly planted in the rich traditions of our race and our soil and, at the same time, to function on the revolutionary plane. Above all, he laid stress on truth and peaceful means.

Thus, he built on old foundations, and at the same time, oriented the structure towards the future.

When Islam came to India in the form of political conquest it brought conflict. It had a twofold effect. On the one hand, it encouraged the tendency of Hindu society to shrink still further within its shell; on the other, it brought a breath of fresh air and fresh ideals, and thus had a certain rejuvenating influence. Hindu society had become a closed system. The Muslims who came from outside brought their own closed system with them. Hence, the great problem that faced India during the medieval period was how these two closed systems, each with its strong roots, could develop a healthy relationship. Wise rulers like Akbar and others realized that the only hope for the future lay in some kind of harmony being established.

The philosophy and the world outlook of the old Hindus was amazingly tolerant; and yet they had divided themselves up into numerous separate caste groups and hierarchies. The Muslims had to face a new problem, namely how to live with others as equals. In other countries where they had gone, their success was so great that this problem did not really arise. They came into conflict with Christendom and through hundreds of years the problem was never solved. In India, slowly a synthesis was developed. But before this could be completed, other influences came into play.

The new liberal thought of the West and industrial processes began to affect the mind and life of India. A new nationalism developed, which was inevitably against colonialism and sought independence, and yet which was being progressively affected by the new industrial civilization as well as the language, literature and ways of the West.

Ram Mohun Roy came, seeking some kind of a synthesis between old India and modern trends. Vivekananda brought back something of the vigor of old Indian thought and dressed it in a modern garb. Political and cultural movements grew up and culminated in Gandhiji and Rabindranath Tagore.

In Europe there had been a fierce conflict between science and traditional religion, and the cosmology of Christianity did not fit in at all with scientific theories. Science did not produce that sense of conflict in India and Indian philosophy could easily accept it without doing any vital injury to its basic conceptions. In India, as elsewhere, two forces developed—the growth of nationalism and the urge for social justice. Socialism and Marxism became the symbol of this urge for social justice and, apart from their scientific content, had a tremendous emotional appeal for the masses....

In India we have had most distressing spectacles of conflict based on provincialism or linguism. In the main, it is the conflict of class interests that poses problems today, and in such cases vested interests are not easy to displace. Yet we have seen in India powerful vested interests like those of the old princes and of the big jagirdars, talukdars and zamindars being removed by peaceful methods, even though that meant a break-up of a well-established system which favored a privileged few. While, therefore, we must recognize that there is class conflict, there is no reason why we should not deal with it through these peaceful methods. They will only succeed, however, if we have a proper objective in view, clearly understood by the people.

We have deliberately laid down as our objective a socialist pattern of society. Personally I think that the acquisitive society, which is the base of capitalism, is no longer suited to the present age. We have to evolve a higher order more in keeping with modern trends and conditions and involving not so much competition but much greater cooperation. We have accepted socialism as our goal not only because it seems to us right and beneficial but because there is no other way for the solution of our economic problems. It is sometimes said that rapid progress cannot take place by peaceful and democratic methods. I do not accept this proposition. Indeed, in India today any attempt to discard democratic methods would lead to disruption and would thus put an end to any immediate prospect of progress....

What will emerge from the labor and the tumults of the present generation? I cannot say what will tomorrow's India be like. I can only express my hopes and wishes. I want India to advance on the material plane—to fulfill her Five Year Plans to raise the standards of living of her vast population; I want the narrow conflicts of today in the name of religion or caste, language or province, to cease, and a classless and casteless society to be built up where every individual has full opportunity to grow according to his worth and ability. In particular, I hope that the curse of caste will be ended, for there cannot be either democracy or socialism on the basis of caste.

Four great religions have influenced India—two emerging from her own thought, Hinduism and Buddhism, and two coming from abroad but establishing themselves firmly in India, Christianity and Islam. Science today challenges the old concept of religion. But if religion deals not with dogmas and ceremonials, but rather with the higher things of life, there should be no conflict with science or *inter se* between religions. It might be the high privilege of India to help in bringing out this synthesis. That would be in India's ancient tradition inscribed on Asoka's edicts.

■

NATIONAL SOLIDARITY

Why, indeed, should we have to take a pledge of solidarity? Solidarity is a natural thing which the people of every nation must possess because the whole concept of a nation is that the people hold together, that the people have many common features, that the people attain freedom and retain it, and the people realize that in the freedom of the nation and in the progress of the nation lies their progress and advancement; and if anything ill happens to the nation, that is an ill to them all. If in a country there is no proper solidarity among its people, that country is doomed. It will go to pieces. It cannot fight the many dangers that beset it. If a country is united, if there is solidarity among the people, then no amount of arms can conquer it.

So, while we prepare for strengthening our army and air force, all of us must always remember that real strength will come from the unity of the country and from the hard work that we put in. We possess, I think, that basic solidarity in our people. We saw that at the moment of danger last year. When the Chinese invaded our country, suddenly the people rose to the occasion and pledged themselves to meet this menace with all their might.

That was a heartening sight, but some time later when the immediate danger seemed to have passed, when there was no actual fighting going on, many of our people relapsed into complacency and started forgetting the menace and the dangers, although they were still there. They lost themselves in mutual squabbles, complaints, slogans and the like. That shows that although we are basically united and there is something in us which makes us rise when danger threatens us, we soften and go back to our petty thoughts and conflicts when the threat does not appear to be so obvious.

We have the Chinese menace before us. Even before this menace occurred, we had, and continue to have, the real menace of poverty. We have to fight that as stoutly and as bravely as we fight any enemy who invades our country. We can build our nation only when we build our people and make them happy and contented.

Therefore, this habit of ours to slacken, when no immediate danger threatens us, is bad. We must get over it. We talk of solidarity and unity, and yet we know that in our country, behind this certain feeling of solidarity and unity, there are many forces which are fissiparous and which interested people use for separating us. It is unfortunate that some people forget the essential unity of the country by encouraging these forces.

Sometimes religion is employed in this behalf; sometimes caste, sometimes language; sometimes there is conflict between states and so on.

We are a great country, a country with enormous variety, a variety that is good. There is no reason why we should be regimented and be made to look like one person. We should keep the variety, but that variety is only good when we are united and there is an essential unity behind it.

I am not asking you to forget this rich variety, but I am asking you to remember that this variety itself, along with everything that we value, will go if we do not remember that unity is essential. That unity is not a superficial unity on the map or of some constitution, but the unity of heart and mind, which makes us feel like a large family which has to be defended, which has to be worked for and which will lead us to cooperate with one another.

■

■ PART TWO ■

■ MODERNIZATION AND ITS DISCONTENTS ■

13

A.K. SARAN

A.K. Saran belongs to the forefront of sociologists and social theorists in post-independence India. He began his teaching and research career at Lucknow University in the 1960s. Subsequently, he served as professor of sociology at the University of Jodhpur, from which he retired in 1980. He has been a visiting fellow at Harvard University, at the Indian Institute of Advanced Study, Shimla, and at the Indian Institute of Education, Pune.

Among his publications is a book he edited with V.B. Singh entitled *Industrial Labour in India* (New York: Asia Publishing House, 1960). The following essay is taken from L.P. Vidyarthi et al., eds, *Gandhi and the Social Sciences*, New Delhi, Bookhive Publishers, 1970, pp. 47–62.

GANDHI'S THEORY OF SOCIETY AND OUR TIMES

Gandhi is a world–historical figure. Though he refused to formulate a religious or philosophical system, he did stand throughout his life for certain ideas, which are nothing if not of universal significance. In order to see this clearly, let us review very briefly the nature and context of the challenge to which his life and thought were a dedicated response.

Within the limited scope of this paper, it is not possible to begin at the beginning of Gandhi's political career in South Africa; we cannot even review his role in the Indian Independence movement in any systematic way. All that can be done is to indicate some salient features of India's freedom struggle at the time Gandhi entered the scene as a major figure after World War I.

The Indian reform movement was a number of different things at the same time. It was a reform, a renaissance, and a nationalist movement. At the same time it was also a movement for religious revivalism under the name of Hindu nationalism. At the time Gandhi came on the Indian political scene, it was dominated by Gokhale and Tilak: Gokhale [Gopal Krishna Gokhale, 1866–1915] leading the reformist and secularist or non-religious form of nationalism and Tilak [Bal Gangadhar Tilak, 1856–1920] leading the religio-social revivalist interpretation of the nationalist movement. The tension that developed between Gokhale and Tilak as leaders of the Indian freedom struggle, reflected something far deeper than a clash of personalities. It signified the essential incompatibility between the idea of nationalism and Hinduism, and for that matter, Islam. In other words, while Hindu nationalism or Islamic nationalism is a contradiction in terms, both nationalism and Hinduism had necessarily to be emphasized by the anti-imperialist forces in the Indian political and social movement.

At one level, Hinduism and Hindu society are inseparable and hence to strengthen or weaken the one has profound significance for the other. Now, Hindu society being a caste society, an outcaste, though a Hindu is really an outsider and hence he can be easily lured into other religions. For this reason certain reforms became necessary and urgent, for Hinduism at this time was being threatened not only by Christianity and Islam, but also by Western rationalism. But this reform of Hinduism had at the same time to be a kind of revivalism, for that was the only way to unify, to get a collective identity and to rouse and gear the society to act against foreign rule. In other words, in the specific historical context of India under modern Western Imperial rule, reformist and modernist forces could work only within very great limitations. Thus, Gokhale's correct non-religious interpretation of nationalism was bound to develop serious inner tensions in the Indian situation for, given the history of Hindu–Muslim relations, it was impossible to forge a truly national identity in terms of a common historical past. Hence, there was not only the appeal, but a kind of irrefutability in Tilak's idea of nationalism as the completion of S[h]ivaji's [1627–1680] task—an interpretation, however, which can have meaning only within Hinduism and must be rejected by the Muslims. This inner schism in the freedom-cum-nationalist movement of India has persisted all the way down up to date. After Gokhale and Tilak, the two inconsistent aspects of the nationalist movement were represented by Nehru and Patel [Sardar Vallabhai Patel, 1875–1950], and even though Patel died in 1950, the ideological forces which he represented are very much alive and strong.

The immediate successor of both Gokhale and Tilak was, of course, Gandhi. How did he heal, or at any rate, deal with this inner schism?

Gandhi's response to this crucial challenge was threefold. He radically changed the basis, the scope and the nature of the Indian freedom movement.

Basis: With Gandhi the Indian National Congress became a mass party. At any rate, it ceased to be confined to upper and middle educated classes.

Scope: He universalized the scope of Indian politics, emphasizing the world–historical character of the Indian struggle as representing the struggle of the oppressed and the exploited against all oppressors and exploiters. He thought of himself as fighting for a better world order and not simply for a free India. Indeed, until comparatively late in his political career, he did not emphasize so much the freedom of India, as he did a reformed British Commonweal in which India could be a self-respecting and valuable partner. In his own view, the Indian movement was not national but universal–human—one global in scope and paralleling the Marxist movement.

Nature: Gandhi changed the nature of Indian politics by spiritualizing it. By this I refer to the Gandhian principles of Truth and Non-violence as the basis of social order and the instruments of socio-political dynamics. In other words, Gandhi stood for the substitution of power politics by goodness politics in terms of his doctrine of the integrality and symmetry of ends and means. Gandhi repudiated the idea that morality is simply an individual affair; on the contrary, he emphasized the idea that a moral and spiritual social order was a *sine qua non* for human life at its proper level. Accordingly, he firmly believed in and straightforwardly advocated a socio-economic order and a political system based on the traditional virtues: *satya* (truth), *ahimsa* (non-violence), *aparigraha* (non-possession), *asteya* (non-covetousness), and *brahmacharya* (self-control of the senses and, particularly, the sex impulse).

The significance of this threefold Gandhian revolution can hardly be exaggerated. It is crucial not only for understanding the nature, the success and the failure of the Indian freedom movement but also, and no less important, for understanding the relevance of Gandhism to contemporary India and the world. Suffer me to offer a brief analysis of this Gandhian revolution:

First, by emphasizing the people, their needs and aspirations, he at one stroke cut through the Gokhale–Tilak or the rationalism/tradition, or the reform/revival antitheses. To the masses, Hindu or Muslim or Sikh or Buddhist or Christian, religion was real and meaningful: thus, by emphasizing the truth in Hinduism and Islam, indeed in all religions, and by extending political thought and action from the classes to the common people, the peasantry, he modified, in a major way, the nature of both Indian nationalism and Hindu revivalism. He sought to accomplish the dual transformation by taking the religiousness and misery of the Indian common people as the given basis for a community of fate; the specific religious differences between Hinduism and Islam he attempted to resolve by a transcendent religion, or better, spiritual catholicism. In effect, Gandhi sought to minimize the twin problems of unity and identity of India which, he rightly thought, were at the root of the tension between nationalism and revivalism. His method was to universalize the perspective for the identity problem, so that the specific burden of India's history will not be felt as a dead weight. This was reinforced by the effect of his second revolution, namely, the universalization of the freedom struggle, making his ideal essentially the foundation of a new stage in human history. It thus undermines the idea of nationalism which is both parochial and retrograde when viewed independently of its colonial or anti-imperialist context.

The viability of the second revolution depends in fact on his third revolution: the spiritualization of politics. This is the foundation of Gandhi's thought. If there can be a goodness politics, then the idea of nation states can be used creatively: in the absence of a spiritual social-political order, as distinguished from a religious one, the concept of nation must be maintained for the solution of the identity problem, if a universal context is not found, that is, one that will replace the imperial context. Religion and communism have been so far the supranational context for unity and identity. In his idea of spiritualization of politics Gandhi seeks to provide a renewal and a reinterpretation of the religious context which will at the same time supersede the communist context. He attempted to do this by going beyond both the modern Western theory of the state as the embodiment of the will of the people, and the Hindu theory of state as the embodiment of the *dharma*. He thought of non-violence and truth as the foundation of state as well as of social order, interpreting these as universal spiritual principles independent of all formulated religions. The idea, however, led him ultimately to the theory of a stateless society—a development that paralleled the Marxist theory of the withering away of the state. Though Gandhi was never a Marxist, this parallelism is not a mere chance convergence: it is inherent in all universalization of politics.

Another concept that Gandhi evolved in his effort to provide a non-Marxian solution to the inherent problems of modern political–social theory is that of trusteeship. In Gandhian thinking it has two fundamental roles: socio-economically, the concept of trusteeship is designed to prevent a productive society from becoming acquisitive and exploitative, and politically it is meant to resolve a major difficulty in the modern Western theory of democracy. The difficulty is this. The relationship between the state (ruler) and the people (ruled) in a democratic socio-political system ought not to be that of guardian and ward, doctor–patient, educator–educated. However, in modern democratic societies, this is precisely the nature of the relation between the state and the people. Indeed, the key institution of modern democratic process, viz., leadership may, strictly speaking, be said to be undemocratic, a point often indirectly conceded through opposition to what is called the cult of personality and the proposals for collective leadership. Indeed, the more technologically advanced a society is, the more have the people to be managed, the greater the need for protection, and thus the relation between the people and the state tends to be increasingly that of ward and guardian.

The Gandhian theory of trusteeship tries to resolve this dilemma by replacing the concept of representation by that of trusteeship. However, for this change of concepts to have more than a technological significance it is necessary that the idea of trusteeship be an organic part of the Gandhian theory of a society based both individually and collectively on the virtues of self-suffering and non-possession. This approach was profound, broad-based, farsighted, and a failure. Gandhi himself was the most self-aware, anguished and undespairing witness to the grandeur and misery of his life's work: the grandeur, transfer of power to India, largely through a non-violent freedom struggle; the misery, the communal disharmony culminating in the partition of India.

Gandhi wanted two things: the restoration of a spiritual or normal social order in India and, by extension, in the world, and second, to free India from foreign rule; this freedom according to Gandhi was a pre-condition for his first goal.

He did not succeed. For Gandhi the Partition robbed India's freedom of its full truth and the socio-historical process culminating in the division and the post-independence Indian society signified the failure of his main mission: the spiritual renewal of man. Too saintly to lose faith and too great to feel frustrated, Gandhi nevertheless knew that his vision had suffered a great setback; indeed, he knew it with a clarity rare among the great.

If Gandhi was simply a survival produced by the liberal, civilized British rule in India, if his cardinal spiritual quest and mission were in the last analysis a clever Hindu's embellishments of his political struggle and hence a distraction for the social scientist, if Gandhi was just a parochial figure trying to do something good to the Hindu character under colonial rule—in a word, if the failure of the Gandhian idea are synonymous, then Gandhi's life and thought are irrelevant to our times. And if I, for one, believed this, I would see no reason to be interested in talking at all about Gandhi or Gandhism.

If, however, the Gandhian revolutions about which we have been speaking constitute a real revolution with world–historical significance, if Gandhi was *not* just a colonial leader who happened to achieve some kind of world fame, but, on the contrary, is a universal figure with relentless and steadfast concern with the destiny of man, then the central question raised by Gandhi, his thought, life and work is the question of its relevance to our times, and this is nothing else or no less than this: Has the voice of sanity any chance at all against the dark, demonic powers of our times?

It is a terrible question. Apart from the fact that like everybody else I am deeply involved in the question, I have no competence to answer it. What I have to say in the rest of the time available to me is nothing more than an analysis of the question itself. Let me repeat, the observations that follow make no claim to answering the question that has just been put. All I attempt to do is to explore a little the implications of this question from the Gandhian stand-point. I said that to ask the question of the contemporary relevance of Gandhism is really to ask the question about society and sur-vival. To see this, and to understand the question of Gandhism's contemporary relevance in its proper perspective, it is essential to speak briefly about the Gandhian vision of a normal society—the kind of society for which Gandhi lived and died.

Gandhi did not believe in the co-existence of moral man and immoral society. In fact, one of his most important contributions to political thought and action is the idea that ways of moral ac-tion and resistance could be transferred from the individual to the collective plane and be used as powerful forms of political action. Indeed, the technique of *satyagraha* (fast, civil disobedience, *dharna*, roughly sit-in and other variants) presuppose this basic idea. Gandhi believed that society could be and should be moral. Did he also hold that man as an individual needed a moral society in order to be moral himself? I think this is a fundamental point in understanding Gandhi's sociological thought. Let us, therefore, ponder [over] it a moment.

Gandhi was a great believer in the virtues of compromise, not only in the political but in almost all spheres; it was part of his political theory and practice to lay the greatest stress on sincerity and the purity of the personal lives of every political actor. In a more general way too, he gave all possible emphasis and atten-tion to political participants as persons. Looking at his thought and practice from this point of view, it may look as if Gandhi did not rule out the possibility of moral men in a not-so-moral society. In further support of such an interpretation of Gandhi's thought, it could be pointed out that the ultimate orientation of Gandhi's po-litical action was towards effecting a change of heart of the other party. Both his thinking and the forms of political action that he developed imply, it may be argued, a cumulative process of social change.

All this is correct. However, I would like to argue that it does not invalidate my thesis that Gandhi did not think that individually man could be moral in a non-moral, immoral or unjust society, that is, he did not believe in the Niebuhrian antithesis of moral man and immoral society.[1] I want to show that in any analysis of his thought and work the co-existence (of moral man and im-moral society) theory would be seriously misleading.

Gandhi did place man as person in the forefront. But this was only a powerful and realistic way of focusing attention on what may be called the principle of normalcy. A normal society is simply a society. Opposed to it are what have been called mass-society and mass-man—and mass, or what is currently called pop culture. The mass and the society used to be contrary to each other. They have been hyphenated today. A society has an intelligible order and an overall purpose. A mass lacks both. It follows that members of a society have their own place and function in it. Not so in a mass.

A society whose members are humans is a human society. When man is called a social animal, the reference obviously is to his innate love of order and purpose and not to any 'herd' instinct or some 'natural' inclination for the company of his own kind, for these propensities are by no means exclusively human. Man, unlike many other animals, cannot suffer to live merely as a unit, for the love of order and purpose are given to him in his self-consciousness.

Those who talk of mass-society certainly recognize the distinction between mass and society. They are often aware—implicitly, if not always explicitly—that mass undermines society. They understand that the mass-man is not human—at least not fully human. They had learnt to admire certain things, certain states of affairs, certain states of mind which they conceptualized as civilization. They now realize that the mass will destroy this civilization more effectively, in fact, than any barbarian onslaught could ever do. They are not unaware that the barbarian has entered the soul. Somewhere at some time modern man was lured into the magician's bargain: give up your soul, get power over everything in return. Anxiously aware of the deadening influence of this demonic deal, modern thinkers are nonetheless too much under its spell to believe in the possibility of its total repudiation. Through a variety of ideas, they search for a synthesis of mass and society, that is, of the anti-human and the human: they are exploring the possibility of a mass that will have just enough of the social to save it from withering away.

Gandhi wanted to break the spell. He would disown and destroy this diabolic bond. Herein lies the basic difference between Gandhi's critique of modern society and those of most other modern thinkers. And what is even more important, this also defines the difference between Gandhi and Gandhism in India today.

Gandhi was against 'mass-society'. He was uncompromisingly opposed to modern industrial technological society and civilization. He knew what forces, what propensities underlie such a socio-cultural system; and unlike most contemporary thinkers and leaders, he remained relentlessly consistent and thoroughgoing in his opposition to these forces. He went to the root of the matter and attacked the very concept of a rising standard of living. He could see most clearly what this really meant, viz., a continually rising standard of consumption even to the point when rapid, built-in obsolescence and wanton destruction become the controlling principles of the economy. In opposition to this economic theory, he boldly set up the theory of *aparigraha* (non-possession, non-acquisitiveness) and the minimization of wants. The principle of *aparigraha*, it is to be noted, is one that emphasizes the present and hence it severely limits the cumulative process and thus undermines a capitalist as well as a state-planned 'socialist' production system. Indeed, the ideas of minimal wants and of non-possession presuppose a world outlook that is quite incompatible with the currently accepted ideology for a planned society.

It is in this context that Gandhi's emphasis on the individual person should be understood. From the Gandhian point of view, the modern industrial–technological mass-society is really a collectivity of sub-humans. Gandhi thought steadfastly in terms of a society of men: a society in which there will be no mechanical equality, but at the same time nobody will be forced to live at a sub-human level; a society in which every member will be a full member according to his own place and specific competence.

Contrary to a prevalent interpretation, I think that Gandhi did not believe in the individual as the source of social change. Absolutely believing in God and providential guidance, Gandhi thought that man could only be an instrument of God's will. He emphasized purity of heart and mind so that one could attain to the highest point of human creativity and get a correct intimation of the divine will and act efficiently according to it. Gandhi believed that a supra-human order was the common ground of both man and society. Given this frame of reference, the antithesis of man and society cannot arise, unless one held, as Gandhi *did not*, that a social order could not be built on moral and metaphysical principles, like truth and non-violence. In fact, a whole social order based on truth and non-violence—and not merely individual truthfulness and non-violence—is the very cornerstone of Gandhian sociology.

In summary form, the Gandhian socio-economic system can be described in terms of the following ideas and principles:

(1) Means and ends should be seen as parts of a whole which has a transcendental reference.
(2) The production system should be based on the ideal of progressive and regulated minimization of needs (and not on that of multiplication of wants).
(3) The economy should be life-centered (and not one that is oriented to commodity production). This means that the socio-economic system should operate on the principle of a metaphysically grounded optimum (and not on the principle of maximization).
(4) Consequently, it is to be a non-exploitative economy based on simple and limited technology.
(5) Social and economic organization should be decentralized, based on the principle of optimum autonomy.
(6) Truth and non-violence should form the foundation of the political order.
(7) Satyagraha (the determined pursuit of truth or the right path) should be the chief form of political vigilance and protest.
(8) The social and the economic systems should be hierarchical, non-competitive and non-acquisitive, based on the principle of trusteeship. Ideally, it should be a stateless society.

What has been the impact on our times of Gandhian economics and sociology, or better, of Gandhi's life and thought as a whole? The question has two parts, the first about the role of Gandhi's ideas in the independence movement of India and the second about the relevance of Gandhism to Free India and to our times in general.

The role of Gandhi and his ideas in the Indian freedom movement is greatly important; however, to determine the precise nature of his role and its relation with other factors and forces operating to shape the Indian freedom movement, is by no means easy. It requires difficult and careful analysis. However, it must be pointed out here that even though throughout his life Gandhi thought and worked in the context of a relentless struggle against imperialist forces, the question of the contemporary relevance of his thought is not bound by this historical context. In other words, the question of the validity of Gandhism is inseparable from that of its universality.

I say this for two closely related reasons. First, Gandhi's thought and work developed in the context of an encounter between India and the West, tradition and modernity, and his stand was not simply that the Indians should not be forced to accept Western civilization through British rule; much more important was his conviction that the modern industrial–technological civilization is not good for man, Eastern or Western. He increasingly made India's freedom struggle something subsidiary to a struggle and movement for a normal world society. Second, the principles on which he based his political action, as well as those in terms of which he constructed his vision of free India were universal by their very nature; and Gandhi always made it clear that he did not regard his fundamental ideas as merely matters of policy or suitable strategy in the Indian freedom struggle.

To return to the question of the impact of Gandhism. In my opinion, Gandhi's life and thought were completely repudiated by independent India. I am aware that Nehru often denied this but I do not know what he was talking about. If the present interpretation of the essentials of Gandhi's social, political, and economic thought is correct, the state-planned centralized industrial–technological society which India adopted as her goal, is quite contrary to Gandhi's vision of free India. As to the political order, non-violence and truth have not at all been accepted as its foundation. In fact, today there is a great deal of violence simply in running the government: much more than any democratic people should tolerate, whether or not they believe in non-violence. Gandhi would not have supported a government which needed this kind of violence as its sanction not only in extreme situations, but for its day-to-day running. And, in the so-called conquest of Goa, the Government of India explicitly, though unnecessarily, repudiated truth and non-violence as principles of state policy.

It is often said that Gandhi was not wholly uncompromising in his doctrine of non-violence, that he would make exceptions, that, in fact, he did not oppose the Kashmir war in 1947. Such a view can be a complete misunderstanding. I think it can be confidently stated that Gandhi made no exceptions whatsoever to his doctrine of truth and non-violence. A full defense of the above statement will need another paper; however, a brief explanation may be attempted here.

Non-violence sounds as if it were a negative concept, but it is not. It is violence that is negative in nature; for, essentially, every violent act or thought violates reality. All violence is fundamentally violence against reality. Non-violence is thus acceptance of reality as it is. This is why Gandhi always emphasized the equation—indeed, the essential synonymy—of non-violence and truth.

In the sphere of human relationship—leaving aside for the moment that of man–nature relationship—violence arises only when there is a failure of rational communication: it is one of the forms of infra-rational communication. So, in all such situations, instead of violence, Gandhi recommended without exception resort to non-violence. What does this mean? It means this: [...] when parties to a situation do not see the relevant reality in a mutually acceptable way, the believer in non-violence, that is one who wants to accept reality as it is, will voluntarily undertake to suffer for his vision of reality (that is, instead of trying to forcibly impose it on the other party, he will accept temporarily the other party's view of reality under protest and on pain of self-suffering). This will bring about a change of heart and mind in the other party, or in the sufferer, or in both, and thus a common vision of a reality will emerge, eliminating any imposition of a supervening reality by the use of superior physical force.

This implies that non-violence can only be an expression of the inner truth of the non-violent actor. Otherwise, his suffering cannot be said to be really voluntary, for if it (non-violence) is not the externalization of his inner vision, it can only be something forced upon him by external or even extraneous circumstances.

This is why Gandhi said that when non-violence does not express the inner truth of the person, it will be cowardly to stick to it. If the unity of truth and non-violence is disrupted and a choice is to be made between the two, Gandhi would be for truth. In other words, he preferred a straightforward and honest rejection of a fundamental principle to its half-hearted or insincere acceptance and lukewarm opportunistic or compulsive application.

By the dictum, rather kill than be a coward, Gandhi expressed his refusal to compromise with the purity of non-violence. He did not mean any approval of violence in assorted situations. This is why he stood steadfastly for a non-exploitative socio-economic order, for he understood perfectly well that violence is built into an exploitative social system. And holding fast to the doctrine of integrality of means and ends, he adhered throughout to the view that a technology-centered socio-economic system could not but be an exploitative society.

Do Vinoba Bhave [1895–1982] and his movement represent the Gandhian spirit today? I wish it were possible to answer this question with a plain 'yes' or 'no'. Unfortunately, the position is complicated. Even though in his vision of a normal human society Vinoba seems committed to the Gandhian principles, I think there are crucial differences between his thinking and that of Gandhi.

In his later thinking Vinoba has been inclined to emphasize the purely instrumental nature of technology and modern natural science. He distinguishes constructive and destructive types of technology and is really opposed only to the last type. He believes in the well-known argument that technology by itself is just a set of means; hence everything depends upon how and for what ends it is used. He also believes that man can develop the kind of spiritual power that can contain and control technology and technological power. He thinks that the Hindu tradition (in fact, all traditions) is not yet complete in its development. He hopes for a future development of metaphysics and religion which will be [a] synthesis of spirituality, science, and technology.

In this paper, I cannot examine this theory in any systematic manner. It may be pointed out, however, that Vinoba's thinking is inconsistent here, for it violates the principle of the integrality of means and ends which he does accept. In other words, Vinoba fails to see that a technological system is not a free gift from above or from the USA to be used in the chosen manner; it has to be produced by the society which uses it, and its *production*, apart from use, alters the nature of that society. A society based on the principles of the minimization of wants and non-possession is a society with a low level of technological development; it cannot be otherwise. By the same token, if one wants a Gandhian society, one has to be opposed to the development and production of technology beyond a certain fairly low level.

In talking about spirituality, natural science, and technology, we must remember that the essential (spiritual) question is not how and for what purpose technological power is to be used. The crucial question is: what kind of power and in what measure ought man to acquire it. It seems to me that Vinoba's views on modern natural science and technology are not sufficiently sensitive to the traditional principle that man's knowledge must never exceed his being.

The other fundamental departure from Gandhian principles is Vinoba's support for a government which bases itself on a fundamental negation of the principles of Gandhism and *sarvodaya*. Whether the revolution for which Vinoba is working should necessarily involve a large-scale non-violent movement aiming at the complete overthrow of the present government is an open question. In any case, it can certainly be argued that it is not the only alternative in the present situation. However, what cannot be justified, I think, is the open and positive support Vinoba gave to the government and the Indo–Pakistan War (1965). Nor is it possible to understand why Vinoba and other *sarvodaya* leaders have not yet straightforwardly rejected and opposed the government's socio-economic principles and plans.

I can only briefly touch upon the question of the impact of Gandhism on the contemporary Western world. I think the most important thing to note here is the general narrowness of the Western response. Gandhism calls for a radical revolution, for a complete transformation of man's thinking and way of life, social as well as individual. In a word, it aims at *metanoia*. But apart from the theoretical interest of certain European philosophers, like Arne Naess, the major Western interest in Gandhi, when it is not historical or aesthetic, is predominantly in Gandhian techniques that may be tried for resolving certain problems and tensions of the modern society for which local methods have been proving increasingly inadequate.

With Gandhism as a way of life, that is, with a Gandhian socio-economic system, the West so far has been concerned only rarely. By and large, its interest in Gandhism and non-violent techniques has been experimental in nature and approach.

By virtue of its all-embracing scope and radical nature, the Gandhian vision is an alternative to both world views: the liberal democratic and the Marxian. The one question about Gandhism and our times is, therefore, simply this: can Gandhism work as the new world-view? Is there a possibility of a radical change in the orientation and structure of contemporary society? Can we hope for *metanoia*?

Standing at the brink of an abyss, the next step lies not forward but backward. Did Gandhi then want to put the hands of the clock back? No, he wanted to set them to another noonday.

■

■ Note ■

[1] The reference is to Reinhold Niebuhr, *Moral Man and Immoral Society: A Study in Ethics and Politics*, New York, Scribner, 1932.

■

14

■ THOMAS PANTHAM ■

Born in 1938 in Kerala, Thomas Pantham was educated at St. Anselm's High School in Ajmer, and later at the M.S. University of Baroda where he obtained his doctorate in political science. He has been teaching at the M.S. University since 1966, serving recently for several years as departmental chair. He has held visiting fellowships at Princeton University, the University of Essex, the University of Heidelberg, and St. John's College in Cambridge (UK).

Among his publications are *Political Theories and Social Reconstruction: A Critical Survey of the Literature on India* (New Delhi: Sage, 1995), and *Political Parties and Democratic Consensus* (Delhi, Macmillan, 1976). With Kenneth L. Deutsch he has edited *Political Thought in Modern India* (New Delhi: Sage, 1986), and with Bhikhu Parekh *Political Discourse: Explorations in Indian and Western Political Thought* (New Delhi: Sage, 1987). The following essay is taken from Amal Ray et al., eds, *The Nehru Legacy: An Appraisal* (New Delhi: Oxford and IBH Publishers, 1991), pp. 171–92.

UNDERSTANDING NEHRU'S POLITICAL IDEOLOGY

I

Jawaharlal Nehru's intervention in the political thought and practice of our times has been interpreted differently by the liberal rationalists and the Marxist subalternists. According to the former, Nehru's political ideology is neither original nor autonomous as it is wholly derived from the political thought of European post-Enlightenment rationalism and industrial modernity.[1] The Marxist subalternists deny or de-emphasize the progressive character of Nehru's political ideology on the ground that it is simply a child or stepchild of the marriage of Reason and Capital—on the ground, in other words, that it is not an ideology of 'the violent struggle between classes' for the establishment of socialism.[2]

Against these interpretations, I shall try to show firstly that, though derived largely from the political thought of European post-Enlightenment modernity, Nehru's political ideology is an 'odd mixture' of liberalism, Marxism and Gandhism which has a radical transformative thrust against Western modernity. Nehru, in other words, as I shall try to show, regarded India's modernizing nationalism as inextricably linked with the radical transformation of Western modernity.[3] He perceived the need for a fusion of horizons between the scientific spirit of post-Enlightenment modernity and 'the deeper lessons of life, which have absorbed the minds of thinkers in *all* ages and in *all* countries.'[4] Secondly, I shall suggest that the implications of the 'relative autonomy' of the Nehruvian state from the imperialist reason of capital is not given adequate appreciation by his Marxist–subalternist critics.

II

According to the liberal–rationalists/structural–functionalists, Nehru was simply a 'modernizing elite', acting under the universal imperative of post-Enlightenment modernity, the justificatory ideology of which he simply borrowed from the modern Western tradition of political thought. The Nehruvian 'model' of nationalism and industrial modernity, in other words, are said to be cast in the Enlightenment's theory of progress, which was based on the eighteenth century West-European ideas about man, society and the good or happy life.

The philosophers of the Enlightenment, we are reminded, inaugurated modernity and set global, universal standards of progress for the whole of humanity by emancipating the individual and his reason from faith, custom and authority. They thereby paved the way for man's scientific knowledge of, and technical mastery over, physical nature and social life. The resultant industrial civilization was a universalizing civilization, respecting no territorial barriers. Nehru, like other 'modernizing elites' of the Third World, we are told, did not have to do any original political–ideological thinking; it had already been done for them by the philosophers of the European Enlightenment! The modernizing role of the former was simply to grasp and bring about the sociological or functional conditions of Western-type industrial modernity in their own societies. In other words, they were simply required to act under the universal imperative of modernization or Westernization. Given the compelling world-wide sweep of Western industrial modernity, the political–philosophical competences or persuasions of Nehru or any other Third World nationalist leader are said to be of no consequence. Adopting this liberal-optimist interpretive position, Ernest Gellner writes:

> It is not so much that the prophets of nationalism were not anywhere near the First Division, when it came to the business of thinking.... It is rather that these thinkers did not really make much difference. If one of them had fallen, others would have stepped into his place.... The quality of nationalist thought would hardly have been affected much by such substitutions. Their precise doctrines are hardly worth analyzing.[5]

According to this view, Nehru's contribution pertains to the 'political sociology' or 'political science' of modernization or development, and not to the intellectual activity of political thinking or political ideologizing. We are told that whatever their rhetoric, the so-called philosopher kings of the Third World 'all act as Westerners'! *All!*

The only innovativeness that the liberal–rationalists see in Nehru and the other nationalist leaders of the Third World is that they *reversed* the imperialist or colonial orientalism of the European or occidental powers; while the colonizing orientalist political ideology regarded the oriental as a passive object to be civilized by the active, occidental subject, Nehru and the other Third World nationalists are said to have merely reversed that orientalism by asserting and acting out the subjectivity of the oriental. The epistemological and philosophical categories of this newly proclaimed subjectivity of the Third World countries, we are told, are all borrowed from modern Western political philosophy. Hence according to the liberal–rationalists, while Nehru's 'role' as a modernizing or Westernizing elite may be a fit subject of study by the students of the political sociology or of the functionalist theory of political development, his political ideology is said to be wholly lacking in originality or creativity and therefore not worth even a mention in the study of political thought.

III

In this and the next sections, I shall attempt a review of aspects of Nehru's political thinking with a view to highlighting its essential tension between derivative–nationalist modernization and a complex of pre-modern/post-modern ideas.

Nehru saw important socio-historical differences between India and the modern West. He admired the scientific, technological and industrial advances of the latter and bemoaned their absence in the former. Lacking the scientific, technological and industrial advances of post-Enlightenment modernity, the Indian people, he felt, have remained poor, backward and subjugated.

Unlike the colonialist orientalists, Nehru does not attribute the poverty, backwardness and subjugation of the Indian people to their *human nature*; he attributes them rather to the rigid and progress-inhibiting social structures that have either evolved historically from within India or have been imposed from outside. It is important to stress Nehru's rejection of the imperialist–orientalist thesis of *essential differences in human nature* between India and the West; the differences for him are socio-historical, and not ontological or natural. According to him, both the oriental and occidental people share a common humanity and they can and must widen their horizons by learning from each others' socio-historical experiences. It is only from *this* perspective, he believes, that we can overcome racialism, cultural arrogance and structural oppression. Rejecting the thesis of 'essential difference between the East and West', Nehru writes:

> I do not understand the use of the words Orient and Occident, except in the sense that Europe and America are highly industrialized and Asia is backward in this respect. This industrialization is something new in the world's history.... There is no organic connection between Hellenic civilization and modern European and American civilization.[6]

Ridiculing the orientalist thesis that the backwardness and poverty of the Indian people are a consequence of their essential or ontological other-worldliness, Nehru writes:

> India, it is said, is religious, philosophical, speculative, metaphysical, unconcerned with this world, and lost in dreams of the beyond and the hereafter. So we are told, and perhaps those who tell us so would like India to remain plunged in thought and entangled in speculation, so that they might possess this world and the fullness thereof, unhindered by these thinkers, and take their joy of it.[7]

Nehru believed that the European Enlightenment and industrial modernity was a progressive step not only for Europe but for the entire world. For him, in other words, post-Enlightenment modernity represents 'the spirit of the age' for the whole of humanity, and India, he says, is under the imperative of modernization:

> The modern mind, that is to say the better type of the modern mind, is practical and pragmatic, ethical, and social, altruistic and humanitarian. It is governed by a practical idealism for social betterment. The ideals which move it represent the spirit of the age, the Zeitgeist, the *Yugadharma*. It has discarded to a large extent the philosophical approach of the ancients, their search for ultimate reality, as well as the devotionalism and mysticism of the medieval period. Humanity is its god and social service its religion....
>
> We have therefore to function in line with the highest ideals of the age we live in.... Those ideals may be classed under two heads: humanism and the scientific spirit.[8]

The Indian people's participating in, and benefiting from, 'the spirit of the age', Nehru felt, were blocked or prevented not by their human nature, but by both the rigid, indigenous socio-political structure and the engulfing structure of Western imperialism. While a certain conjuncture of historical forces led to the Enlightenment and modernity of Western Europe, a different historical conjuncture, says Nehru, brought about in India a 'slow and creeping inner weakness ... which affects not only her political status but her creative activities'.[9] In his *Discovery of India*, after noting 'the growing rigidity and exclusiveness of the Indian social structure as represented chiefly by the caste system', he goes on to point out:

> Life became all cut up into set frames where each man's job was fixed and permanent and he had little concern with others.... Thus particular types of activity became hereditary, and there was a tendency to avoid new types of work and activity and to confine oneself to the old groove, to restrict initiative and the spirit of innovation.... So long as that structure afforded avenues for growth and expansion, it was progressive; when it reached the limits of expansion open to it, it became stationary, unprogressive, and later, inevitably regressive.

> Because of this there was decline all along the line—intellectual, philosophical, political, in technique and methods of warfare, in knowledge of and contacts with the outside world, in shrinking economy, and there was a growth of local sentiments and feudal and small-group feeling at the expense of the larger conceptions of India as a whole.[10]

These progress-inhibiting rigidities and exclusivisms of Indian social structure, Nehru finds, are supported and reinforced by the engulfing structure of colonial rule, which is based on force and which, besides blocking growth and industrialization, is supporting the 'groups and classes which had ceased to have any real significance'. Ending colonial rule therefore becomes an absolute precondition for the modernization of the Indian society. In his historic presidential address to the 1936 Lucknow session of the Indian National Congress, he said: 'I work for Indian independence because the nationalist in me cannot tolerate alien domination; *I work for it even more because for me it is the inevitable step to social and economic change.*'[11]

Since the opposition to India's political independence comes both from the indigenous reactionary groups and classes and from the foreign capitalist–imperialist classes, Indian national movement for Nehru becomes a revolutionary movement directed as much against reactionary traditionalism as against the decaying structures of Western post-Enlightenment capitalist–industrial modernity. He could sincerely claim: 'I wanted India's freedom for India's sake of course; but I also wanted it for England's sake.'[12] Thus, modernizing nationalism and critical modernity become the two sides of the Nehruvian political ideology; according to him, India cannot modernize without at the same time bringing about a socialist turn of Western capitalist-imperialist modernity.

Nehru owed his world-historical-structural perspective on India's revolutionary nationalism to Marxism–Leninism, which also made him realize the inevitability of socialism. On his return from Europe in 1927 after visiting the Soviet Union and attending the Brussels Congress of Opposed Nationalities, he wrote:

> My outlook was wider, and nationalism by itself seemed to me definitely a narrow and insufficient creed. Political freedom, independence, were no doubt essential, but they were steps only in the right direction; without social freedom and a socialistic structure of society and the State, neither the country nor the individual could develop much.[13]

Later, in prison, he wrote in his *An Autobiography*:

> Russia apart, the theory and philosophy of Marxism lightened up many a dark corner of my mind. History came to have a new meaning for me. The Marxist interpretation threw a flood of light on it, and it became an unfolding drama with some order and purpose, however unconscious behind it....[14]

The twin objectives of India's revolutionary nationalism, according to Nehru, were (i) to extend the *bright side* of European post-Enlightenment modernity, and (ii) to cause a revolutionary-socialist ending of its *dark side*, namely the imperialist and fascist side. Of these twin goals, Nehru assigned strategic priority to the second one because the colonialist state, as the chief instrument of the 'decaying stage' of the world capitalist system, was preventing the spread of post-Enlightenment progress to the colonized peoples. A politically independent national state, Nehru believed, can reform and modernize the Indian society in a socialist direction. 'I do not think it very difficult', he wrote in his *An Autobiography*:

> to convert the masses to social reform if the State takes the matter in hand. But alien rulers are always suspect, and they

cannot go far in the process of conversion. If the alien element was removed and economic changes were given precedence, an energetic administration could easily introduce far-reaching social reforms.[15]

Nehru's revolutionary nationalism thus called for mobilizing the Indian people for emulating and furthering the *bright side* of Western post-Enlightenment modernity by opposing and destroying its *dark side*. Such a discriminating attitude to modernization might have been alright for the intellectual classes, but not for the poor and ignorant masses of India, who, at any rate, had to be mobilized against the colonialist state. Any attempt to mobilize them against the 'wrong England' by telling them of the values and potential socialist virtues of the 'right England' would have been an unrealistic approach. In this moment of intellectual dilemma, Nehru found a temporary, strategic solution in Gandhi's mobilization of the peasantry against the colonialist state. Even though he did not appreciate or agree with Gandhi's non-discriminating, outright condemnation of Western modernity, or his non-socialist attitude, or his individual-based rather than structural approach to social change, Nehru *accepted* Gandhi's supreme leadership of the national movement against the chief impediment to the modernization of the Indian society.

IV

Because of Gandhi's leadership, the Congress, Nehru realized, was able to produce 'a wonderful awakening of the masses', and in spite of its vague bourgeois ideology it had served a revolutionary purpose.[16] The socialist component of his own project of revolutionary nationalism, Nehru reasoned, had to await the formation of the politically independent national state. He assured himself with the resolve that after Independence his modernity and socialism, and not Gandhi's 'fads', were to be pursued. In his *An Autobiography*, Nehru wrote:

He was a very difficult person to understand, sometimes his language was almost incomprehensible to an average modern. But we felt that we knew him well enough to realize he was a great and unique man and a glorious leader, and having

put our faith in him we gave an almost blank cheque, for the
time being at least. Often we discussed his fads and peculiarities among ourselves and said, half-humorously, that when
swaraj came these fads must not be encouraged.[17]

Nehru also entertained the belief that in the actual course of the
political mobilization of the masses, Gandhi would himself move
a step or two toward or in favor of modernization and socialism.
'Gandhi', Nehru wrote:

was a unique personality, and it was impossible to judge him
by the usual standards, or even to apply the ordinary canons
of logic to him. But because he was a revolutionary at bottom
and was pledged to political independence for India, he was
bound to play an uncompromising role till that independence
was achieved. And in this very process he would ... himself
advance step by step toward the social goal.[18]

I cannot pursue here the question of whether or not in the
course of the freedom struggle Gandhi did in fact move toward an
appreciation of the Nehruvian 'model'.[19] It is, however, pertinent
to note that both Gandhi and Nehru regarded 'parliamentary
swaraj' to be of crucial importance to the realization of their fuller
model of *swaraj*. In the case of Nehru, it can be asserted that he
not only appropriated the masses mobilized by Gandhi but also
came to imbibe aspects of Gandhi's social and political philosophy, especially the principles of non-violence, the purity of means,
the 'divinity' of all life and the necessity to integrate politics and
science with *dharma*. In 1939, Nehru stated:

I have been and am a convinced socialist and a believer in
democracy and have at the same time accepted wholeheartedly the peaceful technique of non-violent action which
Gandhi has practiced so successfully during the past twenty
years.[20]

Similarly, in his *Discovery of India*, he affirmed: 'I have been
attracted by Gandhi's stress on right means and I think one of his
greatest contributions to our public life has been this emphasis.'[21]
As I indicated earlier, Nehru rejected the orientalist or colonialist
thesis of essential or ontological differences in human nature be-

tween India and the West. However, he did not fail to recognize that in their different socio-historical experiences, India and the modern West have come to stress or emphasize different values and norms. Nehru's critique, as an Indian, of Western modernity, and his critique, as a Westernized/modernized bi-cultural person, of Indian tradition made him aware of some of the strengths and weaknesses of both 'systems'. Instead of either orientalizing or occidentalizing the other, he maintained that both the orient and the occident must learn from each other. In his *Discovery of India*, which he wrote after he came under Gandhi's influence he wrote:

India, as well as China, must learn from the West, for the modern West has much to teach, and the spirit of the age is represented by the West. But the West is also obviously in need of learning, and its advances in technology will bring it little comfort if it does not learn some of the deeper lessons of life, which have absorbed the minds of thinkers in all ages and in all countries.[22]

In the pre-Gandhian phase of his political thought, Nehru had dismissed metaphysics, mysticism and 'religiosity' as the concerns of the anti-scientific traditionalist. Under Gandhi's impact, Nehru came to appreciate the interrelationship between physics and metaphysics, and politics and 'spirituality'. In 1958, enunciating his 'Basic Approach', Nehru stated:

The law of life should not be competition or acquisitiveness but cooperation, the good of each contributing to the good of all. In such a society the emphasis will be on duties, not on rights; the rights will follow the performance of the duties. We have to give a new direction to education and evolve a new type of humanity.

This argument led to the old Vedantic conception that everything, whether sentient or insentient, finds a place in the organic whole; that everything has a spark of what might be called the divine impulse or the basic energy or life force which pervades the universe. This leads to metaphysical regions which tend to take us away from the problems of life which face us. I suppose that any life of thought, sufficiently pursued, leads us in some measure to metaphysics. Even

science today is almost on the verge of all manner of impon-
derables. I do not propose to discuss these metaphysical
aspects, but this very argument indicates how the mind
searches for something basic underlying the physical world. If
we really believed in this all-pervading concept of the principles of life, it might help us to get rid of some of our narrowness of race, caste or class and make us more tolerant and
understanding in our approaches to life's problems.[23]

V

From the foregoing interpretive reconstruction of Nehru's political
thinking, it is clear that his 'odd mixture' of liberalism, Marxism
and Gandhism was an innovative ideology of essential tension
between modernizing nationalism and pre-modern/post-modern
ideas. He admitted his inability to theoretically resolve all the tensions among these ideological currents of his thought. But he did
not remain an inactive prisoner of that theoretical tension. An
independent, democratic–socialist and secular state, he believed,
constituted a practical moment of commonality to the emancipatory-progressive goals of all those ideologies. To historically and
contextually conceive such a practical, emancipatory-progressive
ideological commonality and to put it into practice was Nehru's
distinctive contribution to the political thought and practice of our
times. This was indeed a 'gradual' approach, but it had the merit
of being able to reach a large number of people towards the long-
term goal of democratic socialism. Underlining this aspect of
Nehru's political ideology, S. Gopal writes:

> It was not an intellectual framework of logical consistency but
> a sense of what he regarded as essential values which held
> together all these elements in Nehru's mental make-up. It
> made him a Marxist who rejected regimentation, a socialist
> who was wholly committed to civil liberties, a radical who
> accepted non-violence, an international statesman with a
> total involvement in India and, above all, a leader who
> believed in carrying his people with him even if it slowed
> down the pace of progress.[24]

A defense of his slow practical–idealist approach to social transformation was provided by Nehru in 1936, when Krishna Menon

complained about his 'hob-nobbing with ministerialism'. 'Try to image', Nehru wrote to Menon,

> what the human material is in India. How they think, how they act, what moves them, what does not affect them. It is easy enough to take up a theoretically correct attitude, which has little effect on anybody. We have to do something much more important and difficult and that is to move large numbers of people, to make them act....[25]

In which ideological direction then was Nehru attempting to 'move large numbers of people'? Was it, as his Marxist–subalternist critics say, simply towards an *etatisme* that remains wedded to capitalism? These critics say that Nehru simply crowned the passive, capitalist revolution of India with a sovereign national state, which he legitimized 'by a specifically nationalist marriage between the ideas of progress and social justice'.[26] This is the view of Partha Chatterjee who, in his path-breaking study of Indian nationalist thought, maintains that Nehru's political ideology is that of 'the final, fully mature stage' of the 'passive revolution' of capital in colonial/post-colonial India. Following Gramsci's ideas, Partha points out that the Indian *bourgeoisie*, blocked by imperialism and the colonial state, was unable to carry out any full-scale (*bourgeois*) revolution against the old, pre-capitalist dominant classes. Thus, failing to establish hegemony over the 'civil society', it tried to bring about a passive revolution by spearheading an all-class nationalist struggle against the colonial state so that a politically independent national state can be set up and used for establishing capitalism as the dominant mode of production. In this 'passive revolution', the *bourgeoisie* makes a political appropriation of the masses or the peasantry, and brings about 'a "molecular transformation" of the old dominant classes into "partners in a new historical bloc"'. What is particularly noteworthy, according to Partha, is that the political independence that is thus brought about 'does not attempt to break up or transform in any radical way the institutional structures of "rational" authority set up in the period of colonial rule, whether in the domain of administration and law or in the realm of economic institutions or in the structure of education, scientific research and cultural organization'.[27] Those 'institutional structures of "rational" authority', we are reminded, are subservient to capitalist-imperialism.

Gandhi, according to Partha, was the supreme leader of the penultimate phase or 'moment of maneuver' of India's passive capitalist revolution in the sense that he 'succeeded in opening up the historical possibility by which the largest popular element of the nation—the peasantry—could be appropriated within the evolving forms of the new Indian state'. In other words, Gandhi is said to have made the peasantry 'willing participants in a struggle wholly conceived and directed by *others*', namely, the *bourgeoisie*. To Nehru, according to Partha, the Indian passive revolution of capital owes its 'moment of arrival' or 'the final, fully mature' phase; he appropriated the Gandhian political legacy of the partially mobilized peasantry and crowned it with a sovereign national state, assigning to it a 'central, autonomous and directing role in the further development of capitalism', which he legitimized 'by a specifically nationalist marriage between the ideas of progress and social justice'.[28] Partha sums up the Nehruvian, *etatist* phase of the Indian passive revolution of capital, in the following manner:

> It is now a discourse of order, of the rational organization of power. Here the discourse is not only conducted in a single, consistent, unambiguous voice, it also succeeds in glossing over all earlier contradictions, divergences and differences and incorporating within the body of a unified discourse every aspect and stage in the history of its formation. This ideological unity of nationalist thought it seeks to actualize in the unified life of the state. Nationalist discourse at its moment of arrival is passive revolution uttering its own life-history.[29]

Partha goes on to argue that after Independence Nehru abandoned socialism and that instead of pursuing equality 'by means of politics, through the violent struggle between classes', he left it to the rational, realistic management of the government by the technicians of power. Since the Age of Enlightenment, there has been, he notes, an historical partnership between the universal march of Reason and the universalist urge of Capital. Anti-imperialist nationalism, of which the paradigmatic case is the Indian one, did, according to Partha, administer 'a check on a specific political form of metropolitan capitalist dominance' and gave a 'death-blow ... to such blatantly ethnic slogans as the civilizing mission of the West, the white man's burden, etc'. But all this, Partha maintains, has been achieved in the name of capitalistic rationality. 'Nowhere in the world', he writes, 'has nationalism qua nationalism challenged the legitimacy of the marriage between Reason and Capital'.[30] Nationalist thought, according to him, has lacked the ideological means to make such a challenge.

In an insightful attempt to uncover the 'apparent paradoxes' of Jawaharlal Nehru, Sudipta Kaviraj gives him credit for his innovativeness in setting up a politically independent *bourgeois* state and pursuing a relatively independent path of reformist–welfarist capitalist development. Nehru however, according to Kaviraj, resorted to an 'irresponsible' technique of legitimation, namely 'a manipulation of the evident appeal of the socialist idea in a poor and illiterate country'. Nehru's 'socialism', Kaviraj notes, brought him political success in the electoral arena but historical failure against such impersonal or 'structural problems' of capitalism as poverty, inequality, exploitation, etc. 'Nehru', writes Kaviraj, 'was a political success and at the same time a historical failure.'[31]

This conclusion seems to me to be too sweeping and not quite in keeping with the theory of the 'relative autonomy' of the political. If (as Kaviraj rightly maintains) the political is relatively autonomous from the economic and if Nehru is credited with political success, then that success must be seen as altering the economic in some significant way. Nehru's political success, in other words, cannot be said to be without any historical consequence. The Nehruvian ideology of anti-imperialist democratic socialism has indeed served as 'a guarantee against the selling out of national economic and political interests by small elite groups or authoritarian regimes'.[32] It has in fact given the Indian state 'greater political and economic bargaining power' vis-à-vis the advanced nations and the international financial agencies. It has also led to a considerable sharing of the fruits of economic growth with the disadvantaged sections of the Indian society.[33]

Partha and Kaviraj are indeed right in pointing out that the Nehruvian state and ideology have not transcended capitalist–technological rationality or that they have not established socialism. Nehru himself admitted it.[34] I would, however, urge an appreciation of the implications of the greater relative autonomy which the Nehruvian state has from the imperialist reason of capital than the other form of the capitalist state which was not only a clear alternative historical possibility in Nehru's time but also actively campaigned for. As both Partha and Kaviraj admit, the independent, national, non-aligned, democratic state, in setting up which Gandhi and Nehru played a world-historic role, braving strong opposition from within and outside the country, has a greater relative autonomy from imperialist capital than would have been the case if a non-democratic, 'non-socialistic', aligned, satellite-type or neo-colonial state had been set up. In bringing about that 'greater relative autonomy' or, in other words, the 'decolonization' or dissociation of the identity of the reason of the state system from the imperialist–global reason. of capital,[35] the Nehruvian 'mixture' of liberalism, Marxism and Gandhism did play a historic role.

This ideological 'mixture' was correctly seen by Nehru to be constituting a necessary, though far from sufficient, condition for the politics of transition to a post-capitalist or 'socialistic' social order. He as well as Gandhi correctly perceived that the minimal requirement for the politics of exit or transition from the capitalist–imperialist system of states was the setting up of independent, non-aligned, democratic nation states that were to constitute the counter-hegemonic points against that system. In the post-World War II context of emerging bipolar super-powerism that was beginning to engulf the whole world, Nehru's overarching concern was to create and nurture the independent, non-aligned democratic national state, and to use it both as a counter-hegemonic political space against the alignment systems of the super-powers and as an instrument for bringing about social and economic change at both national and transnational levels.[36]

Even though Nehru did not pursue socialism 'through the violent struggle between classes', the non-aligned, democratic–socialist state which he strove to institutionalize does constitute a crucial step in a larger political movement of exit or transition from the two interrelated versions of imperialism which the two super-powers have been trying to impose on the rest of the world since the end of World War II. That political movement, I would say, is not devoid of post-capitalist potentialities; the Gandhi–Nehru complementarity in 'modern' Indian political thought sought to legitimize a 'third way' of constituting the reason of the state from out of the life concerns of the people.[37]

This is not to claim that the Nehruvian state and ideology constitute, in any unambiguous or non-paradoxical sense, a political step towards post-capitalism or post-modernity. Is not the post-modern state or ideology necessarily paradoxical or in essence a tension between capitalistic and post-capitalistic logics? Such an ambiguity or tension is indeed a characteristic not only of Nehru's 'mixed economy' and non-alignment but also of his commitment to science and technology. While he was deeply committed to the rationality of science and technology, he did not put absolute faith in it; he was not a fanatic of progress. He rejected the doctrine of the amoral or non-political sovereignty of science and technology. His commitment to science and technology, in other words, was not at the expense of his commitment to democratic politics or spiritual values. In his 1959 Azad Memorial Lecture, after expressing his confidence that India would advance in science and technology, he went on to say:

> What I am concerned with is not merely our material progress, but the quality and depth of our people.... Power is necessary, but wisdom is essential. It is only power with wisdom that is good.... Can we combine the progress of science and technology with this progress of the mind and spirit also?[38]

In one of his very last writings, he emphasized that while we must use the advances in science and technology for increasing production, 'we must not forget that the essential objective to be aimed at is the quality of the individual and the concept of *dharma* underlying it'.[39]

■

■ Notes ■

[1] Without going into the question of the appropriateness of labeling his position 'liberal–rationalist', I wish to note that K.P. Karunakaran finds Nehru's 'rootless' cosmopolitanism a justification for the comment that he was 'more the last British Viceroy in India, and not the first Prime Minister of independent India'. K.P. Karunakaran, *The Phenomenon of Nehru*, New Delhi, Gitanjali Prakashan, 1979, p. 17. In a recent article, however, Karunakaran emphasizes the fact that Nehru was a 'meeting ground for ... different and apparently conflicting strands of thought'. See idem, 'Nehru: A Meeting Ground for Different Political Forces', *Gandhi Marg*, May, 1987, p. 79.

[2] This position is advanced in Partha Chatterjee's *Nationalist Thought and the Colonial World: A Derivative Discourse?* New Delhi, Oxford University Press, 1987.

[3] Within the modern societies themselves there has been a shift, since the mid-1970s from 'modernization euphoria' to 'modernity critique'. This is discussed in Claus Offe, 'The Utopia of the Zero-Option: Modernity and Modernization as Normative Political Criteria', *Praxis International*, Vol. 7, No. 1, April 1987.

[4] Jawaharlal Nehru, *The Discovery of India*, New York, John Day, 1946, 517–18, emphasis added.

[5] Ernest Gellner, *Nations and Nationalism*, Oxford, Basil Blackwell, 1983, p. 124.

[6] Nehru, *The Discovery of India*, p. 142.

[7] *Ibid.*, p. 143.

[8] *Ibid.*, pp. 517–18.

[9] *Ibid.*, p. 217.

[10] *Ibid.*, pp. 221–22.

[11] Nehru, 'Socialism and Internationalism' (1936), reproduced in Karunakaran, *The Phenomenon of Nehru*, p. 133, emphasis added.

[12] Nehru, as cited in W. Range, *Jawaharlal Nehru's World-View*, Athens, University of Georgia Press, 1961, p. 49.

[13] Nehru, *Towards Freedom: The Autobiography of Jawaharlal Nehru*, New York, John Day, 1941, p. 128.

[14] *Ibid.*, pp. 362–63.

[15] Nehru, *Autobiography*, p. 384.

[16] Nehru, *Mahatma Gandhi*, Bombay, Asia Publishing House, 1966, p. 107.

[17] *Ibid.*, p. 73.

[18] *Ibid.*, pp. 107–08.

[19] The complementarity/polarity between Gandhian and Nehruvian ideas are dealt with in B.R. Nanda, P.C. Joshi and Raj Krishna, *Gandhi and Nehru*, Delhi, Oxford University Press, 1979; and Bimal Prasad, *Gandhi, Nehru and JP*, Delhi, Chanakya Publications, 1985.

[20] *Selected Works of Jawaharlal Nehru*, New Delhi, Orient Longman, 1978, Vol. IX, p. 487.

[21] Nehru, *Discovery of India*, p. 29.

[22] *Ibid.*, pp. 517–18.

[23] Reproduced in Karunakaran, *The Phenomenon of Nehru*, pp. 156–57.

[24] S. Gopal, 'The Formative Ideology of Jawaharlal Nehru', in K.N. Panikar, *National and Left Movement in India*, Delhi, Vikas, 1980, p. 13.

[25] *Selected Works of Jawaharlal Nehru*, Vol. VII, p. 471.

[26] Chatterjee, *Nationalist Thought and the Colonial World*, p. 132.

[27] *Ibid.*, pp. 30, 49.

[28] *Ibid.*, pp. 124, 132.

[29] *Ibid.*, p. 51.

[30] *Ibid.*, pp. 161, 168.

[31] Sudipta Kaviraj, 'Apparent Paradoxes of Jawaharlal Nehru', *Mainstream*, November 15, 22, and 29, 1980; and December 6 and 13, 1980.

[32] Aditya Mukherjee and Mridula Mukherjee, 'Imperialism and Growth of Indian Capitalism in Twentieth Century', *Economic and Political Weekly*, Vol. XXIII, No. 11, 12 March 1988, p. 541.

[33] *Ibid.* That Nehru's ideology gave an 'instrumental–socialist orientation' to India's mixed economy is argued in Baldev Raj Nayar, *India's Mixed Economy: The Role of Ideology and Interest in its Development*, Bombay, Popular Prakashan, 1989, chapters 4 and 5. Cf. also Sukhamoy Chakravarty, *Development Planning: The Indian Experience*, Oxford, Clarendon Press, 1987, chapter 2.

[34] In 1964, when asked if he was satisfied with the gains of socialism over the three Five Year Plans, Nehru admitted that 'the gap between the 'haves' and the 'have nots' has widened'. See R.K. Karanjia, *The Philosophy of Mr Nehru*, London, Allen and Unwin, 1966, p. 154.

[35] The thesis that the interstate system and the capitalist world market constitute one integrated logic is advanced in Christopher Chase–Dunn, 'Inter-State System and Capitalist-World-Economy: One Logic or Two?', *International Studies Quarterly*, Vol. 25, No. 1, March 1981. That they constitute relatively autonomous logics or subsystems is maintained in T. Skocpol, *States and Social Revolutions*, Cambridge, Cambridge University Press, 1979; A.R. Zolberg, 'Origins of the Modern World System: A Missing Link', *World Politics*, January 1981; and Anthony Giddens, *Nation-State and Violence*, Cambridge, Polity Press, 1985.

[36] These two dimensions of the transformative tasks of Nehru's foreign policy of non-alignment are discussed in A.P. Rana, 'Non-Alignment and International Change: Strategic and Socio-Economic Dimensions', *The Non-Aligned World*, Vol. I, No. 3, July–September 1983; and A.P. Rana, 'The Non-Aligned Regulation of India's National Security Problematic, and the Universalization of International Society: A Conceptual Study of Nehru's International Legacy', Paper presented at the seminar on Nehru Legacy, Institute for Social and Economic Change, Bangalore, February 1989.

[37] Some of the implications of Gandhian thought for a post-Western world order are discussed in Thomas Pantham, 'Beyond Liberal Democracy: Thinking with Mahatma Gandhi', in T. Pantham and K.L. Deutsch, eds, *Political Thought in Modern India*, New Delhi, Sage Publications India Pvt Ltd, 1986; T. Pantham, 'Habermas's Practical Discourse and Gandhi's Satyagraha', in B. Parekh and T. Pantham, eds, *Political Discourse: Explorations in Indian and Western Political Thought*, New Delhi, Sage Publications India Pvt Ltd, 1987; and T. Pantham, 'On Modernity, Rationality and Morality: Habermas and Gandhi', *Indian Journal of Social Science*, Vol. I, No. 2, April–June 1988. Cf. also Bhikhu Parekh, *Gandhi's Political Philosophy*, London, Macmillan, 1989.

[38] Cited in *Nehru and the Modern World*, International Round Table on Jawaharlal Nehru, New Delhi, September 1966, New Delhi Indian National Commission for Cooperation with UNESCO, 1967, p. 105.

[39] Nehru's foreword to Shriman Narayan, *Socialism in Indian Planning*, New York, Asia Publishing House, 1964.

15

■ RAJNI KOTHARI ■

Born in Palanpur, Gujarat, in 1928, Rajni Kothari is one of the leading social theorists and social reformers in post-independence India. Trained both in India and the West, he is a prolific scholar, an institution builder, and a social activist at the local, national and international levels of politics. In 1963 he established the Centre for the Study of Developing Societies in Delhi, an institute devoted to interdisciplinary research and social praxis. In 1975, he was instrumental in launching the journal *Alternatives*; in the same year he emerged as a vocal spokesman of the campaign against the Emergency (imposed by Indira Gandhi) and one of the chief leaders of the civil liberties movement. He subsequently became associated with the formation of the Janata Party. In 1980 he inaugurated 'Lokayan' (meaning 'dialogue among peoples') as an arena for the meeting of scholars, policy-makers and activists concerned with local grassroots initiatives. In 1989 he joined the National Front government led by the Janata Dal as a member of the National Planning Commission.

For primary and secondary sources see Rajni Kothari, *Politics in India*, Boston, Little Brown, 1970; *Footsteps into the Future*, New York, Free Press, 1974; *Towards a Just World*, New York, Institute of World Order, 1980; *State against Democracy: In Search of Humane Governance*, Delhi, Ajanta, 1988; *Transformation and Survival: In Search of a Humane World Order*, Delhi, Ajanta, 1988; *Rethinking Development: In Search of Humane Alternatives*, New York, New Horizons, 1989; *Politics and the People: In Search of Humane India*, New York, New Horizons, 1989; *Growing Amnesia: An Essay on Poverty and the Human Consciousness*, Delhi,

Viking, 1993; and D.L. Sheth and Ashis Nandy, eds., *The Multiverse of Democracy: Essays in Honour of Rajni Kothari*, New Delhi, Sage Publications India Pvt Ltd, 1996. The following is taken from *Growing Amnesia*, pp. 165–180.

ETHICAL IMPERATIVES

Beyond the institutional steps needed to restructure the processes of power and root out its worst pathologies like endemic corruption and criminalization, there is a need to enlist human sensitivity on behalf of the poor at more basic levels. There is a need to go beyond the political, the social and the ecological domains and tap the moral and ethical domain. It is not enough to provide an intellectual profile of an alternative model, or to inject into the dominant intellectual paradigm and the economistic ethic of our time social and ecological considerations. The essential task that faces us is to render the actions of the state and other corporate entities humane, to ensure that the processes generated by 'development' do not destroy diverse cultures and their roots both in nature and in unique human beings in the name of some abstract idea, be it of profit or of some absolutist ideology.

Keeping Hope Alive

Central to such a task is the paramount need of the time we find ourselves in: how to keep *hope* alive. As stated by the leading educationist Denis Goulet, by a purely rational calculus of future probabilities, the development enterprise of most countries is doomed to fail. The poor can never cope so long as the rich continue to consume wastefully and to devise ideological justifications for the same. In all probability, technological and resource gaps will continue to widen and vast resources will continue to be devoted to destructive armaments. Exacerbated feelings of national sovereignty will, in all likelihood, continue to co-exist alongside an ever more urgent need to institute new forms of governance and problem-solving. By any rational scenario projectible over the next fifty years, development will continue to wreak ecological destruction, and it will remain the privilege of a relative few, while underdevelopment will continue to be the lot of the vast majority. Only through a major act of imagination and a new stirring of consciousness can even a candle of hope be generated. The French social critic Jacques Ellul [has written] eloquently of the need for hope in a time of abandonment.

Indeed, it is precisely when it is becoming clear that the present is not sustainable and when realistic projections indicate a dismal scenario for the future, at any rate for the suffering part of humanity, that we need to remind ourselves, based on the totality of human experience, that the future has never been predestined and can be reordained, if only we have the confidence—based on hope—that this is possible. And not just that it is possible but that it is *necessary* and indeed inherent in the scheme of things, and hence incumbent upon us all. As the title of this chapter says, it is an ethical imperative.

Such an imperative cannot be in the form of a disembodied and abstract idea. It must arise out of a certain process of history, of not just being but becoming, emerging out of a collective experience of something that is at once organic and specific, located at once in the mind as in the reality 'out there', evolved over time and hence real, yet continuously evoking new definitions of the challenge that lies ahead. Discovering new priorities, particularly on the margins of society, not necessarily through great events as through small signs of ordinary assertion, all of it as part of a larger reawakening and restructuring of civil society.

The First Indian Enterprise

Independent India started with two projects—partly interrelated but in many ways different from each other—viz., the project of building a state and the project of Development, one promising an all-encompassing presence in a plural society, and the other promising a major *economic* (and technological) transformation of a traditional society toward a modernist paradigm helped by education, urbanization, mass media exposure and, in Karl Deutsch, the political scientist's terms, 'social mobilization' through which the mass of the people 'become available for new patterns of socialization and behavior'.

Conceptually, 'development' was to be a project of the state (this was central to the Nehruvian vision) but as the state had not really come through in any organic sense (encompassing the enormous cultural diversity of the land), development became a project of the elite or rather, a self-appointed arm of the elite, viz., the bureaucratic administration which, as it was by its very nature colonial and remote, led to an increasingly exclusivist structure of power. In the process, the state too got reduced into a mere government, a government from one center—*the* center with a capital 'C', a colonial and colonizing Center.

The only way an enduring structure of a state could be built was by drawing into its corpus the various cultural and regional identities that obtained in the socio-political space that it had inherited from colonial administration—and the ethical systems that they embodied—and providing them with a sense of authenticity and a measure of self-governance. Only through such an organic corpus could a humane state have been built. Failing that all you could have was an administration, based on files and procedures, not a State as a moral presence.

The pursuit of a monolithic (hence socially steamrollering and homogeneous) model of the state necessarily precluded a diversified and plural approach to 'development', thus leading to the inevitable neglect of (in turn promoting ignorance of and distancing from) the ground realities that were obtained in various cultural and ethical domains. In turn, this led to a reflection of abstractions at the top in abstractions at the bottom. Thus, the pursuit of 'prosperity' in macro terms of necessity produced 'poverty' in macro terms too—the same scenario of high-rise and hi-tech industrialization alongside malnutrition, ill-health, hunger and starvation deaths. Even the scenario of 'exploitation' and 'marginalization' turned out to be standardized: enforced unemployment, forced evictions from land, forced immigration following destruction of ecologies and the village social nexus, low-paid wages (even below 'minimum wages' which are themselves exploitative), growth of child labor and of prostitution not as a vocation but for sheer physical survival. With all this the scope for culture-specific and ethical responses to deprivation and disparities became marginalized too.

Over time, such a texturing of poverty and disempowerment led, first, to an incredible expansion of the human machine (the bureaucracy) with the ostensible purpose of dealing with 'poverty' defined in standardized patterns and through centrally-sponsored schemes. And, then, after it was demonstrated to these bureaucracies that these methods were not working and were ill-suited to remove poverty or reduce disparities, deciding to concentrate on the modern sector and leaving the poor out of the purview of the state (and, without admitting it, out of the purview of the market too).

Unfortunately, in the meanwhile, the exploited, the deprived and dispossessed and socially uprooted people have also been brainwashed into thinking of themselves in one single *leitmotif* of being the 'poor', the 'poor wretches', the 'poor things'—being induced to be pitied and patronized. They seem to have lost their capacity to endure and find their own diverse ways of dealing with their reality. Even their 'struggles' are no more than 'demands'.

Is a New Indian Enterprise on the Anvil?

Not quite, fortunately. While I do not want to be misunderstood as romanticizing their plight, I happen to believe that the so-called 'poor' are the true bearers of India's cultural resilience; they are slowly realizing that there is no 'place' for them in this system and will soon arrive at two simultaneous judgments: first, that as there is no justice in the system there is little point in keeping on hoping that something will be 'delivered' by the rich and the powerful; and, second, that this does not mean the end of the world and that they should work out their own path to salvation—they know how to, they are convinced the rich and the powerful do not!

Nor is it just a question of the so-called 'poor' seeking a way out of both the injustices of the state and the tapestries of development. It is also a series of other social groups and communities (and not just the poor among each of them)—the artisans, the farmers, the women, the millions of children and adolescents and the grown-up 'youth', the educated unemployed, many of whom are being forced to take to crime and 'terrorism'. They are all, on the one hand, feeling exploited and excluded, yet, on the other hand, seeking their own ethical domains which are providing them with their own 'models' for moving along. Of in fact creating 'alternatives' without ever (unlike academic pundits) using that kind of upstart terminology.

The point is that if the state in India has both failed to provide itself with an appropriate structure and in turn created a model of development that is equally disembodied and culturally and ethically adrift, the people of India will soon have to decide to pursue a course quite different to what recent history has laid out for them. And there is no need necessarily to take this as a setback to the much proclaimed projects of 'nation building', 'development' and 'democracy'. It could be seen as providing new openings and ethical spaces for creating new ways of dealing with the problems faced by the people. One could almost say: one phase of the Indian enterprise has failed; another is beginning. One is not sure it will make it, but there certainly is something under way that we should try and unravel…. The imagery of the poor being 'marginalized', dropped out, excluded, forced to 'stew in their own juice', becoming victims of not just discrimination and displacement but also the fact that they are considered dispensable by the ruling class, has its own relevance and validity. This makes them targets of pity, analysis, at best compassion, at worst contempt, of being thought of as culturally backward and irrational and lethargic, etc. It is an imagery that the supposedly most empathetic and radical segment of the intelligentsia has promoted. There is need to look at how in fact the poor themselves 'cope' (despite they themselves being prone to accept the imagery).

Two Distinct Enterprises

The point is that we have two quite different perceptions of the poverty situation and the two have produced quite distinct responses. One is the way the 'problem of poverty' has been conceived by professionals coming from the relatively well-off and often richer sections of society (including a whole set of social workers and activists). These have tried to identify, define and analyze the phenomenon of poverty and sought to both 'manage' the same within a given system and tried to 'alleviate' the same through the project of economic development in which needs (presumably limitless) are matched with resources (presumably scarce) and efforts made to improve living conditions within the constraints of the state under which they operate and the interests that the state serves.

Now, while it is increasingly realized that this particular model of 'dealing with' poverty has not worked as was desired, what is not equally realized is that large sections of the poor are poor *because* of development, because they are the victims of the particular model of economic development that was adopted. Severed from their cultural roots, dispossessed of their own resources, drop-outs (forced out) from the very system that was designed to serve them, although designated as 'poor' and accepted as 'target groups' of various development projects, they are increasingly being perceived by sections of the ruling class as threats to stability and 'peace'. Treated as pathologies (inherently backward, inert and lazy, lacking motivation, merit and having no work ethic), they are, over time, considered parasites that are best excluded from that very model of development that had originally been devised for them. The model has since been penetrated by external agents who treat the poor as both a 'resource'—cheap while they last, dispensed with when not needed—and a pretext for turning every deprivation of the poor into an opportunity for the rich. This is found, for instance, with housing where shortages are announced and the builders' lobby moves in, or when nutritional impoverishment is caused by food processing industries.

It seems clear by now that if we were to follow this particular Indian enterprise based on the project of economic development, we would be trapped. And, the poor would be worst affected. Should we be at all concerned with their fate beyond the make-believe of this project or should we allow them to continue to be left to the inexorable logic of the project? In that lies the crucial ethical question. The questions that the poor themselves face are less ethical than political and strategic in terms of their own strategy of dealing with their reality; the ones we, the non-poor, face are ethical. We need to ask ourselves with a certain sense of history: Is poverty, as we know it today, not basically a modern phenomenon? What, if any, is the link between poverty of the traditional type and modern poverty? While for heuristic purposes and for holding out warnings and signals, comparison with the older reality or even tracing some of today's indicators of inequity and deprivation to the older reality may be worth exploring, is not the phenomenon that is unfolding before our eyes—a phenomenon that links the local, the national and the global—one of contemporary making and is it not likely (if we go about dealing with it the way we have so far) to endure in the future, indeed get worse? Given the fact that the development model that we have adopted has led to more and more resources and opportunities being available for smaller and smaller sections of the people, can we not visualize a growing interest in sustaining poverty and not just neglecting it but actually using it for perpetuating and enhancing the parasitic lifestyles of both Indians and non-Indians through an 'integration' of the Indian economy into the 'world market'? Is there not a critical need to devise new strategies (beyond the usual ones of lobbying in the corridors of power and the Planning Commission) of resistance aimed at the reversal of present reality?

We seem to have arrived at a moment in history in which positioning ourselves *vis-à-vis* the poor has increasingly meant that leaving them out of the purview of the state and the development process is not only considered both economically and politically necessary but also legitimate, given the growing perception that in the modern and post-modern paradigm of the world and 'world order' they are proving to be a drag and an obstacle, a 'noise factor' like an unwanted relation. If one takes the role the state in such a world, one moves from a liberating and empowering one to a repressive and dominating one, and if the role is of capitalism and its relations of production, it is from one of functional exploitation in which the poor and the working class were considered necessary to the economy to one in which the latter are seen as sources of growing demands and conflicts and violence that one moves. Hence, substitutes are imperative. Even the 'movements' waged in the name of the poor—and the various development NGOs—seem to, on the whole, leave out the real poor, not necessarily out of design or deceit (though this too cannot be ruled out in all cases) but because there is no larger and comprehensive ethical movement any more that is coherent and capable of mobilizing diverse social and political constituencies on the basis of being rooted in civil society.

The Other Indian Enterprise

That takes us to the other Indian enterprise that I spoke of earlier. While some of us still continue to feel concerned about the burning issues of our time—including poverty, the root of them all—and may feel ethically driven to effectively intervene in the moment of history that was spoken of above, it is increasingly becoming clear that if we are to prove relevant or, rather, not become irrelevant and filled with a sense of despair devoid of 'hope', we need to see how the poor themselves are thinking of the situation they face. Is it in any way different from the prescriptions held out by planners and developers, is it that over time the poor too have been made to think in the same way, of trying to find a 'place in the system', which means getting merged into the global poverty ghetto? Or is it that the poor are likely to become the main instrument of creating an alternative, both for them-selves and hence necessarily—through the various struggles and strategies of sustaining themselves despite everything—for the world around them. Are the strategies of survival (including the struggles), at least some of them, emanating from the victims of the system, the state and the global establishment as against those devised by the latter? Increasingly, the poor (when not fully margi-nalized and excluded) are being imposed upon and taken for a ride both by their exploiters and by their liberators (not just the do-gooders but even the 'revolutionaries'). What, then, is the enterprise in which the poor themselves, with their diverse politi-cal, social and spatial networks, are found? After all, let us face it, they have survived for a long time, and are not exactly being liquidated (except for some of them). Why? How have they managed?

Any attempt to answer this question must go beyond mere reci-pes or formulae for 'dealing with' poverty, 'managing' it or even 'countering' present structures which are all of course involved in moving towards both a new understanding and a new enterprise based on a new interpretation of the unfolding reality, of the na-ture of the transition that lies ahead. Nor can such an enterprise be exclusively focusing on poverty in any narrow economistic sense, leaving out all other considerations that are pressing for at-tention. It is only the rich who have both an exclusive and an ex-cluding mindset. Not the poor, who must of necessity relate to the whole and try to transform the whole, for then only can things change. Last, such an enterprise must begin with a degree of hope rather than in despair.

As we look at the whole matter within an overall sense of the historical process within the specific Indian setting of today, we find that there are two possible interpretations of 'India-in-transition', and two different strategies of intervening in its evolving future. According to one, the India one knew is in shambles, a tottering subcontinent, ill at ease with other states and nations on its pe-ripheries, internally disintegrating (both territorially and socially), unable to 'hold' politically. Culturally too, even as a civilization—which most people think will somehow survive, weathered, as it has, so many onslaughts—it is being subjected to multiple pressures that could well upset its traditional balance and staying power: consumerism and globalization, on the one hand, and the internal tearing apart of its social fabric under the rising cult of violence unleashed by multiple confrontations, on the other. The India that we know is, then, not just in 'crisis', it is entering a terminal phase.

But there is quite another way of interpreting the transition, namely, that a new India is struggling to be born. It will be an India that is more complex and both multilayered and multifaceted, not amenable to neat and confident portrayal, perhaps. But this may well be because of our failure, intellectually, to grasp, and socially to come to terms with and accept, a different kind of reality, bearing the impact of the rise of the poor and the unorganized peripheries, having been so long used to looking at the country from the apex and all along looking for 'order' and 'orderly change'. This view is held by not just national politicians and bureaucrats and planners but academic and media dons too, and even social workers and activists occupying various NGO citadels from where so much social change is being engineered.

Discomfort in the Old Order

There has been much bemoaning by each of these high towers of public 'concern'. We are told that no one obeys the law, long accepted public norms are continuously violated, there has been a great decline in moral standards, everyone seems to be flouting the basic framework of values and commitments enshrined in the 'Constitution'. And yet, could this be because the issues people have to face and grapple with are fundamentally different from the ones they faced and dealt with even ten or fifteen years ago? Are they not caught in a twilight zone, where one moral code is no longer found relevant, and a new code is yet to be born? The bemoaning comes from the elite that is too tied to a value system—and an 'order'—that has lost its meaning for a majority of the people.

Underlying such anxiety lies the end of our self-confidence as a nation, till recently governed by an identifiable set of people—centrists and nationalists, all of them—and according to set norms and predictable ways, in a world that appeared stable, and was sustaining 'growth' and 'development' and the nation state.

We also face an end of not just confidence but hope as well, of a chance for most people to make it in life (almost for everyone, except for the very down and out who are excluded and for whom few care anyway; but even for them, there was 'hope' that the development paradigm would one day give scope for them). Of belonging to a nation that was somehow holding. Of minimum conditions of health and education and well-being, with all the indices showing up—life expectancy, decline in infant mortality, crossing the poverty line, stable prices, even literacy, slow as the upswing was, growth of cities which, with all their squalor and emptiness, still gave one a 'chance', the slow improvement in the condition of the 'weaker sections', oppressed no doubt, yet fighting for their 'rights'. Much of this is still there and even growing but without that basic *élan* and confidence of it all being in one piece, together transforming the Indian landscape, and not falling apart; that coherence and confidence is no longer there.

This is particularly the case among the 'upwardly mobile' middle class professionals, not just the lawyers and the doctors and the corrupt Public Works Department (PWD) engineers but also the university academics and the journalists and the NGO-types, and those who have access to either foreign jobs or foreign jaunts *ad nauseum*. But then, even in this hitherto upwardly mobile class there has started taking place a downward mobility, with the specters of unemployment, inflation, high costs of luxury items like petrol and housing and decline of various services like education and health haunting them, unsettling their long held assumptions about progress and the good life.

With this decline in the earlier confidence about the 'system' and optimism about one's life chances, there is taking place a growing questioning of the ability of the state to deliver the goods, and alongside an erosion of identities—national identity in particular, but also a variety of institutional, professional and other secondary identities.

New Strivings, New Sensibility

Instead, there is a search for new identities, new relationships across existing identities, a new understanding of emerging shifts in relationships. The majority is still unsure of the new understandings, because of so much bickering and insecurity, and an almost total lack of new leadership, and even more of a new vision, but it is still showing signs of some new *sense* and *sensibility*, a sense of becoming free of older constraints, though no doubt anxious about new constraints that may emerge and unsettle existing arrangements, including possible erosion and even chaos. A growing combination of both a sense of liberation from the old and fear of the new: the typical 'fear of freedom', yet also the possibility of 'freedom from fear', fear that so far held back so many from exploring so much.

For a majority of the people the future seems uncertain and it seems futile to project either a pessimistic or an optimistic sense about it. There is a mood of deep ambivalence on the part of all—left or right, religious or 'secular', traditional or Westernized. While not new for the Indian personality (on which more soon), the new ambivalence presents itself in a drastically changed social and political setting. Also, while there is a growing sense that institutions are no longer operating according to expectations, there seem to be basic differences on how to take it all. For the many who think things are falling apart, there are many others who see value in that happening. After all, there isn't much for them in the way things are!

This is particularly the case in urban areas, especially in the larger cities. We have not yet realized the real import of the fast growing numbers of those living in the cities, of the fact that it is from here that the growing turbulence among the poor will find new outlets and completely new types of community and new expressions of social diversity are likely to emerge in these cities that are on so many indicators 'post-modern nightmares'. Our long neglect of the urban in a period of still greater neglect of rural areas and the environment which is forcing the active population to migrate to the cities is going to force on our attention a completely different set of issues that one did not ordinarily associate with urbanization.

New configurations of caste and community identities will take shape, both within the large and growing backwaters of the 'unorganized sector', and the increasing presence within the migrant communities of the backwards, the *Dalits*, the socially uprooted and increasingly defiant hordes of women and the (literally) millions of homeless children selling their labor and their bodies while at the same time defying conventional norms and experimenting with a new set of ideas and behavior patterns.

As the contours of the new norms and patterns of behavior are not clear, and as the new actors in the new social and spatial arenas—the young, the women employed from the poor classes, traditional artisans and 'artists' finding wholly new openings—have no models to fall back on except the continuing hold of caste and family, and as religious beliefs will prove less and less useful in facing the new challenges, we are likely to encounter wholly new contexts given to economic life and new structures provided for secular politics and the composition of civil society.

The 'Mandal phenomenon' has far more to it than mere job reservations or economic threats to the middle class. It signifies the political and social assertion of the poor at a time when both the economic policy of liberalization and the social challenge of 'Hindutva' are threatening their very survival. Needless to say, the India of today has little to offer to this new configuration of social forces which is bound to ask for a new definition of both secular identity and the democratic process.

The Poor and the Young

It was Indira Gandhi who had said that the two majorities of India were the poor and the young. While the claims of the poor as such are increasingly pushed aside and the moral sensitivity of middle classes has suffered erosion, when the majority of the poor happen to be young—growing young with every decade—they become a force to reckon with, even if their growing assertions tend to be increasingly turbulent and unsettling for established structures. In any case, for any appraisal of the future to be adequate, it must take full account of the young generation, its motifs and cultural contours, its internal composition—with respect to both class and community—and the various cross-currents to which it is likely to be subjected....

It is against this backdrop of the emerging interface of class, youth, gender and ethnicity that the real challenge of restructuring the Indian enterprise will be faced in the years and decades to come. As the state is found more and more to be abdicating its role in ensuring justice and providing social minima of welfare (even in things like education and health, housing and basic amenities), new institutional models will be needed, new self-help collectives in the form of a new genre of cooperatives and 'workers control' devised, leading to new structuring of the spaces provided by civil society which were till now dominated by a centralized state and a colonial bureaucracy but which are now likely to get a new lease of life, a new 'liberation'.

Rise of New Politics, New Identity

From this may well emerge a new and different political structure too. There is already under way an incremental withdrawal from New Delhi on the part of not just movements of ethnic identity and regional self-determination but also those of social and economic justice. Be it Mandalism or tribal struggles against displacement and forced evictions; or, the completely new kinds of assertions of feminine personality (deeply ingrained in the revolts against indigenous structures of oppression) than found in the struggles of metropolitan and global-oriented feminists (the latter no doubt opening up spaces for the former); or, the reassertion of 'Bharat' ... as laid out by a real and genuine search for 'cultural democracy' in the yearnings of traditional artisan communities struggling against urban and 'global' tycoons trying to export Indian art and culture, but also of deeply frustrated artists and activists and 'alternate media' exponents seeking a new identity for themselves as well as for the country.

As all this will also militate against the new 'special interests' of professionals and business groups lobbying in the corridors of power and—more pertinently—against new collaborationists with foreign interests masquerading as 'nationalist' politicians (chastising real movements of cultures and nationalities as being 'anti-national'), and as it will also find it difficult to swallow the old socialist rhetoric (which had generated so many expectations which were just let down), a completely new alignment of forces is likely to find fruition.

How does it all sound? At once unsettling for the modernist generation which has lost its moorings and yet opening up new possibilities, new hopes, that may well move the country towards fresh thresholds of democratic self-realization. For so many forces that appeared to run helter-skelter that may now get poised to take on new roles and, by so doing, find a new comprehension, a new cohesion. Despite so much uncertainty, so much ambiguity.

One of the continuing cultural traits of the Indian civilization has all along been in terms of its high tolerance of ambiguity. Only the modern hi-tech elite wants to regulate things, 'resolve' contradictions along some rationalist calculus, live by the logic of the excluded middle. The age of these modernists—and their 'post-modern' inheritors—is fast coming to a close here and elsewhere in the world. This does not mean any return to some pristine past as if such a past were ever there for us to 'revive'. This, then, is the ambience of a new awakening, a redefinition of Indian identity, one that is at once so uncertain about what lies in store and so pregnant with possibilities. This will call for a series of conceptual efforts—reconstructing national identity, restructuring the state, at once decentering and recentering the federal polity. Federating from below, federating regionally (that being the challenge of Punjab and Kashmir and Tamil Nadu) and federating socially (that being the challenge of Mandal), with a deep ecological content (that being the challenge of Narmada) and an extensive economic rationale (that being the challenge of the struggle against globalization), together creating a new and refashioned democratic structure, drawing on fresh convulsions in the social fabric occasioned by new assertions of the poor and the various peripheries.

It is through such a conception of 'a new India (that) is struggling to be born' that we can have some glimpses of a future that could take shape. Hopefully, such a future can be fashioned on the basis of a timely sense of how to respond to a historical reality, and to enable the right actors to so respond. From both the bottoms of the social hierarchy—the poor—and the diverse ethnics and the 'backwards', together announcing a new consolidation of forces.

The Call of the Ethical Imperative

If this be the new enterprise based on a new interpretation of the emerging reality, what should be the role of those among us who till recently held on to the old and yet have, for some time now, been wanting to become part of the new? It is here that the ethical imperative comes into force: how to, at once, communicate and commiserate with the new strivings and the new assertions, 'sacrifice' the lifestyles that divide us from them on an almost permanent basis, and do this not just as ecological prudence and the aesthetics of frugality and limits but as ethical choices made out of a sense of sharing and solidarity, of inhabiting a common world which we are together trying to reshape—despite the continuing gaps and cultural distances. The condition of the poor and the cultural correlates of poverty do indeed entail the former, but the ethical imperative is essentially based on the latter. By themselves the former exclude class. The latter necessarily includes it. And that is what provides the cutting edge of the politics of poverty. And of the ethics thereof.

Before concluding I should like to make two vital points. First, the new enterprise we have in mind is cast in modest and achievable terms—a lot better and different than where we are today but not necessarily aiming at some golden utopia. This is where the practical ontological perspective of the poor must guide us, not the 'perfect state' neurosis of the affluent. As in many other enterprises, here too the best can be the enemy of the good. And to the extent the 'best' is interpreted as 'most' in the sense of more and more consumption of finite resources, it excludes the rights of others because, in sheer gratification of what Gandhi called 'greed', it becomes blind to others' needs. Also, those who have sought the best, for themselves or for 'mankind', have, in fact, produced a world full of iniquity and exploitation. We should aim at a world of greater equity and less affluence, at an ethic of concern for all, instead of an ethic of gratification of individualized selves.

Second, our approach to the ethical imperative is also not cast in abstract philosophical terms but in terms of *active* interventions. And these too not by a select few who alone (like the traditional Brahmans) are supposed to provide ethical directions and guidance to society but by ordinary people—by those who have suffered from the course of secular history so far, have been victims of the historical process. For them the ethical intervention consists in recharting the course of history. If that is aiming high, so be it.

■

16

■ASHIS NANDY■

Born in 1937 in Bihar, Ashis Nandy is a leading social theorist and social psychologist in post-independence India. Trained in social science and psychoanalysis in Calcutta, Nagpur and Ahmedabad, he is one of the vocal critics of the legacy of colonialism and its embroilment with central features of Western modernity, like centralized state government, worship of reason and science, and disdain of vernacular traditions. In 1965 he joined the Centre for the Study of Developing Societies in Delhi under Rajni Kothari's leadership. Having served as Kothari's associate for many years, he is now a senior member and intermittent director of the Centre.

For primary and secondary sources see Ashis Nandy, *At the Edge of Psychology: Essays in Politics and Culture*, Delhi, Oxford University Press, 1980; *The Intimate Enemy: Loss and Recovery of Self under Colonialism*, Delhi, Oxford University Press, 1983; *Traditions, Tyranny and Utopias: Essays in the Politics of Awareness*, Delhi, Oxford University Press, 1987; 'Cultural Frames for Social Transformation: A Credo', *Alternatives*, Vol. 12, 1987, pp. 113–23; *The Illegitimacy of Nationalism: Rabindranath Tagore and the Politics of Self*, Delhi, Oxford University Press, 1994; *The Savage Freud*, Princeton, Princeton University Press, 1995; Fred Dallmayr, 'Global Development? Alternative Voices from Delhi', *Alternatives*, Vol. 21, 1996, pp. 259–82. The following is taken from 'Cultural Frames for Social Transformation'.

CULTURAL FRAMES FOR SOCIAL TRANSFORMATION: A CREDO

I. Culture, Critical Consciousness and Resistance

Amilcar Cabral, the African freedom fighter, spoke of the 'permanent, organized repression of the cultural life of the people' as the very core of colonialism. 'To take up arms to dominate a people is', he said, 'to take arms to destroy, or at least to neutralize ... its cultural life'. Cabral also seemingly recognized the corollary of such an understanding: that the reaffirmation of cultural traditions could not but be the heart of all authentic anti-colonialism. In many ways, however, Cabral borrowed heavily from nineteenth century Europe's world image. He could not be fully sensitive to the other reason why a theory of culture has to be the core of any theory of oppression in our times: a stress on culture reinstates the categories used by the victims, a stress on cultural traditions is a defiance of the modern idea of expertise, an idea which demands that even resistance be uncontaminated by the 'inferior' cognition or 'unripe' revolutionary consciousness of the oppressed. A stress on culture is a repudiation of the post-Renaissance European faith that only that dissent is true which is rational, sane, scientific, adult and expert—according to Europe's concepts of rationality, sanity, science, adulthood and expertise.

Viewed thus, the links between culture, critical consciousness and social change in India become, not a unique experience, but a general response of societies which have been the victims of history and are now trying to rediscover their own visions of a desirable society, less burdened by the post-Enlightenment hope of 'one world', and by the post-colonial idea of cultural relativism.

II. Criticisms of Modernity: Internal and External

Cultural survival is, increasingly, a potent political slogan in India. When the religious reformers of nineteenth century India spoke of protecting cultures, it seemed an obscurantist ploy. Today, when the juggernaut of modernity threatens every non-Western culture, the slogan no longer seems a revivalist conspiracy. It has become a plea for minimum cultural plurality in an increasingly uniformized world.

The plea has been accompanied by a growing concern with native resources and ideas, even though only to the extent they serve causes such as development, growth, national integration, security and even revolution. As if culture were only an instrument! Perhaps the time has come to pose the issue in a different way. I shall do so here in terms of the binary choices which underlie most responses to modernity in complex non-Western societies.

Unmixed modernism is no longer fashionable, not even in the modern world. The ultra-positivists and the Marxists, once so proudly anti-traditional, have begun to produce schools which criticize, if not the modernist vision in its entirety, at least crucial parts of it. Lionel Trilling and Peter Gay have gone so far as to call such criticisms—and the modernist dislike for modernity—a unique feature and a mark of modernity. One can off-hand think of several examples: the 'solar plexus' of D.H. Lawrence; the crypto-Luddite critique of industrialism by Charles Chaplin in *Modern Times*; the 'primitivism' of Pablo Picasso; and the defiance of science and rationality in the surrealist manifestos of André Breton, *et al*. They are all indicators of how modernity, at its most creative, cannot do without its opposite: anti-modernity.

However, to the extent these criticisms try to abide by or use as their reference the values of European Enlightenment, and to the extent modernization is an attempt to realize these values, such criticisms are internal to modernity. Let us call them forms of critical modernism. Examples of such critical modernism are: those models of scientific growth or technological transfer in the Third World which do not challenge the content or epistemology of modern science; critiques of the existing world order which take for granted the modern nation state system; and the social criticisms which vend the belief that if you displaced the elites or classes which control the global political economy, you could live happily with the modern urban–industrial vision ever after.

At the other end of the spectrum are the criticisms of modernity from outside. These criticisms reject the Enlightenment values and thus seem insane or bizarre to the modern man. Blake, Carlyle, Emerson, Thoreau, Ruskin and Tolstoy have been some of the better-known external critics of modernity in the West. In our times, Gandhi has been by far the most consistent and savage critic of modernity and of its best-known cultural product: the modern West. Gandhi called the modern culture satanic; and though he changed his mind about many things, on this point he remained firm. Many Gandhians cannot swallow this part of him. Either they read him as a nation-builder who, beneath his spiritual façade, was a hard-headed modernist wedded to the nation state system. Or they see him as a great man pursuing crazy civilizational goals (the way Isaac Newton, when not working on proper mathematical physics, worked on alchemy and on the science of trinity). They divide Gandhi into the normal and the abnormal, and reject the latter either as an aberration or as an embarrassment. 'Bapu, you are far greater than your little books', Nehru once charmingly said.

An unabashed Gandhi, however, took his 'insanity' to its logical conclusion. He rejected the modern innovations such as the nation state system, modern science and technology, urban–industrialism and evolutionism (without rejecting the traditional ideas of the state, science and technology, civic living and social transformation). Not being a Gandhian, I often watch and applaud from a distance the contortionist acts many modernists put up to fit Gandhi and his strange views into the modern paradigm. They can neither disown the Mahatma, nor digest him.

Yet, Gandhi was no Ananda Coomaraswamy. Both hated modernity, but they parted company when it came to traditions. Coomaraswamy theoretically kept open the possibility of assessing or altering traditions from the point of view of traditions. But perhaps because he was single-handedly trying to do for past times what the anthropologists as a community were trying to do for distant cultures, there was no criticism, or at least no significant criticism, of traditions in his works. The attitude was unashamedly defensive (examine, for instance, his comments on the concept and practice of *suttee* [i.e., *sati*, self-immolation of widows]).

Gandhi never eulogized the Indian village, nor called for a return to the past. He supported the ideas of the village and traditions, and India's traditional villagers, but not the extant Indian villages or traditions. Coomaraswamy, too, at one plane made this distinction, but the tone was different. This would be obvious to anyone who reads Coomaraswamy and Gandhi on caste. Coomaraswamy defended the pre-modern caste system because he found it more human than the modern class system. Gandhi also did so but went further, i.e., he sought to reorder the hierarchy of skills—to re-legitimize the manual and the unclean and delegitimize the Brahmanic and the clean. (I remember anthropologist Surajit Sinha once saying that while Rabindranath Tagore wanted to turn all Indians into Brahmans, Gandhi sought to turn them into Shudras. This can be read as an indictment of Gandhi; it can be read as a homage. And every Indian social thinker and activist has to make his or her choice some time or other; for, to say glibly that one must in the long run abolish both the categories is to fight in the short run for the Brahmanic world view. Exactly as to work for the future removal of poverty without touching the super-rich, in the present, is to collaborate with the latter.)

Such examples can be multiplied. Compare Coomaraswamy's appraisal of the Indian village—or Nehru's—with Gandhi's description of Indian villages as 'dung-heaps'; compare Dhanagopal Mukherji's passionate defense of India against the attack of Catherine Mayo in her *Mother India* with Gandhi's advice to every Indian to read what he called Mayo's 'drain-inspector's report'. Recently, sociologist T.N. Madan, analyzing Raja Rao's *Kanthapura*, has shown how the novelist construes Gandhi's movement against the tradition of untouchability as the other side of his struggle against modern imperialism, to stress the point that neither of the two struggles could be conceived of without the other.

Unlike Coomaraswamy, Gandhi did not want to defend traditions; he lived with them. Nor did he, like Nehru, want to museumize cultures within a modern frame. Gandhi's frame was traditional, but he was willing to criticize some traditions violently. He was even willing to include in his frame elements of modernity as critical vectors. He found no dissonance between his rejection of modern technology and his advocacy of the bicycle, the lathe and the sewing machine. Gandhi defied the modern world by opting for an alternative frame; the specifics in his frame were frequently modern. (The modernists find this hypocritical but they do not object to similar eclecticism when the framework is modern. Witness their attitude to the inclusion of Sarpagandha in modern pharmacology as reserpine, even though the drug has been traditionally a part of Ayurveda.)

Today, the battle of minds rarely involves a choice between modernity and traditions in their pure forms. The ravages of modernity are known and, since the past cannot be resurrected but only owned up, pure traditions, too, are a choice not given to us. Even if such a choice were given, I doubt if going back 2,500 years into the past is any better than going 5,000 miles to the West for ideas, especially in a post-Einsteinian world in which space and time are inter-translatable variables. Ultimately, the choice is between critical modernism and critical traditionalism. It is a choice between two frames of reference and two world views.

III. Oppression, Innocence and Voice

Some scholars object to the foregoing formulation. They find the concept of critical traditionality soft on obscurantism and internally inconsistent. One of them, T.G. Vaidyanathan, has suggested that I should use the expression 'critical insider' instead of 'critical traditionalist'.

Frankly, I have little attachment to the words I use. If by changing them some processes can be described better, I have no objection. I recognize that my descriptive categories are partly the ashes of my long romance with some versions of the critical theory, especially the early influence on me of scholars such as Theodor Adorno, Herbert Marcuse and Erich Fromm. They are not always adequate for non-Western realities. However, my categories are also partly a response to the argument of some scholars—Pratima Bowes being the last in the series—that traditional Indian thought never really developed a true critical component. I argue that (i) Indian thought, including many of its *puranic* and folk elements, can be and has been used as a critical base, because critical rationality is the monopoly neither of modern times nor of the Graeco–Roman tradition; and (ii) that some aspects of some exogenous traditions of criticism can be accommodated in non-Western terms within the non-Western civilizations.

Let me further clarify my position by restating it differently. Critical traditionality refers to the living traditions which include a theory of oppression, overt and/or covert. No tradition is valid or useful for our times unless it has, or can be made to have, an awareness of the nature of evil in modern times. If the term 'evil' seems too Judaeo–Christian to Indian ears—it should not, though, in a civilization which has known and included the Judaeo–Christian traditions longer than Europe has—one can talk of the nature of man-made *dukkha* or suffering in our times. This is the obverse of the point that no theory of oppression can make sense unless it is cast in native terms or categories, that is, in terms and categories used by the victims of our times. As a corollary, no native theory can be taken seriously unless it includes a subtheory of oppression.

This is not an odd restatement of the ideology of instrumentalism which dominates most modern, secular theories of oppression. I am not speaking here of a strategy of mass mobilization which includes certain compromises with the language, or the so-called false consciousness of the ahistorical societies. I am speaking of the more holistic or comprehensive cognition of those at the receiving end of the present world system. I am speaking of the primacy that should be given to the political consciousness of those who have been forced to develop categories to understand their own suffering and who reject the pseudo-indigenity of modern theories of oppression using—merely using—native idioms to conscientize, brainwash, educate, indoctrinate the oppressed or to museumize their cultures. The resistance to modern oppression has to involve, in our part of the world, some resistance to modernity and to important aspects of the modern theories of oppression. The resistance must deny in particular the connotative meanings of concepts such as development, growth, history, science and technology. These concepts have become not only new 'reasons of the state', but mystifications for new forms of violence and injustice. The resistance must also simultaneously subsume—and here pure traditionalism fails to meet our needs—a sensitivity to the links between cultural survival and global structures of oppression in our times. The critical traditionality I have in mind is akin to Rollo May's concept of authentic innocence, as opposed to what he calls pseudo-innocence. Authentic innocence is marked by an updated sense of evil; pseudo-innocence is not, for it thrives on what psychoanalysis calls 'secondary gains' for the victim from the oppressive system.

This also means that the living traditions of the non-Western civilizations must include a theory of the West. This is not to make the facile point that the West is a demon, but to recognize that the West and its relationship with the non-West has become deeply intertwined with the problem of evil in our times—according both to the West and to the non-West. Contrary to what the modern world believes, this non-Western construction of the West is not morally naive either. It does draw a line between the Western mainstream and the cultural underground of the West, between the masculine West and the feminine—exactly as it draws a line between the authenticity and pseudo-innocence of the non-West.

All said, it is the culturally rooted, non-modern understanding of the civilizational encounters of our times for which I am trying to create a space in public discourse. I am not trying to provide a new theory of oppression from within the social sciences.

IV. Language, Survival and the Language of Survival

Is there an Indian tradition with a built-in theory of oppression? The question is not relevant. The real issue is: can we construe a tradition which will yield a native theory of oppression? The issue is the political will to read traditions as an open-ended text rather than as a closed book.

This civilization has survived not only because of the 'valid', 'true' or 'proper' exegesis of the traditional texts (though a sophisticated hermeneutic tradition has always existed in India), but also because of the 'improper', 'far-fetched' and 'deviant' reinterpretations of the sacred and the canonical. If Chaitanya's dualist concept of *bhakti* (evolved partly as a response to the pure monism of Advaita that had till then dominated the Indian scene) seems to have been posed too far in the past, there is the instance of the *smarta* text, *Gita*, acquiring the canonical status of a *shruti* text in the nineteenth and early twentieth century India. And, of course, there is the instance of the first great social and religious reformer of modern India, Ram Mohun Roy (1777–1833), 'legitimately' interpreting Shankara's monism as monotheism, and the instance of Gandhi 'legitimately' borrowing his concept of *ahimsa* or nonviolence from the Sermon on the Mount and claiming it to be the core concept of orthodox Hinduism. Howsoever odd such 'distortions' may seem to the Westernized Indian or to the scholastic, Brahmanic traditionalist, they are the means the Indian civilization has repeatedly used to update its theories of evil and to ensure cultural survival while allowing large-scale social interventions.

To appreciate such reinterpretations, we must learn to acknowledge or decode three languages which often hide the implicit native theories of oppression in many non-Western traditions. These are the language of continuity, the language of spiritualism and the language of self. They may look like aspects of a primitive false consciousness to the moderns, but they continue to be the means of indirectly articulating the problems of survival for the non-modern victims of history.

The language of continuity (which accounts for the image of the savage as change-resisting and stagnant) assumes that all changes can be seen, discussed or analyzed as aspects of deeper continuities. In other words, the language assumes that every change, howsoever enormous, is only a special case of continuity. The perennial problems of human living and the perennial questions about human self-definition are common to all ages and cultures, and all disjunctions are a part of a continuous effort to grapple with these problems and questions. This position is radically different from the modern Western concept of continuity as only a special case of change or as only a transient period in time which is only overtly continuous or which, if it is truly continuous, is for that reason less valuable. In the dominant Indic tradition, each change is just another form of the unchanging and another reprioritization or revaluation of the existent.

At one plane the difference between the languages is exactly that: a difference in language. Yet, the fact remains that the language of continuity is mostly spoken by the victims of the present global system; the language of disjunction by the powerful and the rich and by those dominating the discourse on cultures. The fact also remains that the language of disjunction today has been successfully, though not wholly, coopted by those who are for the status quo. The Shah of Iran spoke of modernization and social change; his opponents spoke of cultural survival and conservation; the military juntas in South America and in the ASEAN countries speak of changing their societies into powerful nation states; their opponents speak of American Indian rights and of the traditions of non-white cultures; Ronald Reagan and Indira Gandhi have spoken of scientific and technical growth, their critics of ecological issues, traditional sciences and rural technologies. For a long time the weights were differently distributed: the language of continuity was mainly used by those who ran the older oppressive systems. Now, development, maturity, scientific temper, revolutionary consciousness—these are key words in the vocabulary of those who see themselves either as deservedly ruling the world or as its future rulers.

The language of spirit, including both its 'respectable' versions and the versions which the spiritually-minded themselves reject as confidence tricks, serves a number of this-worldly purposes of the oppressed. It often expresses, when decoded, an analysis of oppression which rejects the analytic categories popular with the oppressors and with the modern sectors from which the oppressors come. Such analysis in the language of spirit is seen by us as a

camouflaged statement of hard self-interest and *simultaneously*—
and here lies a fundamental contradiction in the modern concept
of the politics of cultures—as woolly sentimentalism and a subjectivist hoax. Obviously, if it is only woolly sentimentalism it cannot
at the same time be a camouflaged statement of self-interest; and
if it is an indirect statement of self-interest it is not that subjectivist,
after all. Marx recognized this when he spoke of religion as expressing the pain of the oppressed. But he was mired too deeply
in Eurocentric nineteenth century scientism and evolutionism. He
did not go so far as to take seriously the cognitive frame which
went with the pain. Nor did he notice (*i*) that the frame often used
the language of spirit to articulate a set of values which criticized
or defied the society as it existed; (*ii*) that it rejected the conventional concepts of science and rationality as potentially irrational,
inhuman, sectarian and collaborationist; and (*iii*) that it included
the potentiality, as Gandhi was to later demonstrate, of a renunciation of renunciation which would shun spiritual exercises for
the sake of political intervention on the assumption that suffering
is never unreal and a moral truth has to be acted out at both the
subjective and the objective planes.

A subcategory of the language of spirit in societies like ours is
the language of anti-history that rejects the idea of history, especially the idea of historical laws, as a new tool of oppression. The
language seeks to reinstate the mythopoetic language which is
closer to the victims of history. The understanding of oppression
expressed in myths and other forms of shared fantasies—or
expressed through alterations in existing myths and shared fantasies—transcends the barriers of regions and subcultures in a complex civilization. For most savages, myths communicate life
experiences and cultural roots; history hides them. That is why the
theory of oppression expressed in the mythopoetic language does
not come as a special module prepared by outsiders (to which the
oppressed must learn to adapt); it comes as an analytic statement
of the emic kind which may or may not be translatable into the
languages used by the dominant theories of man-made suffering.
History, as a modern myth, selects for us what should be remem-
bered on grounds of objectivity. Myths, as self-consciously selective memories, not only aid memory but also select for us what
should be forgotten on grounds of compassion.

Finally, the language of self in which the oppressed often pack-
age their story. It includes, as does the language of spiritualism,

the so-called fatalism of the savage and the primitive against which conscientization and other similar processes seem such good medicines. The language of self emphasizes variables such as self-control, self-realization, self-actualization and self-enrichment, and it apparently underplays changes in the non-self or the outer world. The language has been especially emphasized by the humanistic psychologists and others who have tried to base their theories of consciousness, psychological health and human creativity on insights into self processes rather than on insights into psycho-pathologies of social life. I am, however, drawing attention to the language from another vantage ground. The language of self, I want to stress, also has an implicit theory of the not-self—of oppression and social transformation. To borrow words from modern psychology, autoplasticity does in this case include alloplasticity. In many of the non-Western traditions the self is not only included in 'external' laws of nature and society; nature and society, in turn, are subsumed in the self. Self-correction and self-realization include the principle of intervention in the outside world as we have come to understand the world in post-Galilean and post-Cartesian cosmologies. Bhikhu Parekh has drawn my attention to the Gandhian emphasis on purifying the self as a means of serving the world, and serving the world as a means of purifying the self. The emphasis is built into the more sensitive traditional theories of self-in-society.

V. Critiques of Critiques

Modern theories of oppression may or may not help the oppressed; but they certainly help the theorists a lot. To the extent they speak the language of discontinuity, ultra-materialism or impersonality, they become a part, often a fashionable part, of the modern world and of the valued streams of dissent within that world. To the extent they presume to represent the sanity of the oppressed, these theories sometimes become the livery of a new elite—whether known as the revolutionary vanguard, the expert demystifier, the trained psychotherapist, or the scientist trying to break down the prescientific temper of the masses. Perhaps we have reached the point where one must learn to take more seriously other categories used by those victimized by the modern oppressive systems. For these systems not only oppress in the way older oppressive systems did—by openly legitimizing violence, greed and dominance. These systems successfully tap the human ingenuity (i) to produce systems that are unjust, expropriatory and violent in the name of liberation or freedom; and (ii) to develop a public consciousness which would include an explicit model of proper dissent. In such a world, dissent, unless it seeks to subvert the rules of the game and the language in which the rules are framed, becomes another form of conformity.

George Orwell realized this. He felt that the oppressed, when faced with problems of survival, had no obligation to follow any model or any rule of the game. Now, it is possible to argue that this 'methodological anarchism', too, can, in turn, produce over time its own special brand of violence. I have no fool-proof answer to that argument. But I like to believe that perhaps one way of containing such second-order violence is to work with a perspective which (i) retains, and persistently struggles to retain, the sense of immediacy and directness of the experience or per-ception of man-made suffering; and (ii) keeps open the scope for criticism of every criticism.

In the short run, however, one may have to be even less de-manding. Protest or dissent cannot, and should not, wait for that golden moment when the protestor or the dissenter gets hold of, or is converted to, the correct theory in the correct way, be that theory modern or traditional. In fact, any theory which believes that such correctness or conversion must come before liberation can be talked about is, to that extent, an incorrect theory, follow-ing the Orwellian principle mentioned above. Yet, some stipula-tions can perhaps be made about the minimum scepticism towards contemporary structures of authority and authoritative-ness which an activist or a social critic must show in order to qual-ify as useful for our times. Such stipulations may give meaning, not only to the resistance of the illiterate savage pitting his naked body against the might of the high technology of his oppressors, but also to the passions of the young activist moved by the plight of his fellow humans and trying to understand that plight in terms of the highly technical modern theories of liberation.

First, scepticism has to be directed at the modern nation state. This, I am aware, is easier said than done in post-colonial socie-ties. The folk-theories of politics popular among the middle classes in these societies would have us believe that all the ills of these societies are due to their inability to produce or to sustain proper nation states. Once such nation states are built, the argument goes, the first problem of social engineering and collective survival would be solved. Scepticism towards the nation state in such an environment looks, at best, simple-minded; at worst, treacherous. Yet, the fact remains that in most Asian and African societies, the state has increasingly become not only the major instrument of corruption, expropriation and violence towards their own people, but also increasingly ethnocidal. Even if one does not take an anarchist position on the state in such societies, one could at least be wary of the idea of nation state as an end in itself and be sceptical of state-sponsored anxieties about national security, specially when this concept of security is invoked to demand sacrifices from social sectors least able to make them.

Second, there must be scepticism towards modern science. I am not speaking of the usual scepticism about some forms of technology or about the usual criticisms of the control on science exercised by social forces. I am speaking of modern science as the basic model of domination in our times and as the ultimate justification for all institutionalized violence. I am speaking of the criticism of criticism which is aware that the acceptance of the social determination of science and technology can hide the refusal to be sceptical about the philosophical assumptions and texts of modern science, about the modern scientific imagination itself. Unless one builds checks against the basic model of domination in modern science, I doubt if one can have any check on the newer forms of institutionalized violence.

Third, there must be scepticism towards history, specially towards the so-called larger forces of history, unless the awareness of such larger forces is matched by an awareness of their implications in everyday life. I am not very clear here. Let me try again. I have mentioned here and there in this essay the name of Gandhi; and it may be appropriate to end this statement with a reference to his attitude to history. One reason why Gandhi aroused deep anxieties in Indian middle class *literati* was that he always pushed social analysis to the level of personal lifestyle, to the level of what can be called the smaller forces of history. Gandhi did not allow the rhetoric of historical awareness to be a substitute for the political morality of everyday life. He was willing to suspend his suspicion of history, but he was unwilling to let anyone forget one's personal responsibility to live out one's understanding of historical and/or perennial truths. This terribly, terribly fuddy-duddy demand for internal consistency—between the public and the private, and between the collective and the personal—is particularly anxiety-provoking to those who specialize in speaking the language of making history while only passively living in history. Now, it is possible to argue that all accountability is odious, that ideas are important in themselves and independent of the personal lives of their proponents. But Gandhi was always sceptical of the modern claim that perfect institutions would one day eliminate the social need for individual morality. He therefore believed that accountability should be demanded at least of those whose theories of social intervention demand sacrifices and accountability of others. He believed, too, that accountability should likewise be demanded of those whose theories claim to bridge the private and the public, and the personal and the historical.

For those who feel uneasy with any talk of personal morality in the public realm I can word the issue differently. Many political economists, Immanuel Wallerstein being a recent example, have drawn attention to the fact—uncomfortable to the Third World elites and intellectuals—that the Third World societies usually maintain within their borders exactly the same violent, exploitative, ethnocidal systems which they confront in the larger world: the same center and periphery, the same myth that the sacrifices made by people in the short run will lead to the beatitude of development and scientific advancement in the long run, the same story of over-consuming elites fattening themselves to early death at the center, and starvation, victimhood and slow death at the periphery. Because of this, the demands of the Third World for more equitable and just terms in North–South exchanges often sound dishonest or hollow. I believe that many traditional as well as some modern systems of psychology allow us to extend the argument to the level of the individual. In other words, they allow us to claim (i) that we model our interventions in the world on our interventions in our own selves; and (ii) that the world does to us what we do to ourselves. This is the reverse of what I have called elsewhere the principle of isomorphic oppression, according to which each level of an integrated social structure neatly reproduces within it the oppressive dynamics of the whole. The principle of isomorphism says: what you do to others you ultimately do to yourself, for 'the wages of sin is the kind of person you are'. When reversed, the principle becomes: what you do to yourself or to your kind cannot but invite others to do the same to you and to your kind.

It should be obvious that this way of looking at social intervention and culpability dissolves the crude dichotomy between the study of the elites and the study of the masses or, for that matter, between elitism and mass-line. Following traditional wisdom, I like to believe that the story of the prince can never be told without telling the story of the pauper, and that the cause of the pauper can never be independent of the cause of the prince. My life's ambition is to write an interpretation of poverty by focusing entirely on the lifestyle of the super-rich. As Frantz Fanon recognized, the suffering of the victims cannot but be the sickness of their oppressors and the intertranslatability between two sets of life experiences is complete once the rules of translation are identified.

The three scepticisms are tied together in my case—I have a right to end a credo on a personal note—by a general scepticism towards all ideas which are used as sources of legitimacy by the winners of the world. I should like to believe that the task of a person living a life of the mind is to make greater demands on those who mouth the certitudes of their times and are closer to the powerful and the rich, than on the faiths and ideas of the powerless and the marginalized. That way lie freedom, compassion and justice.

■

17

■ ROMILA THAPAR ■

Born in 1931 in Lucknow, Romila Thapar enjoys a solid reputation as a leading historian in post-independence India. She studied history first at Punjab University, and then at the University of London where she received her doctorate in 1958. Subsequently, she taught at Kurukshetra University and Delhi University. In 1970 she joined the Jawaharlal Nehru University in Delhi as professor of ancient Indian history and was instrumental in establishing there the Centre for Historical Studies. In 1983, she served as general president of the Indian History Congress. She retired from teaching in 1993.

For literature see Romila Thapar, *A History of India*, 2 vols, Baltimore, Penguin Books, 1965–66; *Asoka and the Decline of the Mauryas*, 2nd ed., Delhi, Oxford University Press, 1973; *Ancient Indian Social History*, New Delhi, Orient Longman, 1978; *Cultural Transaction in Early India: Tradition and Patronage*, Delhi, Oxford University Press, 1987; *Interpreting Early India*, New York, Oxford University Press, 1992; *Time as a Metaphor of History*, Delhi, Oxford University Press, 1996; R. Champakalakshmi and S. Gopal, eds, *Tradition, Dissent and Ideology: Essays in Honour of Romila Thapar*, New York, Oxford University Press, 1996. The following selection is taken from *Cultural Transaction in Early India*, pp. 7–24.

TRADITION

A variety of beliefs about India's past have simmered over the last couple of hundred years. Some among them have come to be accepted as part of the country's cultural tradition and have been accorded the status of tradition. It may be argued that this happens when societies are searching for identity and the pronouncements of historians, particularly of cultural historians, come to be accepted as axioms. It becomes necessary therefore for historians to pause from time to time to take stock as it were by asking whether what has come to be accepted as tradition deserves to be so accepted. This is what I propose to attempt in the two lectures. The change of focus becomes imperative either when there is new information on the past or when the process of interpreting the past undergoes change. It is primarily the latter which in this case suggests a reassessment.

A consideration of cultural history would have to begin with an attempt at defining culture and this has been the subject of much discussion in recent decades. I can at best attempt a very brief summary.

The term culture itself has it own history. The primary meaning of culture is the cultivating of natural growth, and by extension in recent times it has come to mean the cultivating of the human mind. Among historians of the eighteenth and nineteenth centuries culture and civilization became synonymous. The association of culture was, however, with superior social groups. The inadequacy of this limitation contributed towards the redefinition of the term in which it was extended to include all patterns of behavior and ways of life. Culture therefore refers to behavior patterns socially acquired and socially transmitted by means of symbols. It includes language, tradition, customs and institutions. It is in the wider sense that I am using the term.

Furthermore, culture in relation to tradition links the past to the present. It has therefore a historical context which is as significant as the cultural form itself.

The historical process is decisive to the definition of culture, yet the understanding of Indian culture is poorly served in this respect, for it is assumed that the historical process has a static interpretation and has remained broadly unchanged over the last century, or, that culture is a one-time event which has survived untampered with from the past to the present. From newspaper editors to prime ministers everyone pronounces on the civilization and culture of the Indian past, unblushingly unconcerned with their historical basis. There are now, at least among historians, new kinds of analyses of cultural institutions and forms. Cultural history and its analysis juxtaposes the form with those who create it and those who order its creation, and also attempts to see it as a social signal.

The continuity of culture is generally related to traditions which, in turn, are made up of cultural forms. Tradition is defined as the handing down of knowledge or the passing on of a doctrine or a technique. Cultural history implies looking analytically both at what goes into the making of a tradition as well as that which is interpreted by historians as tradition. We often assume that a form is handed down in an unchanging fashion and that what comes to us is its pristine form. However, the sheer act of handing on a tradition introduces change, and not every tradition is meticulously bonded by mnemonic or other devices to prevent interpolations or change. A tradition, therefore, has to be seen in its various phases. Even the concept of *parampara*, which at one level appears to be frozen knowledge, reveals, on investigation, variations and change. Traditions which we today believe have long pedigrees may, on an historical analysis, be found to be an invention of yesterday. In other words, what we regard as tradition may well turn out to be our contemporary requirements fashioned by the way we wish to interpret the past. Interpretations of the past have also come to be treated as knowledge and are handed down as tradition. I would like to consider some of these interpretations in their historical context, for this may clarify their validity or otherwise to being regarded as tradition.

Let me illustrate these ideas with a few examples.

The disjuncture between normative values and social reality is often so evident that it is sometimes surprising to come across normative values being taken for descriptions of reality. But it is necessary to distinguish between the organization of external reality as a theory and the reality itself. Thus, the *dharmashastras*, the normative texts *par excellence*, inform us of the rules of varna [caste]. It is assumed that at least the members of the higher varna observe these rules. However, from the earliest times there are certain discrepancies. The Vedic texts refer to various important Vedic Rishis as *dasiputrah*, being born of *dasis*.[1] Dirghatamas, who is described as the son of a *dasi*, in turn married a *dasi* whom he is said to have found among strange people in the east, and she was mother to his son, the respected Rishi Kaksivant. Evidently these Brahmans took the rule of exogamy literally, and married far out. But equally intriguing is the origin of the compiler of the *Mahabharata*, the learned Veda Vyasa. His father, the Rishi Parasara, became enamoured of a girl of a fisherman's community as she rowed him across the river. Despite her fishy odor he made his intentions clear. She resisted him at first, but finally accepted his advances when he promised that she would be rid of the odor of fish. The boat was enveloped in a discreet curtain of clouds and the now sweet-scented girl eventually gave birth to Veda Vyasa. The ambiguity of his mother's origins is further complicated by the story that she had been an *apsara*'s [celestial nymph] daughter abandoned as a foundling among fisher folk.[2] And this becomes a stereotype among such origin myths, raising a host of questions regarding the treatment of identity.

How are we to interpret this? First of all, and certainly, that our ancestors had a sense of humor and were willing to invent stories about these lapses from the normative perspective of even those whom they revered—a quality which is difficult to find in contemporary India, for such stories would be unheard of today. But, what is more important, and once we get past the symbolic meaning, is that origins obviously do not have to conform to normative rules, and are possibly not very significant.

This is even more marked in the origin myths of a variety of royal families claiming *Kshatriya* status in the post-Gupta period.[3] Prior to the Gupta dynasty the *Puranas* refer to such families being of Brahman and even *Shudra* origin. Few in fact were *Kshatriya* in spite of the insistence of the normative texts on the *Kshatriya* origins of ruling families. The myths of many such families of the later period, as those of the Guhilla and Gandella, make one suspect that the families may have been obscure and that they sought status through fabricated genealogies, linking them to the Suryavamsi and Candravamsi lineages, which lineages seem also to have been an invention of a particular historical time.

In shying away from coming to terms with this divergence, we blind ourselves to the possible flexibility of a society which, in certain situations, was probably as important a characteristic as the theoretical insistence on the minutiae of rules of social behavior. We thereby provide a simplistic explanation for a complex arrangement. The concession to the Brahman that he could marry into any varna was in some ways parallel to the incorporation of belief and ritual from a variety of sources in the making of religious sects—an incorporation which defies the forcing of what we call Hindu sects into a homogeneous, uniform, clearly identifiable and ecclesiastically organized religious entity. This epitomizes a perspective different from that of the Semitic model.

But how are we to interpret high culture literature which mocks the Brahman? In the plays of Kalidasa, the *vidushaka*—the stereotype of companion or fool—is a Brahman unable to speak Sanskrit and mocking the essence of Brahmanism as contained in the *dharmashastras*. The normative texts, of course, do not carry even a hint of the *vidushaka* as a category of Brahman. Admittedly, in a literature intended for the royal court, the foil to the king could only be a Brahman, since a member of another caste would amount to *lèse majesté*. But did he have to be such a non-Brahmanical Brahman that even the king mocks the Brahman in him? Was this an ironic commentary on the *purohita* or on particular categories of Brahmans elsewhere taken more seriously? So distinct a contravention of the norm can only point to the norm not being pervasive.

Talking of Kalidasa, we assume that his version of the story of Shakuntala was the one made familiar to people of all ages since the writing of the play. Yet Kalidasa was himself taking an existing tradition and transforming it into something new and in keeping with his own time and place. There were two versions of the Shakuntala story in circulation with two different audiences. The earlier version occurs in the *Mahabharata*, where the origin myth of the founder of the Puru lineage, Bharata, is recited.[4] The story begins with a massive hunt led by the Raja Duhsanta, where we are told that many families of tigers were laid low and many hundreds of deer killed. The hunt, as hunts in epic literature often go, is a war against nature, causing havoc and destruction all round. Arriving at the hermitage of Kanva, Duhsanta is welcomed in the absence of the Rishi by Shakuntala, who happily converses with him without any reservation. When asked about her parentage, she explains that she is the natural child of the *apsara* Menaka and the Rishi Visvamitra and was left a foundling at the hermitage of Kanva. When Duhsanta, attracted by her beauty, proposes a Gandharva marriage, she replies in a spirited fashion that she will agree only on condition that her son is declared the *yuvaraja*, which condition Duhsanta accepts. A few years later she arrives at his court with their son Bharata. Although he recognizes her, Duhsanta pretends not to know her and, even as she argues her rights, he abuses her parents, referring to Menaka as a slut and to Visvamitra as a lecher, and dismisses her as a whore. Whereupon a celestial voice proclaims that the boy is in fact the child of Duh-santa. He then accepts both mother and son, maintaining that his earlier pretence was merely to ensure that the legitimacy of the child would be declared before his people. The story may well have been introduced as a form of genealogical latching on.

Kalidasa introduces the sub-plot of the signet ring which drops off Shakuntala's finger; and Duhsyanta (as the name occurs in Kalidasa) loses his memory owing to a curse and does not re-member the association with Shakuntala until he sees the signet ring. In effect, the feel of the play is completely different from the epic version of the story.

Shakuntala in the epic is a confident, high-spirited, assertive young woman who knows what she is about and is not going to be taken for a ride. In the play she is submissive, shy, reserved, perhaps even a little frightened and cowed down by her love for the king. She is the new subservient woman of upper caste courtly culture who is incapable of arguing in defence of her rights or ob-jecting to the treatment by Duhsyanta. Kalidasa has invested Shakuntala with status. The king's major concern is the need for an heir, unlike in the epic where it is Shakuntala who is anxious that her son be declared the *yuvaraja*. Today, we have accepted Kalidasa's depiction of the submissive woman and have ignored the far more independent characterization of the epic version, in part at least for reasons which have to do with attempts to justify the subservience of women with an appeal to what is regarded as 'our tradition'....

Normative texts and creative literature differ in the handling of those who live in the hermitage. The normative curriculum refers, of course, only to males of the upper caste and requires a life cycle which covers the well-known four stages of studentship, house-holder, renouncer, and ascetic. Written into this life cycle is the opposition of *grihastha* to *sannyasa*, of householder to ascetic.[5]....
In the normative tradition renunciation was the prelude to asceti-cism and the means of achieving personal salvation. The distance from society was intended to underline the need for isolation and contemplation in pursuit of the goal of salvation. In a sense it was a selfish act as much as it was social. In effect, however, as is clear from descriptive passages referring to asceticism, the supernormal powers became an asset on which the power of the ascetic was based.... As a source of alternative authority, the renouncer is dis-tinct from both priestly power and the coercive authority of the

state.[6] The socio-political role of the renouncer is, it seems to me, a characteristic feature of Indian civilization and requires a more thorough analysis. This would question the notion that Indian society has always been other-worldly because of the attraction of renunciation. Instead, it requires that we examine more analytically the many dimensions to the role of the renouncer in society....

I have already mentioned that, in creating a tradition, we sometimes select from the past those normative values which may have a contemporary appeal but which may even be contrary to historical actuality. The insistence on the tradition of religious tolerance and non-violence as characteristic of Hinduism, which is built on a selection of normative values emphasizing *ahimsa*, is not borne out by the historical evidence. The theory is so deeply ingrained among most Indians that there is a failure to see the reverse of it even when it stares them in the face. The extremity of intolerance implicit in the notion of untouchability was glossed over by regarding it as a function of society and caste. The fact of this intolerance is now conceded so casually, that the concession is almost beginning to lose meaning. Apart from this, we also need to look at more direct examples of religious persecution. Curiously, even when historians have referred to such activities as indications of intolerance and persecution,[7] there has been a firm refusal on the part of popular opinion to concede that Hindu sects did indulge in religious persecution.

The persecution of Buddhists in Kashmir is referred to by Hsuan Tsang; but, lest it be thought that he being a Chinese Buddhist monk was prejudiced, the testimony of Kalhana in the *Rajatarangini* should be more acceptable. Hsuan Tsang refers to the atrocities of Mihirakula against the Buddhists both in Punjab and in Kashmir in the sixth century A.D. Hsuan Tsang may well have been exaggerating when he lists the destruction of 1,600 Buddhist *stupas* and *sangharamas*, and the killing of many thousands of Buddhist monks and lay-followers.[8] Kalhana gives an even fuller account of the king killing innocent people by the hundreds.[9] This is often dismissed by attributing the anti-Buddhist actions of Mihirakula to his being a Huna. But it should not be forgotten that he was also an ardent Shaiva and gave grants of land in the form of *agraharas* to the Brahmans. It is possible that the recently discovered *stupa* at Sanghol in Punjab, where sculpted railings were found in the vicinity of a *stupa* dismantled and packed away, indicates this persecution of the Buddhists. Kalhana writes of an earlier persecution of Buddhists in Kashmir and the willful destruction of a *vihara* again by a Shaivite king. But on this occasion the king repented and built a new monastery for the Buddhist monks....

My purpose in drawing attention to the Shaivite persecution of Buddhists and Jainas is not an attempt at being provocative. We have here a major historical problem which requires detailed investigation. The desire to portray tolerance and non-violence as the eternal values of the Hindu tradition has led to the pushing aside of such evidence. That there were mutual intellectual borrowings in certain philosophical schools should not prevent us from seeing the reality on the ground. If there were cases of diverse religious sects co-existing, there were also situations of antagonism. The evidence of persecution raises the question of the degree to which such activities on the part of various religious groups were seen as a way of claiming ascendancy and power.

A related question is whether the Hindus as a community were aware of or perpetrated this hostility, or whether it was perpetrated only by a segment of the Hindu community, substantially the Shaivas. An historical evaluation of such persecutions would be required to ascertain the sects involved, and their social affinities. If only certain segments of society, whether castes or sects, were involved, the effect of these on other segments would be worth inquiring into, as also the influence of religious militancy on the segment itself. Would these actions have had an impact on the values associated with the Hindu community, assuming, of course, that there was at this time the consciousness of a single Hindu community? The argument put forward in recent times that the Buddhists, Jainas and a variety of Hindu sects were all part of the compendium religion we call Hinduism has also contributed to these animosities being dismissed as minor sectarian rivalries, whereas the evidence points to a different assessment.

It is historically important to know why this persecution of the Buddhists and Jainas occurred in particular by the Shaivas. I can only offer a few comments. At the religious level, it may have had to do with asceticism. Was Shiva seen as the ascetic *par excellence* and the patron deity of ascetics, and were Buddhist and Jaina monks seen as imposters? Did Buddhist and Jaina monks find the worship of the lingam offensive owing to the puritanism inherent in both these systems? Yet the Tantric versions of these systems conceded to practices and ideas which were opposed to puritanism. If the hostility related only to religious differences, then it should have surfaced earlier in time. It is interesting that it begins about the middle of the first millennium A.D. and gains force through the centuries until Buddhism eventually fled the country and Jainism was effectively limited to a few pockets. The persecution predates the coming of Islam to these areas, so that the convenient excuse that Islamic persecution caused the decline of these religions is not applicable....

I have been emphasizing Shaiva hostility, which is not to suggest that the Vaishnavas were altogether partial to Buddhists and Jainas. But there seem to be fewer examples of persecution by the Vaishnavas. This, too, requires an explanation. An obvious explanation is that the *avatara* theory of Vaishnavism made it an assimilative religion except, of course, that the incorporation of a cult was generally after it had been emasculated. Thus, the Buddha in some late texts came to be treated as an *avatara* of Vishnu. The underlying strength of this religious induction was that the *avatara* was ahistorical, in other words, the historicity of the *avatara* and his being located in space and time was irrelevant to the religious process. This was, of course, in striking contrast to the historicity of the founders of various Vaishnava sects. Unlike contemporary Hindu movements today, which seek to find birth places and historicity for the *avataras* of Vishnu and even drag in archaeology in the attempt to prove this, such searches were of little concern to the majority of the Vaishnavas in the past. It becomes pertinent, therefore, to inquire into the question of the period of history when the need for historicity enters belief in the *avataras*, and why.

The persecution of Buddhists and Jainas was not a principal concern with all Hindu sects; nevertheless, it was socially important enough to be recorded by some. If there had been a Hindu community with an all-India identity, it would have been aware of the intolerance of some of its constituents and pronounced upon it. That this intolerance is not characteristic of the entire community does not suggest the tolerance of Hindus, but, rather, that the consciousness of community determined by a religious identity, based on certain essential uniformities and cutting across segmental differences, may not have been prevalent.

The term 'Hindu' is used for the first time in Arabic sources referring to the inhabitants of the subcontinent across the Indus. For them it simply meant the indigenous. It does not appear to have been appropriated by those who constitute what we today call the

Hindu community until very much later. The historical context suggests that it did not connote a specific identity but was intended to include those who were neither Muslim nor Christian. It would be worth investigating whether historically the label 'Hindu' became a convenient umbrella under which to include a large number of segments which lay outside the more identifiable followers of Islam and Christianity. In the case of Islam and Christianity, religious identity cut across caste and sectarian concerns. There was no such clear-cut religious identity among what have been called Hindu castes and sects where the caste and sectarian identity was primary. Perhaps it would be more appropriate to see the latter as separate communities. The putting together of these latter groups into what came to be seen as the Hindu community was, however, important to the process of nation-building in recent times.

The religious identity among groups which had constituted what has come to be called the Hindus was earlier a series of sectarian identities rather than one of a universalizing kind.... There appear, instead, to have been a number of segments largely determined by caste, custom, language and region; and only at certain levels were religious identities recognizable as being similar. For the rest, caste identities probably were more significant and the religious belief systems and actions of particular castes may have had some common features. There was certainly geographical mobility among Brahmans and a certain degree of universality among them too, but this was not a Hindu identity in the sense of enveloping people at all levels in all sects. Shankaracharya, for instance, organized a Shaivite Brahman identity which was only a segment of and did not include the totality of what is today called a Hindu identity. Even the observance of varna-*ashrama-dharma* remained a normative aspiration. Differences of language, customary law and worship kept the segments segregated.

It is important to differentiate between common civilizational symbols, which are recognized over an area, and the consciousness of a community acting towards common social and religious goals. Whereas the former was evident in India the latter appears not to have been so. It is also worth examining the possibly different role of the inter-relation between religion and society in such a caste and sect-based system. Historians have long looked at religions in India, whether indigenous or imported, from the perspective of the teachings of the texts. If religion in the past has to be

properly understood, this obviously has to be related to the practice and perceptions of the religious groups. Tolerance and persecution has to do with such perceptions. It is worth noticing, for
example, that in the early encounter between religious sects in
India and Islam, Muslims were rarely referred to as such. The
terms used were either ethnic—Turuska/Turk, or geographical—
Yavana/West Asian, or the more generalized *mleccha*, meaning
impure and covering a wide range of non-Muslims as well. This is
a very different perception of 'the other' from what we have tried
to make of it by postulating a society divided into Hindus and
Muslims.

The Hindu community as an all-India phenomenon identifying
itself as a large community encompassing all aspects of 'Hindu'
belief and worship appears to have been a development of recent
centuries. The notion may well have been encouraged not only
by the adoption of the label 'Hindu', but also by the use of this
label by orientalist scholarship, which attempted to format Hinduism as an historically evolved religion along the lines of Christianity,
and by the demands of political representation as they emerged in
the nineteenth century. Here the term 'Hindu' connotes effectively the capturing and claiming of almost all religious belief and
practice other than that associated with Islam and Christianity. It
bunches together a range of religious sects, some so antithetical to
each other that it is difficult to accept them under one label. This
perhaps also explains the ease with which that pre-eminent institution, the Ramakrishna Mission, can claim to be both Hindu and
non-Hindu.

For such a diverse community to create a uniform cultural tradition for itself can become an exercise in juggling with history. Traditions are not self-created: they are consciously chosen, and the
choice from the past is enormous. We tend, therefore, to choose
that which suits our present needs. The choice has its own logic
and we are perhaps not fully aware of the directions which such
choices may take. If we are to understand the role of religion in
the Indian society of earlier times we may have to move away
from the paradigm of Hinduism and the other religions in India as
projected in the colonial period. There has to be an awareness of
social relations actually experienced and the representation of
these by particular social groups. In the search for a cultural tradition Hindus turn to normative texts and the Brahmanical tradition
as the exemplars from the past. This has the advantage that it acts
as a kind of all-purpose Sanskritization. But it excludes a large

range of both valuable and essential cultural experience. Complex societies have competing value systems and attempts are made by the more established to delete ideologies of protest or of divergent values, as I have tried to show. The awareness of the historical context of a cultural form or an ideological supposition may help us understand that cultural forms change their function over time, both through the internal development of the form and through the imprint of external factors. In other words, cultural forms are embedded in social realities and when we consciously choose a cultural form we should be aware of this reality. It is only then that the choice becomes intelligible.

In this lecture I have attempted to show that we have a variety of beliefs about India's past which have been projected as part of our cultural traditions. We speak of a well-regulated society characterized in all cases by an observance of caste rules, but we pay less attention to instances where these rules were not observed. The latter would go contrary to the tradition, but would provide insights into nuances of social dispositions and perhaps foster a variant set of tradition about the functioning of society. We see the tradition of renunciation largely as a search for individual salvation with an emphasis on the value of other-worldliness, but miss out the importance of the seemingly contradictory role of the renouncer as a figure of authority in society. We insist on the tradition of tolerance and non-violence as an essential feature of Hindu practice and, by neglecting the evidence to the contrary, diminish our understanding of the religious and social interrelations of a major part of India's cultural past. This aspect would be further illuminated if we had a more precise historical view of at least the concept of community, instead of assuming its existence in a particular form from earlier times. Communities in contemporary India, be they Hindu, Muslim, Sikh, Christian or whatever, seek legitimacy by asserting a long history for their existence. This claim relates closely to our understanding of a secular society in the present. A more precise comprehension of the community in Indian history would clarify some of the problems of the present day as well. Our understanding of all these institutions from the past is closely related to our perceptions of ourselves in the present. It is imperative therefore that historical legitimacy should not be given arbitrarily without first ascertaining its historical viability.

■ Notes ■

[1] *Pancavimsa Brahmana*, 14.6.6; *Brhad-devata*, 4.11.15; 21.25; *Rg Veda*, 7.33.

[2] *Mahabharata, Adiparvan*, 63.

[3] Romila Thapar, 'Genealogy as a Source of Social History', in *Ancient Indian Social History: Some Interpretations*, New Delhi, Orient Longman, 1978, pp. 326–60.

[4] *Mahabharata, Adiparvan*, 71.

[5] Romila Thapar, 'Householders and Renouncers in the Brahmanical and Buddhist Tradition', in T.N. Madan (ed.), *Way of Life*, New Delhi, Manohar, 1982, pp. 273–98.

[6] Romila Thapar, 'Renunciation: The Making of a Counter-Culture?', in *Ancient Indian Social History: Some Interpretations*, pp. 63–104.

[7] e.g., K.A. Nilakanta Sastri, *The Colas*, Madras, Oxford University Press, 1955, pp. 636, 645.

[8] *Si–yu–ki*, I.xcix.

[9] *Rajatarangini*, I. 307.

■

18

■ RANAJIT GUHA ■

Ranajit Guha was born in 1922 in eastern Bengal into a family of medium-sized landowners, lower government officials and lawyers. Being educated first at a village school and then at a secondary school in Calcutta, he entered Presidency College, Calcutta in 1938 to study history, with a focus on the history of Bengal. While at college, he became a Marxist and joined the Communist Party of India. After receiving his Master's degree from Calcutta University in 1946, he worked briefly for the communist paper *Swadhinata*, and then left India for extensive travels to Paris, Eastern Europe, the Middle East, Africa, and China. On returning to India in 1953 he taught at a number of colleges in Calcutta; in 1956 he resigned from the Communist Party over the Soviet invasion of Hungary. In 1959 he left for England, teaching first at the University of Manchester and then at Sussex University. During 1979–80 he and a group of younger historians conceived the idea of 'Subaltern Studies' whose first volume, edited by Guha, appeared in 1982. In late 1980 he went as Senior Research Fellow to the Australian National University in Canberra. In 1989 he relinquished overall charge of editing *Subaltern Studies*.

For primary and secondary sources see Ranajit Guha, *A Rule of Property for Bengal*, Paris, Mouton, 1963; *Elementary Aspects of Peasant Insurgency in Colonial India*, Delhi, Oxford University Press, 1983; Guha, ed., *Subaltern Studies*, Vols 1–6, Delhi, Oxford University Press, 1982–89; Guha and Gayatri C. Spivak, eds, *Selected Subaltern Studies*, New York, Oxford University Press, 1988; David Arnold and David Hardiman, eds, *Essays in Honour of Ranajit Guha*, New York, Oxford University Press, 1994. The following selection is taken from *Selected Subaltern Studies*, pp. 37–44.

ON SOME ASPECTS OF THE HISTORIOGRAPHY OF COLONIAL INDIA[1]

1. The historiography of Indian nationalism has for a long time been dominated by elitism—colonialist elitism and bourgeois-nationalist elitism.[2] Both originated as the ideological product of British rule in India, but have survived the transfer of power and been assimilated to neo-colonialist and neo-nationalist forms of discourse in Britain and India respectively. Elitist historiography of the colonialist or neo-colonialist type counts British writers and institutions among its principal protagonists, but has its imitators in India and other countries too. Elitist historiography of the nationalist or neo-nationalist type is primarily an Indian practice but not without imitators in the ranks of liberal historians in Britain and elsewhere.

2. Both these varieties of elitism share the prejudice that the making of the Indian nation and the development of the consciousness—nationalism—which informed this process were exclusively or predominantly elite achievements. In the colonialist and neo-colonialist historiographies these achievements are credited to British colonial rulers, administrators, policies, institutions and culture; in the nationalist and neo-nationalist writings—to Indian elite personalities, institutions, activities and ideas.

3. The first of these two historiographies defines Indian nationalism primarily as a function of stimulus and response. Based on a narrowly behavioristic approach this represents nationalism as the sum of the activities and ideas by which the Indian elite responded to the institutions, resources, etc., generated by colonialism. There are several versions of this historiography, but the central modality common to them is to describe Indian nationalism as a sort of 'learning process' through which the native elite became involved in politics by trying to negotiate the maze of institutions and the corresponding cultural complex introduced by the colonial authorities in order to govern the country. What made the elite go through this process was, according to this historiography, no lofty

idealism addressed to the general good of the nation but simply the expectation of rewards in the form of a share in the wealth, power and prestige created by and associated with colonial rule; and it was the drive for such rewards with all its concomitant play of collaboration and competition between the ruling power and the native elite as well as between various elements among the latter themselves, which, we are told, was what constituted Indian nationalism.

4. The general orientation of the other kind of elitist historiography is to represent Indian nationalism as primarily an idealist venture in which the indigenous elite led the people from subjugation to freedom. There are several versions of this historiography which differ from each other in the degree of their emphasis on the role of individual leaders or elite organizations and institutions as the main or motivating force in this venture. However, the modality common to them all is to uphold Indian nationalism as a phenomenal expression of the goodness of the native elite with the antagonistic aspect of their relation to the colonial regime made, against all evidence, to look larger than its collaborationist aspect, their role as promoters of the cause of the people than that as exploiters and oppressors, their altruism and self-abnegation than their scramble for the modicum of power and privilege granted by the rulers in order to make sure of their support for the Raj. The history of Indian nationalism is thus written up as a sort of spiritual biography of the Indian elite.

5. Elitist historiography is of course not without its uses. It helps us to know more of the structure of the colonial state, the operation of its various organs in certain historical circumstances, the nature of the alignment of classes which sustained it; of some aspects of the ideology of the elite as the dominant ideology of the period; of the contradictions between the two elites and the complexities of their mutual oppositions and coalitions; of the role of some of the more important British and Indian personalities and elite organizations. Above all, it helps us to understand the ideological character of historiography itself.

6. What, however, historical writings of this kind cannot do is to explain Indian nationalism for us. For it fails to acknowledge, far less interpret, the contribution made by the people *on their own*, that is, *independently of the elite* to the making and development of this nationalism. In this particular respect the poverty of this historiography is demonstrated beyond doubt by its failure to

understand and assess the mass articulation of this nationalism except, negatively, as a law and order problem, and positively, if at all, either as a response to the charisma of certain elite leaders or in the currently more fashionable terms of vertical mobilization by the manipulation of factions. The involvement of the Indian people in vast numbers, sometimes in hundreds of thousands or even millions, in nationalist activities and ideas is thus represented as a diversion from a supposedly 'real' political process, that is, the grinding away of the wheels of the state apparatus and of elite institutions geared to it, or it is simply credited, as an act of ideological appropriation, to the influence and initiative of the elite themselves. The bankruptcy of this historiography is clearly exposed when it is called upon to explain such phenomena as the anti-Rowlatt upsurge of 1919 and the Quit India movement of 1942—to name only two of numerous instances of popular initiative asserting itself in the course of nationalist campaigns in defiance or absence of elite control. How can such one-sided and blinkered historiography help us to understand the profound displacements, well below the surface of elite politics, which made Chauri–Chaura or the militant demonstrations of solidarity with the RIN mutineers possible?

7. This inadequacy of elitist historiography follows directly from the narrow and partial view of politics to which it is committed by virtue of its class outlook. In all writings of this kind the parameters of Indian politics are assumed to be or enunciated as exclusively or primarily those of the institutions introduced by the British for the government of the country and the corresponding sets of laws, policies, attitudes and other elements of the superstructure. Inevitably, therefore, a historiography hamstrung by such a definition can do no more than to equate politics with the aggregation of activities and ideas of those who were directly involved in operating these institutions, that is, the colonial rulers and their *élèves*— the dominant groups in native society. To the extent that their mutual transactions were thought to be all there was to Indian nationalism, the domain of the latter is regarded as coincident with that of politics.

8. What clearly is left out of this un-historical historiography is the *politics of the people*. For, parallel to the domain of elite politics there existed throughout the colonial period another domain of Indian politics in which the principal actors were not the dominant groups of the indigenous society or the colonial authorities

but the subaltern classes and groups constituting the mass of the laboring population and the intermediate strata in town and country—that is, the people. This was an *autonomous* domain, for it neither originated from elite politics nor did its existence depend on the latter. It was traditional only in so far as its roots could be traced back to pre-colonial times, but it was by no means archaic in the sense of being outmoded. Far from being destroyed or rendered virtually ineffective, as was elite politics of the traditional type by the intrusion of colonialism, it continued to operate vigorously in spite of the latter, adjusting itself to the conditions prevailing under the Raj, and in many respects developing entirely new strains in both form and content. As modern as indigenous elite politics, it was distinguished by its relatively greater depth in time as well as in structure.

9. One of the more important factors of this politics related precisely to those aspects of mobilization which are so little explained by elitist historiography. Mobilization in the domain of elite politics was achieved vertically whereas in that of subaltern politics this was achieved horizontally. The instrumentation of the former was characterized by a relatively greater reliance on the colonial adaptations of British parliamentary institutions and the residua of semi-feudal political institutions of the pre-colonial period; that of the latter relied rather more on the traditional organization of kinship and territoriality or on class associations depending on the level of the consciousness of the people involved. Elite mobilization tended to be relatively more legalistic and constitutionalist in orientation, subaltern mobilization relatively more violent. The former was, on the whole, more cautious and controlled, the latter more spontaneous. Popular mobilization in the colonial period was realized in its most comprehensive form in peasant uprisings. However, in many historic instances involving large masses of the working people and petty bourgeoisie in the urban areas too, the figure of mobilization derived directly from the paradigm of peasant insurgency.

10. The ideology operative in this domain, taken as a whole, reflected the diversity of its social composition with the outlook of its leading elements dominating that of the others at any particular time and within any particular event. However, in spite of such diversity one of its invariant features was a notion of resistance to elite domination. This followed from the subalternity common to all the social constituents of this domain, and as such distinguished

it sharply from that of elite politics. This ideological element was of course not uniform in quality or density in all instances. In the best of cases it enhanced the concreteness, focus and tension of subaltern political action. However, there were occasions when its emphasis on sectional interests disequilibrated popular movements in such a way as to create economistic diversions and sectarian splits, and generally to undermine horizontal alliances.

11. Yet another set of the distinctive features of this politics derived from the conditions of exploitation to which the subaltern classes were subjected in varying degrees as well as from its relation to the productive labor of the majority of its protagonists, that is, workers and peasants, and to the manual and intellectual labor respectively of the non-industrial urban poor and the lower sections of the petty bourgeoisie. The experience of exploitation and labor endowed this politics with many idioms, norms and values which put it in a category apart from elite politics.

12. These and other distinctive features (the list is by no means exhaustive) of the politics of the people did not of course appear always in the pure state described in the last three paragraphs. The impact of living contradictions modified them in the course of their actualization in history. However, with all such modifications they still helped to demarcate the domain of subaltern politics from that of elite politics. The co-existence of these two domains or streams, which can be sensed by intuition and proved by demonstration as well, was the index of an important historical truth, that is, the *failure of the Indian bourgeoisie to speak for the nation*. There were vast areas in the life and consciousness of the people which were never integrated into their hegemony. The *structural dichotomy* that arose from this is a datum of Indian history of the colonial period, which no one who sets out to interpret it can ignore without falling into error.

13. Such dichotomy did not, however, mean that these two domains were hermetically sealed off from each other and there was no contact between them. On the contrary, there was a great deal of overlap arising precisely from the effort made from time to time by the more advanced elements among the indigenous elite, especially the bourgeoisie, to integrate them. Such efforts when linked to struggles which had more or less clearly defined anti-imperialist objectives and were consistently waged, produced some splendid results. Linked, on other occasions, to movements which either had no firm anti-imperialist objectives at all or had

lost them in the course of their development and deviated into legalist, constitutionalist or some other kind of compromise with the colonial government, they produced some spectacular retreats and nasty reversions in the form of sectarian strife. In either case, the braiding together of the two strands of elite and subaltern politics led invariably to explosive situations indicating that the masses mobilized by the elite to fight for their own objectives managed to break away from their control and put the characteristic imprint of popular politics on campaigns initiated by the upper classes.

14. However, the initiatives which originated from the domain of subaltern politics were not, on their part, powerful enough to develop the nationalist movement into a full-fledged struggle for national liberation. The working class was still not sufficiently mature in the objective conditions of its social being and in its consciousness as a class-for-itself, nor was it firmly allied yet with the peasantry. As a result, it could do nothing to take over and complete the mission which the bourgeoisie had failed to realize. The outcome of it all was that the numerous peasant uprisings of the period, some of them massive in scope and rich in anti-colonialist consciousness, waited in vain for a leadership to raise them above localism and generalize them into a nationwide anti-imperialist campaign. In the event, much of the sectional struggle of workers, peasants and the urban petty bourgeoisie either got entangled in economism or, wherever politicized, remained, for want of a revolutionary leadership, far too fragmented to form effectively into anything like a national liberation movement.

15. It is the study of this *historic failure of the nation to come to its own*, a failure due to the inadequacy of the bourgeoisie as well as of the working class to lead it into a decisive victory over colonialism and a bourgeois–democratic revolution of either the classic nineteenth-century type under the hegemony of the bourgeoisie or a more modern type under the hegemony of workers and peasants, that is, a 'new democracy'—*it is the study of this failure which constitutes the central problematic of the historiography of colonial India.* There is no one given way of investigating this problematic. Let a hundred flowers blossom and we do not mind even the weeds. Indeed, we believe that in the practice of historiography even the elitists have a part to play if only by way of teaching by negative examples. But we are also convinced that elitist historiography should be resolutely fought by developing an

alternative discourse based on the rejection of the spurious and un-historical monism characteristic of its view of Indian nationalism and on the recognition of the co-existence and interaction of the elite and subaltern domains of politics.

16. We are sure that we are not alone in our concern about the present state of the political historiography of colonial India and in seeking a way out. The elitism of modern Indian historiography is an oppressive fact resented by many others, students, teachers and writers like ourselves. They may not all subscribe to what has been said above on this subject in exactly the way in which we have said it. However, we have no doubt that many other historiographical points of view and practices are likely to converge close to where we stand. Our purpose in making our own views known is to promote such a convergence. We claim no more than to try and indicate an orientation and hope to demonstrate in practice that this is feasible. In any discussion which may ensue we expect to learn a great deal not only from the agreement of those who think like us but also from the criticism of those who do not.

A Note on the Terms 'Elite', 'People', 'Subaltern', etc. as used above

The term 'elite' has been used in this statement to signify *dominant* groups, foreign as well as indigenous. The *dominant foreign* groups included foreign industrialists, merchants, financiers, planters, landlords and missionaries.

The *dominant indigenous* groups included classes and interests operating at two levels. At the *all-India level* they included the biggest feudal magnates, the most important representatives of the industrial and mercantile bourgeoisie, and native recruits to the uppermost levels of the bureaucracy.

At the *regional and local levels* they represented such classes and other elements as were *either* members of the dominant all-India groups included in the previous category *or* if belonging to social strata hierarchically inferior to those of the dominant all-India groups, still *acted in the interests of the latter and not in conformity to interests corresponding truly to their own social being.*

Taken as a whole and in the abstract this last category of the elite was *heterogeneous* in its composition and, thanks to the uneven character of regional economic and social developments, *differed from area to area.* The same class or element which was dominant in one area according to the definition given above, could be among the dominated in another. This could and did create many ambiguities and contradictions in attitudes and alliances, especially among the lowest strata of the rural gentry, impoverished landlords, rich peasants and upper-middle peasants, all of whom belonged, *ideally speaking*, to the category of 'people' or 'subaltern classes', as defined below. It is the task of research to investigate, identify and measure the *specific* nature and degree of the *deviation* of these elements from the ideal and situate it historically.

The terms 'people' and 'subaltern classes' have been used as synonymous throughout this note. The social groups and elements included in this category represent *the demographic difference between the total Indian population and all those whom we have described as the 'elite'.* Some of these classes and groups such as the lesser rural gentry, impoverished landlords, rich peasants and upper-middle peasants who 'naturally' ranked among the 'people' and the 'subaltern', could under certain circumstances act for the 'elite', as explained above, and therefore be classified as such in some local or regional situations—an ambiguity which it is up to the historian to sort out on the basis of a close and judicious reading of his evidence.

■

■ Notes ■

[1] The author is grateful to all the other contributors to this volume, as well as to Gautam Bhadra, Dipesh Chakrabarty and Raghabendra Chattopadhyay for their comments on an earlier version of this statement.

[2] For a definition of the terms 'elite', 'people', 'subaltern', etc., as used in these paragraphs the reader may kindly turn to the note printed at the end of this statement.

■

19

■ SUDHIR CHANDRA ■

Born in 1941 in Allahabad, Sudhir Chandra studied modern Indian history at Allahabad University and at Kurukshetra University where he received his doctorate in 1970. He has taught at the Jamia Millia Islamia and at Aligarh Muslim University, and is now a Senior Fellow at the Centre for Social Studies, Surat. He has been a Senior Fellow at the Centre for the Study of Developing Societies, Delhi, and at the Indian Institute of Advanced Study, Shimla; he has also served as a visiting professor at the Institute for the Study of Languages and Cultures of Asia and Africa in Tokyo, at the South Asia Institute of the University of Heidelberg, and at the Maison des Sciences de l'Homme in Paris.

Among his publications are *Dependence and Disillusionment: Emergence of National Consciousness in Later Nineteenth Century India*, New Delhi, Manas, 1975; *The Oppressive Present: Literature and Social Consciousness in Colonial India*, New Delhi, Oxford University Press, 1992; and *Enslaved Daughters: Law, Colonialism and Women's Rights*, New Delhi, Oxford University Press, 1997. The following selection is taken from *The Oppressive Present*, pp. 1–16.

THE OPPRESSIVE PRESENT

I

Historiography tends to highlight change, for it is drawn by the logic of conventional conceptions to those aspects of man-in-society that reflect movement. Being concerned, by the same logic, with the particular as against the general, historians tend to stress variety and contrast more than uniformity and similarity. However, underlying processes of change and the existence of variety there exist various dimensions of the same social reality that represent continuity and uniformity. Depending upon the questions one asks and the vantage point one chooses, one may discern, within any segment of social reality, apparently contradictory indices of change and continuity, or similarity and variety; apparently contradictory because, inasmuch as they are aspects of the same entity, they are not mutually exclusive. They need to be ordered into one whole.

In seeking to understand the dominant structure of social consciousness in modern India, the present book traces the patterns of synchrony in the face of obvious diachrony. It concentrates on the later nineteenth century, when, following the colonial encounter, the dominant structure of social consciousness crystallized as part of the general shaping of modern Indian society. This structure neither presupposed nor effected an undifferentiated social consciousness that characterized all the dominant sections within Indian society. It consisted, rather, in an arrangement of the constitutive elements of this consciousness. While the relative value of the constitutive elements fluctuated and produced varying manifestations in terms of individual responses to a whole range of issues, I argue that the basic mode of these responses remained the same.

The concept of structure resonates with the idea of synchrony. But synchrony is not stasis. It does not negate temporality. Nor is a structure—a social structure—something eternal. Structures follow temporal courses and come about through a process.

While this more 'dynamic' view of structure informs my study, it does not deal primarily with change, dissimilarity and contrast. Assuming the existence of such features, and occasionally referring to these explicitly, I delineate the making of a structure of social consciousness that initially characterized the literati, and in course of time influenced the rest of Indian society.

The justification for this selective stress constitutes the very raison d'être of this inquiry. Change and variety have been the center of concern within historical and sociological works on modern India. This has generated some widely accepted stereotypes on the nature of society in colonial and independent India. These stereotypes often appear as a series of binary pairs, in terms of which the whole society is seen as divided. Individuals, groups and movements are, accordingly, categorized as progressive or revivalist, reformist or reactionary, secular or communal, nationalist or communalist, and so on. These pairs are not treated as isolated dyads. They are assumed to be logically and empirically interconnected in such a way that qualities associated with the first category of any pair imply, in an individual or a group or a movement, the existence of qualities associated with the first categories of the other pairs. Thus, for example, those who are seen as progressive are presumed to have been reformist, secular and nationalist; and, in the same way, revivalism is presumed to have been accompanied by reactionary and communal tendencies.

In this normative–descriptive scheme the first categories are invested with positive properties while the counter-categories are charged with negative properties. This follows from the fact that the scheme is part of a larger explanatory dyad in which modernization is historically poised to get the better of tradition. Naturally enough, the first categories in the binary pairs are related to modernization and the counter-categories to tradition. The whole world, in this monolithic framework, is living through a teleology of which the end is not only inevitable but also desirable.

Even though it may often remain unstated, the normative bias of this framework is clear from the valorization of modernity at the expense of tradition. The acceptance of this framework may well demonstrate the predominance of a particular ethical choice in the world as it is today. It could, though, as well be the result of acquiescence in a situation seemingly permitting no viable alternative accounts to oppose the dominant theory. Be that as it may, individuals can be either resigned or enthusiastic *vis-à-vis* the underlying moral imperialism of the modernity–tradition polarity. But that is a matter of ideological freedom; one ought to ensure that people do actually exercise such a freedom, even if the exercise leads to the despairing realization that choice is only an illusion.

This, however, is more than just an ideological matter, for the modernity–tradition polarity introduces a serious perceptual limitation: the dichotomy is projected back to explain and categorize even those actions, attitudes, beliefs and values that did not rest on, or stem from, such a polarity. After all, people can—as often happened in nineteenth century India—view the phenomena designated 'modernity' and 'tradition' without opposing them to each other. In such perceptions there may even be a reversing of the way in which these two constituent units figure in the explanatory framework of modernization. If change is not seen as external to tradition, a precedence is accorded to tradition over change. The word 'change' has not always been synonymous, or associated, with modernity; it has in the past been conjoined equally well with 'tradition'.

This is a mentality which, without being necessarily hostile to modernity, neither treats tradition as a counter-category, nor eschews change per se. In fact, even when hostile to modernity, it is not necessarily opposed to change. Thus, tradition and change are not oppositional categories in such a world-view. Change, in this view, does not mean going back to an earlier 'purer' tradition.

Within the available modernity–tradition polarity framework, it is difficult to see this mentality in anything other than dichotomous terms. Ideologically, with its totalitarian moral presuppositions, those who see the world from this polarized perspective can only approve of a change that is in consonance with modernity; the only destiny they envisage for tradition is that it be 'modernized'. At the methodological plane such a perspective presents in neat oppositional categories the forces that contribute to the co-existence of tradition and change.

There is admittedly some schematic simplification in this description of the modernity–tradition polarity. During its development, especially after it shed its earlier nomenclature of 'Westernization', the modernization approach has acquired the sophistication to recognize the complexity of actual human and social situations. It is, for example, willing to recognize the co-existence of change and persistence and realize that the same person, group of persons or movements may be both progressive and revivalist, reformist and reactionary, secular and communal, and so on. Nevertheless, its basic ideological and methodological blocks are untouched. With all its sophistication, the modernization approach continues to proceed along normatively inspired dichotomous divisions.

If the forces of change and persistence are conceived of as dichotomous, the co-existence of these dichotomies can be explained in terms of either a thematic or a chronological divide. The thematic divide suggests that in certain issues one may be secular, progressive and reformist while in certain other respects the same person may be revivalist, reactionary and communal.

The chronological divide explains the same phenomenon in terms of life stages: a person who displays, up to a certain point in life (usually youth and early middle age), the positive traits of the first categories in the pairings used by the modernization framework may subsequently lapse into their opposites; the lapse may be gradual or abrupt.

Within the context of the modernity–tradition polarity, this is an important advance. It imparts to the concept of modernization sufficient resilience to accommodate a variety of situations and details produced by the complex simultaneity of change and continuity. And yet it does not go far enough. It remains incapable of understanding terms that are not its own, or a world-view different from its own. While all understanding is eventually in one's own terms, any encounter with the Other, i.e., the alien and the unfamiliar, ought to result in a process of questioning, modifying and extension of these terms, and of incorporating new terms from the Other. If one merely attempts to comprehend the unfamiliar by translating it in terms of what is familiar, no proper understanding of it is possible. One needs to be aware that there are no exact equivalents for the Other in one's own language. The finer such an awareness, the greater the possibility of the translation being faithful; and the more faithful the translation, the less the degree of violence and mutilation done to the Other.

It is this important epistemological effort that eludes the modernization approach. Given its self-besotted belief in the global character of the teleology that it sees itself as embodying, it is immune to the kind of self-doubt required for such an effort.

If understanding is possible only in one's own terms, what are the terms that we—the English-educated Indian scholars who seek to understand the making of a structure of social consciousness that we have inherited—can call our own and employ in order to understand? The question is not posed as a routine exercise. It is a response to the perception of a danger: the danger is that the terms of modernity–tradition polarity are also our own terms. This is the blunt answer. There is, consequently, the danger that an understanding in terms of the modernity–tradition polarity will help perpetuate the polarity. But human perception is often marked by an effort to break through the perceptual constraints of given cognitive categories, an endeavor that corrodes procrustean constructs. I hope this [essay] makes some headway in that sort of direction.

This hope must be incorporated within my answer to the question of the terms we use, and this may be put like this: the terms of the modernity–tradition polarity are our terms, but the realization that this is so carries the possibility of varying degrees of freedom from these terms. Such freedom is not unlimited, and we shall soon see that it may not include, for the time being, the possibility of formulating an alternative world-view....

In foisting upon our nineteenth century forebears the dichotomy of a West, with its civilizing mission, and an East that needed to be 'civilized', colonial mediation helped create in Indian minds the idea of a traditional India. This initiated a momentous epistemological change. At the plane of collective cultural life, time was fractured into past, present and future; and tradition, plucked out of this continuum, was created selectively out of different points in times past. Alienation from tradition—from one's own culture—lay in a consciousness of the need to belong to this newly constructed tradition.

A similar tension marked the relationship with Western culture, the nineteenth century homologue of modernity. Contrary to received wisdom, the Indian response to the West was not along the exclusive lines of either accepting or rejecting the West. Paradigmatically, this is supposedly represented by Raja Ram Mohun Roy and Raja Radhakanta Deb [1784–1867]. The stereotypical image of Radhakanta Deb as the archetypal figure who rejected the West, intriguingly enough, remains unaffected by the knowledge of his celebrated role in the introduction of English education in early nineteenth century Bengal, and by his less known initial support to Ishwarchandra Vidyasagar when [the latter] wrote his historic pamphlet in favor of widow marriage.[1]...

When even 'rebels' and 'apostates' belie the conventional image of having been mesmerized by the West, it would be laboring the obvious to argue that what Ram Mohun Roy—the archetypal adversary of Radhakanta Deb—embodied was the best of both the West and of his own culture. And similarly, if even Radhakanta Deb did not symbolize a complete rejection of the West, it is reasonable to assume that the dominant Indian responses to the West, as to traditional culture, need to be seen not as exclusive acceptances or rejections, but as different mixes of acceptance and rejection.

As colonialism progressed, a dual tension with regard to the West and to indigenous culture came about. With the intensification of political conflict against alien rulers, the emotional need for cultural belonging deepened. At the same time, and paradoxically, familiarity with indigenous culture diminished progressively. The state of being organically, and unselfconsciously, related to indigenous culture was so transformed that it required consciously designed links for the relationship to exist between individuals and their culture. This was paralleled by a reverse paradoxical development: as the political confrontation against alien rule gained momentum, an intellectual proximity with the West—the center of modernization—became greater.

The fate of Gandhi's *Hind Swaraj* is an ironic epitome of this paradox: within a decade of formulating his radical critique of modern Western civilization, Gandhi became supreme leader of the Indian national movement and, barring occasional eclipses and voluntary withdrawals, he held this position for close to three decades. These were the decades when, during the struggle against the Raj, the conception of a free India took shape. This conception replicated the modernization model and bore little resemblance to the civilizational alternative enunciated in *Hind Swaraj*, a fact that reflects the growing hold of the West upon the indigenous social consciousness that crystallized through the colonial period.

The depth of this paradox is illustrated by the ineffectiveness of Gandhi's final bid to have the *Hind Swaraj* blueprint accepted as the pattern for social reconstruction in free India. Realizing that freedom was round the corner, he broached the issue with his 'heir', Jawaharlal Nehru. In a letter dated 5 October 1945 he referred to a 'major difference of opinion between us'. If the difference really existed, he said, he wanted the fact to be known to people, for otherwise the task of *swaraj* would be adversely affected. The difference related to the vision that these two protagonists of Indian nationalism had of India after independence. The vision articulated by Gandhi in this letter was the same as the one he had envisaged in *Hind Swaraj*. In the materialization of this vision, Gandhi told Nehru, lay the true freedom of India, and through India of the world at large. The village was to be the basic unit of the society so reconstructed; the village as a unit within which everyone knew everyone else. Gandhi warned Nehru not to mistake the village he was referring to with actual villages in the country, for then his vision could not be grasped. 'My village today', he clarified, 'exists only in my imagination'; and pertinently, he added: 'Eventually every man lives in the world of his own imagination.'[2]

It was an exasperated Nehru who replied to this momentous letter four days later. The exasperation resulted from Nehru's incomprehension of the idiom and categories employed by Gandhi. Even the basic idea that the village invoked by Gandhi existed only in his imagination, waiting to be realized in free India, was misunderstood by Nehru to mean actual villages with their depressing poverty, squalor, disease and superstitions. Was this what the master wanted to build the new India upon, Nehru asked with self-righteous bewilderment.[3]

Barely five weeks after he had first sounded Nehru on this issue, Gandhi reverted to the question of the concrete meaning that was to be given to Indian freedom. He met Nehru on 12 November 1945 and wrote to him the following day to say that their conversation had made him, 'at least', very happy. Nehru's reaction to this meeting is not known. Gandhi's happiness, however, was restrained by his awareness of a gap between himself and Nehru that, he feared, might widen damagingly. For, while granting that the issue could not be resolved in one meeting, Gandhi admitted that, even as they stood on the threshold of freedom after years of intimacy and political association, he and Nehru might have to part company on the issue of what ought to constitute their country's freedom. For the time being, though, Gandhi hoped there were no great differences between Nehru and him. His hope, like his happiness, was tempered with scepticism. Gandhi felt it necessary to summarize, point by point, the previous day's discussions so that Nehru could tell whether his position had been correctly understood by Gandhi.[4]

Little ensued thereafter. The follow-up meetings hoped for by Gandhi as a sequel to their inconclusive discussions on 12 November 1945 never materialized. This was scarcely surprising in view of Nehru's unconcealed chagrin that Gandhi should have chosen to rake up this issue at a time when, with freedom imminent, the Congress leadership was confronted with a whole range of difficult problems. Gandhi gave up quietly. He did not even press his suggestion, made in the letter of 5 October 1945, for a two- or three-day session of the Congress Working Committee to discuss the issue. Neither his political heir nor the national organization that had for so long looked up to him could comprehend his vision of freedom. Nehru's incomprehension was evidently widely shared.

Before coming to what this incomprehension meant, an answer may be suggested for Nehru's objection to the timing of Gandhi's move. The abortive dialogue of 1945 repeated a similar exchange, in 1928, between the two leaders; except that, on that occasion, their roles were reversed. Being impatient with prevailing inequalities and injustices, Nehru wanted the Congress in 1928 to wage a crusade against the dominant interests within Indian society. He told Gandhi that 'we must clearly lay down an economic program for the masses with socialism as its ideal.'[5] Gandhi's reply was laconic and decisive: 'I am quite of your opinion that some day we shall have to start an intensive movement without the rich people and without the vocal educated class. But the time is not yet.'[6]

As colonialism came closer to ending, Gandhi offered an exposition of freedom from the viewpoint of the poor and the oppressed. On the other hand, having fumed in favor of the adoption of socialism as an ideal at a time when the Congress was not required to implement it, Nehru now fretted that Gandhi saw in the prospect of political power an obligation to define freedom from the viewpoint of the masses. This radical difference in the priorities that the imminence of freedom impressed upon Gandhi and Nehru, and subsequently its quick resolution, reflect the turn taken by nationalist ideology with regard to the nature of the sovereign Indian state, as well as social relations in independent India.

Though this aspect of the dominant nationalist ideological concern for the poor is important, what is relevant for our purpose is the fact that the timing of Gandhi's move had nothing to do with the Nehruvian rejection of his blueprint for post-independence social reconstruction. Gandhi's view was rejected not because Nehru, representing the dominant world-view, found the move ill-timed—the matter could, in that case, have been deferred to a more propitious time, and not irrevocably settled, as it was. The Gandhian blueprint was rejected because it was seen as completely out of tune with the dominant world-view. It was rejected without being understood. Its obvious 'absurdity' was seen as sufficient argument against the need to understand it....

The Nehruvian incomprehension of the *Hind Swaraj* alternative defines the extent to which imperialist discourse had succeeded in controlling the minds of the colonized intelligentsia.

Despite its debt to Western critiques of modern industrial civilization, *Hind Swaraj* represented an aspect of Gandhian thought
that—during its refinement from the first enunciation in 1908 to
the final formulation in the 1945 letters to Nehru—had become
progressively self-assured in its assertion of an indigenous vision.
Gandhi's was a language, an ensemble of assumptions and ideals, that lay essentially outside the cognitive and normative field of
imperialist discourse.

If the fate of the Gandhian alternative is taken as an index, the
hold of the colonial modernization world-view upon the minds of
the colonized was all but complete on the eve of Indian independence. All but complete because, despite the effectiveness of
imperialist discourse, the structure of social consciousness that
crystallized in colonial India was one in which notions of both the
'alien' and the 'indigenous' had been inscribed. This meant that
even the summary rejection of the Gandhian alternative marked
neither the complete triumph of modernization nor the total rout
of tradition. It meant that indigenous assumptions and categories
gradually receded from the vision of those who continued to feel
drawn towards tradition. It is ironic that the advent of freedom
was also the high water mark of the hold of imperialist discourse
upon a dominant section of India's intelligentsia....

So complete, in fact, was the power of the imperialist discourse
to determine the criteria of valorization that even when a kind of
superiority was claimed for tradition by rejecting the West, the
terms by which India's superiority was proposed were those that
the West valued. This is exemplified by an argument that began
during the later nineteenth century and subsequently became
fairly common, more so during the decade-and-a-half preceding
independence. At this time, following the rise of the Congress Socialist Party, a socialist veneer was sought to be provided to the
dominant nationalist ideology. The argument was that while the
West prided itself on its individualism and the spirit of competition
that sustained its progress, Indian culture was organized on a principle of cooperation that resulted in harmonious social existence.
The argument was further extended towards the conclusion that
whereas the West was fumbling its way to socialism, the same
ideal had already been woven into the institutional fabric of
Indian culture.

Given the reproductive power of imperialist discourse, which
could even convert challenges to its authority into instruments of

its own perpetuation, it was not easy to recognize or resist the ways in which it corroded the cultural–intellectual sovereignty of the colonized. Gandhi could do this, but only at an individual, and therefore localized, plane. Among the few like him who understood the cultural–intellectual dimension of subjection was Krishna Chandra Bhattacharya (1875–1949). Addressing his students some time between 1928 and 1930, when the demand for *purna swaraj* [complete self-rule] had fired the country politically, this philosopher stressed the need for '*swaraj* in ideas' and cautioned against the subterranean workings of the cultural subjugation that came in the wake of political subjection. 'Political subjection', he argued, 'primarily means restraint on the outer life of a people and although it tends gradually to sink into the inner life of the soul, the fact that one is conscious of it operates against this tendency'. But the 'subtler domination exercised in the sphere of ideas by one culture on another' was 'all the more serious in the consequence, because it is not ordinarily felt'. 'Slavery', he continued, 'begins when one ceases to feel the evil and it deepens when the evil is accepted as a good. Cultural subjection is ordinarily of an unconscious character and it implies slavery from the very start'.

Bhattacharya did not support an unquestioning rejection of the 'alien', nor a blind acceptance of the 'indigenous'. Cultural autarky was not his ideal. Cultural assimilation, he believed, 'may be positively necessary for healthy progress and in any case it does not mean a lapse of freedom'. Subjugation of one's culture occurred 'only when one's traditional cast of ideas and sentiments is superseded without comparison or competition by a new set representing an alien culture which possesses one like a ghost.'...

Though he did not put it so sharply, Bhattacharya came very close to suggesting that the secret of the power exercised by imperialist discourse lay in the universality claimed by the West for its ideas and ideals. Aggressive interests were supported by aggressive ideals, and Bhattacharya felt impelled to expose the falsity of such totalitarian universalism. Arguing in general that, despite their assumed universality, Western political and social principles were culture-specific, he singled out for refutation, by way of example, one of the cardinal universals put forward by the West— that of rationalism—and showed that the Western mode was not the only mode of rationalism.[7]

II

The recovery of the 'vernacular mind', then, was the solution. But that was also the problem. Already in the 1920s, when Bhattacharya called for '*swaraj* in ideas', the 'vernacular mind' had sunk below the conscious level of culture. It had sunk still deeper by the time Gandhi decided to present for practical acceptance his alternative civilizational model. And today, when we, English-educated Indians, seek to understand our not-so-remote past, we are faced with the task of excavating that buried 'vernacular mind'.

The loss of traditional categories of thought had advanced far enough by 1945 to make the Gandhian alternative generally incomprehensible. Nor, even now, has the hold of the modernization world-view slackened in any significant sense. How, then, do we resolve the dilemma?

A propitious starting point is provided by the recent emergence of a concern for alternatives. This has lent respectability to inquiries into 'tradition', as against modernity, that do not *ipso facto* assign an inferior status to tradition. But despite some open-mindedness, the concern for alternatives really springs from the West, the sanctuary of the discourse with global claims. Indeed, the concern for alternatives there is more pronounced than in the Third World, where, in several quarters, it is seen as part of a Western design to keep the post-colonial world backward and amenable to manipulation. So, despite the new quest for alternatives, imperialist discourse is far from overthrown and we are still mainly left with a dominant notion of development: development through large-scale industrial modernization. The only admissible debate is whether this ought to be achieved through capitalism or through socialism....

Important though it may be as a starting point, something more than the will to understand tradition is required. A project involving the recovery of a world that remains ours, despite having been nearly lost to us intellectually, is needed. This should attempt an understanding of the world of tradition in its own terms, although it may thereafter reject that world as anachronistic. Given that the terms we use cannot be too different from those within the modernity–tradition frame, any project to understand tradition in its own terms can hope at best for partial success....

The triumphant course of the imperialist modernization discourse is one of the subjects of this book. A generation, which is the product virtually of this discourse, is seeking to understand the discourse of its ancestors, in their terms, and looking at people who were among the first to be exposed to this discourse. Still one of their own culture, these people faced an alien culture and were forced to adjust. Much happened in their own day that was beyond their ken, but there also happened things that they either consciously chose or were keenly aware of. Irrespective of the extent to which they were conscious of the political and cultural world around them, or of the nature and implications of their own positions, their idiom was predominantly indigenous.

Their idiom produces in our minds resonances that are tantalizingly familiar. The familiar tone, we realize, is not related to the space that colonialism had begun carving out within this idiom. It is related, rather, to the parts of our being that still reverberate to indigenous idioms at a subconscious plane.... Vague and tenuous though they may be, our links with the fast disappearing world of our nineteenth century forebears offer us clues to work our way back into their idiom. As a possible beginning towards the retrieval of that repressed and powerful stratum of our being, we need to watch out for those moments when familiar resonances tend to leave us as we fail to follow their trail, and to see that we do not treat what we do not comprehend as irrational or obscurantist. We could learn also to be wary of yet another sequel to this failure of understanding: the tendency to ascribe our own meanings to terms that we do not quite understand.

My formulation of the persistence of a dominant structure of social consciousness may seem objectionable on the grounds of there being an ideological-theoretical correlation, which is believed to exist axiomatically, between a given socio-economic reality and· its universe of values, beliefs and attitudes. But I argue that this, by itself, cannot be a reason for revising the argument about the persistence of a dominant social consciousness. Nor is this an argument for the total autonomy of the world of ideas, attitudes and beliefs. What my formulation does is attempt to support the shift towards arguing for a more dialectical relationship between the material and cultural–ideological realms of Indian society.

■

■ Notes ■

[1] Realizing that Raja Radhakanta Deb carried influence with both Hindu society and the government, Vidyasagar sent him a copy of the pamphlet in favor of widow marriage. The Raja was so pleased with the pamphlet that he sent for Vidyasagar and, to help the latter in his cause, organized a meeting of the learned pundits to discuss the matter. As often happened at such public discussions, a great deal of passion was generated but no decision could be reached. However, Radhakanta Deb made no secret of his own preference when, at the end of the debate, he rewarded Vidyasagar with a pair of shawls. Soon thereafter he extended his support to organized orthodoxy; but that is a different matter. See S.C. Mitra, *Isvar Chandra Vidyasagar: A Story of His Life and Work*, 1902; rpt., Delhi, 1975, pp. 266–67.

[2] For the original letter in Hindustani, see *Jawaharlal Nehru Papers*, Pt. 1, Vol. 26, Nehru Memorial Museum and Library, New Delhi. I have used my own translation of the letter. Differently translated, the letter has been included in *The Collected Works of Mahatma Gandhi*, New Delhi, Government of India, Publications Division, 1980, Vol. 81, pp. 319–21. The date of *Hind Swaraj* as given by Gandhi in this letter is 1908 and not 1909.

[3] See S. Gopal (ed.), *Selected Works of Jawaharlal Nehru*, New Delhi, Orient Longman, 1981, Vol. 14, pp. 554–57. 'I do not understand', wrote Nehru—despite Gandhi's warning that he was not writing about the Indian villages as they existed—'why a village should necessarily embody truth and non-violence. A village, normally speaking, is backward intellectually and culturally and no progress can be made from a backward environment. Narrow-minded people are much more likely to be untruthful and violent.'

[4] *Jawaharlal Nehru Papers*, Pt. 1, Vol. 26; also *The Collected Works of Mahatma Gandhi*, New Delhi, 1980, Vol. 82, pp. 71–72.

[5] 'Our educated classes', Nehru wrote further, 'have so far taken the lead in the fight for Swaraj, but in doing so they have seldom paid heed to the needs of the masses.... But what shall it profit the masses of India—the peasantry, the landless labourers, the artisans—if every one of the offices held by Englishmen in India today is held by an Indian.' S. Gopal (ed.), *Selected Works*, Vol. 3, p. 371.

[6] *The Collected Works of Mahatma Gandhi*, New Delhi, 1970, Vol. 36, p. 174.

[7] For Bhattacharya's discourse, see *Indian Philosophical Quarterly*, Vol. 11, October–December, 1984, pp. 383–93.

■

20

■ RAMCHANDRA GANDHI ■

Ramchandra Gandhi was born in 1937 in Madras, the son of a prominent newspaper editor, and grandson of Mahatma Gandhi. He studied philosophy in Delhi and at Oxford, and received doctorates from both universities in 1966 and 1971. Subsequently, he has taught at various universities in India, Britain, and the United States. From 1977 to 1996 he was professor of South Asian and Comparative Philosophy at the California Institute of Integral Studies in San Francisco. He is now an independent scholar and writer in Delhi.

Among his publications are *Two Essays on Whitehead's Philosophic Approach*, Shimla, Indian Institute of Advanced Study, 1973; *Presuppositions of Human Communication*, Delhi, Oxford University Press, 1974; *The Availability of Religious Ideas*, New York, Barnes & Noble, 1976; *I am Thou: Meditations on the Truth of India*, Pune, Indian Philosophical Quarterly, 1984; *Sita's Kitchen: A Testimony of Faith and Inquiry*, Albany, New York, SUNY Press, 1992. He has also edited *Language, Tradition and Modern Civilization*, Pune, Indian Philosophical Quarterly, 1984. In addition, Ramchandra Gandhi has written and produced a film on Mahatma Gandhi (1992) and written a number of plays, including 'The Sadhu and the Sage' and 'The Temptation of Vivekananda'. The following essay is taken from *Indian Philosophical Quarterly* (Pune), Vol. 11, October 1984, pp. 461–71.

THE SWARAJ OF INDIA

I

What could be the significance, the esoteric and civilizational significance, of the remarkable coincidence that precisely during the half-century when Mahatma Gandhi was steering India's struggle for at least political *swaraj*, Sri Ramana Maharshi [1879–1950] mightily witnessed to the truth of *svanubhuti*, self-realization, radical freedom from all delusion and ignorance of not-self, alienation? The answer should be obvious to anyone who has not lost a sense of the truth of India, the *advaitin* (not *advaitic* which has the bad suggestion of 'smacking of *advaita*') truth of India, and it is this: *swaraj* in politics or economics or in ideas or whatever is etymologically the kingdom or order or dispensation of *sva*, self, myself; consequently, in all seeking of *swaraj* I seek, *sva* seeks, to be the ruler, center, source of all things; and this seeking is wisdom and not paranoia, health, i.e., *svasthya* or self-situatedness, and not sickness, *sarvodaya* and not selfishness, only in and through the truth of *advaita*, *the truth that you and I are not other than one another*.

Thus the Gandhian struggle for *swaraj*, and indeed the Indian struggle for *swaraj* under the leadership of thinkers and revolutionaries rooted in Indian metaphysics and spirituality such as Lokamanya Tilak and Sri Aurobindo, is always implicitly an *advaitin* struggle, a struggle for the kingdom of self or autonomy and identity as opposed to the delusion and chaos and dishonor of not-self or heteronomy and divisiveness. British rule or modern industrial civilization and its imperialism and materialism, missionary Christianity and Islam and their soul-lust, the self-contradictariness and shame of *advaitin* Hinduism's practice of untouchability, etc., are symbols and powers of illusion of not-self, otherness, Maya; and the historical struggles of metaphysical Indian civilization have always been, not excluding the modern period, attempted overcomings of all such Maya so as to see God face to face in the truth of self-realization. Such alone is the *swaraj* of India, at least such.

Sri Ramana Maharshi's towering presence in the background of modern India's struggle for *swaraj* in outer life is no coincidence; it was meant to draw attention to the deeper *advaitin* implications and responsibilities of the outer struggle, and it was meant to be a promise of the possibility of victory. Really, the outer struggle gathered momentum only after 1896 when Sri Ramana arrived in Tiruvannamalai. Indeed, it is only in 1897 that Swami Vivekananda establishes the Ramakrishna Math and Mission, and metaphysical Indian thought, *advaitin* thought, is world news, good news, great news. Renaissance is not rebirth but second-birth, *dvijatva*, birth into Brahmanhood. Nationally, in the modern period of history, Indian *dvijatva* is promised by Sri Ramakrishna's catholic spirituality and marked by Sri Ramana's unambiguous, effortless, *sahaja* self-realization at the end of the nineteenth century. Brahmo Samaj and Arya Samaj, powerful self-images of defensive Indian self-confidence, lose catholicity in their flight from the truth of image worship, and lose Indian distinctiveness and truth's ultimacy in their flight from *advaita*. It is only in the post-Vivekananda and post-Ramana phase of Indian awakening that social awareness begins to acquire the catholic *advaitin shakti* of *swaraj*. Aurobindo and Tilak and Gandhi are inconceivable before Ramana and Ramakrishna, and without them.

It is important, following K.C. Bhattacharya's lead, to examine the whole corpus of our indigenous thought and ideas with a view to ascertaining whether this storehouse of truth cannot serve our civilization's needs better than imported knowledge and experience and enthusiasm, and whether our intellectual inheritance needs renewal and reorientation in the light of our encounter with the modern world's alluring intellectual and civilizational foreignness. It would be a great pity, however, if we were to allow ourselves in this exercise to get stuck with lists of what is native and yet serviceable, and what is alien and yet available in the world market today as civilization, important though it is to be mindful of these things even in a list-making way. It would be a great pity if such list-making, whatever its importance, were to obscure from our view the root obligation and meaning of *swaraj*, the obligation to repudiate the so-called law of identity, that old testament of unadventurousness which is at the foundation of alienating modern civilization, i.e., *that everyone is what he is and not someone else, that everything is what it is and not another thing.* In so far as we choose not to repudiate this manifesto of monadism, we are hardly entitled to speak and dream of *swaraj* in ideas or life, of a jealous self-sufficiency which is at the same time exploding uncoercing uncovetous caring. *Advaitin* India must boldly embrace the new testament of identity, which is really *anadi* and new only in rediscovery and abiding freshness, *that everyone and everything is both what he is and it is and also everyone and everything else.* For *swaraj* is simultaneously autonomy *and* love, radical *and* universal, and these are impossible of realization without transcending in *advaita* the old order of isolationism and hegemonism, tribalism and imperialism.

II

'Nativism!' is how a friend only half-humorously derisively characterized the defense of *swaraj* in ideas generally, and not only K.C. Bhattacharya's plea for it. What is 'nativism' as a dirty word and thing? Perhaps the following things: (*i*) A mulish disregard of truth and worth which originate and flourish elsewhere than in one's own nation or civilization or general cultural milieu, irrationally and unexaminedly reserving regard only for indigenousness in all spheres of life and thought; (*ii*) An almost pathological womb-returning life-style which chooses the timid security of familiarity and kinship and abandons the adventure of growth and rebelliousness and novelty, impervious to rational and ethical and general social and existential considerations in the matter; (*iii*) A failure of cosmopolitanism and internationalism and cultural freedom, a blindness to the universalism of science and a deafness to contemporary imperatives and invitations of justice and freedom and enjoyment.

I suppose there is some dark truth in the above characterizations of what might be called degenerate nativism, although I think one should here be very wary of implicit assumptions such as the following which are worse than fallen nativism and often pass as adequate criticisms of it: that to prefer one's own truth and *dharma* to another's is unmitigated selfishness, or that faithfulness to the familiar is less adventurous spiritually than being magnetized by novelty; that conformity to truth as one sees it is less demanding morally and intellectually than the rebelliousness of egoistic heterodoxy, or that the metaphor of 'returning to the womb' cannot be a term of praise and celebration, that the world is less cocooning in its worldliness than the womb in its nourishment of a soul; that internationalism, which is mostly superpower nationalism in disguise, is less parochial than the patriotism of dateless national traditions; that Eurocentrism is universalism; that class war and race war and arrogant species-centeredness are more redeemable than, e.g., the merely fallen but not false sociology and ecology of Indian civilization.

Unfortunately, those who pejoratively shout 'Nativism!' are not only not wary of the dangers listed above, constantly succumbing to them in high places, they have no notion at all of unfallen or regenerate or true nativism, for such a thing and truth there really is, and it is the highest truth and thing too. There is no need to abandon even the word 'nativism' falsely defensively in favor of words of euphemism and growing respectability such as 'tradition', 'aboriginality', 'ethnicity', etc., because there is always greater hope for the fallen and abused than the secure and unharmed in language as in spiritual life! Take the word 'untouchable', vehicle in use of tragic sinful disrespect of a whole category of human beings in our country even today, alas! Yet ironically, the word 'untouchable' itself truly designates *atman*, which alone cannot be touched, seen, heard, etc., and is what each one of us really is. Thus, when we would-be-derisively call somebody an untouchable, we acknowledge him in perfection of phrase as *atman* and he deserves our obeisance, and not ostracization. Untouchability will be defeated by the word 'untouchability'. Likewise, narrow unadventurous isolationism is overcome by nothing more effectively than by etymologically self-conscious 'nativism', which is loyalty to what is most *native* to myself, i.e., selfhood and self-consciousness, one in and as all.

Consider further the *swaraj*ist magic of nativism. Even if what I am exhorted to return to, or to race towards, is as exotic as the idea of a golden age of Indian civilization, *Ramarajya*, both as symbol and reality, or the idea of a human future beyond history and without inhumanity and alienation, without fear and delusion, e.g., communism, but if what I am exhorted to return to, or to race towards, is not myself, my own essential truth of self, the retreat and the adventure cannot be enduringly satisfying to me because they will prove to be forms of otherness capable of unexpected power of oppression over self, myself and yourself. Only if a golden age of the past or of the future can be seen by me as the unfurling in manifestation of myself, the truth of me, the being of me, can they be unalienatingly acceptable to me. Dualistic nativism or dualistic universalism and futurism are by this token equally alienating and unacceptable to the core of my being. But 'nativism' has this edge over universalism and futurism: it suggests powerfully, as earlier pointed out, the idea of that which is native to myself, that which is in no manner alienatingly other than myself, i.e., that which is myself, i.e., I, self-consciousness, *atman*. Existentially and metaphysically, nativism is *advaita*, *atmanubhuti* in all its forms and figurings. Nativism become self-conscious ceases to be fallen, resurrects as the truth of *atman-Brahman*. Nativity becomes Resurrection! Self-conscious Indian nativism cannot, therefore, be any of the narrow things possible to it in ignorance of itself, in fallenness.

Advaita is a *Shruti*-sanctified tradition of India revivified down the ages, not excluding our own age where Jnani Ramana reigns supreme in *swarajya* unlike elsewhere in civilizational time and space where *advaitins* appear but *advaita* does not receive the status and sanctification of *Shruti*. Christ is at the head of a long line of *advaitins* martyred by the absence of appropriate *advaitin Shruti*. Indian nativism, because of its inescapable *advaitin* dimension, unlike fallible dualistic localism of all varieties, *including its Indian equivalent*, is the very opposite of irrationality and exclusivism and infantilism; it is, on the contrary, a *Shruti*-sustained far-flung sourcewardness, the heterodoxy of orthodoxy, the rebelliousness of conformity. Faith in *atman*, one in all and as all, is the most seditious and iconoclastic and cosmic, not merely universalist, revolutionary *shakti* conceivable, but it is not hubris-inviting world-remaking arrogance because it is indistinguishable from the timelessness of self-realization which is no worshipper of times, past or present or future, while caring for all time, and because of its rootedness in one nation of the earth, Bharata, spiritually omnipotent but geographically uncovetous. K.C. Bhattacharya's or Gandhiji's invitation to *swaraj*, in ideas or civilization, is unalluring without *advaita*, run-of-the-mill traditionalism and not a summons to Indian self-realization. Mercifully *advaita* is at the heart of the philosopher's thought and the Mahatma's life.

III

I can hear the following strident objection straightaway to what has been said above. 'You are unjustifiably *advaitizing* the Indian tradition of thought and aspiration. The *vishishtadvaitin* and *dvaitin* traditions of metaphysics and meditation, thought and aspiration, are as fundamental a part of Indian consciousness as *advaita*, no less *Shruti*-supported than the latter. Nativism of the Indian variety is a return to the entire corpus of our legacy and inspiration, not only to those portions of revelation that sustain a Shankaracharya or a Ramana Maharshi, but also those sources which uphold a Ramanujacharya, a Madhvacharya, a Chaitanya Mahaprabhu, and a Sri Aurobindo. Indian groundedness is larger than *advaitin* self-realization. Even K.C. Bhattacharya in 'Swaraj in Ideas' is not flying exclusively the *advaitin* flag, he is not unfurling a Shankar-ite umbrella and pretending to be able to give shelter under it to the totality of tradition. We have roots to return to, not just one trunk of one tree but roots that nourish a whole orchard of trees and fruits and flowers. Tradition is an ocean, not one or two rivers, howsoever mighty. Neo-Vedanta is a caricature of the complexity of Indian civilization. Off with your head!'

Without losing my head, and without denying the complexity—and oceanic unity—of Indian consciousness, I would like to suggest that the above diatribe is shot through with misunderstanding. *Advaita* is a distinctive identifying feature of Indian consciousness, not a mere fringe indulgence as it is elsewhere, and dualism of all types in India defines itself most intimately by reference to *advaitin* thought. If Indian nativism is a distinctive sourceward turn, and not merely an instance essentially indistinguishable from other instances in the modern world of a harking back to the truths of the past, if it is a rootedness not to be confused with mere chauvinism, it cannot hope to avoid acknowledging the centrality of *advaita* in Indian *Shruti* and civilization and the *advaita* inherent in the very idea of nativism, i.e., of that which is truly native to oneself, i.e., self-realization. Non-*advaitin* Indian thought and aspiration cannot claim to be nativist in this deep sense of the word. Dualism of all kinds requires reference beyond oneself to something other than oneself, God or heaven, which dualistically conceived are not the self-consciousness which is what is most fundamentally native to oneself. Only in a watered-down sense of nativism can a dualistically envisioned deity be regarded as my native being. Such a deity and his abode may be my native place, but even my native place will alienate me if it does not disclose itself as the unfurling of my native being, self-hood and self-consciousness. I am not here concerned to argue against the truth-claim of dualism. I am merely suggesting that dualism and nativism do not go well together at any level of depth, and that for better or for worse, metaphysical nativism is unavailable as a principle or a platform to dualism. As for qualified non-dualism, *vishishtadvaita*, it can only lay claim to a qualified, not a full-blown, nativism and it is for my purpose sufficient to point this out and not attempt metaphysically to quarrel here with *vishishtadvaita*.

I believe that it is possible to cast apparently dualistic Vaishnava *bhakti* and thought in a strictly *advaitin* mould, taking metaphysically seriously Sri Krishna's declaration 'Vasudeva Sarvam Iti' [God is (in) everything], but it is not necessary for me to attempt such an exercise here or even to indicate its possible outlines. My limited purpose here is to argue that Indian nativism which is not the *mumuksatva* [desire for liberation] of *advaita sadhana* is not the kind of Indian sourcewardness in thought and life which is likely in India and elsewhere to be a winning power of correcting the costly self-obscuring absentmindedness of modern civilization. K.C. Bhattacharya's plea for *swaraj* in ideas has many dimensions, but its worth would diminish in my judgment if it is not understood as taking for granted that *advaita* is the true philosophy of nativism, and that Indian nativism because of the centrality of *advaita* in Indian civilization is more likely than any other kind of nativism to be the genuine thing. The imagined diatribe against *advaita* quoted earlier invoked Ramanujacharya, Madhvacharya, Chaitanya Mahaprabhu and Sri Aurobindo. It is my belief that their implicit and esoteric *advaita* (*advaita* is not synonymous with Shankaracharya) tends to be forgotten in *shastratha* [scriptural dispute] between doctrinaire dualism and non-dualism, and in any case my plea that *swaraj* in ideas or *swaraj* in general in India is unintelligible without *advaita* is not an undermining of their truth and vision.

The boy Mohandas who later became Mahatma Gandhi confessed to his father the sin of stealing and selling some of the latter's gold ornaments and spending the ill-gotten money on meat-eating forbidden to Vaishnavas such as his family, and his father forgave him the transgression with tears of joy at the nascent saint's contriteness and purity of heart. Gold symbolizes the native wealth of the soul, i.e., self-realization, and selling gold dramatizes the obscuration of *advaitin* self-realization in exchange for the glitter and litter of worldliness, which includes meat-eating, symbolizing lack of faith in the soul's capacity for nourishing itself without avoidable violence. Gandhian nativism, esoteric *Hind*

Swaraj, in ideas and in other things, is, therefore, *advaitin* faith together with a search for autonomy in all spheres of life, an unexploiting idiom of living with which to battle and cure, hopefully, the heteronomous megalomania of modern civilization; it is the faith that within the soul of man and in the intimacy of community life are available all the resources of survival and growth in love and truth that mankind needs. *Advaitin* conviction is what prevents intimacy from becoming isolationism, and uncovetous intimacy is what prevents *advaita* from becoming expansionist in morally risky ways.

IV

On the subject of *swaraj* and India, I can think of nothing more instructive than stories, true stories, from the lives of saints and *jnanis* [sages]. Even more powerfully instructive than the Gandhi story I recalled in the last section is the following outwardly innocuous incident from the life of Sri Ramana Maharshi. Ramana was but a boy biologically, although a *jnani*, when, magnetized by Arunacala Shiva, he made the sacred hill his home, inhabiting its caves and groves, instructing its animals and devotees, communing with its spirits and *siddhas*, one with Shiva in essence, and in manifestation the most ardent *bhakta* cleaving inextricably to his Lover Hill. One day the boy Ramana, bare-headed and barefoot, *kaupina* his sole garment, is wandering in the hot sun up and down all over the hill as any boy would, *jnani* or no *jnani*, as any child should. From nowhere a *chandala* old woman appears and fires a volley of abuse at Ramana, the gist of her vigorous speech being: 'And why don't you sit in one place, are you off your head?' At first puzzled by the undeserved abuse, the boy *jnani* realizes that the strong words are good advice to a *jnani* who must exemplify sufficiently outwardly too his inward truth of still-centeredness, so that everything about him, the style of his rest and movement no less than the power of his words and silence, are a complete *upadesha* [instruction], a complete *upanishad*. But the incident is a volume of esoteric instruction on our civilization and its future, on the truth and fate of India, and not merely good advice to a *sadhu* in the sun.

The *chandala* woman is surely Parvati, mother of Kartikeya Ramana or Ganapati Ramana, protectively scolding her son for avoidably risking life and health. But why has she assumed the form of a *candala* woman and why is her speech so strong? To the believing heart of India the answer should be plain, and it is this. Essentially, every woman is Parvati herself, Godhead, and not only half of Shiva; this is the first lesson which the incident teaches us, that all women, and especially urgently, all ill-treated and exploited women, are in truth to be seen as the Divine Mother, *atman-Brahman*, if we would wish to put right our society's injustice to them not in the style of metaphysically uprooted feminism, but in absolute harmony with the nature of things. Again, quite rightly roughly, for politeness and the urgency of truth do not go together, she orders the *jnani* to sit in one place and conserve the truth of *atman-Brahman* and not let it die in the hot sun of aimless do-gooding, the exploited of the world being quite capable of fighting their battles without such misdirected help. (Ramana is not guilty of any of this. He only occasions in *lila* Parvati's warning to mankind.) What the exploited, the wretched of the earth cannot hope to do without, what no one can do without, is the truth of *advaita* which must continue to be exemplified in the lives of *jnanis*, who must not be allowed prematurely physically to disappear, something which in their utter forgetfulness of bodily need they may let happen. A *jnani* like Sri Ramana Maharshi arrives once in a millennium and the *candala* needs him no less than the *Brahmana*. *Swaraj* in ideas, in everything, requires the uncompromised exemplification of the reality and possibility of *advaita-siddhi*, self-realization ablaze with the gospel of identity, contemporary battles for freedom and justice in India and the world requiring the light and fire of such self-realization no less than the battles of other ages. It would be a false activism which would make of all contemplatives political revolutionaries, and it would be a false *jnana marga* which would seek to make all activists yogis. Arunachala means 'The Red Hill', 'Aruna' symbolizing the activist *shakti* of truth, as does the *chandala* woman; and 'achala' images truth's still-centered, yet omnipresent, immovability, Ramana–Shiva. 'Arunacala' is the motto of Indian civilization's revolutionary conservatism and its saving, conserving, *Shakti*. Shiva and Parvati. *Swaraj*.

A final story and reading of outwardly trivial things which are yet monumental in their significance for us, an incident from the life of Ramakrishna Paramahamsa. When it was reported to Sri Ramakrishna that one of his devotees had started, quite avoidably, to learn English, the Paramahamsa made the comment: 'Now he will start whistling and wear[ing] boots!' That comment of Sri Ramakrishna's goes to the heart of the subject of Indian *swaraj*. Whistling represents frivolousness, especially of thought and speaking, inquiry and learning, which is what our servile and supercilious English speaking symbolizes with deadly accuracy. Boots represent grossness and insensitivity, the trampling upon native soil which borrowed authority so painfully truthfully represents, the authority of sundry '–isms' of importation without examination and assimilation. They are a caricature of the substantiality, *gambhirya*, which and not whistling, ought to characterize our speaking and life of mind and ideas. And whistling in the context caricatures the lightness, the uncoerciveness, which should be our gentle walking upon this sacred earth. The absence of *swaraj* results in comic costly inversion of the truth of things, trivializing levity where deep-going seriousness is in place, i.e., in thought and speech, and trampling burdensomeness, weight of insensitivity, where the lightness of the Paramahamsa's feet, which shuddered even at the thought of stepping on grass, is called for. The setting right side up of things is no Marxist discovery, it is the ancient Indian tantric discipline of *svatantrya*.

May K.C. Bhattacharya's plea for *swaraj* in ideas occasion a deep-going Indian inquiry into the idea of *swaraj* as our birth-right to second-birth, *dvijatva*, true renaissance. May we rediscover and celebrate the distinctive *advaitin* politics and metaphysics of Indian civilization.

21

■ U.R. ANANTHA MURTHY ■

Born in 1932, Anantha Murthy grew up in a village in Karnataka. He later studied English literature at the University of Mysore, and then at the University of Birmingham where he received his doctorate. After serving as a visiting professor in Iowa, Anantha Murthy became Professor of English at the University of Mysore. Later, he moved to Kottayam in Kerala to serve as Vice-Chancellor of Gandhi University. Subsequently, he became Chairman of the National Book Trust and President of the Sahitya Akademi (India's National Academy of Letters). He was awarded the Jnanpith Award in recognition of his contribution to Indian literature in 1995. In 1991 he returned to Mysore.

Anantha Murthy is recognized as one of the leading contemporary writers in the Kannada language. His works include collections of short stories, several major novels, two volumes of critical essays, some stage plays, and a book of poems. Among his writings, the novel *Samskara* has gained particularly wide acclaim; it was made into an award-winning film and later was translated into English by A.K. Ramanujan. Among his other novels are *Avasthe* (translated into English by Shantinath Desai), *Bharathipura* and *Ghatashradda*. Anantha Murthy also enjoys a wide reputation as a socially minded intellectual and activist, siding in his views with the 'radical humanism' associated with the names of M.N. Roy and Ram Manohar Lohia. The following essay is taken from the journal *Bahuvachan*, February 1988, pp. 95–117, an occasional publication of the Bharat Bhavan in Bhopal.

WHY NOT WORSHIP IN THE NUDE?
REFLECTIONS OF A NOVELIST IN HIS TIME

The reality for a novelist in India—I am speaking from my Kannada experience—is so complex as to disallow the comforts of either status-quoist acceptance or of revolutionary ruthlessness. R.K. Narayan can afford to say 'India will go on' only as a comic realist, in his inimitable low mimetic mode. But when his insightful Indian experience is translated into ideas in a polemical context, it is difficult to defend them. The same is true of Naipaul's indictment of Indian reality. He can afford to speak angrily and ruthlessly and plead for a thorough-going modernization in India— only in a polemical context. I wonder if he can maintain his position unambiguously in a novel where his imaginative sympathies are fully engaged.

All of us share this dilemma. What we *feel* and what we *think* are often in conflict. Even while I am writing this I am engaged in a bewilderingly confusing discussion with my radical friends about an incident in Chandragutti, a village of my district 85 kilometers from Shimoga—where every year, in March, men and women of all ages offer naked worship to a goddess in fulfillment of a vow. Early morning they take a dip in the river, Varada, wait in the water to get possessed, and then run four or five kilometres and go up a picturesque hill, 800 metres above sea level to worship *Renukamba*. Last month many young men and women belonging to radical and rationalist organizations went there, with the encouragement of the social welfare department of the government, to plead with these 'backward caste' worshippers that nude worship was 'wrong' and 'inhuman'. This attracted wide media attention and journalists went there too, with their cameras. Earlier, two weeklies run by rationalists and Scheduled Caste activists had also carried pictures of nude worshippers on their colorful cover pages. These weeklies published articles attacking what, for them, seemed an inhuman 'superstitious' practice, while they also aimed at increasing their circulation with the nude pictures.

The encounter between the illiterate believers and the educated middle-class rationalists was both fierce and unexpected. The worshippers broke through the physical barricade of the rationalists who stood on the bank of the river pleading with them to wear clothes. And then they ran to the hill in frenzied possession. Some worshippers even turned violent. The deputy superintendent of police was stripped forcibly of his khaki uniform and forced to go naked in procession with the worshippers. The women police were also mercilessly stripped by the dancing priestesses, called *jogithis*. A policewoman, it was reported, felt so humiliated and helpless that she wanted to kill herself. The *jogithis* with their matted hair and red-and-yellow powder-smeared faces danced gleefully waving police pants and helmets and iron *trishulas*. The clothed devotees and pilgrims who had gathered in Chandragutti from far and near by foot, on bullock carts, buses and lorries ascribed the mass hysteria to the fury of the Goddess *Renukamba*, even while they felt sympathy for the victims. Nobody seemed to have any sympathy for the photographers whose expensive cameras were smashed like the coconut offerings to the Goddess.

I must not offer myself as typical but my personal feelings and my stance as a novelist—which are related of course, but in a complex manner—have always reacted in an ambivalent manner to conflicts of this kind in my culture. Twenty years ago when I wrote my first novel *Samskara*, my conscious motivation was more rationalist than what it is today, and I acted culturally and politically from that standpoint. But, even then, I was still moved by the mystical elements in my religious world, which entered into my writing despite myself.

In my second novel *Bharathipura* I set out with a conscious rationalist purpose. My Western-educated hero, Jagannath, returns to his temple-town in search of his identity. He wants to authenticate his existence through action in the world of his childhood, the temple-town. He feels this can be done only by destroying his relation to the God of the temple-town who controls not only the emotional life of the inhabitants but the economic realities of the place also. The god, *Manjunatha*, had been installed some centuries ago in the temple as the overlord of an indigenous deity, *Bhootharaya*, whom the original inhabitants—now the untouchables—had once worshipped. Jagannath wants this cultural colonization to end and he sets out to demythify the power of the temple. On the *Jatra* day he wants to take the untouchables, to whom the indigenous god, *Bhootharaya*, belongs, into the temple and prove to the devotees that the belief that the untouchables would vomit blood if they enter the *sanctum* is unfounded. As he prepares the untouchables for the event he passes through agonizing conflicts, personally, in the process of decasteing himself. Before taking them into the temple, a symbol of the collective belief, he wants to destroy the myth surrounding the stone *saligram* of his family, the personal deity for which the sacred lamp has burned ceaselessly for generations. He takes the *saligram* on his palm and walks out of the house to the untouchables standing outside the gate of his compound. His blood relations and servants of the house look on bewildered and frightened, for the *saligram* had never been taken out of the ancient house and desecrated like this.

The whole situation gets charged. Jagannath wants to prove that it is a mere rounded piece of stone, and not a sacred object. But the intensity of the gaze of his relations and his servants—belonging to several castes—turns the stone into a *saligram*. The very attempt to destroy the myth, paradoxically, enhances the sacredness of the stone. The still unawakened untouchables are mesmerised by the intensity of the whole situation. The hero stretches his hand and asks them to touch it and thus make it what it truly is—a mere stone. But they dare not touch it and hence the stone is transformed into a *saligram*, more potent than what it was, untested. Jagannath feels so disgusted and angry with the untouchables that for a moment he feels like killing them. His fury, which for the hapless untouchables is after all the wrath of a landlord—for he still stands to them in that economic relation—cows them down and then they touch the *saligram* passively! The hero suddenly realizes that his old aunt whom he loves, and who is superstitious and doesn't touch the pariah, is humanly kinder to them than he is.

I shall not go into the details of what happens in the novel. Suffice it to say, the myth triumphs in the end. There is also a hint that with education and unavoidable social processes the untouchables will become touchables some time in the future, and they will also become respectable like the other middle class peoples. In the meanwhile, *Manjunatha*, the god, is reinstalled in the temple. The priest's son who throws the idol into the river for personal vengeance against his domineering father gets deified in an absurd series of events. Does any change take place in Bharathipura?

'Yes' and 'No' is the answer of the novel, *Bharathipura*. Of course I pleased no one, neither my radical friends nor the reactionary status-quoists, by this. I was putting my own rationalism and political radicalism to test in the novel. The form and content of the novel, with its blend of allegory and realism, didn't seem to work as satisfactorily as in *Samskara*. I was biting more than I could chew—which I do not regret.

In my political action—whatever little a full-time teacher like me can do—I have not wavered all these thirty years; I remain a democratic socialist. But with regard to cultural questions I am increasingly and agonizingly growing ambivalent. *Bharathipura* was written about a decade ago, at a time which also saw the rise of activism among the Scheduled Caste radicals and rationalists in Karnataka. Some of my intimate friends whom I respect and with whom, politically, I have a lot in common are among these activist groups, and, therefore, my dilemmas cause me and also my friends bafflement and pain. They feel often very angry and also, naturally, intolerant with my dilemmas.

The papers are full of the Chandragutti episode and we meet in a committee room of the Central Institute of Indian Languages in Mysore, under the auspices of a journal that I edit, to discuss the happenings. Our small group consists of two anthropologists, liberals of different persuasions, and a woman activist of great courage and commitment who has luckily come back unscathed from Chandragutti. We are eager to hear the anthropologists and the woman activist. We already have some anthropological data regarding the Chandragutti worship. *The Hindu*, a solidly middle class, even conservative, South Indian newspaper with a Marxist on its editorial board has published a report with the headline, 'Were the volunteers over-enthusiastic?', *The Hindu*, Monday, March 24, 1986. The report tells us that we have records of Chandragutti dating back to 1396 AD. It was an early stronghold of the Kadamba kings of Banavasi. The mythological references of Chandragutti date back to the pre-*Kruta yuga* days. This was the sage Jamadagni's hermitage, according to legend. His wife Renuka went to bring water from the river as she did daily, but one day she failed to repeat the miracle of carrying water in a basket as she had lost her purity. She had seen a Kshatriya king bathing in the river and she was for a moment attracted by him. Her husband Jamadagni perceived what had happened and he ordered his son Parsurama to kill his mother. There are several stories about this. He obeyed his father, and from the pleased father earned the boon of getting his mother back to life, but had to wander round the world in expiation, vainly trying to wash clean the axe of his mother's blood. He also killed all the Kshatriyas and spared only

Rama, who, like him, is an avatar of Vishnu. But the legend in Chandragutti is vivid and dramatic. As the son pursued Renuka to behead her, she ran recklessly and in the process lost all her clothes. She hid herself in the Shiva temple, naked. There is still a cave in Chandragutti below which is a rock shaped like two giant hips, believed to be those of Renuka. There is another legend linking Renuka with Matangi, who was Renuka's maidservant. Parasurama, before leaving on his mission of killing Kshatriyas, entrusted his mother to the care of Matangi's son, Beerappa. But he grows into a sex maniac and Matangi, moved by the plight of helpless women, provided them with clothes.

Even today, as the naked women come to the temple of Matangi they are provided with new clothes. Many of these worshippers are also devotees of Yellamma of Saundatti in Belgaum district. The two are believed to be sisters. There is also a legend that Renuka of *Kruta yuga* took the form of Yellamma in *Kaliyuga*. The radical activists are up against practices observed to propitiate Yellamma of Saundatti. Young girls offer themselves as prostitutes in observation of a vow and many of them now-a-days find their ways into Bombay's flesh market owing to commercial exploitation. There are *Jagithis* and *Khojas* in the Yellamma temple, too. Some activists who went to Chandragutti associate the nude worship with the likely enticement into prostitution.

In our meeting, the anthropologists offer proper technical explanations: for the way in which Dravidian culture has interacted with the Aryan in Chandragutti, and for the unique survival of age-old practices like possession-worship, owing to the inaccessibility of the hilly regions of the Sahyadri range of mountains. And, of course, they ask what is the cultural significance of mother-worship in general, and what it may mean to the lower castes in Chandragutti. And they offer guesses regarding the private psychological problems of the devotees and the therapeutic nature of the nude worship. They speculate on how some women offer their hair, some others their nudity—whatever is held to be most valuable to themselves, to the goddess, and so on. And, finally, the anthropologists add: it is futile to attempt to stop a practice until you study in depth what the practice means to the actual believers. But change they must, some day—and their quarrel is only with the tactics employed by the over-enthusiastic activists. They concur with the first sentence of the *The Hindu* report: 'Can

a deep-seated superstition handed down the centuries be eradicated overnight?'

The woman activist is impatient. We should make a beginning
somewhere, shouldn't we? In the name of culture and belief do
we tolerate untouchability and *sati*? Have we not legislated against
such evil practices? She is also angry with the Government that
they did not take enough precautions by way of extra police force.
Although she did not actually say so in the meeting, many of the
activists are attacking the Government that the police did not even
burst tear gas shells, and they had rifles in vain. Some activists
suspect the hand of Hindu revivalists in the attack, but one of
them also acknowledges that the Vishwa Hindu Parishad, a militant revivalist organisation, had published pamphlets calling upon
the devotees to give up nude worship.

The woman activist is still under shock from what she has seen
and one of the anthropologists tries to persuade her that the practice of untouchability which is a social evil should not be equated
with nude worship. Yet he agrees with her that it *must* go, and that
it *will* go with education and civilization spreading into the area.
Another anthropologist speaks of the practice of hooking oneself
up in the air on the back and being turned round in the observation of a vow and how the worshipper does not even bleed with
the hook pierced into the flesh. Such is the intensity of faith in
some lower castes, and such is the power of possession.

The woman activist looks on bewildered as he goes on to nar-
rate a famous Kannada story by Ananda, 'The Girl I Killed'. In the
story, the girl is a prostitute from a respectable and rich landlord
family. She is given over to the temple in fulfillment of a vow. The
story is narrated by a traveller—that he is a superior 'outsider' and
a city person is important—collecting historical information on a
temple in the vicinity. (Also note that his interest in the temple is
aesthetic and historical—not religious.) He stays as a guest in her
father's house. The girl, in her innocence and gratitude for the
affection shown by the sophisticated guest from the city, offers
herself to him. He does not know what she is. Being a stranger to
such practices and a rationalist-moralist, he is shocked by the inhumanity of the practice. He convinces her how despicable the
superstitious practice is, only to find her drowned in a well the
next morning. The anthropologist implies by his story that we do
not have any right to interfere with the belief-pattern of others.
But the story also implies a point I feel that the anthropologist has

missed: that one cannot help interacting—although the result is tragic.

The woman activist is so possessed by her conviction in the rational approach to life that she is too impatient to pay attention to the subtleties of the story's message. I understand how she feels, and why the cool distance and objectivity that the anthropologist enjoys by virtue of his discipline sounds somewhat inauthentic to her.

We have in our midst a linguist belonging to the Sikh faith. Only a week earlier he had spoken with great feeling how his people were driven to fundamentalism because of the desecration of the Golden temple of Amritsar. Today he surprises me with his argument. How can we, in India, afford to have the objectivity of the anthropologists? The terrorists strike in Punjab because of their faith. Do we merely look on? The *jogithis* in Chandragutti defend nudity with the tridents. Can we merely look on? The anthropologist does not answer him but argues: do we not tolerate the nude sages of the *Digambara* Jain cult? When thousands of them congregated in Sravanabelagola, did not our late prime minister, Indira Gandhi, pay them a visit and get blessed by them? What about the great saint poet, Mahadevi of the twelfth century, who wandered naked and when questioned by her Guru, Allama— how could her nudity be genuine when she still covered her genitals with her long hair?—she answered: 'Lest its sight embarrass you, Sir?' Why do we tolerate practices of All India Communities, and attack only those of small groups of low castes? Why this double standard? Moreover, do we sell today anything—a soap, a toothbrush, a screwdriver, a shampoo or even a plastic bucket without the help of a nude? What about striptease clubs?

We get heated up in cross-talk and the weary woman activist answers that her group has also protested against commercial exploitations of nudity.

As the anthropologists shift from the position that we should preserve what is unique in a culture, to the other position that we must try to change them slowly through sympathetic understanding and education, and as the Sikh linguist argues passionately for a firm position from us who form the national mainstream— which I suspect he will not hold on to, firmly, as the situation in Punjab changes—I am reminded of a story by A.K. Ramanujan.

The story is entitled 'Annaiah's Anthropology', and had I narrated it at the meeting it could have perhaps induced a deeper self-reflection on the part of the anthropologists present there. Or merely confirmed their own sophisticated scepticism—I do not know. The tone of the narration, as is often the case in Ramanujan's Kannada poetry too, is cool, witty and low-keyed, and, therefore, its end becomes all the more terrifying. Annaiah, who had never taken much interest in India while he lived there, begins to devour books on Indian anthropology when he comes to Chicago as an economist. He reads with admiration the American academics who write books on Indian rituals with such eye for detail and such interest. A recent book by one, Ferguson, fascinates him. Annaiah's orthodox parents live in Mysore and he has also a cousin, Sundara Rao who owns a photo studio in Hunsur. He is piqued to read that Ferguson got much of his material on funeral rites from his cousin. Annaiah reads on, with an uneasy curiosity and finds photographs of houses and streets that are familiar to him. Could the picture of the burning corpse be of his own father whose death must have been kept a secret from the son, as he lives far away for his studies? Yes, that was a picture taken by his cousin Sundara Rao who owned a studio. Annaiah is frightened. The book falls down. He picks it up and opens it to read about 'widowhood' and he sees the picture of his shaven mother in red saree as a gratefully acknowledged illustration of widowhood. Annaiah is aghast.

The story works at many levels and symbolizes much more than Annaiah's particular predicament. Annaiah is the modern Indian, fascinated by the West, ignorant of his own culture, yet attached to it emotionally. He dislikes India while he lives there, but loves the country when he goes abroad as is the case with most of us, and there is desecration and corruption deep down in the encounter of East and West. He recovers through anthropology what he has lost in reality, but the anthropology itself is the result of a profound betrayal and also a product of an inauthentic relation with the self. You cannot have an anthropological sympathy or curiosity for your own culture, when it hurts you.

I came out of the meeting feeling that the woman activist's position was more authentic than the tolerance and curiosity of an anthropologist. 'But don't you see', I had yet asked the woman activist, 'something positive in those nude worshippers, a feeling of religious awe that you and I have unfortunately lost? A woman's naked body is an erotic object for us; or exceptionally an aesthetic experience only if it is handled by a great painter or sculptor. It is neither aesthetic nor erotic for the worshippers. Isn't that profoundly moving?—And can that happen anywhere else in the world? A naked body is *sacred* for them.' One of my friends whose old aunt lives in a village had told me what the old woman had said after witnessing the procession. For her the beautiful and healthy young women who overcome their shame and walk naked had seemed like goddesses with flower garlands round their necks. Moreover, the processionists were old and young of both sexes including children, and they walked naked not anywhere and not any time, but only in Chandragutti on a particular day— rehearsing an event of the timeless past of India—reverentially.

My feelings must seem like poetic romanticism to the woman activist, naturally. I seek to find out how my friend Devanuru Mahadeva feels about the whole episode. Mahadeva is an activist himself of the Scheduled Caste group. He is perhaps the best fiction writer among Kannada writers in their thirties. He has written two novelettes and a collection of stories. He writes about the actual condition and the slow awakening of the untouchables with a depth of poetic feeling and objectivity that is all the more remarkable considering his passionate political engagement with the day-to-day struggle of the untouchable castes for equality and self-respect. His stories abound in rituals and intimate description of the everyday life of his characters in their misery as well as their ecstasy. The success of his daring is largely due to the low mimetic mode he employs. The novelette, *Odalala*, where a hungry family eats up a whole bagful of peanuts sitting around a fire without leaving a trace of their theft to the police who search their poor cottage in the morning is a moving story of the revolutionary potentiality of the untouchable castes even in the midst of their misery. The old woman in *Odalala* who goes in search of a lost cock she has lovingly reared grows in the story into the proportions of the mythological mother symbolizing the elemental urge of *caring*. She quarrels, weeps loudly, admonishes her children, tells mythical stories, curses heartily and yet what is remarkable about this earthy woman is that she cares. A young girl in the family draws the picture of a peacock on the wall, a school-going child marvels at his sister's creation, the old woman who has no time for nonsense like a peacock dancing on the mud wall still tells him a mythical story where the child becomes a potential prince—and at night they all sit and eat the stolen peanuts around a fire, forgetting the lacerating quarrels and frustrations of the day. The peanut

eating is as intense a creative act—almost an *yajna*—as the peacock drawing in the story. In this world of simple ritualistic folk-life
is also heard the rumblings of the coming change. One of the peanut eaters, who wears a wrist-watch, entertains the family crowd
with his story of defying a hotelier and demanding respectful service along with others.

Mahadeva cannot afford to look on the nude worshippers,
many of whom belong to his caste, with anthropological curiosity.
Nor can he want them to stay put in a magical world. He wants
them to become conscious of their rights in the modern democratic society. Yet I feel he ought to be able, the kind of poetic
novelist that he is, to see the grandeur of the souls of the nude
worshippers—however necessary and inevitable it is for them to
come out of their magical universe—a universe that Blake and
Lawrence and Yeats had longed for in the analytical and scientific
Western civilization. Mahadeva tells me it would have been all
right for them to worship in the nude, if the onlookers were also
nude, and if some of the girls were not forced or dragged to go
nude. I understand what he means; I add, sadly, it cannot remain
the same particularly after what had happened, and the nude
worshippers displayed on cover pages.

I ask myself another question—which is very important for me.
How would the *Vacanakaras* of the twelfth century, particularly
the great mystic poets, Basava and Allama, who protested against
the 'little' as well as 'great' traditions have reacted to the nude
worshipers? I can only speculate. They would have perhaps
pleaded with them for a less magical and a more spiritual God-
awareness. And that could have been a more meaningful encounter in our tradition than between our modernizers and the magical
worshippers.

I dare to tell 'yes' in a young poet's ear alone when he accosts
me with the question: 'Is Renuka true? Is Yellamma true?' I am
alone with him and so I say 'yes'. I am surprised at the leap I have
taken, but I have hopes of striking a chord in his heart, for he is a
poet. He looks uncomprehendingly at my flushed face. Have I
betrayed a part of me, the ever vigilant sceptic in me whom the
Baconian–Cartesian epistemology of the scientific West has nourished with a good salary and comfortable working conditions?
Have not I become what I am by demythifying, even desecrating
the world of my childhood? As a boy growing up in my village did
not I urinate stealthily and secretly on sacred stones under trees to

prove to myself that they have no power over me? I remember the terror I had overcome spending sleepless nights, and consequently the ambivalence that enters into my youthful stories and novels. No, I cannot be an absolutist, for I am a novelist, and not a poet. My dream of combining Marxism with mysticism in actual praxis will never come true. In a literary work, perhaps, but not in actual life. Only as a poet Wordsworth cried in weary despair, 'Great God, I would rather be a pagan suckled in a creed outworn'. Nor can one be indifferent, or merely curious, or patronizingly tolerant. Chandragutti is no longer inaccessible. There are buses plying from Shimoga and the once thick forests surrounding the village are now thin, thanks to the greedy contractors and corrupt timber merchants and forest officials. The quick growing, inhospitable eucalyptus are planted everywhere with World Bank aid for the multi-millionaire Birla's factories. The *jogithis*—the matted haired, fierce priestesses of Yellamma of Saundatti—are under suspicion of girls for the flourishing flesh trade in Bombay. And Bombay attracts fun-seeking tourists from all over the world.

Yet, I dared to write a long story a couple of years ago into which I have put, I hope, all my agonizing perplexities. I was prompted to write it when a grasshopper accidentally hopped into my sunlit room and I told my daughter that the dear thing is called, in Kannada, *suryana kudure*, the sun-horse. And that started the story. Was not Marx wrong to say that the rural calm can only produce idiocy? Has not the rural culture dared to connect the sun with an otherwise insignificant and vulnerable insect? The joy and reverence for life and the daring imagination seen in the naming of an insect profoundly moved me and I wrote *Suryana Kudure*. The story took me back into the magical universe of my childhood. The restless son of my hero is willing even to commit patricide, such is the threat to my hero's way of life, and a sensibility that has become comically impractical. Yet I am temporarily won over by him, after a ritualistic magical oil bath and the serenity with which he overcomes the violent encounter between him and his son who wants to get away from the idiocy of the limited village life. His son, after all, is on the path I have myself walked, yet the father makes me see, by his own ecstatic absorption, the wonder of the Surya's horse perched on a hedge. The story has moved many of my critics, only as momentarily as myself, under the charm of my hero, but the next moment the implicit ideas in the story make way for angry polemics. As my other novel *Awasthe* too did, where my political hero, wearied by the corruptions of parliamentary democracy, wants to return to the glowing quotidian of his boyhood days in the village. He wants to organize the unorganized poor of the village for revolutionary change rather than reformistic modernization, perhaps a weak resolve—but no critic recognizes it even. Such is the hold of modernization on us that we feel there is no other viable path. Look at what is happening in China—they say....

Mahatma Gandhi back from South Africa entered Indian politics not with a religious book, but with a political tract, *Hind Swaraj*. This is in the form of a dialogue with a terrorist. Mahatma Gandhi asks the question why the British are in India and answers himself—because we Indians are in love with modern civilization. If modern civilization is bad for us it is bad for the British, too. Like all great visionaries, Mahatma Gandhi is also an extremist. No one in India has paid any heed to the Mahatma about what he thinks are the evils of modern civilization and its unimportance to human happiness or search for truth. Not even his dearest disciple, Nehru, paid any heed to him. We are all in love with the modern civilization in India, whether we are capitalists, communists or liberals. But the masses of the Indian subcontinent, with their innumerable children, poverty, superstitious practices and caste-bound loyalties are quite content in their lives. Because of them 'India will go on', as she is, the immemorial past just repeated in the present, for they expect nothing more from life than the bare necessities that a backward subsistence economy can give them. Gods are still propitiated by these masses of people, and their humdrum life glows at such moments.

No wonder this inertia enrages the energetic modernizers. The Emergency that Mrs Gandhi proclaimed in 1975 gave full expression to this rage in some of Sanjay Gandhi's programs. People were operated upon forcibly to bring population down, and roads were broadened removing hutment dwellers mercilessly beyond the city limits. These words of a sociologist at Delhi University quoted by Shiva Naipaul ('The Emergency and the Meteor', *The Observer*, 11 January 1981) express what many felt at that time:

> Sanjay did express a certain dark side of the Indian personality. I recognize that darkness in myself. 'Sometimes', he said slowly, deliberately, 'when you look around you, when you see the decay and pointlessness, when you see, year after year, this

grotesque beggarly mass ceaselessly reproducing itself like some … like some kind of vegetable gone out of control … suddenly there comes an overwhelming hatred. Crush the brutes! Stamp them out! It's a racial self-disgust some of us develop towards ourselves … that is the darkness I speak about'….

Yes—all of us are modernizers in one way or the other, but with an uneasy conscience, if we are sensitive. The great writers among us see it as inevitable and search for ways to preserve what is best and unique in Indian Civilization. The novelists of the pre-independence idealism who had begun to write before I was born are still with us. Masti Venkatesha Iyengar is 95 years old. He has a gentle and profound insight into what lasts in India, and what elements inherent in human nature threaten it. Shakespeare, Wordsworth, Leslie Stephen, Arnold and Valmiki—the best in the traditions of the East and the West—have gone into the making of his liberal humanist sensibility. His novel, *Chickadeva Raya*, is about colonization (like Achebe's *Things Fall Apart*), how a decadent kingdom is manipulated into submission by the British. Some of its passages of inhuman cruelty juxtaposed against divine tolerance and love have a Dostoeyeskian intensity about them. A large number of his better stories deal with cultural amnesia, and how it is overcome, thanks to the positively beneficial result of our encounter with the West. Masti, still orthodox in his ways, reminds us that tradition and modernization need not be always antagonistic. He has read Valmiki and Shakespeare as if they were his contemporaries. The crisis of modern life confirms his faith in tradition. But there is only one Masti in my language, and his simple faith and certainty is impossible for any of us….

Mistah Kurtz went with his great idealism and empty rhetoric to bring the sanity of modern Christian civilization to Africa, but ended up crying, 'Exterminate the brutes'. In our times, the Chinese have invaded Tibet, the Russians are in Afghanistan, and the Americans are everywhere except where the Russians are, and the elite in India are no exception in their relation to the masses.

If I write further I may begin to say more than I mean. I would not have been a fiction writer if it were not for the impact of the scepticism of the modern civilization on me. And also, I must add, the kind of fiction writer I am is due to my quarrel with modern civilization.

■

22

▪ NIRMAL VERMA ▪

Nirmal Verma was born in 1929 in Simla. He studied history at Delhi University where he received his M.A. degree. He is acknowledged as one of the leading contemporary writers in the Hindi language. In addition to important works of fiction, his writings include critical essays, travelogues, and translations. He is particularly renowned for his collections of short stories, among which the following stand out: *Parinde* (1959), *Jalati Jhadi* (1965), *Beech Bahas Mein* (1972), and *Kavve aur Kala Pani* (1978; winner of the Sahitya Academi Award). Among his works of literary criticism, these collections are specially significant: *Shabd aur Smriti* (1976), *Kala ka Jokhim* (1981), and *Dhalaan se Utarte Huye, Kala, Smriti aur Akanksha* (1991). As an intellectual and writer, Nirmal Verma emphasizes the tensional relation between tradition and modernity, between indigenous culture and (Western-style) globalization. The following essay, which is the text of a lecture delivered at the University of Heidelberg, Germany, is taken from the journal *Kavita Asia* (Bhopal 1990), pp. 121–144.

INDIA AND EUROPE—SOME REFLECTIONS ON SELF AND OTHER

I am grateful to the South Asia Institute of Heidelberg University[1] for having invited me to talk on a subject which was very close to the heart of the writer in whose memory the present series of lectures is being organized. Ajneya, as indeed most of you know, was one of those remarkable writers who embodied within himself the rare quality of the mind which reaches out to the other without ceasing to be itself; or, to be more precise, a mind which feels at home with itself only when it reaches out to the other. In this sense, perhaps, he was one of the most paradoxic writers on the contemporary Indian scene: to most of the Indians he seemed to be a 'homeless' writer, to Europeans an Indian writer who never left home.

In his early writings Ajneya was deeply influenced by the modern European literature, for which he was often criticized by the critics who found a lot in his early writings which was 'un-Indian'. Ironically, the same critics felt equally disturbed by the Hindu traditionalism in his later work. How to explain the strange development from one extreme of 'Westernization' to the other extreme of 'Indianness' in the single life-span of the same person? Was it a journey peculiar to Ajneya, as a modern Indian writer, or was it in some way symbolic of a situation peculiar to India, where, as a result of colonial uprootedness, an Indian writer has to pass through various stages of metamorphosis before he could finally arrive at his authentic 'self'? I wonder how Ajneya himself would have reacted to the observation of his contemporary Indian philosopher who said: 'there is no other way open to us in the East, but to go along with Europeanization and to go through it. Only through this voyage into the foreign and strange can we win back our own selfhood: hence here as elsewhere, the way to do what is closest to us is the longest way back.'[2]

It would be a very long voyage, indeed, to pass through all the stations of European culture, in order to arrive ultimately at one's own destination. India, whatever it has been in the past, has never had a good reputation for its adventures abroad. Neither driven by the zeal of proselytization nor by any desire of conquest of foreign lands, India has shown any desire to make its presence felt in the world. Could there be anything more remarkable than the fact that without war or any military aggression, Indian culture could spread over vast areas of Asia, what is since known as the concept of *Greater India*, and yet, such an extraordinary historical phenomenon, if ever noticed by Indians at home was soon forgotten, buried in oblivion for centuries, till they were reminded of it by Vivekananda as late as in the late nineteenth century. The fact, that they were reminded of their 'past glories' only under the threat of European civilization is as significant as the fact of their 'forgetfulness', when no such threat existed. It also goes a long way to demonstrate the crucial difference the Indians felt in their attitude to the Western civilization as against the other 'alien' cultures of the past.

It sometimes seems to me that for India to be 'discovered' by Europe was more a misfortune than a blessing, a misfortune far more calamitous than for some other countries of the East who had no heritage of the 'past' to go back to or to be reminded of. If it was left to themselves, Indians, like some plants or animals in a forest, would blissfully have chosen to be invisible to the outside world, their scriptures and shastras hidden 'behind the dark culture of Sanskrit language'. Not that they ever succeeded in remaining aloof from the others. The others were always there. There was hardly any time during the last three thousand years when India was not beleaguered by the yavanas[3] and mlechhas:[4] first by the Greeks and the Huns, then by Islam, closely followed by the Christian missionaries and European conquerors. However, the unusual feature of the Hindu culture is not how it survived the continuous and violent incursions of the foreigners over the centuries, but the way it could remain immune to them even when it failed to resist their physical or political domination. Even the legendary biography of Alexander, which became so well known in large parts of Asia, was totally disregarded by Hindu India. We can know all that we need to quench our curiosity about the Hindus and their ancient customs from the Greek and Chinese travellers or later from the chronicles of Muslim historians, but there is hardly any account available to us about what the Hindu natives thought of their 'guests' from abroad. Not even about the Muslims with whom they co-existed for so long and who presided over their destinies by a supreme coercive power and an aggressive religious ideology, which they could not have easily ignored. Nor do we find any account of philosophical or religious debates with ulemas[5] in traditional Hindu literature. This is all the more striking, for Hindu pundits, whatever their other weaknesses, rarely suffered from intellectual humility when it came to metaphysical discussions, which they conducted with such vigor with their Buddhist opponents in the past and where destined to continue, in a limited manner, with the Christian missionaries in the future.

The reason for this silence and evasiveness towards the other cultures and religions among the Hindus is often attributed to their complete lack of interest or curiosity about the others. Possibly it is true. Perhaps it is equally true that Indians had already built up (or thought that they had built up) such a self-contained, sophisticated metaphysical system which answers to all their needs and enquiries and they had nothing more or new or important to learn from the other. But perhaps there was a more profound reason for their so-called 'indifference' to other cultures: not so much the lack of curiosity or a smug sense of perfection, but the fact that *for them the 'other' was never a source of reference to define their own identity as it was for the Europeans*. But the 'self' was always accepted as self-referential, the 'other' was neither a threat to their identity nor a source of confirmation of their uniqueness. This was very different from the European notion of the 'other', an inalienable entity external to oneself, both a source of terror and an object of desire. Sartre's famous statement, 'hell is the other', carries a strong echo of Hegel who always defines one's identity as 'identity against the other, either to be appropriated, or to be destroyed'. But here, as I pointed out elsewhere, the European man gets himself entrapped in his own contradiction; if he succeeds in completely subjugating the 'other', the identity of his own self becomes dubious. He wants to become whole by destroying the other, but without the other, he becomes nothing.

Buddhism, however, posed a challenge which was quite different from other traditions, both in its origins and its philosophical content. It was both the other and not the other. If Hindu scholars and seers felt compelled to engage themselves in passionate intellectual discussions with their Buddhist counterpart, it is precisely because Buddhism, while being other, also at the same time shared with Hinduism some most fundamental concepts of common reference, the questions of *moksha* (liberation) and *nirvana*, of 'self' and 'nothingness'.

If Islam and Christianity failed to arouse the same interest or curiosity, it is because they were 'other' in the absolute sense of the term. The extent to which semitic religions denuded themselves from their ontological moorings, to that extent they lost much of their challenging power and attraction for Hindu traditionalists. So far as Buddhism posed a philosophical threat to Hinduism, the 'otherness' of it became redundant for Hindus and ultimately disappeared from India. On the other hand, Islam and

Christianity, who in their indubitable otherness never posed such a threat, continue to exist as institutionalized religions even to this day.

Here, one may point out a dimension of Hinduism which is uniquely its own: for other cultures, particularly European, the 'other' becomes an object of inquiry only in its 'unassimilable otherness', while for Hindus, unless the 'other' is in some way assimilated or internalized within its system, it does not acquire the weight or visibility of a system to which it could make a meaningful response. If the problem of 'untouchability' caused such a fierce controversy in Hindu society, it is because the *shudras*, though an assimilated part of the caste system, always remained very much on the periphery of the society, not really outsiders like *mlechhas*, but not exactly 'insiders' either. Similarly, in the nineteenth century India, it was not the Christian missionaries who in their tirade against the ancient customs of Hindus could succeed in stirring up any response from traditional pundits. They were treated simply as misguided outsiders. The abusive epithets they used for Hindu gods like 'horrid Kali, scandalous Shivlingam, ridiculous Ganpati and lecherous Krishna'[6] were received more in the spirit of amusement rather than in anger. If there was any anger or bitterness, it was reflected in the debates the orthodox Hindus carried on against the Hindu reformist sects like Brahmo Samaj in Bengal and Arya Samaj in north India; for they were the people who, in the name of 'progress' and 'enlightenment', were trying to recast the Hindu society in the alien mold of semitic religions. They were the real blasphemers, precisely because they were the real insiders. Rabindranath Thakur's [Tagore] first major novel, *Gora*, gives a vivid account of the most anguished debates which were raging within the Hindu society at the beginning of the twentieth century—no less passionate and self-searching than what Thomas Mann was to depict later in his famous novel *The Magic Mountain* concerning the dark and troubled state of European civilization. Two novels about two destinies: Mann brooding over the threatened collapse of the civilized values which constitute the identity of Europe, Tagore, on the other hand, reflecting on the crisis of Hindu identity which is being threatened precisely by those 'civilized values' which were being forced on a society that had no choice to accept or reject them.

This brings me to the point which has played such a crucial role in determining the basic 'repertoire of images' which both India and Europe fabricated for each other when they came in contact with one another for the first time. The fact that they oscillated so wildly from one extreme of exaggerated praise and admiration to another extreme of contempt and rejection only proves that they were *fantasized* images which had very little to do with reality. Indeed, if anything, reality itself was fantasized to an extent where it became actually embarrassing for both to see each other as they were, and not what they thought they *ought* to be. The embarrassment arose not from any lack of desire on the part of India and Europe to relate to one another, but from the nature of the relation in which they found one another historically bound—India serving the role of an undeveloped Asian colony; Britain, the dominant ruling partner representing all that Europe stood for—power, wealth, intellectual enlightenment—a sole repository of humanist values of freedom, equality and justice. The images were distorted precisely because the way in which India and Europe saw one another had a seed of perversion within it—some parts were exaggerated out of proportions at the expense of other parts which remained totally invisible.

What could be a more glaring example of 'invisibility' than the fact that even for those who otherwise were quite unaffected by colonial deceit, e.g., Hegel and Max Müller, 'real' India existed only *in the past*, a rich site of excavation, from where the treasures of ancient philosophy and literary classics can be dug up, but the *link* that connected the past with the *present*—the network of beliefs, myths and rituals which provided a continuous cultural and spiritual nourishment to millions of Indians—was not only *not seen*, but it was firmly believed that it did *not exist*. No wonder Max Müller, with all his sympathetic insights into India's tradition, never bothered to visit the land where it flowered and still survived, for the simple reason that no such 'land' existed for him; it was washed away long ago by the waves of history, leaving behind the 'ruins' which were the only object of his interest and fascination. Europe, which claimed to discover India's 'past', is also to be rightly credited to abolish its 'present'.

Never before such a violent cultural rupture—a rupture between its past and present—had ever taken place in India's psyche, not even under the most intolerant Islamic rulers. Hindus could have been forced to be converted to Islam, but those who refused and resisted enjoyed all the 'civilizational space', in which their past could breathe into their present, their present drawing sustenance from the myths and symbols of the past. It was not the 'past' discovered by the Western orientalists, to be displayed in museums or to be deciphered from the ancient Sanskrit texts; it was not a body of mummified memories to be excavated from the dead and long buried civilizations; India's 'past' was not like the past of Egypt and Greece, segments of ancient memory to be recovered from oblivion; *it could not be excavated because it was never entirely buried*. Past, in India, was eternally contemporaneous even as present was eternally alive in the beliefs and customs of the past embodied in *dharma*[7] which is *sanatan*,[8] knowing no beginning and no end.

Europe, however, had a very different vision of history which could deal with time only as neatly separated categories, a vision nurtured in them by their Judaic-Christian tradition. To determine their identity vis-à-vis India, they perforce had to make India recognizable as a 'historical entity' which had nothing in common with the way the Indians looked at themselves.

Europe's colonization of India was not merely confined to some 'territorial space' but went much further and deeper; it sought to 'colonize' India's sense of *time*, its present being merely a corruption of the past, its past, though glorious, believed to be dead and gone. Thus arose the age-old romantic notion of India 'speaking from the position in the remote past via *its distorted present* to (the) European present'.

Deprived of its 'home' both in terms of space and time, India became a reflected image in the multiple mirrors of European civilization. To Marx, it was a moribund culture of outlived feudalism seething with savage gods and dark superstitions. To Hegel, Indian thought was reduced to an abstract 'dream image', never reaching the level of philosophy which was regarded as a uniquely European achievement. For European merchant conquerors, India was an object of desire. Between an object of desire to be appropriated and a beautiful dream that has passed, India as it existed in the present remained largely invisible to the European eye. India would once again acquire 'visibility', as Hegel then believed and which was confirmed by Husserl and Heidegger in our time, if *its past is transformed into European present*. It was in Europe alone where they saw the power for the 'appropriation, actualization and rebirth' of India's past. India's present would have any meaning if only it could be recast in the ideal image of Europe.

Such was the 'idealized image' of Europe that was presented to Indians when, two hundred years ago, they first saw the white men as their rulers. Today, after the two World Wars and the horrors of holocaust and Hiroshima and the gulags, such an image of 'a civilized European' may have lost much of its shine and glory, but to Indians at the time Europe, as no other part of the world, symbolized what could be only the pinnacle of human civilization—both in the sphere of material progress and intellectual achievements. I think Bankim Chandra Chatterji, one of the most acute and alert minds of Bengali intelligentsia in the nineteenth century, accurately summed up the Indian reaction to Europe when he said: 'Never before has the world witnessed such material progress as has been achieved by the civilization of modern Europe, nor had the earlier generations of mankind even hoped for such progress.'

But with the passage of time, as the native crafts were swamped by the cheap merchandise of Manchester and 'Indian plains littered with the bones of Indian craftsmen', as Marx so vividly describes the appalling nature of devastation brought in the wake of British colonialism, Bankim Chandra Chatterji's words of adulation lost much of their splendor. The economic penury to which India was reduced was accompanied by a sense of spiritual desolation, even as the centuries of traditional learning were gradually replaced by the European system of education with the English language as the compulsory medium of instruction. Of course, there was the famous Raja Ram Mohun Roy, the first Indian modernist who saw in these Western institutions the source of enlightenment which would bring Indians out of the darkness of their superstitions. This was the view of a learned Hindu who was steeped deep in his tradition, but was totally overwhelmed by his first encounter with Europe. Not many Hindu contemporaries agreed with his view of Europe. Nor did a sensitive middle class Indian find the Englishmen, 'the light givers', very enlightened either in their conduct or manners. As we approach the end of the nineteenth century, the romanticized image of the European has suffered many a setback.

Vivekananda gives in a very vivid, though slightly exaggerated manner, the perceptions of an average Indian about their white rulers, 'intoxicated by the heady wine of newly acquired power, fearsome like wild animals who see no difference between good and evil, slaves to women, insane in their lust, drenched in alcohol from head to foot, without any norms of ritual conduct, unclean, materialistic, grabbing other people's territory and wealth by hook or by crook, without any faith in life to come'.

Not really a happy portrait of an Englishman as seen through the eyes of an Indian. But however he may be looked upon, in a spirit of awe and servile adoration or bitterness and resentment, the fact remains that for the first time the presence of alien culture shook the Indians from their apathy and indifference. For the first time in their long history Indians had to cope with the 'other' as the other, which could neither be immunized through assimilation nor could it be treated like Islam with which they could live in peaceful co-existence. They could have effectively ignored or faced the religious dimension of a Europe embodied in Christianity. It was the 'other side of Europe', its enlightened rationalism and material advancement which posed a challenge towards which they felt attracted and repelled at the same time. Most of the time they felt baffled by the two contradictory images of Europe, one the bearer of humanist values of freedom and justice, something about which they read in the books in their colleges and universities, the other image being the dark, supercilious, arrogant power which they encountered face to face in their own country. It was difficult for them to reconcile these two images as twin aspects of a single cultural phenomenon.

Perhaps they would have had a more coherent and balanced view of Europe if they had come into contact with its culture directly and not through the distorted image of British colonialism. The nature of distortion was further aggravated by the context in which they had to encounter and interpret Europe. It was not the context given by their tradition which would have enabled them to see Europe both as the 'other' as well as a part of their worldview. Instead, it was a context built upon the European categories of thought, science and philosophy. Indians were supposed to respond to Europe through the language which was not their own, in terms of categories of thought which were European, in a social setting which was colonial. No wonder that, under these circumstances, India developed its own images of Europe which were as fragmented and reductive as the European images of India. If Europe nourished the fantasized image of India's present cutting it from its past, India was left no option but to develop its own fantasized image of European culture as it was 'presented to Indians' in their country, blocking their normal view of the European horizons from which it acquired its distinctive and complex character.

It was a strange situation where two cultures had to live in a state of togetherness which was demeaning to both, loving and hating each other mostly for wrong reasons, entrapped like two animals in a cage, grinning and growling at alternate intervals, evolving unique strategies to be 'invisible' to one another and yet bound and bewitched by one another under a hallucinating spell from which there was no escape. It has always been difficult for me to agree with Nirad Chaudhuri about his observations on the British role in India, but he was right when he deplored their failure to strike roots in India, their spirit of eternal self-isolation which was so different from Islam. Islam, though it could never overcome its 'otherness' in the Hindu framework of life, gradually got itself 'Indianized' over the centuries to the extent that it felt absolutely at home in India and stopped looking back to its foreign roots from where it had emerged. The British, on the other hand, never forgot to stress their otherness as outsiders as representatives of a superior race and advanced civilization. But they also genuinely felt as strangers in a country whose climate they found so detestable, its landscape so desolate, the people so docile, and sometimes so treacherous, whose customs were so fascinating and yet so quaint, so incomprehensible. That was the reason why, despite his power and authority, an Englishman looked so insecurely ill-at-ease and nervous in India. E.M. Forster brings out most perceptively in his novel *Passage to India* both the supercilious snobbery and pathetic diffidence of an English official in India. Mr Nirad Chaudhuri was amazed to see how kind and cheerful an Englishman could look in his own country, while in India he gave the impression of always being so tense, jittery and irritable.

What really went wrong? Why was it that Hinduism, so well-known for its pluralistic ethos and spirit of tolerance, failed to accommodate a civilization which was rightly famous for its humanist values of equality and brotherhood, and that the British felt so bewildered and beleaguered in a country where they came not of any compulsion but of their own choice? Did the dialogue never take place between the two cultures or did the colonial setting, in which it took place, entail that only the worst of both cultures could come out on the surface? Or perhaps there was something basically wrong in the European obsession with the concept of 'dialogue' itself as the only means of knowing the other and identifying oneself? To go all around the world for the appropriation of the other cultures to affirm one's own identity on the earth—this has never been India's way to enter into any meaningful dialogue with the other traditions, but then what was the Indian way to know the truth of the other—in its 'unassimilable otherness'? The Western sceptics have always found the Indian way of dealing with other cultures and religions slightly devious and evasive, terming it the 'inclusiveness' of Indian tradition, by which, instead of facing the 'other' in a direct encounter, it tends to bypass it, as it were, by 'including' it as a lower 'stage' in its own system.

If the Christian missionaries could not get very far in converting the Hindus to their faith, it was not that they, the Hindus, offered a greater degree of resistance to the message of Christ, but they incorporated the message itself within their pluralist hierarchy of beliefs, including the person of Christ himself as one of the gods within their pantheon of gods. By such ways of inclusive identification, the Hindus seem to avoid the real dialogue with the West which could enable them to understand the truth of others in their own terms and come to grips with it in all its uniqueness. By such indifference to other civilizations, it is alleged, 'the Indian cultural tradition has retained its identity and continuity, but it has at no time *defined itself* in relation to the other'.[9]

If this were true, how shall we then explain the extraordinary cultural phenomenon like 'Bengal renaissance' which was nothing else but the massive intellectual endeavor on the part of the Hindus to respond and relate to Europe in order to redefine their past and assert their national identity? The response was, of course, not uniform; it varied from one section of Hindus to another, ranging from the most orthodox traditional pundits like Bhudev Mukhopadhya and Radhakant Dev to the most Westernized scholars like Raja Ram Mohun Roy and Devendranath Tagore. Whatever their personal background or private prejudices might have been, they were the most brilliant luminaries in the intellectual firmament trying to define the nature of Indian 'selfhood' both in terms of European categories of thought, as well as in defiance of it. Each one of them encountered Europe to pick and choose from its culture which could help him to confirm and rationalize what he already cherished—a traditionalist to glorify his past, a patriot to affirm his nationalism, a nationalist intellectual to emphasize the 'secular' nature of his Vedic heritage. One could see the portraits of Garibaldi and Mazzini in the same Hindu household where the books of Mill and Bentham rested side by side with the ancient texts of *Upanishads* and *Bhagavad Gita*. It was a type of cultural ferment which India had never seen before—as never before its intelligentsia had let itself be so freely exposed to an alien civilization. How deeply Europe could penetrate into the psyche of the urban middle class is revealed by the fact that the first number of one of the 'enlightened' Bengali journals described itself as an organ of people who were 'Hindu by birth yet European by education'.

The small, apparently cynical dictum of a magazine perhaps most lucidly sums up the position of the liberal Westernized Hindus who were in the forefront of the so-called resurgence movement in India. It was a position of increasing accommodation and assimilation of the 'humanist' ideals of European civilization. To be 'Europeanized by education' essentially implied acceptance of the historical idea of progress which established Europe as the vanguard in the field of knowledge and enlightenment. From this position, it was just a small step to accept the 'self image' of Europe as the ideal image of man himself. It was but logical that this would lead the Hindus—at least the most enlightened of them—to radically revise their traditional conception of the 'self'. It ceased to be what it had always been in the past, a part of a larger reality, *atman* as a mirror-image of *parmatma*, a microcosm within a macrocosm. The idealized image of the European man subverted the Hindu image of his own 'self', reducing it to a state of 'sub-self', a minor accessory to a larger reality, not of *Brahman*, but of the *spirit of History* moving across the earth through centuries, to seek its ultimate fulfillment in the European man. Whatever divergent views of Europe the Indians might have had, they all seemed to be committed to and fascinated by the 'positivist' vision of history as advanced by Auguste Comte according to which humanity advances from the theological and metaphysical stage and achieves adulthood in the final scientific stage of Western civilization.

Today we might find this view very naive and outdated, but it would be a wisdom of hindsight; for the enlightened Indians of the last century, as different as Raja Ram Mohun Roy on one end and Vivekananda on the other, faith in such a historical fiction seemed to be the only source of liberation from all the other fictions—they called them 'superstitions'—which had engulfed India in darkness for centuries. When an Indian looked at himself through an historical mirror, he found not only his culture very backward, but even his 'self' in a state of progressive degeneration. 'Three hundred million sub-human creatures, their souls crushed for centuries under the feet of everyone, listless like slaves, without hope, without any past or future, concerned only with bare survival in the present, devoid of any moral stamina, spread all over India like maggots feeding on stinking rotten flesh.' This is how Vivekananda describes the European view of the Indians, but one cannot escape from suspicion that with slight modification this was also the view of many of our enlightened Indians, including Vivekananda himself, about the nature of the Indian 'self' as they saw it from Western eyes—a puny little wretched thing, shivering in darkness, not the *awakened atman* of *Gita*, but the 'maggot' rotting in the putrid flesh of tradition. *This, I believe, was the third and final phase of European 'colonization' of the Indians—not merely of their sense of space and time—to which I referred earlier, but of something much nearer to their bone—colonization of their concept of 'self' itself.*

And yet the self could never be completely colonized, for the identity of a Hindu, unlike that of a European, never resided in the self as an autonomous entity, but in a larger pattern of beliefs, ritualistic observances and caste obligations which constituted his *dharma*. If traditional Hindu pundits never felt threatened by the Western modes of thought and the European concept of history, it was because they never accepted the mode and framework through which those 'thoughts' and 'concepts' were transmitted to them. They refused to buy the 'ideal image of man' which was modeled within the framework of humanistic ideals of the West, where man is supposed to be the ultimate 'end' of the evolution and therefore the measure of all things, a logical extension of its erstwhile belief that the earth is in the center of the universe. From the European conception of 'man', as it was developed in the time of the European Renaissance, it was but a logical step to regard the 'European man' as its highest culmination. Such a step, in the eyes of orthodox Hindus, was fraught with sinister possibilities which may lead not to self-awareness, but to total self-destruction. How justified were their fears and prophetic their warning is proved by the mushroom growth of the totalitarian ideologies in twentieth century Europe: they were but the reflection of a totalitarian image of man, the supreme lord and master of the universe, a self-aggrandized projection of 'God' on earth. Once we accept 'man' as being superior to all living species on earth, then there is nothing to prevent us, logically, from accepting a particular type of man, the European man, as being superior to all the other human species, and within the framework of European civilization itself, one particular image or ideology of the European man, fascism or communism, as superior to all the other ideologies.

This was the primary reason why, unlike the Westernized Indian reformers who were so profoundly enamored by European 'ideals' of humanism, the traditional Hindus found them totally unacceptable. They saw no possibility of harmonization between the European concept of power and the Hindu concept of *dharma* which, while it recognized human beings as the highest bearers of consciousness, precisely for the same reason also regarded them as *responsible* to all the living and apparently 'unliving' phenomena surrounding them; which made no distinctions—at least no value-based distinctions—between human, on the one hand, and non-human or natural, on the other. If man's *dharma* is embodied within the set of responsibilities and obligations to others, then the aggrandized self of man as projected by Europe has no place in it. For the first time, we find two images or concepts of man representing two cultures confronting one another in their crystalline purity and precision—one seeking salvation, *moksha*, through performing one's obligations, enshrined in one's tradition, the other seeking power by asserting its *freedom* sanctioned and sanctified by history.

Here *dharma* and freedom are the key words indicating two different and opposite versions of what constitutes the 'authentic' self which two civilizations were trying to realize for themselves. This did create a distance, in fact an antagonism, between the established goals of two civilizations but by the time the difference was articulated, there were inner rifts and doubts within each civilization about the legitimacy of the goals themselves. Hegel's conviction that Indian civilization is a thing of the past and Europe has nothing to learn from it was seriously challenged by the German romantics for whom India represented not a foreign tradition but the 'forgotten basis and hidden depth of our own European identity', and they invoked this forgotten identity as an argument against the materialism and rationalism of Europe. More fundamentally, freedom itself became a burden, a cause of immense romantic anxiety from which they needed escape and liberation—which they could only find in the Indian concept of the self so different from the individualism of the West.

Similarly, in India, the traditional concept of *dharma* as advocated by orthodox Hindus involved a rejection of Europe as absolute as Hegel's critique of India. With rare confidence in his own tradition Bhudev Mukhopadhya, the nineteenth century Hindu scholar, could declare: 'No other race can match the English in the intensity of their selfishness: no other race ever developed as great a concern for the welfare of others as the Hindus. If through their mutual contact not the Hindu, but the English character underwent a change, that would have been for the best.' Such a voice could have come from the very depth of one's tradition; it had none of the diffidence or the servility of the Westernized Hindu reformers, but its complacent tone about Hinduism would perhaps have invoked a very hostile response from a person like Vivekananda who would give a different interpretation of *dharma* more in correspondence with the concept of human dignity and freedom, values which he had imbibed from Europe. It is a strange irony of history that European romantics would have been fascinated more by Indian traditionalism than by its reformed version, while a Hindu romantic like Vivekananda was more attracted by the positivistic ideals of progress and rationalism which were being so passionately rejected by his Western counterparts, the European romantics. It was no longer a conflict between two civilizations—Indian and European—representing different ideals, the conflict was rather internalized, as it were, within each civilization, each representing a facet frequently in collision with some other facet of the same civilization. At the same time, the conflict was *universalized*, transcending national and cultural boundaries, where a particular image of the ideal self found its confirmation in the spokesman belonging to another civilization, such as Gandhi finding greater affinity with the writings of Thoreau and Tolstoy than with the orthodox pundits representing his own tradition. As if to complete the circle, in our own times of moral crisis many of the European and American social scientists seek inspiration in the teachings of Gandhi himself, rather than from the official spokesman of their own tradition.

Thus, while there was a considerable 'cross-cultural' exchange of ideas between the two civilizations weakening the monolithic authority of 'pro-Europeans' and 'pro-Indians' in both camps, the inner dissensions that we see in the Indian society as a result of foreign intervention were qualitatively different from those that appeared within the overall Western attitudes to India. In Europe, there existed a wide freedom of choices in which Indian metaphysics and civilizational contributions could be accepted or rejected, or accepted in some parts by some section of scholars and rejected in other parts by others. Even within the same school, interpretations of Indian religion or philosophy differed considerably. But whatever the difference and however wide the area of choices, they all emanated from *an integral and unified European consciousness*. Schopenhauer's response to Indian tradition could be radically different from that of Hegel, or as in our day, Heidegger's attitude to the East is different from that of Husserl—at least in its emphasis if not in essence—but all the responses, in spite of their difference, are *embedded* within a common framework of European thought and tradition of thinking to which all of them are loyally committed. Whatever images of India they may have had, their prints, like the negatives of a photograph, would be developed within the laboratory of European consciousness.

India, however, because of its unfortunate historical situation, did not have that 'full space' in which it could freely develop its own images of Europe, negative or positive, for ironically, the space was occupied precisely by the same 'object' whose images India was supposed to take, i.e., Europe. It is one example how a colonial civilization distorts its own image by casting its own shadow between itself and the eye of the receiving subject.

For India, the 'receiving subject', the impact of alien presence disrupted the entire unifying framework of consciousness through which it could have a coherent and integral vision of Europe. Through various administrative and political measures, the occupying power uprooted the Indian culture from the very habitat from which hitherto it had attained its integral character. The constituent elements of myths, symbols, images of gods and beliefs, which acquired a certain unified meaning only within the texture of their togetherness, began to disintegrate once they were displaced from their traditional habitat and put as isolated categories within a historical framework.

As an Indian was 'historicized' in the European context, he was de-Indianized in the context of his own 'traditional' self. With the rise of salvational belief in the powers of science and 'rational' knowledge, the implicit faith of a Hindu in the rites and rituals, the network of myths and symbols which constituted his *dharma*, through which he interpreted and deciphered the 'text' of the world, was seriously undermined. The gods were still there to be revered, the rituals were observed with rigor and reverence, the memory of the 'past' was continuously renewed by a constant process of recovering the 'sacred' through the celebrations of religious festivals where epics and puranic legends interpenetrated with the secular patterns of life. All this was there, but the social institutions in which the Hindu 'self' found its *raison d'être* and through which the institutions themselves acquired the sanction to exist, the essential link between invisible spirit and its visible body was seriously damaged, if not totally destroyed.

The European colonization cast a shadow, a cleavage, right in the middle of the Indian consciousness. Tradition, which was a way of life was 'externalized' as something belonging to the past; Europe, which was an external factor, was 'internalized' as iron in the soul, but not merely that, it was iron in whose mold India was supposed to cast her own future destiny. India, like Janus, looked towards opposite directions at the same time, towards Europe for knowledge and material progress, towards its own tradition for *moksha* and salvation. And since both were totally opposed to one another, it created a schism in the Indian psyche, which has not been bridged even to this day. To crave for 'knowledge' whose end consists in achieving material progress, was this not morally corruptible, symbolizing the power of evil, of which the British rulers at home and Europeans at large were the living examples? And to run after this evil, which destroys the very possibility of attaining *moksha*, was it not a willful attempt on the part of a culture to commit an act of self-annihilation?

Not that the 'modernist' Indian reformers were not conscious of this dilemma: the foremost among them, Vivekananda, made even a more subtle but not a very happy distinction between *dharma* and *moksha*. By the former, he meant the 'ideal of good life', pursued so obsessively by the Europeans. It was essentially action-oriented, embodying the quality of the *rajas*,[10] the element of manly virtues being the dominant trend in European culture driving Western man to the end of the earth in pursuit of material ends. The myth of gods and *asuras* (demons) was repeatedly invoked to exemplify the nature of encounter between Indians and Europeans, the Indians being the 'offsprings of gods', the

Europeans the descendants of *asuras*. Europeans were the children of Virochana, the great demon of Indian mythology who believed that *atman*, the self, was nothing but human body. As against this, for Vivekananda as for other renaissance intellectuals, despite their admiration for European civilization, the 'self' was all, the Vedantic epitome of all that is the supreme discovery of Hindu spiritual tradition.

Such was the Vedantic message of India which Vivekananda propounded with such passion to the Western audiences in America and Europe when he went abroad. At the same time, he was most keenly conscious of the darkness of Indian reality, the *tamas*, the depth of utter decrepitude and degradation, to which Indian society had sunk. The only way, in his view, by which India could come out of this darkness was to inculcate that quality of masculine vigor and dynamism which so fascinated him in the European character, and which he thought could be used as necessary 'transition' to *satva*, the highest stage of spiritual fulfillment. He, like many of his Westernized contemporaries saw no contradiction in the fact that what he most admired in the West, rational positivism and male aggressiveness, could in some way be responsible for precisely those characteristics of European civilization—its spiritual vacuity and crass materialism—which he most deplored. Nor did it even strike him that, what he most bewailed about the Indian society, its spirit of passivity and despair, could be the inevitable outcome of the most ruthless colonial incursions into the traditional pattern of Hindu society which he so deeply admired and wanted to preserve. Of course, he wanted to use the European quality of *rajas* as merely a transitory stage for India's rejuvenation, but could evil means lead to noble ends? And stages which are regarded as transitory have a tendency to get frozen for ages to come, as hard to assimilate as to discard. India is one tragic example of still nurturing a kind of fossilized idea of 'Europeanism' at a time when the idea of Europe as one unified civilization itself seems to have become obsolete.

If I have dwelt at some length on Vivekananda, it is because he of all the enlightened Hindus of the nineteenth century brought into sharp focus the self-contradictions of Indian society in its encounter with Europe. Europe, on the one hand, was the symbol of self-liberation from the servitude of the past; at the same time, it posed a serious threat to the tradition without which no Hindu could feel safe about his identity as a Hindu. Hence, the labored and anxious attempts at a makeshift 'synthesis' between Western rationalism on the one hand, and traditional views of life as described in the *Gita* and *Puranas* on the other. It was a desperate and despairing attempt to seek an answer from a tradition which could at the same time be acceptable to his rationalist mind, thereby redeeming him from his existential *angst*. He seemed to overlook the fact that the *angst* itself was the product of European rationalism which he did not want to abandon. It was like seeking relief from the disease by which one is afflicted. It is said that in some parts of Africa, the hunters devise a clever trick to ensnare monkeys. They make a hole in the coconut to tempt the monkeys to put their hand in it to get its kernel. The hole is big enough to let the open hand slide inside the coconut, but once the kernel is picked up, it is difficult to extract the closed fist out of the hole. The monkey can release himself only by renouncing his temptation for the kernel, otherwise he is caught forever. The Hindus with the 'kernel' of European rationalism in their hands, were faced with a predicament no less painful.

It was, however, not a predicament universally prevalent in Indian society, nor was it shared by that section of Hindu intelligentsia who were known as orthodox traditionalists. The Hindu traditionalists may not have belonged to the mainstream renaissance culture, but for that reason their voice—or silence—was no less significant in the overall ferment of the times. Indeed, they would have been surprised to be called 'traditionalists' at all: what would a Hindu be without his tradition, they would have wondered. How could they have shared a 'predicament' which was not so much the result of a real encounter with Europe, but a consequence of the uprootedness from one's own tradition? To be uprooted from tradition, is tantamount to be alienated from one's self. *Can the chasm between self and tradition be filled up by the European ideal of humanism?* The Indian 'modernizers' were caught in a contradiction from which they could never escape: uprooted from their tradition, they had to seek for a rejuvenation of the self only in Europe; this could not have been done without being assimilated by Europe, as it were, thus making them surrender the self itself, which they sought to rejuvenate. The traditionalists regarded not merely the idea of a 'dialogue' with Europe as futile, the terms of which were borrowed from Europe itself, but also found the entire idea of 'rejuvenation' to be a self-delusion. And they were right for reasons which Europe could never understand.

Tradition makes itself felt only in its invisibility, when it becomes so totally fused with the self that it becomes indistinguishable from it. Thus, the 'dialogue' between the two—tradition and self—often takes place in silence. Silence is to tradition what sleep is to a dream, one becomes aware of it only when one is awake. But, once awakened, one is already outside, alien both to sleep and to tradition; one becomes the 'other', extraordinarily alive and profoundly melancholic: alive as 'conscious self' to interpret one's dreams; melancholic for the loss of the unconscious state which was a part of sleep and of tradition. Perhaps this is what Hegel meant when he characterized the Indian tradition as representing a 'stage of abstraction and beauty', half real, half a dream image.

All the renaissance movements in history are the moments of awakening—moments of self-consciousness. No other civilization made the Indians as keenly self-conscious as the European one: at the same time, never did they feel as painfully lacerated from the self as when they came into contact with it for the first time, as if self-estrangement is the inevitable price history demands before it could bestow the gift of self-consciousness. It was also simultaneously accompanied by the rapturous spirit of self-discovery, particularly true in the case of Indians who for the first time saw their 'face' as it was, in all its glory and horridness. Good or bad, it was their face, warts and all. But somewhere the doubt lurked. Was it the real face? Since the instruments of self-appraisal were borrowed from the West, the face in the very process of uncovering let something of it remain eternally concealed, and what came into the open bore the marks of the instruments that did the uncovering—was it more a 'death-mask' than the face itself?

The cleavage which Europe had caused in the Indian consciousness—one part submerged in tradition, the other trying to cast itself in the image of European man—generated a kind of bad faith which gnawed at the conscience of both the Hindu traditionalists and the neo-Hindus. The former wanted to assert themselves against Europe by idealizing their Hindu past, even though they might have had to falsify some phases of their history, something which Bankim Chandra Chatterji did in his historic romances. The latter, the Hindu modernizers, tried to get rid of the bad faith by becoming more European than the Europeans themselves, a breed of Europeanized Indians who later became so influential in the Indian national movement and were to rule India after Independence. Nehru was after all as much a 'Hindu–European' as was Raja Ram Mohun Roy in the incipient stages of Indian renaissance. The cleavage caused in the Hindu psyche by her 'encounter' with Europe was thus like a crack in the mirror, one part reflecting the glorified image of the past lost for ever, the other reflecting a caricatured image of Europe which was to serve its 'model' that was never to be realized. The Indian 'renaissance' was both a reflection of the Hindu consciousness of the 'self' as well as its estrangement from it.

So, even as the European Renaissance was not merely the 're-birth' of the Greek spirit (the spirit of harmony with nature), for there was a deep touch of melancholy even in the most self-affirmative sculptures of Michelangelo as if the spirit had deserted the stone and the stone was crying for the spirit, so also in the most enlightened moments of the nineteenth century Indian renaissance, despite all the protestations of Indian spirituality and cultural greatness, somewhere there lurked a gloomy doubt that all that was best in the Indian civilization was irrevocably gone, buried in the past, and though it could be invoked on occasions to challenge the self-acclaimed achievements of the West, it could hardly compensate for the wretchedness of the present. If India were totally Westernized, it could be free from her inner anguish, because then, like many Latin American and African countries, it would have sought its salvation in Europe. Such was, however, not the case, for despite all their fascination for European art and culture and scientific achievements, Indians were too conscious of their distinctive identity to surrender their destiny to an alien civilization. On the other hand, if they were totally merged with their tradition, they would have ignored Europe and withdrawn silently into their own self. But under the impact of Europe, the tradition seems to have deserted the self in the same way as under the thrust of the technical revolution the spirit had withdrawn from nature in European civilization. In the first decades of the twentieth century, Europe with all its materialist advancement and prosperity seemed to be haunted by a 'wasteland' feeling of inner desolation—so prominent in her poetry and art—what Heidegger was to call the feeling of 'homelessness'. Was it a nemesis of fate that, through the circuitous paths of history, India and Europe had arrived at a point where the face of the colonizer appeared as ravaged and forlorn as that of the colonized?

At such a crucial juncture, India's response to Europe, if it were to be meaningful, could not be in the conventional and colonial framework of love and hate, of accepting its secular knowledge and rejecting its spiritual debasement; nor could it be in the traditional categories of 'self' against the 'other', for after passing through a cataclysmic relationship with Europe, the self had ceased to be part of the unconscious and became an 'onlooker', i.e., what Europe herself had once been, and which now, after a long habitation with the Indian self, became a part of its 'unconscious', as if the two birds of the *Upanishadic* tale, one being the 'watcher' and the other the 'watched', had been fused into one. Not that India and Europe had ceased to be two distinctive civilizational entities—but now they existed as two facets of a single consciousness. India's response to the West became a kind of inner dialogue of self with its own consciousness.

It is said that Max Müller was pleasantly surprised at discovering in *Rgveda* a documentation of the fact that Indians and Europeans are long-parted brethren, belonging to the same Indo-Aryan family, meeting now after a divided history of four thousand years. But Max Müller's *now* was very much the European present, meeting India in its *past*, while what we are referring to is something quite the contrary—not to slur over the differences of two civilizations under some vague memory of common racial past, but containing the uniqueness of two distinctive cultures within a single experimental framework, where the awareness of the self necessarily involves the awareness of the other and vice-versa.

Such a state of 'shared' consciousness could be achieved neither by going back into some *Rgvedic past* nor by 'going out' for a voyage into the foreign and strange territory of Europe, as Mehta suggests. From the past we have come and to Europe we have gone—if the colonial experience of the past two hundred years was not a 'voyage to Europe', what was it after all? What India needed was to regain her selfhood through a process of decolonization of the self itself, which no outside agency but only their own tradition could have set in motion. It is no accident that the person representing the twentieth century India who was to give a most radical critique of Western civilization was a traditional Hindu like Gandhi who at the same time was also the most passionate critic of the colonized consciousness of the Indians. A colonized state of mind of a Hindu was as much inimical to his authentic 'selfhood' as the materialist mentality of the European is an obstacle to realize the freedom of the soul, which was a part of Christian and

European tradition. The two cultures could share the same consciousness in terms of evolving self-criticism from within their own
traditions. Gandhi would have been baffled by Vivekananda's
statement in America 'I give you spirituality, you give me cash', to
be used for the material welfare of Indians. He would have refused to divide India and Europe under such stereotype labels—
one stamped by spirituality, the other by materialism. Europe
could not have achieved her scientific temper without a rich spiritual and intellectual heritage as India could not have won her
spirituality without a sophisticated system of social relationships
codified by Hindu *dharma*. Gandhi, without being an apologist of
European culture, could see its strength from within the Hindu tradition as, without ceasing to be a Hindu, he could be a critic of
orthodox apologists of Hinduism.

With Gandhi we enter, for the first time, the modern phase of
Indian consciousness—if by *modernity* we mean that form of existential freedom which is not encumbered by external civilizational factors—and yet deeply grounded in one's own tradition.
His 'modernity' was different from that of the modern European
in so far as he never regarded the individual as the sole arbiter of
his freedom. Unless it is sanctified by the code of righteousness,
by one's *dharma*, freedom can acquire an evil character as it had
done in the West; on the other hand, *dharma* in its mere external-
ity cannot be a guide or a discriminate judge between good and
evil, unless it is grounded in one's personal conscience which is
the only truth that counts. It is clear that, here, Gandhi is acting as
a true modernist: operating simultaneously on two levels, a repre-
sentative of European consciousness by introducing the concept
of 'personal conscience' in the codified world of orthodox Hinduism, and on another level using the Hindu concept of *dharma* as
the only valid framework within which the Western concept of individual freedom could acquire its moral legitimacy. Acting as a
free agent between two traditions Gandhi could internalize the
impersonal code of *sanatan dharma* (perennial philosophy) into
an act of personal responsibility, as on the European side he tried
to 'externalize' and enlarge the concept of individual conscience
into concern for all creatures, where Christians are no more soul-
ful and Europeans no more 'privileged' than the others. This was
very different from the monolithic concept of 'humanism' which
Europe wanted to impose upon the entire world; it was rather an
attempt to create a space where each tradition could speak to

another tradition from its own *ground of being* and not from some abstract point of universalism.

This marked the turning point in India's views of the West—a radical departure from an approach arising from colonized consciousness, where the encounter was always conceived between the spirituality of the East and the materialism of the West. It was both a departure from the Hegelian conception of India as it was the rejection of the inclusivist Hindu approach to the 'other' (in this case Europe), where, not unlike Hegel, the other is always assimilated in the 'lower category' of its own system. If Gandhi changed the entire nature of discourse between India and Europe, it is because he radically redefined the categories of the self and the other—not two inclusive autonomous entities but one implicitly inherent in the other.

In this way, while respecting the distinctive qualities of two traditions, Indian and European, Gandhi transformed the 'encounter' between the two from the cultural level of 'mutual questioning' (Heidegger) to the existential level of questioning 'oneself'— thereby reversing the European way of knowing 'oneself' through the other to the way of asking oneself 'who am I?' to be able to know the other. What for Ramana Maharshi was the primary question ('who am I?') to seek the answer of the meaning of one's life, became for Gandhi the crucial civilizational question for both India and Europe to be able to discover the essential truth of their specific traditions.

Gandhi's bold and radical approach to the West, however, failed to elicit any corresponding response from Europe towards India or to other non-European cultures. For Europe, culture— and not the self—continued to remain the crucial reference point to recognize the 'nature' of one's identity on the earth. Language is the medium through which the movement towards understanding between two cultures is realized. Self-understanding thus becomes inseparable from the understanding of the other and it reaches its fulfillment only with the fashioning of a language which mediates us with the other and our present with the past.

This, however, does not solve the problem of 'communication' with those oriental cultures who for centuries have evolved their own 'medium' to communicate with the past and, if the past is not poised at some point back in historical time but actually embodied in the rites and rituals and myths of people by which they live in the present, as is very much the case in India, then the language of such a society invents its own secret code, its signs of speech and silence which remain largely incomprehensible to the historical cultures of the West. In India, as in other oriental cultures, man is not regarded as absolute master of creation, but only as one living species among others. Thus, history no longer remains a circumscribed concept of 'human past', but the past of all species surrounding man at the present moment. The language of 'reason' evolved by the European man fails to provide any key or clue to communicate with this vast, living, mysterious 'non-human' world. The separation of the human world from the non-human has been the most tragic aspect of European civilization which provoked Goethe to make the statement 'In every great separation there lies the seed of madness; one has to be careful not to foster its growth.' Much of modern European art and poetry—we are reminded particularly of the works by Hölderlin and Rilke—is a brooding reflection on this 'separation' and also an attempt to go beyond the dark 'abyss', transcending the separation between the two worlds; if at times it is touched by 'madness' it also enables it to go beyond the abyss, touching the heights of lyrical beauty, unmatched in any literature.

If India did not have to face the abyss, it is because it never abandoned its 'mythical' connections with the non-human world. Actually, it would have surprised a traditional Hindu that any such separation exists at all—so deeply steeped is his 'world-view' in the 'puranic' imagination where there is a continuous series of metamorphoses from one form of life to another, each containing a secret key for the revelation of the other. It is with these keys, the myths, that every Hindu seeks to unlock the connections between man and nature, human and non-human worlds. Nature is mysterious, as every 'other' is, but it holds no terror because it is also a part of man—the human nature....

India has often been called a 'sleeping civilization' by the historically awakened European nations, but of her sleep those dreams are born which have kept in touch with the voices of dark wood and the bright and moving script of the stars. For what are myths if not the dreams of a sleeping culture which has not been awakened by the daylight on-rush of history? History, of course, has its own nightmares, or to be more precise, it is a nightmare, as Marx said in one of his rare, alas, too rare prophetic moments. Perhaps Europe, awakened from the nightmare of history, would be more receptive to understand the underground language of truth which India in her sleep has churned out of her dreams.

This would perhaps be a beginning of a true dialogue, on a civilizational level—but in terms of human consciousness, the dialogue between the two traditions has been going on for centuries. It is not a dialogue based on the concept of 'mutual questioning' between two cultures: rather, the questions are arranged by each tradition in a certain pattern, where they create their own space from which the right answers are elicited—answers not from the 'other' but from the depth of the tradition itself. The form and pattern of questioning is of course deeply colored by the tradition from which it arises, but once the answer is given, it creates its own space of evocations which is infinite, touching the horizons of other traditions. Thus, the *Upanishadic* maxim *tat tvam asi*[11] could be conceived only in a tradition where the question 'who am I?' had such crucial significance; but once the answer was proposed 'I am that', it created its own space of amplitude, causing a resonance even in European cultures, unfamiliar to such a mode of questioning, but became instantly receptive to the answer once it was articulated. European response to the Vedantic dictum was also a fulfillment of a need on some deeper and darker level to overcome her own inability to see the 'other' as oneself. But since this inability, this unbearable anguish of eternal separation from the other, was a product of highly individuated consciousness, it created its own space, in which flowered that strange and sublime notion of 'romantic love' which happens to be one of the most remarkable features of European sensibility.

Once this 'longing to reach out to the other', this desperate need to overcome the dark gulf between two separate and independent selves found its voice in European literature, then its echoes could be heard beyond its own cultural boundaries—in other cultures and other traditions. If generations of Indians have been enthralled and overwhelmed by Dante's beatitude and the sorrows of Werther, the soul-searing jealousy of Othello and self-consuming passion of Anna Karenina, it is not because they were not familiar with such passions in their epics and medieval poetry, but only through European literature; for the first time they were focussed and identified with individual destinies. For the first time, through European poetry and music, the Indian witnessed the 'hungers of the soul', neither fully divine, nor entirely carnal, seeking fulfillment in the fusion of both.

Two traditions, Indian and European, are seeking a sort of completion in one another, not through a philosophical discourse or mutual cross-questioning, but by creating a 'common space' within which the voice of the one evokes a responsive echo in the other, feeling the deprivations of one's own through the longings of the other. There are needs, primal and primordial, which may remain submerged or unexplored in a certain tradition for centuries, and like the keys of a piano, they wait for the right moment and just the right pressure of some 'other hand' to be able to discover the notes, strange and mysterious, though always within us, but never heard before. Such 'listening' is both a discovery and a revelation, a discovery of the other within ourselves and the revelation of ourselves through the other. After all the utterances have been made by the anthropologists, historians and philosophers on either side, perhaps time has come for both India and Europe to pause a little, listening to one another in silence, which may be as 'sound' a method of discourse as any other.

■

■ Notes ■

[1] Nirmal Verma had been invited to deliver the Ajneya memorial lecture at Heidelberg University in 1988.

[2] J.L. Mehta, *India and the West: The Problem of Understanding*, (Chico, CA: Scholars Press, 1985).

[3] Greeks.

[4] Any alien people were called *mlechha* by the Indians; this word had a slight contemptuous ring.

[5] Islamic scholar.

[6] Epithets used by European missionaries for the Indian gods.

[7] Righteousness; nature, disposition; characteristic property, or attribute; duty or prescribed course of conduct.

[8] Perennial.

[9] J.L. Mehta, *India and the West: The Problem of Understanding, passim*.

[10] In classical Indian thought there are three qualities or constituents of everything in creation: *satva*, meaning the quality of goodness or purity regarded as the highest of the three gunas; *rajas*, endowed with or influenced by the quality of passion; and *tamas*, darkness or ignorance.

[11] That art thou.

■

23

■ MAULANA WAHIDUDDIN KHAN ■

Wahiduddin Khan is one of the most respected Muslim intellectuals and maulanas in contemporary India. A profound student of the Qur'an, the Hadith, and the entire Islamic tradition, he is also deeply committed to inter-religious and cross-cultural dialogue and understanding. He is a co-founder of the Islamic Centre in New Delhi, and editor-in-chief of the bi-monthly journal *Al-Risala*. Among the many books authored by Wahiduddin Khan the following stand out: *Islam As It Is*; *Islam: The Voice of Human Nature*; *Muhammad: The Prophet of Revolution*; *Muhammad: The Ideal Character*; *Religion and Science*; *Indian Muslims: The Need for a Positive Outlook*; *Woman in Islamic Shariah*; *Woman between Islam and Western Society*. The following selections are taken from *Al-Risala*, No. 122–123 (March–April 1995), pp. 5–8, and *Al-Risala*, No. 128 (January–February 1996), pp. 13–16.

RELIGION AND POLITICS

With the independence of India in 1947, two countries—India and Pakistan—came into existence on the subcontinent. In both these countries there was a secular group and a religious group. The secular group held that the system of the country's governance should be run along purely secular lines, independently of religion, whereas the thinking of the religious group was quite the contrary. They insisted that the political system of the country should be governed in accordance with the dictates of religion.

This religion-based system was called *Nizam-e-Mustafa* in Pakistan, and *Ram Rajya* in India. Although in both these countries political power fell into the hands of the secular group, in neither country did the religious group remain silent. Rather, they pursued the path of confrontation in order to attain their goal of establishing the system of government on the basis of religion. To put it another way, they opted for the path of force in order to replace the secular system with the system of government of their choice.

This struggle culminated in Pakistan in April 1979 with [Zulfikar Ali] Bhutto's execution, which was termed judicial murder by Bhutto himself. Pakistan's religious class felt that Bhutto's existence presented the greatest obstacle to introducing *Nizam-e-Mustafa*. He had, therefore, to be eliminated. But the experiment revealed that *Nizam-e-Mustafa* could not find a place in the life of the nation even after the removal of Bhutto. The hold of the secular group persisted.

The *Ram Rajya* movement in India culminated in December 1992 with the demolition of the Babri Masjid at Ayodhya. Even after a period of two years, subsequent to the demolition, the *Ram Rajya* movement has not been able to move even one step ahead. The secular group continues to dominate the political arena.

Whether it be right or wrong, from the ideological point of view, to subordinate politics to religion, the experiment of the last fifty years tells us that our present course is certainly not the right one. It would be more true to say that the present course, in terms of non-achievement of goals, has been counter-productive. What has come into being, and what is going to be achieved in the effort to consolidate the position of religion is in no way a religious system, but is rather a course of destruction. This destructive element has only added to the general ruination of the country.

How did all these efforts on our part backfire? It can be traced quite simply to our violation of realities. Innumerable natural causes have to cooperate in this world in order to bring about a significant event. Someone has said very pertinently: 'Politics is the art of the possible'. That is, only when conducive factors are present is a leader able to realize a political event. It is not possible even for the greatest of leaders to bring about a political revolution simply by dint of his own efforts without the cooperation of external elements.

The Islamization of Pakistan and the Hinduization of India simply failed to take shape; despite a fifty-year bloody struggle neither could Pakistan be Islamized nor India Hinduized.

As a result of the intellectual development of the last several hundred years, the world mindset is now entirely against a state based on religion. This worldwide intellectual revolution is known as secularism. While religion is founded on *faith*, secularism is based on *reason*. The majority of the educated classes in modern times has accepted that matters of state should be kept independent of sacred scriptures, and that they should be dealt with on the basis of *reason*. That is to say that world opinion is in favor of the secular rather than the religious state.

India presents no exception to this rule. As a result of the modernization of education over the last two hundred years, the new Indian generation thinks along the same lines as the rest of the world. Like all other countries, India too is a part of the global village.

Given this reality, if a state based on religion had to be established, a sea change in world thinking—on a purely ideological plane—should have to be effected. Without a universal, intellectual revolution, it would be impossible to found a religious state in the manner of a political island even at the level of one's own country.

The only practicable course to follow in this matter is to acknowledge the reality. Besides this, there is almost no other choice. Now the time has come for a true patriot ultimately to change himself in the interests of his country. Accepting his limitations, he should mold himself in accordance with the reality rather than waste time in pursuing the unattainable goal of a reality molded to suit his own purposes.

Having given due consideration to all aspects of this issue, I have come to the conclusion that without going into the ideological discussion of what is right and what is wrong, all the concerned parties should come to agree in this matter on a practicable formula in the wider interests of the country.

What is most important in this connection is to set the election process in motion without any hindrance. Elections should be free and fair. Whichever group is subsequently elected to power should be given full freedom to complete its term.

During this period, the defeated group should never launch a campaign to oust the victor group. It should, on the contrary, direct its efforts to impressing its ideology upon the public which is later to vote it to power. The five-year period should be devoted to bringing about changes in public opinion by peaceful methods. If the defeated group succeeds in influencing the voters, it will automatically be voted to power in the next elections. It will then find the opportunity to reconstruct the country's political and administrative systems along its own ideological lines.

Wholehearted acceptance of election results, followed by the adoption of a waiting policy, while one's own ideology continues to be propagated in a peaceful manner, is the only practicable course. This is the only way to influence the minds of the voters, without running counter to the genuine interests of the country....

According to Ibn Ishaq, a man by the name of Tufail bin Amr Ad Daus of the Daus tribe once visited the Prophet when he was living in Mecca. When the Prophet recited the Qur'an to him, he was so impressed by it that he accepted Islam. Later, with the Prophet's permission, he went back to his tribesmen to call them to Islam. But his people spurned his message and refused to accept it. Tufail now came back to tell the Prophet to curse them. Instead, the Prophet raised his hands and started praying for them: 'O God, guide the Daus tribesmen. O God, guide the Daus people.'

Then he told Tufail to return to his friends and once again call them to the Truth. He also enjoined them to be gentle with them (Seerat Ibn Hisham, I/409).

The prayers and the advice given by the Prophet were not simple matters. They were aimed at correcting the negative attitude developing in Tufail, into a positive approach. The disgust he felt for his people was then converted into a feeling of well-wishing. Whereas Tufail had only been able to see matters in the light of past events, he was now guided by the Prophet to look to the future.

Prayer means not just asking God for something but putting oneself in the correct frame of mind. It is a kind of conditioning towards sound psychology and right thinking. But, most important of all, the act of praying awakens within oneself the divine power. When Tufail returned to his tribe with his new way of thinking, he had acquired a new edge to his personality. He was now better equipped to present the truth to the people in a more effective way. It was inevitable that the whole tribe should respect his call and embrace Islam.

In a society where feelings of goodwill have become so prevalent that people begin to pray for each other, the natural result is the development of positive psychology throughout the entire social fabric. Without this no society can truly better itself.

■

A SILENT REVOLUTION

To a cross-section of educated, socially conscious Kashmiri Muslims (with whom I have had recent contacts), it is a matter of grav-
est concern that the violent *jihad*, unleashed in Kashmir in the
name of freedom in 1989, not only failed in its objective, but
caused the people of that country to suffer irreversible losses.
More than fifty thousand people lost their lives, and all economic
and educational institutions were destroyed. Peace seems to have
vanished forever from Kashmir, and without peace, there can be
no smooth functioning of day-to-day activities, nothing even ap-
proaching normality.

However, there is another aspect to this matter. Many Kashmiris
have been forced by the pressure of circumstances to uproot their
families and re-settle beyond the borders of their own land. At
present, about fifty thousand Kashmiris are living in various
Indian cities. These emigrant Kashmiris—hard workers, as emi-
grants tend to be—are fast becoming an affluent community, running prosperous businesses and owning big houses and Maruti
cars. Their children, too, are receiving a proper education. For
these Kashmiris, the change in their circumstances has turned out
to be a blessing in disguise. It has revealed to them a reality which
had not been apparent to them in Kashmir, namely, that despite
the supposed tyranny inflicted on them and other political problems, there was still the genuine possibility of their thriving in
India. This is a discovery which has brought about a total revolution in Kashmiri thinking. Now, deliberately detaching themselves
from the so-called freedom struggle, they have successfully
plunged into normal economic activity both in India and abroad.

Now—albeit at a late stage—they have realized that their progress had never depended upon the resolution of Kashmir's political problem, and that, as such, these problems have now become
a secondary issue for them.

The same is true to a large extent and, of course, on a large
scale, of Muslims in general. The fault lies with unwise Muslim
leaders who had enmeshed their followers in matters which bore
no relation to reality, tyrannizing them into thinking that the solution to all their problems lay in Pakistan. This explains why they
remained blind to the great opportunities elsewhere, which were

open to all and sundry after 1947. Their blinkered vision caused them to persist in seeing India as a 'problem country'; unrealistically, they looked beyond its borders for a solution to their problems. This rationale did, however, crumble when, in 1971, Pakistan itself was dismembered as the result of a bloody war. Even this cataclysm brought about only a fifty percent shift in Muslim perspectives.

Since that time, it has taken repeated acts of violence in Karachi and other Pakistani cities—in the course of which emigrant Muslims were ruthlessly looted and murdered—to bring them to the realization that, except in India, there was no alternative place for them. It took all these years, all these dastardly events and all the dashing of their hopes to make them emerge from the state of ignorance into which they had been plunged by yellow journalism and the fulminations of unwise leaders. Only then, after all this, did they discover that by seizing the golden opportunities offered them by India, and by working hard, they could be as resoundingly successful there as in former times in Kashmir. That is why, wherever one goes, one finds them prospering in business and acquiring the material symbols of wealth.

The same is also true, but in greater measure, of the Hindus. For the last fifty years, ill-informed and unwise Hindu leaders have been impressing it upon members of their community that Muslims pose a threat to them, and that so long as they tolerate their presence, avenues of Hindu progress will remain blocked. They insist, moreover, that Hindus erase all traces of the Muslim period, and that all possible steps be taken to ensure that Muslims remain as backward as possible. These leaders have even gone so far as to argue that unless the Muslims are crushed, Hindus will never make progress in their own country.

However, the fifty years of baneful activity which culminated in the demolition of the Babri Masjid on 6 December 1992, brought the Hindus a different kind of reward from what they had expected. After the Babri Masjid had been torn down, the riots that took place in different parts of the country caused losses amounting to ten thousand crore rupees—all these were losses which were borne by the Hindus. Where they had expected the automatic opening of doors to economic progress, they now found that this backlash had placed obstacles in their path.

These events, paradoxically, had the effect of causing both communities to arrive at the same conclusion. That is, both realized the futility of negativism and, setting aside such thinking, re-engaged themselves in business and allied activities. The Hindus, too, found that not only did the presence of Muslims in the country do them no harm, but it actually proved to be a positive advantage. For instance, today, millions of Muslim craftsmen and workers are engaged in the manufacture of a variety of goods in many Indian cities. Hindus, for their part, supply them with the raw materials, then market the finished products within the country and abroad. In this way, Muslims have become an indispensable part of the Hindu economic machine. The Muslim, in making one lakh rupees, gives the Hindu the opportunity to make one crore rupees.

This has demonstrated to Hindus that, by adjusting themselves to the 'Muslim problem' (as they see it) they remove all bars to their own advancement, albeit sharing the same territory. This has resulted in former staunch supporters of the plan to demolish the Babri Masjid turning against extremist leaders when they wanted to have a repetition of this incident in Kashi, on 27 March 1994, and in Mathura, on 22 August 1995. Ultimately, fanatical Hindu leaders, deprived of the necessary support, were forced to beat a retreat, leaving unfulfilled their plans for destruction.

The upshot is that a new India has emerged from the debris of the past, the common people having extricated themselves from the clutches of self-serving and incompetent leaders. They have learned that the secret of success in life lies not in groups clashing with each other, but rather in the avoidance of friction and in making full use of whatever opportunities present themselves for individual advancement.

This is a basic, intellectual volte face, which is clearly visible in the people. It is a transformation which has effectively altered the direction in which the country is moving. Now, the people, possibly more as a matter of instinct than of ratiocination, are forging ahead along positive lines. Once the country is well launched on this healthier course, such a revolution will necessarily produce two results: peace and prosperity—the prerequisites for progress. The country is now poised to achieve these goals. Now, not even a horde of wrong-headed leaders should be able to deflect the nation from this path.

In normal circumstances the guidance of nature is sufficient to set mankind on the right course. But this will take place only if the lesson the public has learned about ignoring yellow journalism and the rantings of so-called leaders is a permanent one. At the moment, there are high hopes that the de-railing of the country over communal issues was only a temporary phase.

Again, the checks and balances lie in the system of nature itself. Each wrong course is righted by nature, because horrible consequences prove to be eye-openers to the people. In India, this eye-opening event has already taken place. Its reverberations had barely died down when our countrymen began to abandon the path chalked out by incompetent leaders in favour of the path of nature. This is a silent revolution—a revolution which holds out the greatest hope for the future of this country.

■

24

■ SUSIE THARU AND K. LALITA ■

Susie J. Tharu and K. Lalita are both distinguished literary and
social critics and feminist thinkers. Both hold advanced academic
degrees, the former in English literature, the latter in social science. Tharu was educated both in Oxford and in Hyderabad. She
serves as a member of the Subaltern Studies Editorial Committee
and was a Nehru Fellow in 1995–96; presently she teaches at the
Central Institute of English and Foreign Languages in Hyderabad.
Tharu is known particularly for her book *The Sense of Performance: Post-Artaud Theatre*, New Delhi, Arnold–Heinemann,
1984; with Lalita she has co-published the book *We Were Making
History: Life Stories of Women in the Telangana People's Struggle*, London, Zed Books, 1989. The following selection is taken
from a work co-edited by Tharu and Lalita: *Women Writing in India: 600 B.C. to the Present*, New York, Feminist Press at the City
University of New York, 1991, Vol. 2, pp. 25–37.

WOMEN WRITING IN INDIA

Over the last decade-and-a-half, American feminist criticism
would seem to have arrived at a framework for the study of
women's writing. Tasks have been assigned, themes located, areas of debate defined, and women's writing authoritatively established as an object for disciplined investigation. The confidence of
having drawn up no less than a world picture of the history of
women's literature rings through the introduction of Elaine

Showalter's 1985 collection of essays. 'Since 1979', when *The Madwoman in the Attic* was published, she writes,

> insights have been tested, supplemented, extended, so that we have a coherent, if still incomplete, narrative of female literary history, which describes the evolutionary stages of women's writing during the last 250 years from imitation through protest to self-definition and defines and traces the connections, throughout history and across national boundaries of the recurring images, themes, and plots that emerge from women's social, psychological and aesthetic experience in male-dominated cultures.[1]

The claims are awesome; the tone, one that colonized peoples have heard on many earlier occasions. An anthology of women's writing compiled, as this one was, in the late 1980s, inherits a space—conceptual and political—opened up by these critical initiatives but also shaped by their assumptions. The metaphors we have used state the case too weakly, too neutrally. Feminist criticism has not merely developed a methodology to study a phenomenon that already exists: women's writing. Feminist criticism has actually shaped a new discipline and in the process created, as the object of its study, a new field: women's writing. There is no denying that women have written, or, to put it more accurately in the context of this anthology, that women have created literature in the past. But as those artifacts are studied as *women's writing*, which is charted as an area of study and sculpted into a tradition, they take on a significance that is a contemporary invention. As a discipline, 'gynocritics' has designated its archives, forged its tools, asserted its authority, and made its political alignments.

There are several reasons why artifacts from 'other' cultures might find hospitality in the space created by this new discipline: its self-proclaimed international scope, the increasing self-consciousness among Western liberals about the ethnocentrism of their white middle classes, the wild celebration of pluralism that post-modernism decrees, and the growing multinationalist scope of industry and commerce ensure a ready welcome, at several levels, for other cultures. Yet, the assumptions of this criticism as well as the mode in which it extends a welcome to other literatures make it difficult and compromising terrain for an anthology such as this to enter or negotiate, and we feel the imperative to frame this critical moment and examine in some detail the disciplinary politics of gynocritics as it affects a project such as ours. It is a disturbing step, this, for we are as aware of our solidarities and the need to consolidate them as of our differences. But we hope as we engage critically with the bias of its feminism, and the political agenda hidden in its aesthetic, that we will also open up questions for Western feminism itself and make new, more self-conscious, more risky, and more radical, solidarities possible.

There are several dimensions along which a critique of the discipline as it has established itself might be developed. We have chosen, however, to pick out four major strands in its conceptual weave and tease out the implications of bringing them to bear on the study or reading of women's literature in India. We investigate, first, the idea of loss, which underwrites so much of the 'recovery' of women's writing; second, the notion of release or escape, which tropes itself into a feminist poetics in works such as *The Madwoman in the Attic*; third, the problem that arises as the concept of experience, which in feminist practice has a critical, deconstructive charge, is uncritically conflated with an empiricist privileging of experience as the authentic source of truth and meaning; and finally, the hidden politics of what some strands of Western feminism have set up as women's real experiences, or female nature itself.

(1) Notions of 'loss' and 'exclusion'—for instance lost women writers, lost classics, exclusion from the canon—are always underwritten by a dream of wholeness or completeness. A lost or excluded object can be recognized when it is found, and restored to the place from which it was missed. When it frames the problem as one of loss or exclusion, therefore, contemporary feminism sets up its present and the aspirations that stem from that as a covert norm against which the past is measured. Indeed, what gynocritics actually locates as it raids the past or picks its way through other cultural wares (and even the histories of other peoples) are the scattered fragments of its own dream. As it enumerates the themes and sets up the agenda for women's writing the world over, therefore, the present-day concerns of Western feminists are writ large to encompass the world, and the world collapses into the West. When women's literary history, for instance, culminates in what Showalter categorizes as the 'female phase' turned in on itself, seeking its identity, history becomes a plot that finds its resolution in the current aspirations of Showalter's form of feminism.

If we ask the questions—apparently illegitimate, because the criticism seems to take for granted that the answer is such common knowledge that it does not even need to be stated—who has lost these writers, or rather, to what cause have they been lost, several answers suggest themselves. At one level they are obviously lost to feminists today, lost to a tradition of women's writing, lost to literary studies, lost to the reader's experience. But more significantly they are missing from another, more deeply embedded cultural institution that has, over the last century or so, provided literary studies with its legitimacy. It is this institution feminist scholars must invoke when they voice their grievances. In so doing, of course, they reaffirm its authority and align their concerns with it. These writers, the unstated argument is, are lost to the select company of great (male) writers whose works were charged with the task of providing post-Enlightenment Western society in general, and the nation in particular, with its ethical capital. In other words, even as the feminist act of recovery establishes a historical legitimacy for women's writing, it consolidates the hold of a (liberal) humanism and with it the political imperatives that underwrote the setting up of literary studies as a major agent of that ideology. In a recently published study, Gauri Viswanathan, for instance, argues that 'humanistic functions traditionally associated with the study of literature—for example, the shaping of character, or the development of an aesthetic sense or the disciplines of ethical thinking—are also essential to the process of socio-political control'. Drawing on evidence from parliamentary debates and educational policy, she demonstrates that 'literary study gained enormous cultural strength through its development in a period of territorial expansion and conquest.'[2] Other commentators have explored the process through which the discipline was institutionalized and its imbrication in the shaping of gender and class. The story of its establishment as a humanistic discipline in the 'mother country' and that of its more nakedly dominative functions in the colonies are closely meshed.[3]

Gynocritics forces open the doors of a literary sanctum where only male writers—and that too, only some male writers—seem to have rights of entry, in order to let a few women in. The unwritten rules that once debarred them are cleverly exposed. But the deeper political commitments that govern the teaching of literature are not subjected to serious theoretical scrutiny. Neither the legitimacy nor the function of the sacred monument itself can be radically questioned by those who wish to restore its fullness and thereby endorse its authority.

(2) Structurally, the idea of 'release' is not dissimilar to that of 'loss'. When it asserts the presence of a repressed female creativity struggling over the last two hundred years or more for release, which is recognized at last by the feminist critic and restored through her reading to a female literary tradition, *The Madwoman in the Attic*, for instance, extends the reach of the authors' present-day feminist consciousness to a point where it is naturalized and enshrined as female nature itself. The scope of what they conceive of as women's bondage or imprisonment, however, is clearly laid out. The 'release' is to be principally from 'male houses and male texts'. A further qualification sharpens the focus: an 'escape' through ingenuity and indirection may turn for its metaphors to the other paraphernalia of middle class 'women's place'.

> Ladylike veils and costumes, mirrors, paintings, statues, locked cabinets, drawers, trunks, strong boxes and other domestic furnishings appear and reappear...to signify the woman writer's sense that, as Emily Dickinson put it, her life has been 'shaven and fitted to a frame', a confinement she can only tolerate by believing that 'the soul has moments of escape when bursting all the doors/she dances like a bomb abroad'.[4]

In the process, all women's writing, or at least women's writing that merits serious literary attention, becomes feminist in the precise mode and to the precise extent that the authors themselves understand and experience feminism. Their reading gestures toward history. The subtitle itself indicates the focus as a specific period, the nineteenth century, and the text makes mention of earlier periods. But the past is a collection of intense, more or less univocal moments in which the authors identify the themes and concerns of contemporary American feminism. The paraphernalia of a European middle class woman's place is regarded as an adequate metaphor for all women's worlds. Other times and other places are only a feature of dispersal, not transformation or change. Gender subordination imaged in these domestic, middle class terms defines the entire scope of the woman writer's world, in which, as Gilbert and Gubar image it, there appears to be only the fundamental antagonism repeatedly played out in its primal tune: that of a monolithic, unchanging patriarchy, which would seem to have no connections with other hegemonies, say, of class or race, and an equally fixed and resilient female self: 'The striking coherence we noticed in literature by women could be explained by a common female impulse to struggle free from social and literary confinement through strategic redefinitions of the self, art, and society.'[5]

The idea of a natural being straining for release echoes the Rousseauist formulations of the Enlightenment. But in Gilbert and Gubar's argument, there is a significant reversal of the priorities set up at that time for the emerging bourgeois male. It is a reversal disturbingly reminiscent of the radically different and unequal programs the Enlightenment itself so confidently proposed for men and for women. The man was to direct his revolt outward against the church and the king. *His* natural being, once it was released to enjoy the earth, which was his inheritance, would be governed by reason, which was also part of male nature. Woman, however, and it is important to remember that even the feminist philosopher Mary Wollstonecraft agreed on this, had to turn her energies onto her self. She had to refashion her nature to emerge as fit complement to the new man. The agenda for the colonies was structurally similar. In its most enlightened mode, imperialism regarded the colonized peoples as requiring a remolding, not of course to be fit complement to bourgeois males, but to be fit subjects for its rule. We will have occasion to return to this configuration from the point of view of the middle class woman in India, and for the woman writer—the stresses it set up and the opportunities it opened up. But for the present it is enough to point out that, in Gilbert and Gubar's scheme, as the woman writer struggles for release, she redefines her self and with it the symbolic world of the literary text. As for society, that ghostly appendage does not seem solid enough to throw even a shadow on the imaginative world of the book.

The 'last parable' through which this particular gospel of redemption explicates itself is that of

> the woman artist [who] enters the cavern of her own mind
> and finds there the scattered leaves not only of her own
> power but of the tradition that might have generated that
> power. The body of her precursor's art, and thus the body of

her own art, lies in pieces around her, dismembered, dis-remembered, disintegrated. How can she remember it, and become a member of it, join it, integrate it and in doing so achieve her own integrity, her own selfhood?[6]

Like the messages on the sibylline leaves of Mary Shelley's story on which this 'parable' is based, these fragments are written in several languages. Some of the scripts are faded, others unfa-miliar. But they are inscribed on the elements of the natural world, bark and leaf, and on the secret inner lining of the female body, as Gilbert and Gubar quote Shelly: 'a white filmy substance resem-bling the inner part of the green hood which shelters the grain of unripe Indian corn.'[7] With effort, they can be deciphered. In Gil-bert and Gubar's reading of Shelley, these misunderstood, and therefore scattered, pieces of the woman writer's literary heritage rise now like a 'lost Atlantis...whose wholeness once encom-passed and explained all those figures on the horizon who seemed "odd", fragmentary, incomplete....' Here memory declares itself as an hermeneutic act, for as lost or forgotten works are 'remem-bered...by the community of which they are and were members, such figures gain their full authority.'[8] The cultural context for women's writing is a sort of female enclave untouched by mascu-linist assumptions and the woman writer is imaged as free from ideology. The mystic energy that attends the vision is invoked with a confidence that does not doubt its power to absorb the whole world into its project.

It is not surprising, therefore, to find that their equally monu-mental *The Norton Anthology of Literature by Women*, 1986, which is in many other ways a superb collection, places women from all over the world (who write in English) quite unself-consciously against the backdrop of Euro-American social history.[9] Even the idea that a sizable proportion of British or American society itself does not consider the history or culture of Western Europe as *its* past, that the history and culture of Africa—and not just of the slave trade—may be an important prehistory of the United States, for example, and that of India or the Caribbean of Britain, is sim-ply suppressed. British imperialism is referred to—in one sen-tence—but it does not appear to have touched any of the women writers in a serious way. As the editors project it, the immediate contexts for women's writing are only the images of women in mainstream literature. But nowhere in the book do we find even an awareness that there are many 'mainstream' literatures; or that women who write in English cannot so casually be gathered into the same fold; or that it is not the same essential female nature that is struggling, the world over, to free itself from male bondage.

Like Showalter, Gilbert and Gubar speak as if feminist 'poetics' has finally arrived at its destination. Women writers, they indicate, can now set aside their palimpsestic plots and engage directly with their experience, as male writers whose full authority was never repressed have always been able to do.

(3) Underlying both Showalter's empiricist literary history and Gilbert and Gubar's symbolic recreation of the woman writer's consciousness and her female literary inheritance is an assumption as deeply embedded in the practices of popular reading in the twentieth century (in India as much as in the West) as in literary criticism. Literary texts, the assumption is, express the author's experience and reveal the truth about his or her world, and as they do so, they provide us with access to the universal dimensions of human nature. As an aesthetic theory, expressive realism emerged in the second half of the nineteenth century, more or less in conjunction with the realist novel. It has been subjected to extensive critique in recent times, and its function, in shaping a reader, 'cut to the measure' of the white bourgeois world, analyzed at several levels. The notion is, however, reaffirmed and given new life today by feminist critics who counterpose women's writing, which they choose to read as a transparent expression of women's authentic experience, to the stereotypes of mainstream literature, often spoken of as 'male' literature, which is regarded simply as distorting the reality of women's lives.

Within feminist criticism, the idea that women's experience is a critical resource also draws its strength from the consciousness-raising groups that were so crucial to the development of feminist theory and feminist politics in the United States in the late sixties and early seventies. Several commentators have pointed to the similarities between the politics of consciousness-raising and those of the 'speaking bitterness' campaigns of the Chinese Cultural Revolution.[10] The parallel helps us focus on dimensions of consciousness-raising that are often blurred over as the immediacy, intimacy, and spontaneity of these groups are highlighted. In fact, consciousness-raising was as carefully structured a political exercise as the 'speaking bitterness' campaigns. It worked by challenging and recasting a dominant ideology's characterizations of

women and interrogating authoritative interpretations of every dimension of social and personal experience. The focus was not, as
it tended to become in literary criticism, on distorting stereotypes
but on the wide-ranging strategies, social, economic, and psychic,
through which mastery was exercised and subordination maintained. From the supportive contexts of the consciousness-raising
groups, feminists confronted the institutions and practices of
everyday life, and extended their micropolitical analysis into the
domain of the family and even of desire. Women's experiences
were used as a resource for critical discussion, making it possible
for women to share dimensions of their lives they had earlier kept
secret or felt too insecure to confront or even recognize. Groups
encouraged women to focus on and articulate anger and dissatis-
faction, and evolved through discussion new interpretations of
their experience that questioned and rejected earlier modes of
processing and making sense of what they had observed or felt.
But these sessions were less a spontaneous outburst and more a
reading against the grain, which was often so risky—socially and
psychically—for the individual that they needed the combined resources of a group to make the 'reading' possible. The new 'feminist' significations that emerged were provided legitimacy through
group consent and were consolidated and put into circulation
through active and considered political or personal programs.

Not least among the achievements of consciousness-raising was
the solidarity it generated among women who were closely involved in it, as well as the new self-confidence and sense of power
it produced. Many women felt their lives had been completely
transformed and that they had finally been 'released' from the
constrictions of patriarchal ideology. But consciousness-raising
was also an extremely significant development in political practice. Though the politics of ideology and of representation had
been discussed for well nigh a century, it was in the women's
movement that a critique of culture first emerged as a viable political program. Consistently extended, this attention to the minute,
everyday practices of subordination and expropriation has implications for the politics of class, caste, colonialism, ethnicity, and a
whole range of other structures of domination that determine the
lives of women—and men. But unfortunately the critical use of
experience and the sense of release consciousness-raising generated were quickly annexed in several ways: most blatantly by a
consumerism that addressed and orchestrated women's 'freedom'

in its own interests; but also by a powerful strand of feminist scholarship within several disciplines that naturalized and privileged the
new 'feminist' significations as they conflated the freedom they
experienced, and their sense of having inherited the earth anew,
with an essential—and visionary—femaleness. When the new validity women's experience acquired as a resource that could be
drawn on for critical discussion was conflated with the empiricist
idea that experience was the source of true knowledge, experience lost the critical edge it had acquired as a political tool. And to
the extent that feminism accepted or promoted this conflation and
the consequent valorization of female nature, it acquiesced to and
even collaborated in the annexation of one of the most powerful
political movements of our age into a dominant bourgeois humanist scheme of things. In ways that soon obscured the critical
functions of consciousness-raising, many liberal feminists simply
endorsed the authenticity of what were increasingly referred to in
universalist and naturalistic terms as *women's* experiences. Liberal feminists invented a *female* tradition that was imaged as a lost
city, submerged but intact, unaffected by history, waiting to be recovered, and they spoke of an essential difference between male
and female. They argued for a privileged affinity between women
and peace or women and nature, the body or the unconscious.
When this popular strand of feminism set up its significations, won
no doubt at considerable cost and in the thick of struggle, as a
kind of covert norm, or began to think of these significations as
'natural', or as constituting some sort of female essence struggling
in the work of the woman writer to express itself, it effectively
brought the critical politics feminist practice had so brilliantly
designed and set going in the consciousness-raising groups to a
grinding halt.

(4) We believe that there are powerful alliances feminists of all
classes the world over can make, and equally powerful alliances
feminists can make with other oppressed groups if we accept the
challenges held out to us. But since the kind of feminist criticism
that naturalizes the experiences and issues of Western feminism in
this way is so easily co-opted by the academy and so widely circu-
lated among third world scholars (while the more historically
aware work done by feminist scholars is marginalized), we must
explain in more detail why we find the subsuming of a critical
method into a celebration of female nature so disturbing. We must
also explore why it is that if we simply apply the theories of

women's writing that have been developed over the last decade or so to women's writing in India, we will not merely reproduce its confusions, but compound them.

It might be useful, as a starting point, to unpack the concept of 'reality' as it emerges in the work of the critics we have discussed, whether it is in the idea of 'women's real experiences', which are transparently available in women's writing, especially in realist fiction and in lyric poetry, or in the related idea of a real or authentic female voice that can, if only we pay the right kind of attention, be heard in a woman writer's work.

In gynocritics the real is clearly invested with an oppositional force and with the sense of a knowledge preserved in the face of opposition, and is contrasted with 'unreal' or 'untrue' portrayals of women in the work of most male writers. The idea of the 'real', therefore, carries the impress of a *truth* that emerges as the shackles of prejudice—or false consciousness—are thrown off. As one might have expected, the major contradictions middle class feminists in the West experienced in the initial stages of the movement were those between the promises of freedom and equality that liberalism held out to them and the social and psychic determinations that limited women's access to these rights. Though the movement drew on many existing resources—theoretical and political—to develop a powerful and original critique of patriarchy, when the dominant strand in Western feminism articulated its own solutions to those problems, it did so in a way that only addressed the contradictions principally as women from such social formations experienced them. Other contradictions, which had their source, say, in patriarchy as it was historically constituted by class, by colonialism, or by caste, which would have shaped the subordination of a working-class woman in India—Bangalore Nagaratnamma, for instance—and determined her selfhood or subjectivity, were simply not addressed. Besides, even the contours of what might be more strictly defined as gender subordination were so normatively invoked that they could not accommodate other histories that shaped the contours of desire or of power.

As a result, the shifting reciprocal relationships that determine women's worlds and female subjectivities are obscured. Further, the complicity of white women or middle class women in the structures of domination are never subjected to informed or serious scrutiny. The myriad conflicts women came up against in their everyday lives were invariably woven into a fictional world or a 'real' world in which an adequate 'resolution' to problems was achieved as middle class women uncovered the processes, material and ideological, that had 'excluded' them from full citizenship in their society, and developed strategies to ensure their 'inclusion'.[11] Oppressions of class, of imperialism, of race, which for many women—white middle class women not excluded—compound and reciprocally constitute those of patriarchy, were glossed over in a narrative logic that focused its attention exclusively on what it defined as *women's* concerns. Both the author and the reader, such narratives assumed—and therefore produced and consolidated—as 'woman' belonged to a social configuration the narratives took as norm. Of course, this was precisely how the narrative of the realist novel had a century earlier set up the world as home for its bourgeois hero. That world fell into place and acquired the aura of the real from the viewpoint of the white bourgeois male. Its objects were delineated from his perspective, in his image, and the world was ordered in his interests. Realism was an effect of his gaze. Only from his location could memory, actuality, and language achieve that perfect confluence which produced the 'reality effect'. But feminists who accepted a place in these frameworks and these narratives—whether in the passive sense of allowing them to take over and avoiding more risky initiatives, or in the active sense of choosing their allies—shortchanged feminism too.

We are not, of course, suggesting (what even a decade ago we might have easily been interpreted as doing) that feminism is only a white middle class, or Indian middle class, women's issue. What we are saying is that in the process of posing, elaborating, analyzing, and resolving questions of gender and projecting their resolutions as female reality, Western feminists from the liberal mainstream drew on a whole range of significations and inferential logics attached to them already in circulation, which constituted the common sense of their society. As they did so, they underwrote afresh their society's consensus about the 'real' or the plausible. They questioned the ideological processes that endorsed their subordination as women, but they acquiesced broadly in the consensus on the significations of other cultural and conceptual objects, disciplinary commitments, feelings, tastes, everyday practices, and, indeed, narrative fragments of various kinds that were operative in their society and underwrote the politics of class, race, or imperialism, without subjecting them to the same vigorous critique they had extended to the social construction of middle class femininity. Feminism drew attention in quite spectacular ways to the subtle strategies of power written into the shaping and differentiation of the feminine in the everyday practices of the family, of education, of the workplace, of the law, and of medicine and psychology. But feminisms that projected the results of this initial deconstructive move as *true* or *natural*, as essentially female, projected not only present-day middle class subjectivities as normatively female but also the problem, as they construed it, as the limits of feminism, and their present-day concerns as the great female themes. Such feminism inevitably aligned itself with the many splendored apparatus of power that liberal capitalism, which was also inalienably imperialist, developed over the not inconsequential history through which it established its 'natural' dominions.[12]

■

■ Notes ■

[1] Elaine Showalter, ed., *The New Feminist Criticism*, London, Virage, 1986, p. 6.

[2] Gauri Viswanathan, 'The Beginnings of English Literary Study in British India', *Oxford Literary Review*, 9, 1987, pp. 2–26. Viswanathan argues that the growth of English as a discipline in England took place somewhat later in the nineteenth century, and had as its basis 'a shape and an ideological content developed in the colonial context'. A reader might enjoy the following extract from a toast proposed in 1846 in Edinburgh by Thomas Macaulay (1800–1859), the British statesman and historian who was the principal architect of English education in India and the important spokesman for literary studies in Britain: 'To the literature of Britain, to that literature, the brightest, the purest, the most durable of all the glories of our country, to that literature, so rich in precious truth and precious fiction, to that literature which boasts of the prince of all poets and the prince of all philosophers; to that literature which has exercised an influence wider than that of our commerce and mightier than that of our arms; to that literature which has taught France the principles of liberty and has furnished Germany with models of art; to that literature which forms a tie closer than the tie of consanguinity between us and the commonwealths of the valley of the Mississippi; to that literature before the light of which impious and cruel superstitions are fast taking flight on the banks of the Ganges; to that literature which will in future ages, instruct and delight the unborn millions who will have turned the Australasian and Catfrarian deserts into cities and gardens. To the literature of Britain, then! And wherever the literature of Britain spreads may it be attended by

British virtue and British freedom!' Thomas Macaulay, *Miscellaneous Writings*, Vol. 3, London, Longman's Green and Co., 1880, pp. 398–99.

[3] See Chris Baldick, *The Social Mission of English Criticism, 1848–1932*, Oxford, Clarendon Press, 1983. Francis Mulhern in *The Moment of 'Scrutiny'*, London, Verso, 1981, documents the deep complicity of the Leavisite tradition, often thought of as humanist in contrast to the formalism of American New Criticism, in the ideologies of the Tory middle classes in Britain.

[4] Sandra Gilbert and Susan Gubar, *The Madwoman in the Attic*, New Haven, Yale University Press, 1979, p. 85.

[5] Ibid., p. xi–xii.

[6] Ibid., p. 98.

[7] Ibid., p. 95.

[8] Ibid., p. 99.

[9] Sandra Gilbert and Susan Gubar, *The Norton Anthology of Literature by Women: The Tradition in English*, New York, W.W. Norton, 1985.

[10] According to Florence Howe (in 'Women and the Power to Change', written in 1973), Juliet Mitchell first noted the analogy in *Women's Estate*, New York, Pantheon, 1971, p. 62. Howe adds that there were also 'several elements in the United States culture that allowed for the spread of such groups: the coffee klatch, for example, the quilting bee, and other forms of female social or work groups'. Further, 'in the southern civil rights movement, discussion groups, especially on the subject of racism, also provided a precedent'. *Myths of Coeducation*, Bloomington, Indiana University Press, 1987, p. 172.

[11] Betty Friedan's *The Second Stage*, New York, Summit Books, 1981, represents the anxiety to close the movement off once these initial demands have been met in its most intense and explicit form. Other closures are more subtle and more covert. See Susie Tharu, 'The Second Stage from the Third World', *Indian Journal of American Studies*, 13:2, 1983, pp. 179–84.

[12] For analysis of a replay of the liberal feminist problematic in the 'new realism' of the late 1970s and early 1980s, see Susie Tharu, 'Third World Women's Cinema: Notes on Narrative, Reflections on Opacity', *Economic and Political Weekly*, 21:20, 1986, pp. 864–67.

■

■ ABOUT THE EDITORS ■

Fred Dallmayr is Packee J. Dee Professor of Political Theory at the University of Notre Dame, Indiana, USA. He holds a Doctor of Law degree from the University of Munich, Germany, and a Ph.D. in political science from Duke University, USA. Professor Dallmayr has lectured at various institutions across the world, including Hamburg University in Germany, and the New School of Social Research in New York, USA. He has been a Fellow at Nuffield College, Oxford, and a Fulbright scholar in India. The author of innumerable works, Professor Dallmayr's prominent publications include *Beyond Dogma and Despair* (1981); *Twilight of Subjectivity* (1981); *Polis and Praxis: Exercises in Contemporary Political Theory* (1984); *Critical Encounters: Between Philosophy and Politics* (1987); *Life-World, Modernity and Critique* (1991); *Beyond Orientalism: Essays on Cross-cultural Encounter* (1996); and *Alternative Visions: Paths in the Global Village* (1998).

G.N. Devy is Chairman of the Bhasha Research and Publication Centre, Baroda as well as Director of the Sahitya Academi's Project on Tribal Literature. He was formerly Professor of English at the M.S. University of Baroda, India. His primary interests are literary criticism and tribal culture in India. Dr Devy has been a Commonwealth Academic Staff Fellow at Leeds (1986), a T.H.B. Symons Fellow at Leeds and Coleraine (1991), a Fulbright Exchange Fellow at Yale (1992), and a Jawaharlal Nehru Fellow (1994–96). In 1993, he was awarded the prestigious Sahitya Academi Award for his book *After Amnesia* (1992). His other publications include *Critical Thought* (1987); *In Another Tongue* (1993); and *Of Many Heroes* (1998).

■